Luis Palau:
Calling the Nations
to Christ

Luis Palau:
Calling the Nations to Christ

by
Luis Palau
as told to Jerry B. Jenkins

MOODY PRESS
CHICAGO

To my wife, Pat;
also to Ray Stedman and Dick Hillis

L.P.

To the Tony Martin family,
Aberdeen, Scotland

J.B.J.

© 1980 by Luis Palau and Jerry B. Jenkins
Moody Press Edition, 1983

Unless otherwise identified, Scripture quotations are from the King James Version of the Bible.

Scripture quotations identified NASB are from the *New American Standard Bible,* ©1960, 1962, 1963, 1968, 1971, 1972, 1973, 1975, and 1977 by The Lockman Foundation.

Scripture quotations identified RSV are from the *Revised Standard Version,* ©1946, 1952, 1971, and 1973.

The use of selected references from various versions of the Bible in this publication does not necessarily imply publisher endorsement of the versions in their entirety.

ISBN:0-8024-0461-8

Library of Congress catalog card number 80-22400

Moody Press, a ministry of the Moody Bible Institute, is designed for education, evangelization, and edification. If we may assist you in knowing more about Christ and the Christian life, please write us without obligation: Moody Press, c/o MLM, Chicago, Illinois 60610.

1 2 3 4 5 6 7 Printing/OP/Year 87 86 85 84 83

Printed in the United States of America

Contents

Foreword

I have known Luis Palau for several years, and I have often wished that someone would tell his story. And now, eureka! here it is. Best of all, it is Luis's own story, told in his own words, rather than by an earnest biographer far removed from the real emotions or the facts.

As you read the pages of this book, you are in for a thrilling real-life saga of an excitable Latin American whose character has become well mixed with refreshing dew from heaven. And he is sharing that refreshment with millions.

KENNETH N. TAYLOR

Foreword

Introduction

Few people remember where it started, but several years ago a free-lance journalist first referred to Luis Palau as "the Billy Graham of Latin America." The label stuck, and though flattered by it, Luis is also embarrassed, because people could think that either he or his team was behind it. "I would never dream of drawing such a comparison to a man I have admired for so long," he insists, "but I don't deny that I have been following some of Billy's examples for years."

A quick rundown of the activities of Dr. Palau leaves little question that, indeed, Luis can accurately be called another Billy Graham. Just into his mid-forties, over the last two decades Luis has preached the gospel of Jesus Christ to nearly 5 million people in 39 nations and has reached another 200 million via radio and television.

Luis has written 7 books in English and 5 in Spanish, as well as many booklets, magazine articles, and newspaper columns. His radio programs are heard daily by an estimated 14 million people in 20 Spanish-speaking countries. His team has produced 40 Spanish evangelistic color films and 5 half-hour documentaries in English.

The Palau team is international, with members from Argentina, Australia, Cuba, Guatemala, Mexico, New

Zealand, Sweden, the United Kingdom, and the United States. All over the world, Palau crusades are characterized by their emphasis on mobilizing the entire Body of Christ through church planting and church growth.

More than Luis's preaching style and meeting formats have been compared to Billy Graham. Like Graham, Palau employs every form of mass media to saturate a city, and sometimes a nation, with the gospel. Television, radio, the press, Bible literature, tracts, films, and one-to-one evangelism are all part of the outreach strategy.

But behind this world-renowned man of God is also a husband and father. He's known as a fiery, and even flashy, preacher, but he is also a human being with whom we can easily identify.

Luis Palau is quick to admit his weaknesses and failings. He reveals his battles with pride, anger, impatience, and temptation. Above all, his story contains an element common to almost every Christian's life: his long journey to peace with God.

Even after salvation and rededication and answering a call to ministry, many men and women live in fear and guilt and frustration, because they feel inadequate to live up to God's standards. This conflict clouded Luis Palau's early years, and, in his own telling of it, you'll learn about the intricate, fascinating events that brought an Argentine schoolboy-turned-banking-executive into a ministry of international evangelism.

JERRY B. JENKINS

1

The Little Woman with the Big Facade

And their sins and iniquities will I remember no more.
Hebrews 10:17

It's a huge challenge to counsel people by telephone while all of Ecuador could be watching you on television. I hardly knew if all the calls were legitimate, or if I was talking to someone who merely wanted to be on TV.

In 1965, when I was in my early thirties and had been a missionary-evangelist for a few years, a friend dreamed up the idea of a live counseling program in the HCJB-TV studios in Quito, Ecuador. I had a talent for thinking rapidly under pressure, but this program required quick recall of Scripture. It was good that I enjoyed studying the Bible and had done it for years, but now I was forced to go at it with a vengeance, storing up God's advice for the myriad problems represented by callers from all over South America.

The phones never seemed to stop ringing, once we were on the air. The program was called "Responde," and the people certainly did. Someone near suicide might call, or someone who had just had a fight with

11

his spouse or had just been thrown out of the house. It might be someone who had been to one of our evangelistic services, but who was afraid to come forward and receive Christ.

One November night in 1965, I received two consecutive calls, the first of which was one of the most rewarding ever on the program. The other turned into one of the most bizarre encounters in my entire ministry.

The first caller was a young woman named Ruth, who had seen her parents' marriage break up. She decided that if her father could live in sin, so could she. And so she did. Ruth tearfully told me her whole, sordid story of loose living and immorality in reaction to her father's similar life-style.

Now she was miserable and wanted to be forgiven. It had not been my practice to lead callers to Christ right then, but rather to show them from Scripture how they could begin to turn their lives around. Then I set up in-person appointments, where I could carefully show them the way of salvation in the privacy of the studio counseling office.

But this woman was desperate. When I read to her from the Bible that God loved her and offered His forgiveness and salvation, she wanted to receive Him right then and there. I hesitated. Did I want to do this on the air? Would it look like a setup? Was it a good precedent? It was obvious that she was sincere.

I asked her to pray with me and added that anyone else listening in who wanted to pray along with us and receive Christ could do so. "Dear God," I began, "I know I am a sinner." She repeated each line. "I have abused my body. I have broken sacred marriages." And we prayed on, recounting the sins she had told me. "Father, I need Your forgiveness and Your saving love." It was a tearful, solemn, anointed moment as she prayed to receive Christ.

Those may have been some of the most effective minutes of my ministry. Potentially hundreds of thousands of people were listening in, and who knows how many might have prayed that prayer with us?

Ruth was so excited that she insisted upon an appointment the next morning at nine.

The next caller was brief. A tiny, high-pitched, squeaky voice simply requested an appointment the next day at nine-thirty. No more conversation. When I agreed, the squeaky voice simply thanked me and hung up.

The next morning, after I had counseled Ruth and encouraged her in her new faith, I walked her to the door and was just leaving her with a Bible and some literature when I noticed a little woman walking through the gates of the HCJB property, followed closely by two huge, able-bodied men who could have passed for American football players.

As she entered the office, I asked if the two gentlemen would like to come in, too. "No," she said, "one will stand by the door and the other by the gate." It was the squeaky voice from the night before, and she was right on time.

She brushed past me and felt along the bottom of the edge of my desk top, as if looking for something. Without explanation, she moved to the wall and peeked behind a hanging picture. Her eyes traveled to every corner before she finally sat down. I thought she must be unbalanced.

She crossed her legs like a man and smoked like no one I had ever seen, man or woman. She attacked each cigarette, sucking every last bit from it and then lighting the next with the smoldering butt of the last.

In spite of her tiny voice, she spoke through a sneer, and venom poured out. Her voice dripped with sarcasm and hatred. "You pastors and priests," she began with disgust. "You are a bunch of thieves and liars and crooks. All you want is to deceive people; all you want is money!"

She went on that way for more than twenty minutes, swearing all the while, and accusing, criticizing, and insulting. Bitterness gushed from her and left me speechless. I had no idea how to react and couldn't have got a word in, anyway. I prayed silently, *Lord, how shall I handle this?*

Seemingly exhausted from the ordeal, she finally slumped in her chair like a jogger who has just finished a tough course. She took a deep breath, her eyes still flashing.

"Madam," I began, "is there anything I can do for you? How can I help you?"

She slowly took her cigarette from her lips and sat staring at me for an instant, then suddenly broke into uncontrollable sobs. I continued to pray silently. *Lord, what am I going to do? I'm no psychiatrist. I'm just a preacher. Why did You send her to me?*

When she was composed and could speak again, the edge was gone from her voice. "You know," she said, "in the thirty-eight years I have lived, you are the first person who has ever asked me if he could help me. All my life people have come to me with their hands out, saying, 'Help me, come here, do this, go there, do that.'"

"What is your name?" I asked.

She was suddenly hard again. "Why do you want to

know my name?"

"Well, you've said a lot of things here, and I don't even know you. I just want to know how to address you."

She sat back in her chair and straightened up a bit. Cocking her head and looking at me out of the corner of her eye, she lifted her chin and took yet another drag at her cigarette. Then she said with finality, "I'm going to tell you," as if allowing me a real privilege.

"My name is Maria Benitez-Perez," she said triumphantly. I recognized the name as that of a large family of wealth and influence. "I am the female secretary of the Communist Party here in Ecuador. I am a Marxist-Leninist, and I am a materialist. I don't believe in God."

With that she took off on a breathless tirade against me and all preachers and priests, the church, and anything else she could think of that rivaled her beliefs.

"Why did you come here?" I broke in. "Just to insult me, or what?"

She was thoughtful again. "I'm going to tell you my story," she announced. And for the next three hours, without pause or interruption, she did just that.

She had been a rebellious teenager, who ran away from a religious school and was given a choice by her parents: return to school or leave the family. She left. The Communists befriended her and took her in. Within the next few years, she married and divorced three times and had two children.

Despite her upbringing, she became a party leader and organized student rebellions. Her story was like the plot of a grade-B movie. I let her talk on and on, wondering when her first sign of vulnerabilty would surface.

"When my mother died and the bishop came to officiate at the ceremony, I just stood there and made fun of everything he did. I mocked him while my mother's body lay there in the casket. I made a clown of myself, and I've always felt a little guilty about that. Even though I don't believe in God, of course."

Every time she got onto the subject of God, she became enraged. She repeatedly rattled off her list of titles and beliefs and nonbeliefs. But just as often, she would return to the funeral of her mother and how her mockery of the priest still bothered her.

I kept praying. *When will the opening come?* Three hours after she began, we finally got down to business.

"Hey, Palau," she said. "Supposing there is a God —and I'm not saying there is, because I don't believe in the Bible, and I don't believe there's a God—but just supposing there is. Just for the sake of chatting about it, if there is a God—which there isn't—do you think He would receive a woman like me?"

So this poor, frightened, little woman with the big facade had a chink in her armor, after all. I had read years before that when dealing with a professed atheist, the best approach is to take one truth from the Bible and stay with it, driving it home until it sticks, repeating is as many times as you have to. The Bible says that the law of God converts the soul, not the arguments of men.

What verse suits her? I wondered. The Lord gave me Hebrews 10:17, one of my favorites, because it is so short and says so much: "Their sins and iniquities will I remember no more."

I said, "Look, Maria, don't worry about what to think; look at what God thinks." I opened to the verse and turned the Bible so she could see.

"But I don't believe in the B—"

"You've already told me that," I said. "But we're just supposing there's a God, right? Let's just suppose this is His Word. He says, 'Their sins and iniquities will I remember no more.'"

She waited, as if there had to be more. I said nothing. "But, listen. I've been an adulteress, married three times, and in bed with a lot of different men."

I said, "Their sins and iniquities will I remember no more," and began to count the times I repeated it.

"But I haven't told you half my story. I stabbed a comrade who later committed suicide."

"Their sins and iniquities will I remember no more."

"I've led student riots where people were killed!"

"Their sins and iniquities will I remember no more."

"I egged on my friends and then hid while they were out dying for the cause."

"Their sins and iniquities will I remember no more."

Seventeen times I responded to Maria's objections and confessions with that verse. It was past lunchtime. I was tired and weak. I had no more to offer. I was at the end of my rope. "Would you like Christ to forgive all that you've told me about, and all the rest that I don't even know?"

She was quiet. Finally she spoke softly. "If He could forgive me and change me, it would be the greatest miracle in the world. He can't do it."

"You want to try it?"

"It would be a miracle."

"Take a step of faith. Invite Him into your life and try Him. See what will happen."

Maria stared at me for a long moment and then bowed her head. "All right," she whispered.

I led her in a simple prayer decision, confessing her

17

sins, asking forgiveness, and receiving Christ. By the end she was crying.

She returned, a week later, to tell me she was reading her Bible and that she felt a lot better. A longtime missionary woman from HCJB agreed to follow her up, but I was not prepared for what I would encounter when I saw Maria again, two months later.

2

Divine Ulterior Motives

Blessed is the nation whose God is the Lord; and the
people whom he hath chosen for his own inheritance.

Psalm 33:12

Back in Quito in January 1966, for more television counseling and radio-program taping, I was once again visited by my little revolutionary. I was shocked. She looked happy and had even quit smoking. But, despite a new bounce to her step, her face was a mess of purple blotches and bruises. Several of her front teeth were missing, top and bottom.

Shortly after I had last seen her, she told her comrades of her new faith. At a meeting of all the communist leaders of the country, she told them, "I am no longer an atheist. I believe in God and in Jesus Christ, and I have become a Christian. I am resigning from the party, and I don't want to have anything more to do with it. We are all a bunch of liars. We deceive people when we tell them there is no God.

"Of course there is a God! Do you think flowers created themselves? Are you going to tell me that my beautiful babies are the result of some explosion in space a million years ago?"

It was as if she had let a bunch of hungry lions out of

a cage. The leaders fought among themselves, some trying to shout her down and get at her, others insisting that she should be allowed to speak.

A few days later she was nearly run down by a Jeep full of her former comrades. And the next day four of her former protégés attacked her and smashed her face against a metal electrical box until she was bloody and unconscious.

She was forced to hide out in the basements of evangelical churches and in the homes of missionaries, always on the run. For her and the HCJB missionary to be able to study the Bible, they first had to drive around until they were sure no one was following them.

I was amazed at the persecution she had suffered as such a young believer. "There's going to be a revolution in June," she told me matter-of-factly. "We've had it all planned for months." I shuddered.

It was to be a typical Latin American uprising: students and agitators causing a disturbance in the streets, luring out the army, which would then be attacked and overthrown. The military junta would be forced to leave the country, and the chairman of the Communist Party for Ecuador would come out of his hiding in Colombia and take over the country.

Maria remained on the run until June. The Marxists' network of spies was incredible, and they tracked her down. Rather than letting them take her, however, she talked her four captors into taking a short break from their activities and going to her father's farm in the Ecuadorian interior, where they could rest and read a few books she had chosen for them.

Incredibly, they accepted her offer. On the morning of the revolution, the Communist Party leader came out of Colombia to talk to Maria. In a few hours he was to become the new ruler of the country, but first he wanted to talk to his longtime friend.

"Maria," he asked, "why did you become a Christian?"

"Because I believe in God and in Jesus Christ, and my faith has changed my life."

"You know," he said, "while hiding out, I have been listening to HCJB radio on shortwave, and those—they almost have *me* believing there is a God!"

"There is!" she said. "Why don't you become a Christian and get out of this business? We never had any real convictions about atheism and materialism. And look at all the lives we've ruined and all the terrible things we've been into. Here, take this Bible and this book [*Peace with God*, by Billy Graham]. You can go to my father's farm and read them."

Miraculously, he accepted her offer. Later that morning, the disturbance that was supposed to trigger a revolution fizzled into chaos, because the leaders were off on a farm somewhere, reading.

Of the many, many people I have seen come to Christ over the years, Maria had the wildest story. It solidified in me a burden, not just for individuals, but also for nations, when I saw the effect of the conversion of one woman on the history of an entire country.

Though that was many years ago, the fire still burns in my heart. My desire since my late teens has been not only to see people saved from hell, but also to see nations influenced for the Lord, to live in freedom. Of course the gospel brings salvation to souls; that's fundamental to my calling as an evangelist. But a Christian nation means the people will have better lives.

I want to see more nations turn to God, because that will glorify Him. I love to see nations prosper, and that is God's promise to those who come to Him. People can choose between a miserable life without God or a happy one with Him. What in the world makes millions choose the miserable life?

What drives me most is the conviction that if only people would see the point and get the message, they would be changed. Maybe that's why I—along with many other evangelists—spend so much time literally pleading the case of salvation through Jesus Christ.

Even with my responsibilities as a husband and father and the president of an evangelistic team, I find that I can be distracted for only so long from my burden to preach the gospel to a lost world. I might be busy with business for a while, but then I'll run across something in a magazine or in talking with someone, and the drive deep within me will churn anew, and I'll get anxious to preach.

It seems I have been preaching all my life; but of course I haven't. I wasn't even really a full-time evangelist until I was into my thirties, which is one of the ironies in a story that actually begins in the twelfth century, believe it or not.

That's when the Germans invaded northeast Spain and left a lot of blond, light-skinned progeny. Generations later, my father, Luis Palau, Sr., was born light and fair-haired, like most people in the fishing village of Cataluna. His parents emigrated from Spain to Argentina.

My mother, Matilde Balfour de Palau, was the product of a Scottish-French marriage, her father having served in the British Merchant Marine before settling in Argentina.

Thus, Luis Palau, Jr., born November 27, 1934, as the first—and only—male of six children, never really looked South American.

That is true of many Argentinians, of course. The big landholders in the country are Britishers who settled there. The railroad, the ports, and the meat-packing companies were British-built and became the largest industries. So many Europeans emigrated to work there that they made Argentina more European than South American, in many ways.

So, how does an evangelical Christian preacher emerge from a country where Protestants make up just 6 percent of the population? Well, I'm only a second-generation Christian.

My grandparents on both sides were basically secular, in my opinion, with the possible exception of my maternal grandmother, who was devoted to the French Roman Catholic church. My grandfather always claimed to be "Scotch Presbyterian." If true, he should have brought the gospel with him to Argentina. (In truth, as I tell my friends, he preferred Scotch to Presbyterian.)

My father's parents were nominally religious, as are many Argentinians. They were not committed to the state church and hardly ever attended.

My father's dad died when my father was sixteen, so my father was forced to find work early in life. He purchased a small pickup truck and made enough money hauling materials to buy a piece of land and build a house on it. He sold that, bought more land, built another house, and sold it, eventually developing a thriving construction business.

My dad was a real entrepreneur, in his own quiet way. He was a man's man, self-made, self-taught. He didn't make waves; he just made money. He was good at what he did, and he was a thinker. He supported his whole family by building and selling construction materials, and, by the time he married, he was prosperous, though not showy.

My parents started their family in the small town of Ingeniero-Maschwitz (named after the train station). Around the time of my birth, my father probably would have considered himself a typical nonreligious person. He would have said he believed in God and Christ and probably would have aligned himself with the state church.

My mother was the churchgoer, playing the organ in the local parish church. She was searching for real answers in life, but she told me that at that time neither she nor my dad knew the biblical gospel—at least until they met Mr. Rogers.

Charles Rogers was typical of many British missionaries to South America. He came to Argentina for the express purpose of winning people to Christ and planting local bodies of Christian Brethren assemblies, but he was fully self-supporting as an executive with the Shell Oil Company.

Many Brethren missionaries were European businessmen who had divine ulterior motives for coming to Argentina.

Somehow Mr. Rogers made contact with our family, probably through our Scottish connection, and he began carefully and quietly to cultivate a friendship with my parents until he was able to give them a gospel of Matthew.

My mother was so hungry for God that she would kneel and read this Scripture portion. When she read the Beatitudes and realized that the pure in heart shall see God, she was convicted that she did not have a pure heart.

Mr. Rogers and his wife led my mother to Christ

and, not long after, my grandmother, too, became a Christian. The Rogerses discipled them and got them involved with a few other Christians in the tiny local assembly.

My father said he didn't want anything to do with "this evangelical stuff," but those who knew when to look would occasionally see him standing outside the corrugated-metal shed, on the outskirts of town, that served as the Brethren place of worship.

Mr. Rogers and other preachers like him knew that some townspeople did not want to be seen in the church building, despite the fact that they did want to hear the sermon, so Mr. Rogers turned off the outside lights during the sermon to allow shy listeners to stand close and then steal away before the service ended.

My father listened outside a few times before my mother decided it was time to get him into the chapel for a meeting. He reluctantly agreed, but if my mother had known what he was going to do in the middle of the message, she probably wouldn't have bothered to badger him into coming in the first place.

3

The Classroom of the Soul

And they said, Believe on the Lord Jesus Christ, and thou shalt be saved, and thy house.

Acts 16:31

My mother will never forget the first time Dad walked in and sat beside her in the chapel. And neither will anyone else who was there (except me—I was about a year and a half old). Mr. Rogers was preaching expositionally, as usual, and somehow the combination of what he was saying and what my father had heard during his surreptitious visits in the shadows was used by the Holy Spirit to work in Dad's heart.

The Christian Brethren don't give altar calls, but Dad wouldn't have waited for that, anyway. In the middle of the sermon, he suddenly stood and quoted a phrase often used among evangelicals: "I receive Jesus Christ as my only and sufficient Savior."

My mother nearly fainted. She hadn't expected him to make a scene. When he had made his declaration, he sat down, and that was that. He had believed and accepted and confessed with his mouth the Lord Jesus. And he was saved. Few times does one see such a spontaneous work of conviction, and I long to see it again and again.

With my father also in the fold, both my parents immediately became outspoken and enthusiastic evangelicals. Because there were so few people in the church to begin with, and even fewer converts, the Brethren needed all the help they could get and had a way of pushing new believers into service right away.

It provided a perfect framework for growth, forcing my parents into Bible study and prayer, so they would be equipped to witness and defend their faith, especially now that they were hated minority Protestants.

They were baptized, and soon my father put his trucks at the disposal of the missionary. Every weekend a truckload of local Christians drove to different towns, to witness and pass out tracts.

Some of my earliest memories are of walking to church with my mother. She was so solidly converted that she was eager to stand up for Christ. I know it never happened, but in my mind's eye I picture her walking the family to church with a big Bible held high in front of her. She attended every meeting, and she never minded being insulted and called names. She was never ashamed of Jesus Christ; that I remember most.

When I was a child, there weren't more than a dozen or so people in the Brethren assembly in town, and that included Mr. Rogers and his wife and two children. My mother and dad, my two aunts, and three or four other townspeople made up our congregation, the only one in town.

It's interesting that I would grow up in a unique fellowship like the Christian Brethren. They didn't call themselves a denomination; in fact, they shunned all such labels, including *Brethren*. Their meetings were simple, staid, and sacred, with utmost emphasis placed on the Lord's Supper.

The movement, I learned later, was born in Britain, where many clergymen were not allowed to invite one another into their pulpits. They decided to minister simply to each other, in nonofficial but biblical, private Communion services. It didn't take them long to realize that meeting with no denominational trappings was a vivid, beautiful portrayal of the Body of Christ.

To me, the Lord's Supper is still the greatest service in the church, and I like the way the Brethren do it. We sat in benches and chairs around a table in the middle of the room. It's not at the front, so those serving the bread and the cup are no more prominent than anyone else.

There is no one leader; several men participate. In fact, there is no pastor. The leadership comes from within the assembly, even from my self-conscious father as he matured in the faith. It is simplicity personified. One stands and reads a portion of Scripture. Another prays. Another leads a hymn.

The Communion service might take more than one hour, with songs and Scripture reading. But there is no exhortation or teaching. It is all centered on the person of Christ and the work of the cross. A well-known preacher or teacher within the movement might be visiting the church, but around the Lord's table, everyone is equal. In fact, they would rather that a prominent outsider not lead the service, so he doesn't give the impression that he's any more important than anyone else.

Around that table a person gets the feeling that *Man, I'm one of the brethren.* The little old ladies who couldn't read or write were just as important as Mr. Rogers or Mr. Palau. I knew I wasn't one iota more or less important than any of the adults there; I learned a powerful lesson in my soul, which I never could have learned in a classroom.

During regular worship services, my mother pumped the organ. We children were always embarrassed, because we thought she sang too loudly. But she was always singing, even around the house. That memory blesses me even to this day.

I always thought of my mother as old, but she was just twenty-five when I was born. Frankly, she was plain-looking, average in height and weight, with her hair in a bun at the back of her head. Everyone knew her as a kind, generous, and loving person. She was not loud or quick to laugh, but she was always gentle. My mother was never hard-nosed or unpleasant, but at the same time she wouldn't let anyone's unbiblical comment go unchallenged. Her godliness has always made a strong impression on me.

Mother would not allow herself or those around her to talk about the future without adding, "If the Lord wills." It seemed a bit legalistic to us as we grew older, but she lived that truth. Some of our relatives even made fun of her, because she always delayed her decisions until she had a leading from the Lord. "Hey, Matilde," they would taunt, "has God moved the pillar of fire yet?" She took it well, but I didn't. I resented it, and I hurt for her, but it strengthened my conviction to follow the Lord. I find today that on important decisions I am just as deliberate as my mother was in waiting for clearance from the Lord. (Those relatives are all close to God now, by the way.)

She never missed a church meeting, and I admired that. I thought it was the way a Christian was supposed to be; of course, it was all I knew. When I compared her to other mothers, I did what most kids do: I decided I'd rather have her for my mother than anyone else in the world.

My mother read missionary stories to my sisters and me, over and over, before we went to sleep each night. My favorite was the true story of Mildred Cable and Francesca French, who carried the gospel through Asia in spite of tremendous persecution and physical abuse. That story would come back to me later and convict me of my need to share Christ.

Dad and Mom also insisted that Sunday was absolutely sacred. No sports, no activities except going to church, resting, reading, or participating in gospel street meetings in the middle of hot afternoons. Those meetings were often discouraging, but they helped mold my future.

I recall an active childhood in a happy home. Because of my dad's business, we had many buildings and shops and trucks and employees, including maids and farmhands. I'm often amused that many Americans think anyone who grew up in South America must have been a barefoot, poverty-stricken urchin. When I tell people my father was in business for himself, they say, "Ah, he raised cattle, huh?"

Like all the other kids in the area, I wore short pants—much to my embarrassment, because my skinny legs looked milky white compared to the swarthy brown ones all around. It was good that I was temperamental enough to defend myself when necessary.

My mother is easy-going, so I suppose I inherited my choleric personality from my father. I was exposed to his influence for only ten years, so whatever strengths or weaknesses I got from him had to be more genetic than environmental.

I idolized my father. He was everything I thought a

man should be, even though he was quiet and humble for a man of such stature. I, however, had a quick temper. It is something that, over the years, I have learned I must constantly put under the control of Christ.

When I was a child, my temper flared up every time something went wrong or I didn't get my own way. I was persistent to a fault, moaning and groaning and pestering my mother for days, begging her to give in on some issue or another. In retrospect, I'm sure she was too nice to me.

As a child I was burdened with a tremendous sense of guilt because I couldn't control my tongue. I could shout and say the meanest things. If I felt I had been unfairly treated in a soccer game, I would use some of the worst language on the field.

What always bothered me was that my temper raged over the little things in life, not the big ones. If I were the victim of another driver's carelessness, and he caused an accident, I could be cool as a cucumber. But let me knock a glass over, and suddenly I would fly off the handle. I am not proud of this tendency, but I would be a hypocrite to say it hasn't been a problem.

My temper flare-ups eventually caused problems early in my marriage, as you will see; but my wife's cool head and appropriate reactions and God's continued dealings with me brought control.

I am a professional and a bit of a perfectionist. Seeming stupidity irritates me. Such anger is sin and can't be justified. But God has made me sensitive to the danger of overreacting, to the point where, for the most part, I can still handle situations quickly and decisively, while being careful not to overreact and insult or hurt someone.

Some of my old friends and mentors like to blame that part of my disposition on my Latin heritage, but good things, too, came from my unusual upbringing.

Many traits evident in me today are the results of other events during the 1940s, not the least of which were centered on my father.

4
Briar Bushes and Belt Buckles

Train up a child in the way he should go: and when he is old, he will not depart from it.

Proverbs 22:6

Whenever I heard Dad jingle his belt buckle, I knew I was going to get a whipping. He never disciplined me when I didn't deserve it; in fact, I probably eluded a few spankings I should have received.

My childhood was full of playing marbles and jacks, racing toy cars my dad bought me, and getting into all sorts of mischief with my sisters.

Once my sister Matil and I pretended to run away from home, when actually we were hiding under a sheet of canvas covering some bags of cement and sand my dad had stored. We crouched under that canvas for hours, giggling and holding our breath while my dad searched the neighborhood, calling and calling. We thought it was great, but that was one escapade that ended in the jingling of the belt buckle.

I hardly realized it at the time, but because of my father's business, I'm sure I had things better than most kids in town. I never felt like a rich kid, but even if I had, the daily put-down of being taunted by other kids as an evangelical balanced any feelings of superiority. I was the despised minority—a sign I sometimes wore as a badge of honor.

The badge I wore most proudly, however, was the honor of being Luis Palau, *Hijo,* "the son." My dad was really respected in town, not just because he was a successful businessman, but also because he was honest. I felt that whenever I went into town for anything, I was greeted with respect because of my dad.

One of the things I remember Dad talking about, even when I was a young boy, was that he always paid his bills on time and therefore had no debts. He wanted to die without owing any money. Maybe that's why I had such clear memories of always feeling welcome and loved in town. People called out to me in a kind way, making me proud of my father.

There was little I wanted that I couldn't have, though I think my dad was careful not to indulge me too much. I was thrilled when he finally decided I was old enough to take care of the Scottish-Shetland pony I had always wanted.

The deal was that I would wash it, feed it, groom it, exercise it, and generally be in charge of it, and that he would build me a stall and feeding trough and all the rest. The one rule was that my sisters were not to ride it. There was no way he wanted little girls to ride a skittish, bouncing pony. I was barely big enough myself.

I knew better, of course. Surely Matil was mature enough to handle it. She begged and begged until I gave in. She wound up in a briar bush, and I wound up on the wrong end of the jingling belt.

I had had the pony less than a year when I went out to feed him one morning and found him gasping for breath. I couldn't believe it. We didn't even have time to give him any medicine. I was mad at the world and had to take it out on somebody. I wanted that horse back more than anything, and there was no comforting me.

I stood in the corner all day and cried until I had no more tears. I hardly ate a bite, and no one could talk to me. When I was finally too weak to keep it up, I ate a little. But I demanded to know if I would see the horse in heaven, and through that my mother was able to calm me down.

My dad became an elder in the local assembly and contributed the materials to build a new chapel. In fact, he supervised or did most of the construction work himself. The Brethren believed that plain was beautiful, and although I saw it as a drab Sunday school room, with no pictures or figures and ornaments, I was impressed that my dad had built a structure for God's people, exactly the way they wanted it.

That room—though I grew tired of it and bored with many of the sedate services—had a positive effect on me as a child. The Lord's Supper was so meaningful and filled with long, silent pauses, that I felt we were truly all brothers under the cross, affirming our unity in the Body of Christ. And the fact that my dad and mom were part of it made it all the more significant. I'm sure much of what I learned and took from there is deeply imbedded in my being.

My dad was consistent, the same person at home as he was in the chapel. He rose early on cold winter mornings to start a wood fire in the stove. I should have been sleeping, but often I sneaked out of bed just to watch him putter around the house.

If I watched long enough, I might see him go into his office—a little study he built on one side of the house— and kneel alone. Wrapped in a blanket or poncho, he would read the Bible and pray before going out to work. Though I was not even eight years old yet, I would steal back to my bed, feeling warm and grateful that I had a good dad.

One day he told me that he read a chapter from Proverbs every day, since it has thirty-one chapters and there are thirty-one days in most months. That stuck with me all my life, and I still try to practice it. I have told so many friends and associates that story that many, many people now do the same. In spite of all the other Bible studying and reading I do, I try to start the day with my chapter from Proverbs. And I have learned to do it on my knees, too.

I don't want to be legalistic about it, but there's nothing like studying the Word of God and praying on your knees. I have never shaken the habit of spreading my Bible and study materials out on the bed and kneeling to read and pray. It sure keeps your heart and mind in the right attitude. Sometimes it brings back warm memories of my dad, too.

Even though I had not yet actually trusted Christ as my Savior, I knew my dad and mom were doing the right thing. When we rode on benches in the back of one of my dad's trucks and folded tracts to pass out in a neighboring town, I reacted to the taunts and insults with resolve. I saw the religious parades, common on the many holidays in South America, and I determined that one day Christians would do the same things, emphasizing the Bible and salvation through Jesus Christ.

When a child is thrust into a position in which he must stand firm for the Lord in the face of opposition, I believe he is strengthened by it. It's much more valuable to our spiritual lives when we have to stand up for our beliefs in a non-Christian environment.

So I had an evangelical fervor—perhaps not for the right reason—even before I was actually a Christian.

Much of my life revolved around going, with my parents and friends from the church, on little tent-and-street-corner-meeting evangelism jaunts and helping to pass out tracts, while Mr. Rogers spoke and others led singing or gave testimonies. Often the crowds were small or hardly existent, and sometimes we received threats.

Until Matil joined me a couple of years after I started, I was the only evangelical in the local government public school. I was called names occasionally, even by the teachers, who made me kneel in the corner on corn grains if I misbehaved.

By the time I was eight years old, my dad decided it was time I went to private boarding school. Such schools were run by the British, and I think Dad's main motivation was that I would become bilingual and thus have a better chance in life. He wanted to give me every chance.

My first three boarding-school years were spent at the Quilmes Preparatory School in Quilmes, about twenty miles south of Buenos Aires and a little more than forty miles from my home. My whole family went along on the ride to drop me off, and although it was considered prestigious to be sent to boarding school, I was scared.

To me the British were disciplined and precise, and I feared my poor English would get me into trouble right away. I could go home only one weekend each month, and though my grandmother lived not far from the school, I was not allowed to visit her or call her. When you're there, you're there.

I was one of only fifty boarders at Quilmes. Another two hundred or so boys and girls joined us for day school, and there was a homey atmosphere. With four boys to a dorm, I made friends quickly. But homesickness struck early.

I didn't want anyone to know I was crying at night, so I pulled the covers up over my head and read my Bible by flashlight, not really reading, but just looking at the page numbers. I memorized the books of the Bible by studying the preliminary pages.

Eventually I began to enjoy myself and became active in all the games and sports and classes. It didn't take me long to improve my English, though learning it from Britishers gave me a strange combined accent— strange, at least, to Americans, when I first arrived in the States years later.

I did long for the vacations when I could be home with my family, and then I dreaded the end of the summer, when I had to go back. But Quilmes became my new home and was good preparation for Saint Alban's College, where I was scheduled to go when I was ten years old. I didn't know what Saint Alban's would be like, and I was glad I wouldn't have to think about it until the end of the summer (which in Argentina begins in the middle of December).

Shortly after my tenth birthday, I took all my final exams and began to make preparations for the trip home. A few days before I expected to be picked up by my parents, I received a call from my grandmother. She was not supposed to call me at school, so I knew something was wrong.

"Luis," she said, ignoring any amenities, "your dad is very sick. We really have to pray for him." I had a grave premonition, although she gave me no details. I had the terrible feeling he was dead or dying. The next morning, December 17, 1944, Grandma came to put me on a train for home.

"It's very serious," she said. "Your mom wants you to come and see your dad."

The three-hour trip seemed interminable. I couldn't stand it. I wished I could have engineered the train myself. I really loved my dad more than ever before, although I had seen him so little for three years. We had talked and made a lot of plans.

But now I couldn't shake this ominous feeling. He hadn't even been sick, as far as I knew. Yet I was sure he was already gone.

5

The Palm of Victory,
Which Is Far Better

*I am the resurrection, and the life: he that believeth in
me, though he were dead, yet shall he live: And whosoever liveth and believeth in me shall never die. Believest
thou this?*

John 11:25-26

I sat in silence on the train, staring ahead, yet seeing
nothing. And I remembered.

I was very, very close to my dad. He had always
trusted me and treated me like an adult, when I deserved
it. His workers liked him; his friends respected him; and
he was a good farmer, besides being a good husband
and father.

He may have been a bit too serious—seldom laughing or joking—but having to support a family from age
sixteen on would give anyone a certain sobriety and
singleness of purpose.

Because of him I had many advantages over the other
kids my own age. He had let me drive his new truck,
sitting right there with me, of course, when I was only
eight years old. And he'd promised to buy me a pickup

truck of my own when I turned sixteen.

He would let me crawl in under the hood and pretend to be working on the engine, when about all I could do was check the oil and then try to get the dipstick back in. I was also welcome to sip *mate,* green tea, with the workingmen during their breaks, feeling like a man, treated with respect. That was one of the ways my dad showed his affection for me.

Two years before, Dad had given me a plot of land. It was less than a quarter of an acre, but to me it was huge, endless. He taught me to plant and water and cultivate vegetables and flowers in the six-foot-deep, rich, black, Argentinian soil. Burned into my memory is a picture of him and me standing together among the corn and flowers we had produced together. If he died, I decided, I would never have anything to do with that plot of ground again, that special place I had defended like a castle, making people walk around it.

There was no way I could ignore the dread, the certainty that I would not be there in time to say good-by to my dad. I didn't even know what was wrong with him. I wouldn't learn until later that he had suffered for just ten days, in need of penicillin, so scarce in South America in the 1940s. But something told me he was already gone.

I could hardly stand not being there yet. I've always been a take-charge type. Sometimes it's been embarrassing, even as an adult. But it's part of my nature to feel that, when there is a problem, I can solve it; I can organize people and get things moving. Here was a man about to die, leaving his wife with five children under the age of eleven and one on the way (Ruth). I had to get home and see what could be done.

I was out of my seat and pressing up against the door

of the train by the time it rolled to a stop. I bounded down the steps and strode purposefully toward home. The blast-furnace temperature didn't deter me. It was the hottest day of the year, but to me it seemed wrong to see people lounging around, sipping soft drinks and fanning themselves. Something was terribly wrong at my house, yet people in town were lazing around.

Any shred of hope I might have harbored in the back of my mind during the long train ride was quickly dispelled when I came within earshot of my house and heard the traditional wailing. Some of my non-Christian aunts and uncles were moaning and crying and asking, "Why does God allow this? Oh, what will Matilde do?"

Relatives tried to intercept me as I ran through the gate and up to the house; I brushed past them and was in the door before my mother even knew I was there. And there was my father: yellow, bloated, still secreting fluid, blood drying, lips cracked. His body had dehydrated.

I ran to him, ignoring my sisters Matilde, Martha, Ketty, Margarita, and all my other relatives. My father was still in bed, as if asleep. He had probably just died within the past few hours. His body had not been touched.

I tried to steel myself in the midst of all the crying and sobbing, but I began to shake. I couldn't believe this! I would never talk to my father again. He looked terrible, but I wanted him to be all right. I hugged him and kissed him, but he was gone.

My mother—stunned but not crying—stepped up behind me and put her hands firmly on my shoulders. "Luisito, Luisito," she said softly, pulling me away, "I must talk to you and tell you how it was."

She took me outside, and I tried to stifle my sobs

while listening to her account. She told me that when the doctors had given up hope, they sent my father home. "Papito was yellow even then," she said. "That's when we tried to get in touch with you, so you could hurry home.

"It was obvious that he was dying, and as we gathered around his bed, praying and trying to comfort him, he seemed to fall asleep. He was struggling to breathe, but suddenly he sat up and began to sing."

I looked up at my mother, hardly believing what she was saying.

"Papito began to sing," she said, "'Bright crowns up there, bright crowns for you and me. Then the palm of victory, the palm of victory.' He sang it three times, all the while clapping in time, as you children did when you sang it in Sunday school.

"Then, when Papito could no longer hold up his head, he fell back on the pillow and said, "I'm going to be with Jesus, which is far better.'" Two hours later he had died.

I turned that story over in my mind for days, and even for years. It is still so vivid to me that I sometimes almost feel as if I had been there when he was singing. It was such a contrast to the typical South American scene, in which the dying person cries out in fear of going to hell. It thrilled me that my father was sure of his salvation, and I never doubted that he was in heaven.

Still, my grief devastated me, and I was angry at everything and everybody. It wasn't fair. Why couldn't my father die in old age like everyone else? I locked the gate on my little plot of land, never caring to see it again. (I have never enjoyed working with gardens or plants since that time.)

It was hard to look at the buildings, the metal shop, the garages, and the work areas near our house. It hurt to walk by my father's little study. I didn't want to see anything that reminded me of him. There was no comforting me. My world, my future, had come to an end.

It was painful for me to mull over my mother's story of how my father had died, but I couldn't push it out of my mind. It was the only minutely positive element in the whole ordeal, and it has affected my whole ministry and my whole adult life. My wish and desire is that people get right with God, settle the big question, and die happy, knowing that they will be Jesus, "which is far better."

Even our dog knew my father was dead. He curled up by the front door of the house and refused to move or eat for hours. He cried and moaned all day. The old-timers agreed that this was a dog that had loved his master and sensed when he was gone. It was many days before the dog perked up again.

Because there was no embalming, the dead person had to be buried quickly, usually within twenty-four hours. Once the doctor or undertaker had cleaned up the body and laid it in a casket, the evangelical custom was that friends and relatives sat around it all night, comforting the family.

That was a horrible night. I didn't want to be there, and I didn't want to leave. I was a jumble of ten-year-old emotions. People sat around drinking coffee and talking in whispers. Since there would be very little time before the burial, relatives in distant towns were contacted and began arriving at different times all night.

Many found it difficult to stay awake with my mother, so there were people sleeping in beds, chairs, and on the floor, all over the house. I tried to be an adult and stay awake all night, but eventually the trip and the trauma got to me, and I fell into a fitful sleep.

One thing I had determined, however, was that I would be at the grave site and would toss the first clump of dirt onto my father's casket. I don't know why it became an obsession with me, but I wanted to be the first to say good-by after he was lowered into the ground.

It wasn't going to be easy, though, because the word was out that only the adults would be going to the cemetery the next day.

In the morning the casket was moved into the hallway in our home, and Mr. Rogers came to deliver the message. I don't remember much of what he said, but I remember the atmosphere, because in those days in Argentina, the Protestant missionaries—particularly among the Brethren—took the occasion of a death to preach the gospel.

All the neighbors were crowded into our home, and Mr. Rogers spoke about the resurrection and the fact that Jesus Himself said, "I am the resurrection, and the life: he that believeth in me, though he were dead, yet shall he live: And whosoever liveth and believeth in me shall never die" (John 11:25-26).

At that point I felt complete assurance—even though I had not yet received Christ myself—that to see my dad again, I'd have to see him in heaven. Somehow I knew I would see him again. One of the songs they sang was "Face to Face":

> Face to face with Christ my Savior,
> Face to face—what will it be—
> When with rapture I behold Him,
> Jesus Christ who died for me?

Face to face! O blissful moment!
Face to face—to see and know;
Face to face with my Redeemer,
Jesus Christ who loves me so.
(Carrie E. Breck)

Even today, it's hard for me to recite the words of that song. I clearly remember how it was sung and the assurance it gave me that day.

Then death became, to me, the ultimate reality. Everything else can be rationalized and wondered about and discussed; but death is there, staring you in the face. It's real. It happens. He was there, and now he's gone, and that's it. Without doubt, the death of my father and the two days of mourning and burial had more impact on my future ministry than anything else in my entire life.

The smell of the certain type of flower that surrounded the casket nauseates me even now, nearly four decades later. But what seemed worse then was that somehow my aunts—the ones who were staying with the children while the other adults went to the cemetery —were trying to keep me from going.

We kids were all herded into the kitchen, as the adults —nearly two hundred of them—got into the cars and trucks for the twenty-minute drive to the cemetery in Escobar. I was fuming. I knew exactly what was going on, and I became even more determined to get there and be the first to say good-by.

This is my father, I thought. *And these people are trying to tell me that I can't say good-bye to him? Why? If anyone should be there, it's me. He's my father. I loved him, and he loved me. And I am now the man of the family.* There was no way those people were going to stop me.

The trucks and cars were starting up. I was desperate. A bold run for it would never work; there were too many adults between me and the door, and they were keeping an eye on me, too. Everyone knew I was upset, and they wondered what I would try to pull.

The first vehicles started to pull away, and the others were rolling into line. I grabbed my cousin Robbie. "Distract my aunts," I said frantically. "I'm getting out of here." He loved a good hassle and nodded, smiling. I edged toward the window, where the shutters opened out. Robbie sneaked up behind three or four of the girls.

Quickly he grabbed their hair and yanked hard. They screamed and cried while my aunts charged in to pull him away. Meanwhile, I scampered out through the window. Once I got that far, I was as good as gone. There would have been a fight if they had tried to stop me then.

The line of cars and trucks was rolling away, as I dug in and ran as fast as I could toward the gate. I caught the eye of one of my favorite uncles, Ramon, who was driving the last truck. He immediately sized up the situation and nodded toward the back of the truck. I jumped in and hid under some supplies, and when one of my aunts came running out, demanding to know where I was, no one who knew would tell her. I rode triumphantly, though tearfully, to the burial. *Now just let them try to keep me from throwing the first clump of dirt.*

6

The Best Bargain

But I would not have you to be ignorant, brethren, concerning them which are asleep, that ye sorrow not, even as others which have no hope. For if we believe that Jesus died and rose again, even so them also which sleep in Jesus will God bring with them.

1 Thessalonians 4:13-14

Since Ramon's was the last truck to arrive, we were a little late getting to the graveside. Mr. Rogers was just finishing some remarks as I got to the edge of the crowd. Several were surprised to see me, the only child in the group.

One of my uncles gently put his arm around me, as if to comfort me, in case I broke down. I was just biding my time, waiting for the right moment. Finally, several men began carefully lowering the casket into the ground. All eyes were on them.

I broke away from my uncle and shot through the legs of several adults, squeezing past others, breaking through to find myself at the edge of the grave. The six-foot hole looked so deep. Before anyone could react, I grabbed a handful of dirt and tossed it down onto the casket. It made an unforgettable, dull, echoing thud.

How horrible to be burying my father! When the shovels bit into the pile of dirt and other mourners tossed in handfuls, I was grief-stricken. Yet the words about the resurrection and a heavenly home gave me hope. He was still alive, and I was going to see him.

For days on end that summer, my mother was mercilessly peppered with my questions about heaven and the second coming and the resurrection. It was good that she had been a Christian for more than eight years and had had fine Bible teaching in the assembly, especially from Mr. Rogers. She had the answers I needed to hear again and again.

She had her own grief and loss to deal with, and perhaps this was one way she did it. By reminding me and assuring me of the truths of Scripture all day, every day, she was probably simultaneously applying therapy to her own needs.

She drilled John 14:1-3 into me:

> Let not your heart be troubled: ye believe in God, believe also in me. In my Father's house are many mansions: if it were not so, I would have told you. I go to prepare a place for you. And if I go and prepare a place for you, I will come again, and receive you unto myself; that where I am, there ye may be also.

We memorized that portion, along with 1 Thessalonians 4:13-14, which reminds us that we have hope:

> But I would not have you to be ignorant, brethren, concerning them which are asleep, that ye sorrow not, even as others which have no hope. For if we believe that Jesus died and rose again, even so

them also which sleep in Jesus will God bring
with him.

The things of eternity and heaven became so settled
in my mind during those few months before going off
to a new school that I have never been ashamed to
preach on heaven. Some people have become a little
skittish about it in recent years, claiming that we really
don't know much about it, whether it's literal or symbolic.

I don't believe we should go around mocking the
streets of gold. Even if it *is* symbolic, why mock symbols? Scripture says the streets are gold, so let the
streets be gold. When we get there, we'll find out
exactly what God meant. Anyone with any imagination
should realize that heaven will be fantastic, if God
depicted it as decorated with the most precious metals
and jewels on earth.

I just can't imagine facing eternity or even losing a
loved one without having the absolute assurance of
heaven and all its ramifications. To us it was thrilling,
and through the years I have thought how lucky my
father was to have arrived there so far ahead of the rest
of us. He's in perfect bliss. He's happy. He's having a
great time. He's in the presence of the Father and Jesus
Christ. If I didn't believe that with all my heart, I'd give
it all up.

I know my eyes shall see the King in His beauty. But
you know, for years after that, when we sang, "Face to
face I shall behold Him—" I never bothered to think of
the *Him* as referring to Jesus Christ. I thought it
referred to my father. That's who I wanted to see in
heaven—and I still do.

Seeing the Lord Jesus will be far more meaningful

than seeing my father, of course, but still I look forward to seeing him again. And it's just as real to me as if I said I was going to come to Los Angeles or London and meet you for lunch. When I got off my plane, I would fully expect to see you there, waiting for me. That's the way it will be with seeing Jesus and my father when I die.

Malcolm Muggeridge says, in *A 20th-Century Testimony,*

> Death is a beginning, not an end. The darkness falls, and in the sky is a distant glow, the lights of St. Augustine's City of God. Looking towards them, I say over to myself John Donne's splendid words: *Death thou shalt die.* In the graveyard, the dust settles; in the City of God, eternity begins.

It's hard to understand why more people don't come to Christ just because of heaven. It's the best bargain there is. You give up yourself, let Jesus take over, receive forgiveness of sin, and are assured of eternal life with Him. Frankly, I cannot fathom the logic of people who know all that God is offering and still say they don't want to be saved.

People who know me best say that I preach about heaven with more power and eloquence—not with human words, of course, but with a God-given sense of reality and a passion for souls—than when I preach about anything else. I can feel my heart almost bursting from my body, in an attempt to draw more people to Jesus Christ.

A few years ago I was finishing a crusade in Nicaragua when a woman met me on my way into the stadium. She hugged me in typical Latin fashion and thanked me for presenting the gospel so clearly that her grandson, Danilo, had received the Lord two nights before.

"The next morning he was so happy," she said. "He told me, 'Granny, I've got eternal life.' Then the next day he was run over by a truck and killed while delivering papers."

That story changed my whole sermon that night. I changed the title to "I'll See You in Heaven, Danilo," and I told Danilo's story just the way his grandmother told me. The crowd was shocked. When I said he was out delivering papers the next day, they thought I was going to say that he was inviting more people to the crusade.

But I said, "Then a truck came along, and *pow*!"

Some thirty thousand people gasped, "Ohhh—" They were as shaken by the story as I had been. Then I moved right into John 14. It was a fantastic night, with many people coming to Christ. In addition to the thousands in the stadium, millions heard that night's message as it was transmitted via satellite and shortwave to more than twenty countries. We also released a Spanish film of that message, and people are converted at almost every showing of it.

Some say it's wrong to appeal to people's emotions. Come now. We have emotions, don't we? God gave them to us for a purpose. If the story of the death of a beautiful ten-year-old boy shocks someone into coming to Christ, then I say, so be it. Praise the Lord. Let them come.

Years later people tell me that they still remember that night, whether they were there, heard it on the continent-wide radio broadcast, or saw it on the film. From death comes life. That's what the Bible is all about. Little Danilo did not die in vain.

Neither did my father, for his death forever changed my life and ministry.

I wasn't excited about going off to a different British boarding school: Saint Alban's College, southwest of Buenos Aires and part of the Cambridge University Overseas Program. But my mother said that Dad had already decided to send me there, and she wanted to follow through on his wishes.

Meanwhile, my mother let my uncle take over the family business, because she had never been involved in it and didn't know what else to do. The decision would eventually prove financially disastrous, but none of us knew it then. We had always had all the money we needed, and I didn't have an inkling that it would ever end.

Saint Alban's was a tough, all-boys, Anglican school. The Argentine government required that at least four hours a day, five days a week, be taught in Spanish. Because Saint Alban's was a British school, they met the requirement and then taught the rest of the school day in English.

But we did not study the same lessons in English in the afternoon that we had learned in the morning in Spanish. We moved ahead in our courses. We became totally bilingual, and we got two years of schooling every year. That's one of the reasons the school was called a college, because by the time you were finished, you had the equivalent of four years of high school and four years of college and were qualified for *graduate work* at Cambridge University.

Saint Alban's was an expensive, exclusive private school. (I don't mean that to sound snobbish, but that's what it was.) Fortunately my father provided for me and saw the value in my attending such a place. I became involved in all of the activities, particularly athletics. I missed my mother and sisters, but with my father dead, and my interest in his work and my land diminished, Saint Alban's became my primary home.

About half the students were British, the sons of railway, banking, shipping, or lumber executives. The South American students were from at least middle-class families, because of the cost. All of us—from the youngest to the oldest—wore the typical British private-school uniform. It consisted of gray flannels, and up to age twelve, black shoes, long gray socks, short pants, a light blue shirt, a school tie, and a blazer. The whole school was divided into three houses: Corinth, Sparta, and Athens. I was in Corinth, but my best friend, George James—whom I had known since my Quilmes days—was in Athens.

That hurt, because it was considered treason to have anything to do with someone from another house. You could socialize with him, of course, but to cooperate with him in any way that might contribute to the other house beating your own house in games or contests was taboo.

The houses competed at every level. A house could win points in swimming and cricket and all the rest. The points were tallied at the end of the year, and the winning house received awards. We all got up at the same time, made our beds, cleaned our areas, and brushed and combed our hair just so. We stood in line, marched, and obeyed the masters. And we were disciplined when we didn't.

We both hated and loved it. As we grew older, rebelling or putting down authority became the thing to do.

Yet we were proud of our discipline, of our school, and that we knew what was proper. We had been trained to be responsible, and basically we did what we were told.

We became closer than brothers, spending more than nine months of the year together. Perhaps not everyone belongs in such a boarding school, but for me it was basically good and healthy; and for the most part, I liked it. I hesitate to think what I might have become had I not lived under that discipline and been expected to learn self-control.

Some of the older and more rebellious boys would run off without permission and buy beer, which they drank way up in the woods at the back of the school property. If they were reported, they would more likely lie than admit it, putting off the cricket-bat punishment for as long as they could.

There was nothing like having to bend over and touch your toes and wait for the swing and sting of that massive, flat bat. I ought to know, as you will see.

Though my grades were always pretty good, for a long time I had a bad attitude. My feeling was, "I'll study when I want to and not just because the professor says I have to."

In spite of that, those were happy days for me. We had our fun with the teachers and with one another. Pranks, jokes, traps—anything was fair game.

The British were so well organized that the games and sports were really fun. It was more than a rag-tag bunch of kids running around and screaming and kicking a ball. In fact, soccer was considered inferior. There were teams and clocks and time periods and good equipment. I enjoyed it because it kept me from growing up too fast. And that was a problem.

With my father gone, I felt I got it from every side.

My aunts and uncles always reminded me that I was the man of the family and that I would be expected to take over the business someday and take care of my mother and my sisters. I was just eleven years old, and already I had to try to decide if I thought I could do it. Even thinking of my father's business brought back the painful memories of his death. How could I run a business that carried such memories?

I began to realize that the business was no longer what it had been when my father was alive. Over the summer my mother began to worry about whether she could afford to send me back to Saint Alban's. That nearly made me frantic. That was the world I really knew and loved. And it kept me from having to think about my awesome responsibilities too soon.

My mother wasn't even sure she could afford to send me to a camp that one of my teachers, Charles Cohen, wanted me to go to during school vacation. But she certainly wanted me to go. Mr. Cohen was one of very few evangelicals in our Anglican school, and when he took boys on camping trips, they usually came back as Christians.

My mother knew I had not made a definite commitment to Christ yet, and she encouraged me to go to the camp. I didn't want to go, and I was determined to use our quickly deteriorating financial situation as my alibi.

7

Appointment in the Night

See, I have set before thee this day life and good, and death and evil.

Deuteronomy 30:15

Mr. Cohen taught trigonometry, history, and the gospels at Saint Alban's. He taught the last particularly well; although this was a formal religious course, he was excited about the gospels because he was an evangelical. He even hosted Crusaders—an extracurricular activity for Christian boys—in his home, under the sponsorship of the England-based Children's Special Services Missions (CSSM), today absorbed by Scripture Union, in Great Britain.

After one of those meetings, he had talked privately to me and asked me to come to his two-week CSSM camp in the mountains with some other boys. But I didn't want to go. It would be overtly evangelistic, and someone would put the pressure on me to receive Christ.

I knew the truth of Scripture, but I wasn't really a Christian, although I knew doctrine and all the songs about death and hell; and if anybody asked me a question, it was easy to answer correctly and evade the real issue.

I told Mr. Cohen I would have to write my mother, and when he kept asking if I had written her yet, it forced me to go ahead and do it. She wrote back that she wanted me to go and that we should pray about it—clearly not the answer that I had expected. I avoided praying and told Mr. Cohen that my mother didn't want me to go, taking two weeks out of the summer that were usually spent with her and my sisters. "And, besides, we're short on money."

It was a mistake to emphasize the money part of it, because that was all Mr. Cohen was waiting for. As soon as he sensed a put-off, he waited for me to paint myself into a corner and plead short finances and then he had me. I had pretended to want to go, but that I couldn't because of the money.

He offered to pay, which intimidated me, in his typical, persistent, Anglo-Saxon way that was hard to compete with. He wore me down, lured me into a trap when I was tired of arguing, and then had me. It was off to camp for me, despite my wishes. Even my buddies refused to go with me.

By the end of the school year in 1946 (early in December, just before the South American summer), I had turned twelve and headed home for several weeks before camp began in February. It was annoying to have been caught and forced to go—which was not the "in" thing to do—but by the time February rolled around, I would be anxious to leave for the mountains.

My mother told me straight out that she was glad I was going, because she wasn't sure I was a real, born-again Christian. I responded, "Oh, come on," trying to pretend that I was. But she knew better. And an even more frightening experience at home made my dreaded soul confrontation seem like child's play.

That summer I was eager to get some proper instruction and information about girls, sexuality, birth, and so on. The older kids at school, especially the ones who went home every weekend, always came back with incredible stories about the sexy movies they had seen, or the escapades they had been on with girls.

The full-time boarders were envious, even though we suspected we were getting an exaggerated and very distorted picture. It made me as curious as any twelve-year-old boy, and maybe a bit more so. I just had to know what it was all about, and I hounded my mother for details.

She kept telling me that she would discuss it with me when I was thirteen, probably hoping that someone else would save her the trouble by then. It was too much to ask a widowed mother in those days, but I kept pestering her and pestering her. She would not give in. I wish she had.

I have always resented the fact that at no time—even during all of my teen years—not once did a Christian man take me aside and try to fill my father's shoes in the area of counsel on sex—or anything else, for that matter. I think it's an indictment on the church of Jesus Christ that we let fatherless boys and girls learn about sex from someone outside the church or family. Many of them fail and fall into sin, partially because of their ignorance, and we are quick to condemn them (and abandon them) assuming they should have known something we failed to instruct them in.

Anyway, that summer my sexual advisor was a twenty-year-old worker who drove a truck in the family business. I was helping him deliver a load of cement bags and was really enjoying jumping in and out of the cab and feeling like a man. Then one day he pulled over to the side of the road and pulled a magazine from his pocket. At first I couldn't tell what it was.

"Lusito," he said, "since you are becoming a young man now"—I sat up a bit straighter, appreciating the stroke to my ego—"and you have no father, you need someone to talk to you about the facts of life."

My heart began to pound. I was excited to think that I might get some straight answers from someone who really knew the score. "I want to make a man of you," he said. But instead of telling me anything, he simply opened his magazine and turned the pages while I stared in disbelief. I was shocked and disgusted, but of course I couldn't take my eyes off the page.

I had never seen anything that revealing. I knew it was all wrong; it was dirty; it wasn't pure; yet I was curious. I couldn't sort out my emotions. It was appalling, yet appealing at the same time. I wanted to see it, yet I hated it.

There were fifty or sixty pictures in his magazine. The fact that he would show me something like that shocked me. I couldn't even speak. If he had asked me the next day if I wanted to see the magazine again, I would have run the other way.

I could not push those images out of my mind. I felt horrible, degraded, sinful. My mother would have died, if she'd known what happened. I felt guilty all the time, and especially in the presence of my mother or anyone from the local church. I was certain that Mr. Rogers could read the guilt all over my face.

Impure thoughts invaded my mind. Of course, I had all the usual daydreams about wanting to love someone and marry her, and as my sexual awareness was increased, I even dreamed of romantic love. But now everything had been spoiled. I had been curious before.

Now I was repulsed. And why had I not been able to look away? I was obviously perverted and sinful. I feared the judgment of God.

I was haunted by the idea that others might be thinking the same things about my sisters and my mother that I was thinking about the women in their families. My church taught holiness and purity, and my mother's holy life made me revere the opposite sex. Yet the impulses within me had now been twisted by what I had seen.

Not knowing that I was hardly unique among boys my age who'd had their first shocking encounter with pornography, I could not reconcile it in my mind. It was wrong; it was dirty; it was degrading; and yet it held fascination. I was in such a state that I was actually glad I was going to camp!

I had never been to camp before, so trekking off into southern Argentina to a hilly, mountainous area called Azul carried its own special sense of excitement. I tried to forget about the sins of my mind, because I got a dreadful feeling in the pit of my stomach when I thought of it.

At the CSSM Christian camp run by Mr. Cohen, I recognized several boys from Saint Alban's. We used Argentine army tents and brought our own foldable cots, which we set up ourselves. It was almost like the Scouts.

We set up our tents, dug trenches around them, policed the area, and were generally taught how to "rough it." There were probably fifty or sixty boys in all, supervised by Mr. Cohen and several counselors from different missionary organizations.

The counselors were all Britishers or Americans who were very concerned for the spiritual welfare of their campers. We had Bible lessons, singing, and memorization every day, along with the usual fun and games.

I missed the contact with the outside world. There were no radios, so we couldn't even hear the soccer scores. No newspapers, no nothing. We were totally cut off. We were saturated with the Word of God and with happy, snappy gospel songs, many of which have stuck with me to this day.

One morning an American Bible teacher spoke on purity in that ambiguous, roundabout way many evangelicals have of dealing with the subject of sex. I didn't get too much from it in the way of detailed instruction I needed, but it was very helpful for one reason. It was obvious that this man knew what he was talking about, and even as refined as he was about discussing the subject, his view of its sanctity and sacredness came through. More than anything, I was impressed that he himself was a pure man in an impure world.

I assumed that most people were as coarse as they boasted they were, and I still felt bad about my own confused thoughts on the subject. But this Bible teacher impressed me and gave me hope that there were indeed pure Christian men—men I could model myself after. Though I was attracted by the images in my mind, somehow I knew what was right. And this godly teacher affirmed that.

It was strange to see the stiff, curt, formal, aloof Mr. Cohen—whom I had known from Saint Alban's as someone above it all—in khaki shorts and a totally different setting. It was almost as if he were on our level, though I could never get that image of him to jell in my mind. He even acted a little differently, almost as if he had a sense of humor. The little jokes he cracked were incongruous with his station in life and his personality, and that made them even funnier. I was beginning to like camp, but I knew that soon someone was going to confront me about my faith.

It happened every night. Each counselor had about ten boys in his tent, and each night one boy was taken for a walk and given the opportunity to say yes or no to Christ's claims upon his life. By the second night everyone knew his turn was coming, because the first two kids in each tent were telling everyone what had happened.

If you really didn't want to receive Christ, they wouldn't force you, of course. This was a making-sure exercise. Many of these kids had already received Christ, and the counselors were just helping to solidify it and give them biblical assurance. Then there were the boys like me, who had grown up in solid, evangelical churches and knew the whole story, yet had never accepted it for themselves.

Even the unchurched boys knew the plan of salvation by the end of the two weeks, and many of them became Christians during those little after-dark walks with their counselors. It moves me to think how loving those counselors were and how effective that system was, in spite of its rigid programming. No one was badgered or forced, but no one missed his opportunity to become a Christian, either.

Finally my appointment with destiny arrived. I wished that I could run and hide from it, because I was embarrassed that I had not received Christ yet; still, I would not lie and say that I had.

My counselor, Frank Chandler—whom I thought of as an old man, but who was probably not yet twenty— tried to rouse me from sleep. I had been awake from the beginning, because I was the only one in the tent who hadn't been confronted and I knew it was my turn. There was something about having to go with him that rubbed me the wrong way, even though I knew in the back of my mind that it was inevitable and that I would probably get the matter of eternal life settled once and for all. Still I feigned sleep and would not respond.

"Come one, Luis, get up. I want to talk to you. Come on, up!"

I kept my eyes shut and did not move. He shook me, then shined his flashlight in my eyes. He knew I couldn't be *that* unconscious unless I was dead, so he just tipped my cot over and dumped me out. I rubbed my eyes as if he had just got through to me.

I slipped on my canvas-topped shoes and put on a jacket. The night was cold, and a light rain had begun. We heard thunder in the distance and knew a real rainstorm was coming. Frank was in a hurry. I wasn't.

He walked me to a fallen log, where we sat and talked. There were no preliminaries. The rain was coming, and he had business to cover. "Luis," he began, "if you should die, do you know if you are going to heaven or hell?"

"Yeah," I said.

"And where are you going?"

8

February 12, 1947

*. . . If you confess with your mouth Jesus as Lord, and
believe in your heart that God raised Him from the dead,
you shall be saved; for with the heart man believes,
resulting in righteousness, and with the mouth he confesses, resulting in salvation.*

Romans 10:9-10, NASB

"I'm going to hell," I said.

"Is that where you want to go?"

"No, it's not."

"Then why are you going there?"

"I don't know."

"Would you like to change destinations?" Frank
asked.

"Sure," I answered.

"Do you know what you have to do?"

"Yeah."

"What?"

"Believe on the Lord Jesus Christ and thou shalt be
saved," I said. I knew it all and had known it for as
long as I could remember.

"And have you believed?"

"No."

"Why not?"

"I don't know."

"Would you like to be saved and have your sins forgiven and know that you are going to heaven?"

"Yeah," I said with relief, nodding. I knew I had stepped over the line.

Frank pulled out his New Testament and had me read Romans 10:9-10: "If you confess with your mouth Jesus as Lord, and believe in your heart that God raised Him from the dead, you shall be saved; for with the heart man believes, resulting in righteousness, and with the mouth he confesses, resulting in salvation" (NASB).

Then he read the verses again, but dropped my name, *Luis*, into every pause, making it as personal as it could be. The Scripture was as clear as daylight to my heart, just as it had always been to my head. "Do you believe God raised Jesus from the dead?" he asked.

"I sure do."

"Are you willing to confess Him with your lips?"

"Yep."

I had already begun to cry tears of happiness. Frank then led me in a simple prayer, in which I admitted that I was a sinner and asked God to forgive me. Then I asked His Son, Jesus, to be my Savior.

The rain was cold and getting heavier. Frank flipped quickly to John 1:12 and said, "This is all the assurance you'll ever need: 'But as many as received Him, to them He gave the right to become children of God, even to those who believe in His name'" (NASB).

He prayed, and we hustled back to the tent. I could hardly sleep. I buried myself beneath the covers and, by the light of my flashlight, I wrote the date in my Bible, "February 12, 1947," and, "I received Jesus Christ."

I think of that night often, especially when people criticize speed and technique in evangelism. We worry about hurrying a person in his decision; but, I tell you, when the person is ready to go, just get to the point and help him settle it. When you sense the Holy Spirit at work, time and technique can be irrelevant.

My mother was ecstatic, of course, which was opposite of the reaction I received from my friend George James and others at school. I wasn't obnoxious about it; I was just so thrilled about my commitment that I wanted them to know. I even carried my Bible with me a lot.

I was more active in Crusaders, and the Anglican church services we were required to attend weekly took on a whole new meaning for me. I was even baptized and confirmed. I sang in the choir, until my terrible voice got me drubbed out, and I began to study my Bible every day. I corresponded often with Frank Chandler (I still have many of his letters). And I became a much better student, especially in Mr. Cohen's Acts of the Apostles class.

The biblical classes grew more significant to me, and I really studied hard and learned. I could visualize the cities and movement of the early church in Acts, because it was so clearly taught. Years later, when I studied the same course at the graduate level in the United States, I found that I already knew most of it from that semester as a twelve-year-old, when I was immersed in my first love of Christ. There's not a more open and teachable mind than that of a child still excited over his conversion.

I felt closer to Mr. Cohen and really pitched in to help at Crusaders. I sang out, listened hard, and studied all my Bible lessons. It was a beautiful experience, even though it alienated me from some of my friends who were still into dirty stories and other shenanigans.

That year our Crusader club was visited by two old missionary ladies from China, Mildred Cable and Francesca French. They had tremendous stories to tell of their travels through the Gobi Desert in the interior of China, and of being dragged through the streets of the pagan cities because they insisted upon sharing Christ with the Chinese.

In spite of all the physical abuse and punishment and persecution, they stayed on for years in China, spreading the gospel of Jesus Christ. Their witness hit me at just the right time in my life to make the best impression on me. I thought I had become an outspoken Christian, but what was I doing, compared to these women? Then I remembered that they were the very two missionaries my mother had read about to me and my sisters when we were little.

I began to look for more missionary books; I was inspired to read about how men and women gave up the luxuries of life to minister under adverse conditions, just because they loved the Lord and wanted to serve Him. I prayed that I, too, would love the Lord like that.

I didn't know whether I was going to be a missionary, but I knew that I wanted to do something for God. I was getting the broadest background for it. I was attending one of the "highest" worship services imaginable every week: in the Anglican church. And I had grown up in what might be termed the humblest, most nonconformist church, the Christian Brethren assembly.

I feel I'm in a unique position to love and relate to the entire Body of Christ because of the diversity of my childhood training. From the most hierarchical of Protestant churches in the world to the least organized, plainest assembly, I was an excited, eager listener and learner.

One thing I gained from the Anglican church was an appreciation for the beautiful language possible in prayer. I had been dissatisfied with my prayer life; my prayers seemed to just slip into repetitious blessings of Mom and my sisters and my relatives. The Anglican prayers can be repetitious, too, but what a blessing they can be if you let yourself think about their beautiful and deep content. One of my favorites—and the one I use occasionally in my private devotions even now—was,

> We have left undone those things
>   which we ought to have done;
> And we have done those things
>   which we ought not to have done;
> And there is no health in us.

The loss of that first excitement and love for the gospel is something no one has ever adequately been able to explain. It happens to so many, and when I lost it, it was as if someone had pulled my plug and the lights had gone out. Perhaps I let a cynical attitude get in the way. Perhaps I ignored my mother's counsel to stay away from worldly influences, like listening to soccer matches on Sunday and going to movies, and perhaps I was succumbing to the pressures of my fellow students.

All I know is that one day, coming home from Crusaders, I carelessly left my Bible on a streetcar and was unable to get it back. With that loss went my daily Bible reading, my attendance at Crusaders, my excitement over Bible classes, and almost everything that went along with my commitment to Christ. I still loved and believed and respected the gospel, but I did not let it interfere with my life.

I did not totally understand this quick turn-off myself,

but part of it may have had to do with the punishment I once received at the hands of Mr. Cohen. He was the master on duty one day—a fearful role of disciplinarian that was rotated among the professors. I was in an art class and doing none too well.

I was showing off to some of my friends when Mr. Thompson, the new art teacher, recently come from England, walked over and made a sarcastic remark about my horrible painting of a tree. He was right, of course; it was terrible. But I responded with some foul word in Spanish, which Mr. Thompson was not supposed to understand.

"What did you say, Palau?" he said.

"Oh, nothing, Mr. Thompson, sir. Nothing, really."

"No, what was it, Palau?"

"It was really nothing important, sir."

"I'd really like to hear it again, Palau. Would you mind repeating it?"

"Oh, I don't think it was worth repeating. I—"

"All right," he snapped. "Go see the master on duty."

The class fell silent, and my jaw dropped. That was the ultimate punishment. No one else tells the master on duty why you are there. You must tell him yourself and take whatever punishment he deems necessary. I almost died inside when I saw that Mr. Cohen was on duty.

"Come in, Palau," he said. "Why are you here?"

"Mr. Thompson sent me."

"Why?"

He was being terribly cold, especially for someone I knew and with whom I had spent a lot of time. He was even a fellow Christian, but here he was, aloof and frigid again.

"Well, I said a bad word," I confessed.

70

"Repeat it," he said.

"Oh, I had better not," I said.

"Repeat it," he said.

There was no way out of it. I told him what I had said. He didn't move at first. He just sat there staring at me, obviously disappointed, but mostly disgusted with me. When he finally spoke, it sounded like the voice of God. He reached for the cricket bat—he was a pretty fair player, and he knew how to swing it.

"You know, Palau, I'm going to give you six of the best." It was the extreme amount of swats for any punishment.

I froze.

"Bend and touch your toes, please."

As I bent over, he said, "Before I do it, I want to tell you this, Palau. You are the greatest hypocrite I have ever seen in my life."

I winced. That sounded pretty strong.

"You think you get away with your arrogant, cynical, above-it-all, know-it-all attitude, but I have watched you. You come to the Bible class, but you are a hypocrite."

That hurt almost as much as the six shots I took to my seat. The physical punishment stung for days, and I mean literally *days*. It was hard to sit down, and I slept on my stomach for a week. I cried and cried, as tough as I wanted to be about it. What he said and what he did were both medicine for me, but it took years before I realized it.

For months I hated the man. I wouldn't look at him, let alone say hello or smile at him. I quit going to Crusaders, and I quit paying attention to his Bible classes. I went through the motions of going to church because we had to, but I acted totally indifferent to the services. And I was.

71

Something between God and me had been severed. Not my salvation, of course, but something sweet in the relationship. I started to stretch the limits that had been placed on me by my school and my mother and the church. At that time I believed it was sinful to go to school dances or listen to soccer games on the radio on Sunday, or even to read magazines about car racing and sports on that day, but I did it anyway. I joined my old friends, began talking rough again, and in general developed a bad attitude toward life.

It doesn't sound like much now, but back then it was the height of shaking my fist in the face of all I had been taught. I had been an excited, eager, happy Christian for almost a year. And now I was flat.

I knew the gospel was true, and I never once doubted my salvation, but my thoughts turned to what I thought were practical matters. The family business was failing; my tuition was being subsidized, and no one knew how long that would last. I could be out of school before I wanted to be, just because we no longer could afford it.

I could think of nothing more humiliating. I would rather have been born into poverty than to suddenly find myself in it, after having lived well. But poverty was just around the corner.

9

A Genuine Phony,
Fast and Smooth

For what is a man profited, if he shall gain the whole
world, and lose his own soul? or what shall a man give
in exchange for his soul?

Matthew 16:26

Though I had actually cried when I lost my Bible, it
symbolized a spiritual cooling-off period that lasted
more than three years. I felt worldly and sinful and
guilty, but somehow I couldn't come out of it.

I was frightened that I was falling away from the
Lord, and I wondered what would become of me. Very
simply, I did not live for God during the rest of my
school years at Saint Alban's and my summers at home.
I knew deep down inside that I belonged to Christ, but
to me the pressure to not be considered a fool was too
much.

I stood by and let the two or three other born-again
Christians at St. Alban's carry the ball for the gospel.
Henry Martin and David Leake were two of the other
confessed evangelicals, and I always felt sorry that I
was hardly in their league as a witness.

Leake, now a bishop in the Anglican church, didn't

flaunt his faith. He was just faithful and steady. He never talked piously. He was just himself, and he was admired and respected.

Henry Martin, who now lives in the town I grew up in, was aggressively evangelical. He made a point of the fact that he wouldn't dance or enjoy worldly pleasures on Sunday or engage in the occasional beer-drinking escapades. He never hassled the masters, either, even when everyone else did.

One year we got so tired of having the same menu week after week that we staged a mild rebellion. Everyone took just a few grains of rice and put them on his plate, leaving the huge serving bowls full at each table. When the masters came around and demanded to know why no one was eating rice, everyone pointed at his plate and said, "I had some! See?" Everyone, that is, except Henry Martin. He would not be any part of any disrespectful actions, so he ate a generous portion of the rice. The others threatened to beat the stuffing out of him later, but he told them straight out that he didn't think it was right and that he couldn't go along with them in good conscience because he was a Christian.

Later they made good on their threat. As I stood and watched, several of the bigger boys beat him bloody. I felt so bad for so long about standing by and watching that happen to someone who stood up for the Lord that, twenty years later, I looked Henry up and apologized. He forgave me, but he had totally forgotten the incident.

Over the years I've tried to determine just what went wrong with my spiritual temperature during those last years of school. First, I had no idea about how to live a victorious life. Basically I had been taught well, but I was into a spirituality based on performance. I had no goals and little idea of my own resources. I just knew what I had to do or not do to be a fine Christian.

It was a nice, mild form of legalism. Praying, reading, studying, and going to church can wear thin fast, if that's all there is to a person's faith. I don't recall picking up any instruction on how to enjoy Christ, how to walk with Him and be happy in Him. How to really praise and worship God for who He is slipped past me, and I found myself bored with simply going on and on in the repetition of the routine.

Though I take full responsibility myself, three things contributed to my straying into the world. The first was that my father had not left a will, and my relatives who took over the business ruined it, leaving us destitute. I was not equipped to forgive them, and the rage I felt as a young boy is hard to describe. When I understood more about what had happened, and how they had jeopardized the very survival of my widowed mother and her children, I felt like I could have destroyed them.

Second, there was the lure of the world and non-Christian friends. They seemed to have so much more fun. I was drawn into a life of parties and soccer games and listening to the radio—hardly bad things in themselves, but indicative of my loss of interest in spiritual things.

Because of the business failure, my mother did everything she could to see that I continued in school. Since I was at least part Scottish, the English Aid society gave me a partial subsidy on my tuition. But I was forced to live with my grandparents in Quilmes and commute to school to save money. It was humiliating, and it also put me in a position to be less disciplined about whom I spent my time with.

Fortunately, even my non-Christian friends from my

new neighborhood were pretty straight, or I could have gotten into really big trouble. We wasted time by sitting around and talking for hours, but what really made me feel guilty was spending my Sundays doing something other than Christian work.

My goals were to be a race-car driver, a soccer player, or a big businessman. Even though the family was nearly bankrupt, and the business was virtually finished, I told my friends that it was thriving and just waiting for me to come back and run it.

I was going to be rich and powerful, a self-made businessman. Only I was lying. And it was during those really low years, when I was sixteen and seventeen and living with my grandparents, doing my own things, that I actually blamed God for a lot of our troubles. I had come full circle from my first love of Him to where I thought He had let us down.

Finally things got so bad financially that my mother visited me at school to tell me I could not continue much longer. I could finish what would be the equivalent of a junior college degree, but I would not be able to take the last year and qualify for the graduate program at Cambridge.

Completing the Cambridge program was a dream I had nurtured for years. Even though I was a rebellious student, my grades had been good, and I looked forward to continuing my education in England. Short of that, I at least wanted to go on to college in Buenos Aires; but that was out of the question. I would have to go to work to help support my family, and they were going to have to move several hundred miles north to Cordoba, now that there was nothing left of the business.

About that time my uncle, Arnold Francken, who had married Marjorie, my mother's youngest sister,

76

stepped in and kept the business together for as long as he could, by letting it be known that he was running the place with an iron fist and a gun in his belt. He said he would shoot anyone he caught trying to steal anything, workers included. Occasionally, in the middle of the night, he would empty his gun into the air in the work compound, just in case anyone got the idea he could slip past him. But, despite Uncle Arnold's iron fist and all our efforts, we ended up flat on our backs, destitute.

I felt I had been the victim of a cruel joke. Eight long, double years of schooling in the British boarding schools had left me with an intermediate degree, no money, and no future, as far as I could tell. I still feared God, but I questioned Him daily and was sometimes glad that I had not served Him more. I felt He owed me better than what I was getting, so why should I live for Him? It didn't wash, though. All the while I knew I was wrong and that I should go back to Him.

I never made fun of the church, as some of my friends and relatives did. I knew better than that. But I went sparingly to the Brethren chapel in my grandparents' town, and then only to please my grandmother. I went late and left early, doing my best to appear uninterested. It wasn't difficult.

I worked part-time for my grandfather, in his small business of selling sauces and smoked fish to restaurants, and when my last year of Saint Alban's was over, I considered myself a real British man of the world. My six or eight friends from the neighborhood were from slightly outside the circle of my British contacts, but that just made me feel important.

I joined the local university club and bought myself a pipe. I studied a Dale Carnegie book and learned "how to win friends and influence people," by talking all the time about the other person and acting interested in any small detail about his life. I was a fast-talking, smooth-working phony, and inside I hated myself.

For one thing, I knew that my new friends—even those who didn't speak any English—weren't worth any less than the British people I knew from school and club. And, try as I might to put myself in some aloof category of potentially rich, influential, and educated businessmen, something at the core of me told me that neither I nor any full-blooded Englishman was inherently any better than anyone else.

That was the truth that had been burned in my soul as a child, when rich and poor, old and young, educated and illiterate sat as equals at the Lord's Supper.

My friends, though non-Christians, were really super kids; by most standards, they were straight. They never got drunk, though they drank a little. And what I considered sins—going to soccer games on Sunday, fantasizing about girls, and wasting time—were about the worst things they did.

They danced, too, but dancing embarrassed me—I felt awkward. I used those friends as an excuse to be more worldly than my conscience was comfortable with, but it wouldn't be fair to say they were bad influences on me. In truth, I missed my chance to be a good influence on them. If I had been able to communicate what the Lord could do for them at that stage in their lives, it might have made all the difference in the world.

But I wanted to be "in." I wanted to be "cool." I didn't want them to think I was peculiar. The fear of the Lord kept me from going off the deep end and into any gross sin. Still, I was far from the Lord and ashamed to stand up for Him. In later years, even after I got back into fellowship with God, the memory of the way I shamed the Lord then was a big source of guilt for me.

The turning point came just before Carnival Week in February 1951. Carnival Week is similar to Mardi Gras, in that it is a week of total abandonment. Any business that was not crucial to the festivities was closed for the whole week. It was the week before Lent and would be followed by forty days of confession and penance, so, during the carnival, anything went.

People dressed in costumes and masks and danced around the clock. It was not unusual for a young person to experience his first night of drunkenness during Carnival Week.

I had grown tired of the sophisticated little parties and games the university club offered, so doing something more bizarre with my other friends at first sounded like an exciting alternative. My friends and I made big plans for celebrating Carnival Week of 1951. The more I thought about it, however, the more ominous it became.

Somehow I felt that if I got involved in the carnival, I could be severing my relationship with the Lord. I had already been ignoring God's ownership of my life and soul, and, while in my head I knew that nothing could separate me from the love of Christ, in my heart I feared God might not forgive this out-and-out mockery of everything I had been taught.

What would happen if something snapped within me and I went off the deep end? All of the supposed fun I had been having for months left me bored. I sensed discontentment and emptiness inside, and I knew exactly what it was. I just didn't want to admit it.

Somehow I knew that if I went to Carnival Week, temptation would overwhelm me and I would be engulfed in sin. I knew my mother and other relatives prayed daily that I would walk with the Lord, and the more I thought about it the more panicky I became.

I had to get out of Carnival Week, or I would be swallowed up, finished, sunk. I'm sure the Holy Spirit was convicting me. Toying with the world was one thing, but abandoning self-respect and flaunting God's law was something else. I wanted no part of it.

There was no purpose in my life, nothing to look forward to, except more of the same empty "fun." If I went to Carnival Week, I was convinced I would have gone beyond that point of no return. I had to get out of it.

My grandparents were gone that weekend, and the house was empty. The next day my friends would come by to pick me up for the festivities. I was beside myself. There was no way I had the strength to simply tell them I wasn't going. I had to have a reason.

Falling to my knees by my bed, I pleaded with God: "Get me out of this and I will give up everything that's of the world. I will serve You and give my whole life to You. Just get me out of this!"

10

Big Doors Turn on Small Hinges

Being confident of this very thing, that he which hath begun a good work in you will perform it until the day of Jesus Christ.

Philippians 1:6

I had no idea how God would get me out of my dilemma without my having to lie. I didn't want to do that. To prove that I meant business, I pulled my grandmother's Bible from a drawer and put it on the table beside the bed.

The next morning I awoke on my back in the empty house, staring at the ceiling. I stared. Then I blinked. Slowly I sat up and swung my legs over the side of the bed onto the floor and sat there a moment. I yawned. My mouth felt strange. I touched it. I felt no pain, but it was bloated.

I stumbled to the mirror. My mouth was so swollen it looked as if I had a table-tennis ball in it. Staring straight into the reflection of my own eyes, I worked up a crooked smile. I looked the way you look when you come home from the dentist. "God has answered my prayer," I said aloud.

I called up one of my friends. "I can't go to the dance tonight, and I won't be going to the carnival at all this week."

"Come on, Luis! Everything has been planned!"

"No. I have a good reason, and I will not go."

"I'm coming over," he said. "You must be crazy."

A few minutes later he showed up with three or four of the others. They insisted that the swelling would go down and that I should change my mind, but by then I had a good head of steam going, and I resisted until they left. It was the beginning of the end of my relationship with them.

I should have told them that, because of my faith in the Lord Jesus, I was afraid of the sin I might get involved in. That's what I would tell them today. But I was so spiritually bankrupt then that it took that fat lip to deliver me.

Knowing how good the gospel is, I am ashamed that I was so cowardly. But at least I had made my decision, taken my stand, and broken with the world. I went back into the house, broke my pipe in two, tore up my university-club membership card, and threw away all my soccer and car-racing magazines and many record albums.

The next day I went to church morning and night. The rest of the town, it seemed, was frolicking in sin. I was glad to have escaped. Everything changed. I was excited. Life perked up and had meaning again.

Looking back, I'm so thankful for the promise of Philippians 1:6: "Being confident of this very thing, that he which hath begun a good work in you will perform it until the day of Jesus Christ." Slowly I was seeing that, although I might fail God many times in my life, He would never fail me. I would learn, step by step, what it meant to live a godly life.

I bought myself a new Bible, intentionally choosing one that was written in Spanish. I wanted to get out of the proud little world of people who thought they were superior because they were better educated and more well-to-do. That was a difficult move for me to make, particularly because everything from the Bible and anything else of a spiritual nature had come to me in English.

It was time I started a career in which I could draw a good salary and help to support my family. Because I had been successful in math and business, one of my former professors recommended the Bank of London in Buenos Aires, a huge, block-long complex, with several buildings and more than five hundred employees.

My British education and bilingual abilities made me attractive to the Bank of London, and I was hired as a junior employee in training, at a decent salary for someone my age. I loved being a workingman, traveling on the subway, dressing up, and working in the sophisticated, bustling metropolis I loved. Buenos Aires had 5 million residents back then. It looked a lot like Paris, with its boulevards, sidewalk cafes, and beautiful people.

Working there made it more difficult to break away from the style of life I now despised. The bank was full of office politics, the old-boy system, golf, tennis, card games, drinking, parties, and all the rest. All those things irritated me. The pendulum had swung completely back.

I had got my taste of the world, but now that my family was living from hand-to-mouth in Cordoba, several hundred miles north, I had more important concerns. I dreamed of perhaps becoming a lawyer, of changing the world, and of making South America a decent place for troubled, poor people to live without getting walked on.

I could discuss the subject for hours, and my friends and relatives warned me that I was taking life too seriously. Perhaps I was, but I didn't think so. How could people play and party and carry on, when others were going broke and being cheated and living in hunger? How could they ride around in golf carts, ignoring the lower class, when widows and orphans were begging for help?

I looked for the best way to change my world, and I wasn't sure banking was it, though I loved it in many respects. I was learning more than I ever had in such a short time, and I was a go-getter. When my own work was done, I went to the people above my level in different departments, causing them to be suspicious of my ambition by peppering them with questions about every aspect of their jobs.

I read the banking manuals in Spanish and English, learning the entire international banking system.

My best memories from that brief period revolve around the walks and talks I had with my uncle, Jackie Balfour. He lived in the same house, and after I broke with my worldly friends, he and I would take trips into the night and walk around. We talked for hours. He was very spiritual, and just five years older than I was.

Argentinian cities were exciting in those days. Thousands and thousands of families jammed the walkways and shops, even as late as midnight. There was music and laughter and the smell of food. Jackie and I talked of what we could do to change the world. He was a writer, so we dreamed up a Christian magazine and even made mock-up dummies of the cover and page layouts.

Much of what we talked about and planned for the publication I saw become reality years later, when we launched *Continente Nuevo,* a magazine of teaching and encouragement for Spanish pastors. (In addition, we also began a Spanish and English news publication and developed a wide literature and book ministry. My staff estimates we have distributed over 12 million pieces of gospel literature.)

I was full of idealism and ambition. There were things I wanted to see happen, things that I wanted to do. Someday my chance would come; I was convinced of that. I wanted to learn, to develop, to make a difference in society. But first, I wanted to help my own family.

The best way to do that, in my opinion, was to get away from the old friends and situations in the Buenos Aires area and transfer to a branch bank, where I could start over socially. And the Bank of London had a branch office in Cordoba.

The only people I knew in Cordoba were my mother and sisters, but that seemed like more than I knew in Buenos Aires. Other than Jackie, I had no friends my own age. There just weren't that many young people in the local church. I feared turning back to my non-Christian friends out of sheer boredom, and I had already resigned myself to the fact I would probably not advance far at the headquarters bank.

I determined never to compromise my faith, even if it might someday jeopardize my business future. I just wasn't "one of the boys." I refused to come to the drinking parties and social events. I even avoided coffee breaks and went to the library instead. Still, I received a couple of promotions, mostly because I was bilingual. I was doing all right with a little desk job, but it was time for me to move.

I knew I would probably be laughed out of the office, or even fired, but I decided to ask the personnel department for a transfer to the Cordoba branch. Asking the bank for a transfer simply wasn't done, but I had worked myself into such a frenzy over the state of the world, and especially my own spiritual condition, that it didn't matter. I would have to take that chance.

I filled out an application for transfer and sent it to the personnel department. To me it was a spiritual decision. I would not have been surprised if they had fired me. If that was God's way of getting me out of a situation He didn't want me in, I was willing to accept it. I called my mother and told her I had decided to follow the Lord. I couldn't promise that it would mean a move to Cordoba, but she was thrilled anyway and no doubt started praying for just that.

When I received a memo, asking that I report to the personnel office, my resolve nearly went out the window. *What a fool,* I told myself. *You've been an idiot! These people have been good to you, and now you ask to be transferred to some hick-town branch!* Then I found myself slipping into the spiritual thought patterns of my mother, and my resolve returned. Even if the firing was painful and I had been stupid, I decided it was a sacrifice for the Lord, and He would provide.

"Why do you want to transfer to Cordoba?" the personnel manager asked.

I told him it was because my mother and sisters lived there and needed me, and that I knew it had a good branch bank. I waited in silence for his decision. "You know," he said, "it would be good for you. You can learn banking more quickly, because there are only one or two people in each major department of a branch that size, and there won't be a jungle of people to go around.

"In fact, we'll put this down as if it were our idea, and then we can justify paying for your move and giving you a promotion and raise."

I was flabbergasted. But he wasn't finished. "If you progress as nicely there as you have here, within six months we'll put you in charge of foreign operations of that branch, and in a year we'll bring you back here for a few weeks of specialized training. In our eyes, you will begin as the number-three man in Cordoba."

I was not yet eighteen years old.

A few weeks before leaving, I was lying on the living-room floor at my Uncle Arnold's and Aunt Marjorie's home, listening to an evangelist on HCJB Radio, though at the time I didn't know what it was. I didn't hear the evangelist's name, but I heard him exhorting, preaching, and calling men to come to Christ. Then I heard a man's beautiful voice, singing a song by William T. Sleeper:

> Out of my bondage, sorrow and night,
> Jesus, I come, Jesus, I come;
> Into Thy freedom, gladness and light,
> Jesus, I come to Thee.
> Out of my sickness into Thy health,
> Out of my want and into Thy wealth,
> Out of my sin and into Thyself,
> Jesus, I come to Thee.

The whole program left me exhilarated. Years later I realized that I had been listening to Billy Graham and George Beverly Shea.

Stretched out on that living-room floor, I prayed:

"Jesus, someday use me on the radio to bring others to You, just as this program has strengthened my commitment to You."

I've always believed that big doors turn on small hinges. I recognize a lot of small hinges that the big door of my life turned on in my past, but one of the major ones was the move to Cordoba. It changed me. I became a different person.

I had been through a lot of new beginnings before, but this time I was taking charge of the family. My mother's influence on me would again be for the best. I would find it easier to live for God in a Christian home where that was encouraged and expected.

We were a big family, but we rented a small house because there was little money. My good salary didn't go far, with seven mouths to feed. When I moved in, my family had already stretched the bedrooms to their limits. I took the living room as my bedroom, and the sofa became my bed.

I felt a tremendous responsibility to provide an answer for my family. I was still quite young, but life was a serious matter to me. Once in a while some old business debt would be paid by someone honest enough to look up my mother and take care of it, but otherwise we had no extra money.

I had only a few clothes and made them stretch over a few years. I no longer looked like a banker, and soon banking became secondary to me. First and foremost was the family, and soon after I arrived I dived right into the middle of the local Christian Brethren assembly.

It was a group of about 130 people, probably the biggest local church I had ever seen, and unusually large in South America at that time. They had an exciting program, run totally by the elders and the one full-time missionary, George Mereshian. He took me under his wing immediately, because I expressed a desire to be baptized by immersion so I could become active in the work.

This was a very strict and doctrinally sound body, and they held fast to the rule that a person could not participate in ministry leadership roles unless he had been baptized, served in lesser capabilities, and studied the Word in depth for several years.

The Bible-teaching program was so sound and systematic that it was like attending a seminary. I was thrilled. I don't know where my hunger for the Word had been all those years, but when the elders and the itinerant full-time workers—we called them missionaries —made the rounds with week-long studies of Bible books, I just couldn't get enough.

I began to devour commentaries and supplementary books by great Christian preachers, teachers, and writers. Books such as *Lectures to My Students* and *Treasury of David*, by C. H. Spurgeon; *The Man God Uses* and *The Revival We Need*, by Oswald J. Smith; biographies on D. L. Moody, John Wesley, Charles E. Finney, and Robert Murray M'Cheyne; and the writings of F. B. Meyer, S. I. Ridout, J. I. Packer, Oswald Chambers, and scores of others influenced my life and ministry.

Many of these were precious copies of out-of-print editions, loaned to me by missionaries and national leaders. Today, especially when I'm in Great Britain, I eagerly comb the used-book stores, in search of more of these precious treasures to add to my library.

For a year I was encouraged and watched while studying hard and performing menial tasks around the church.

I worked harder at my Bible-study program than I

did at the bank—not because I was lazy at work, but because I had caught onto that quickly and moved up fast. When I landed the foreign-operations job, I found I could get my work done in a few hours and have the rest of the time to study my Bible and the commentaries, with permission from my supervisors.

I devoured the program, was full to the brim, and was anxious for some of it to spill out of me.

11
Am I a Soldier?

But seek ye first the kingdom of God, and his righteousness; and all these things shall be added unto you.

Matthew 6:33

My insatiable hunger for the Word of God was increasing, and I enjoyed trying to satisfy it. Then came the day we sang the hymn "Am I a Soldier of the Cross?"

I sang with the enthusiasm the tempo demands, but hardly thought about the words. The Lord must have used all the Bible knowledge that was being poured into me to make me sensitive to Him, because suddenly I was overcome with the meaning of the song.

> Am I a soldier of the cross?
> A foll'wer of the Lamb?
> And shall I fear to own His cause
> Or blush to speak His name?
>
> (Isaac Watts)

The lyrics burst into my mind as if God Himself was impressing an exhortation on my heart. "You sing of being a soldier of the cross, and yet you do nothing,"

He seemed to say. "You have never suffered for the Lord; no one has ever said a thing to you against God. Think of Mildred Cable and Francesca French—those two missionary ladies from Asia, whom your mother read to you about and whom you met several years ago."

My thoughts turned to those cowardly years and how little I was now doing, compared to those inspiring women. I could hardly continue singing. *What kind of coward are you?* I asked myself. *When were you ever dragged by the hair or stoned or spat upon for the gospel? You stand here and sing about being soldiers of the cross, but you are no soldier.*

That rebuke did something for me. I began to take seriously the idea that all this Bible study and training under the elders and Mr. Mereshian was a call from the Lord to serve Him and even to suffer for Him, if necessary. It was then I knew that I probably wouldn't be a banker all my life. And I wouldn't be a lawyer or a judge, either. I couldn't change my nation or the world through finances or law or politics or sociology. I was going to have to be a soldier of the cross or quit singing about it.

I had helped out in Sunday-school classes and dusted and moved furniture and done all the studying as enthusiastically as anyone for a year. Finally it was time for my baptism. I was glad. After that I was not restricted from any ministerial activity I wanted.

As a baptismal day gift, my mother gave me my own copy of C. H. Spurgeon's *Lectures to My Students*, a book on preaching and pastoral work for young preachers. That book molded my young life and has marked my ministry.

Probably the most exciting outreach activities were

street meetings, led by George Mereshian. We would drive into neighborhoods, carrying speakers on top of our cars. Someone would start singing and playing an instrument to draw a crowd, while Mr. Mereshian would try to find an electrical outlet for his audio equipment.

He was quite a salesman. He always managed to charm someone into letting him use a wall outlet in a house. Then we were in business.

My first speaking engagement was at one of those street meetings. Those meetings can fizzle fast if they're not kept lively. I was nervous, but I had prepared for days and was more worried about keeping the crowd there than about whether I was saying everything correctly. A lot of our workers went along to make it look like a big crowd.

A close friend and I really started enjoying the street meetings. He was a better speaker than I was, and he could always get the crowd excited. He had a lot of zeal. It was great to plan for these little junkets, although we didn't see many conversions. The experience was probably more beneficial to us and our future ministries than it was to the populace.

The first time I spoke formally in the Brethren assembly was at a youth meeting, which was customarily also attended by adults. There was a crowd of 120, including my beaming relatives. I was scared to death.

I had studied Spurgeon's notes on Psalm 1 from *The Treasury of David* for weeks on my knees. And I had prayed and prayed. For some reason, knowing that everyone in the audience was at least as accomplished a Bible student as I was made this kind of a speaking engagement more frightening than preaching on the street.

It was more than just the delivery of a sermon. It was supposed to be a message from God—which it was—though it came through the lips and pen of C. H. Spurgeon. Still, God had impressed it upon me to preach it, too. I thought I was ready, but I dreaded going through with it.

It was all I could do to talk myself into showing up, but I had my outline and my notes prepared. I figured I was ready with about forty minutes' worth of thoughts and hoped I wouldn't go over my time allotment.

I needn't have worried. My throat was dry. The butterflies never stopped. I practically read my notes verbatim and finished in eleven minutes and a few seconds.

I felt I had failed, even though Spurgeon's thoughts were good. More than anything, I was relieved it was over.

Meanwhile, the financial situation at home wasn't getting any better. The Lord had impressed upon me to take care of my mother and sisters; He would take care of me. And He did, even though we sometimes ate a loaf of French bread with a little garlic for our whole meal, and I wore my Uncle Arnold's discarded suits and my grandfather's old topcoats.

That didn't bother me. I was in the Word and had shaken many of my fears of not being accepted or part of the crowd. I still worked hard at the bank and kept advancing, but the money just didn't stretch far with my five sisters growing up.

I knew God meant it for our good. We had been wealthy, so our poverty was an education. I understand and love the poor so much better now because I have been there. It would have been more difficult for me to identify with them, if I had simply been raised in British boarding schools and lived in wealth until landing a job. The experience taught me to walk humbly before the Lord and to look to Him for everything. There was nowhere else for us to look.

My mother never lost her spiritual sensitivity. She knew it was a blessed experience to trust the Lord for day-to-day provisions. She often quoted Scripture to us during those rough times, and we all grew from it.

Matthew 6:33 was a daily reality to us, "But seek ye first the kingdom of God, and his righteousness; and all these things shall be added unto you."

At the bank my co-workers began to call me the Pastor. While I was now in a position of influence at work and in the community, I no longer denied I was a Christian, as I had done in earlier years. I was associating with wealthy people, but they all knew of my faith.

I still found more and more time, even at the office, to study theology. I studied whole books of the Bible, using works like *Jeremiah*, by F. B. Meyer. I read through Bible commentaries such as Jamieson, Fausset, and Brown on the New Testament, and Bible dictionaries. I studied up to five different subjects a week.

I kept reading and reading and accepting more opportunities to preach and teach at churches, youth meetings, and on the street. I couldn't have studied more or harder or faster if I had been in seminary. In a way I was in seminary. For two years, George Mereshian discipled me, three hours a day, three days a week.

At his house we'd kneel in front of his couch and read the Scriptures. He would then explain the passages and answer my questions. We would look up the comments written by men of God on the passages we studied. We covered a lot of ground in that time. I learned as much from this humble, holy man as I did from the study itself.

I became the Sunday-school superintendent and learned to organize workers and programs. I was tough, too. If teachers couldn't make it to the teachers' meetings, they couldn't teach on Sundays. No exceptions.

By the time I was into my early twenties, the elders felt that many of us younger men could handle the street work by ourselves. My friend and I headed up a team that really made the rounds. We preached all over the place, taking turns drawing the crowd, leading the singing, and then preaching.

Interestingly enough, although I loved to preach and felt burdened to invite people to turn to Christ, my friend was considered the evangelist. People said we made a great team, and that I should be the Bible teacher and he the evangelist. And that's the way it was for a while.

If we had an evangelistic service, I emceed the meeting, and he preached. If our emphasis was on exposition or doctrine or theology, he led the meeting, and I taught. I learned a lot from him. He had tremendous voice projection, was a talented musician and singer, and was very entertaining. We traveled to little chapels all over the countryside and continued our street meetings.

That's really where I began to learn the basics of evangelism. We would run into everything when we preached on the street: laughter, scorn, hecklers, questions that required quick answers, questions that required diplomacy, and all kinds of things. One thing the elders burned into our minds was that we had the truth. We stood on the truth. There was nothing that could stop the power of the Word of God. The Christian can afford to let hecklers and arguers talk their heads off, because when he responds with the Word of God, he slays them. Truth is truth, and any honest person who hears it knows it.

In *The Joyful Christian*, C. S. Lewis said:

> The great difficulty is to get modern audiences to realize that you are preaching Christianity solely and simply because you happen to think it is *true*; they always suppose you are preaching it because you like it or think it is good for society or something of that sort.[1]

My young evangelist friend and I challenged each other to get up early in the morning to pray. He lived a few blocks away, and we traded off meeting at each other's house at 5:00 A.M. Gradually, more and more of our young friends began to join us for Bible studies and prayer. They were committed. They meant business.

Every Friday night we were committed to spending the entire night in prayer. We had cookies and coffee to help keep us awake, and the whole purpose was to help one another, encourage one another, confess our sins, find escapes from temptation, and stay on top spiritually.

We even developed a midday seven-minute radio program called "Christian Meditation," which was aired locally just after the one o'clock news every day. That was the beginning of what would become an extensive broadcast-media involvement for me, but back then I figured that would be the extent of it. I was developing

---

1. C. S. Lewis, *The Joyful Christian: 100 Readings from the Works of C. S. Lewis* (New York: Macmillan, 1977).

an overwhelming desire to win people and nations to Christ, but I didn't know where it would lead.

The other young fellows and I were working in Sunday schools, holding street meetings, leading youth meetings, selling Bibles, and handing out tracts. The church was really hopping. Nevertheless, even with all of that activity, few of us knew yet what true victory in the Spirit was.

We had doctrine, but some of us never did seem to get the point of what it means to walk in the Spirit and not be legalistic. I longed to walk in the power of the Spirit and be free of the self-effort of the flesh. Discipline is good, but in the frenzy of activity I found little sense of victory or powerful living.

Our times of study and prayer and work became a cycle of grim determination to stay with it, to keep on keeping on. We knew the power was to come from the Spirit, but for some reason we weren't experiencing it. We continued to search desperately, when we should have long since found it.

Though we were far ahead of most people our age in serving the Lord, we desperately needed to know how to rely on the indwelling Christ and not on our own efforts. Many of the guys eventually dropped out, tired of the battle. I was on the verge myself, not because I saw any lack in God, but because I was weary of fighting and struggling and seeking on my own to persevere through sheer dedication. I was exhausted, and exhaustion can breed cynicism.

When am I ever going to catch on? I wondered. *Will I give up now, after all I've been through?* I knew the other side of life was hopeless. But there is a monumental emptiness when you know you're looking in the right place and still are not finding the answer.

I wanted victory. I wanted peace. I wanted to rest in Jesus, instead of wrestling with Him. I agonized literally whole nights in prayer, seeking God's power and fire and ability. I wanted to please and love and serve God. I wanted people to be saved. I would sing, "Oh, Jesus, I have promised to serve Thee to the end," and I would think, *Even if it kills me*. It was a gritting-your-teeth kind of hanging in there.

I didn't know how much longer I could take it.

12

Emerging from the
Wilderness

*Go therefore and make disciples of all nations, baptizing
them in the name of the Father and of the Son and of the
Holy Spirit.*

Matthew 28:19, RSV

I kept trying new programs for the Sunday school
and our other ministries, trying to shake loose from the
small potatoes types of results we had been having.
Many of the ideas came from reading materials I got
from the United States, including a whole new concept—to me—that I picked up from a Southern Baptist
publication. The idea? Daily Vacation Bible School.

A Southern Baptist missionary put me onto many
fine Sunday school magazines, including one that was
great for the superintendent, and some Nazarene publi-
cations. The Southern Baptists were so organized that I
was inspired to learn management principles. Our teachers, even those who did not have high-school educa-
tions, found themselves studying child psychology and
pedagogy.

I knew that the program was important and would
work, because, before I had even become Sunday-

school superintendent, I had taken training with the Child Evangelism Fellowship. Two single women in their mid-thirties—Theda Krieger and Margaret Tyson—who were involved with CEF showed such love to children and such belief in training classes that I talked a group of friends and my sisters into attending their training sessions with me. After learning how to prepare a lesson, give an introduction, tell a story, work with the Scriptures, and lead someone to Christ, I was ready to really get rolling in Vacation Bible School.

Praying for ourselves, several of us young people bussed youngsters from all over the area to the country spot where we held VBS. I directed it and also taught a class of about ten boys, aged ten to twelve. When three of them came to Christ by the end of the week, I had developed such a passion for souls that I was ready to burst. This passion for the lost, fanned into flames as we led these youngsters to Christ, has never diminished. Today, as I see the hundreds of people responding to crusade invitations, I get so excited to realize that God is using us to fulfill the Great Commission:

> Go therefore and make disciples of all nations, baptizing them in the name of the Father and of the Son and of the Holy Spirit, teaching them to observe all that I have commanded you; and lo, I am with you always, to the close of the age (RSV).

Nothing is more thrilling.

All my church work and study began to take on a different flavor. In the midst of it all, however, there was far too much backbiting and criticizing of other Christians, other denominations, and even other churches

101

within the group. It was what I call a certain unvictory.

The problem wasn't only among the young adults. We saw it in the older people, too—envy, pride, divisive spirits. And the temptation to fall into immorality was almost unbearable. We had hoped that our being active Christians would somehow diminish the normal thought-life temptations that face young men. But that just didn't happen. We were expecting more than the Bible promised.

All during that time I struggled with the question of whether I was too big a scoundrel for the Lord to work with. Perhaps I was so base that He couldn't give me victory, because I would mess up. I was hot and cold at the same time. I loved God, and I was burdened to share Christ, but I still longed for that inner peace, that feeling of resting in Him even while working hard and fast to spread the gospel.

Unfortunately, most of the key men in our young people's group dropped out under the same burden. Others joined us, but I have always felt sorry that the original core of committed young men broke up after about two years.

I weighed the whole matter for several days, seeking the Lord in prayer. I wound up still frustrated, still short of what I felt the Scripture offered in terms of peace and God and victory and purity in my thought life. Until I found the answer, I would not quit looking for it. Nor would I allow the search for my own victory to get in the way of offering God's love and salvation to people who had a greater need than I.

I had learned so much from George Mereshian that I grew to enjoy calling on the sick and visiting people in their homes. I discovered an evangelical Christian home for aged ladies and decided that I would be their pastor.

I never told anyone I saw it that way, but I took it upon myself to round up some buddies, and we went there every Saturday for three years and held services for them.

It was good practice. I taught them the Word, led hymns, organized the program with the other talent available, and even took them gifts of clothes and food. This was my little parish, and I loved it—not just the experience, but the dear older women, too.

I really tried to get to know them. They had their own particular needs. One night an old French woman's aged sister died, and the woman asked if I would sit with her by the casket through the night, as is the custom. As we sat there, just the two of us with the quite-dead sister, the woman said, "Luis, in France we have a custom, and I promised my sister I would carry it through."

"Oh?" I said. "What's that?"

"We've always been afraid of being buried alive, so I promised my sister that if she died before I did, I would make sure she was dead. The custom is to flex the muscle, and if there is no reflex, you can be sure the person is dead."

"Well then, let's just tap her knee the way the doctors do," I suggested.

"That wouldn't be good enough. She could be alive and still not respond if she's just unconscious."

"What do you want to do, then?"

She pulled a long straight pin out of her hair. "If we stick this deep into the sole of her foot, and she doesn't respond, then I'll be sure. But she's my sister, and I just can't bring myself to do it. Would you do it, please?"

Oh, Lord, I prayed silently. *The things people ask you to do!* There was no way around it. The woman had been dead several hours, but that didn't make it any easier. I lifted her foot and plunged in the pin. It slid as if through butter, right to the bone.

There was no movement. "Now I know she's with the Lord," the grateful old woman affirmed, giving me a kiss. "Thank you, Luis."

"Certainly," I muttered.

There were still frustrations. The weekly prayer meetings had fallen apart. I was saying the same words and reading the books, but my preaching seemed to have no power. I was prepared, psyched up, prayed up, backed up, and zealous. Yet I saw no immediate fruit.

Nothing I did seemed to make any difference. I had just about had it. I was inspired by things I read and heard about Billy Graham's ministry, but it seemed obvious I didn't have what he had.

Finally I gave God a deadline. I felt I had been in the wilderness long enough. If He had been trying to teach me humility, I guess I had learned it. Actually, I couldn't understand why He was withholding His blessing from my preaching. But I felt beaten.

I told the Lord that if I didn't see converts through my preaching by the end of the year, I would quit preaching. I would still be an active Christian, and I would still study and pray and read, but I would resign myself to simply assisting others. There was no sense in preaching evangelistically if no one was coming to Christ.

The end of the year came and went about six weeks later, and I was really low. God had had His chance to prove Himself to me; I had given Him plenty of time. My mind was made up. I was through as a preacher. Who needed it? Obviously I wasn't filled, called, or gifted.

On Saturday morning, about four days into the new year, I bought a Spanish translation of Billy Graham's *The Secret of Happiness,* shut the door so I wouldn't be distracted by my sisters and their friends in the kitchen, and curled up on the couch to read.

As low as I was, I was blessed by Billy's thoughts on the Beatitudes, from Matthew 5. Though depressed and feeling starved for spiritual fruit, my learning techniques kicked into gear and I couldn't help memorizing the points he made on each Beatitude. The book didn't quite make me happy, for I was still mourning the loss of my preaching ministry, but I gained a few things from it.

That night the Brethren had what is called a cottage meeting, run by the elders, at someone's house. I didn't feel like going, but I always went, out of loyalty to the elders. Someone would be preaching the Word, and it was only right to support him. Other elders did the same when I preached.

I dressed slowly and dragged myself out of the house to the bus stop, not even taking my Bible; I would just be there as moral support, anyway. We sang several hymns, but the speaker never showed up. None of the other preachers were there, either, so I was glad I hadn't brought my Bible and wouldn't be able to preach.

Finally one of the elders came to me. "Luis, you're going to have to speak. There's no one else here."

"No, no, I don't want to preach. I'm very low and unhappy right now."

"There's no one else. You have to speak."

"Please," I said, "I am not going to speak; I don't have a message. I didn't even bring my Bible."

He gave me a Bible and demanded that I preach. He was the elder, and I was obedient. I hardly had time to breathe a prayer. As I stood I decided to read the Beatitudes and then—without notes—see how many of Billy

Graham's points I could remember from the book I had read that morning. It was really terrible, because I couldn't work up any enthusiasm. While speaking, I thought how terrible it was to be pretending.

I read a verse, repeated Billy's commentary, read another verse, repeated Billy's commentary, and so on. Finally I came to "Blessed are the pure in heart, for they shall see God" (Matthew 5:8, RSV), and I added a few comments, including the fact that the New Testament also says that "the blood of Jesus His Son cleanses us from all sin" (1 John 1:7, RSV).

Suddenly a non-Christian woman from the neighborhood stood and began to cry. "Well, I'm not pure in heart," she sobbed. "That means I'll never see God. Somebody help me! How am I going to find God? My heart isn't pure. I haven't been cleansed. How do I get cleansed by the blood?"

We led her to Christ right there. What a thrill it was! God really has a sense of humor. He lets me try my humanistic techniques, figuring that if I threaten to quit preaching He will certainly come through and save my talent for His use. Then, when my first adult convert does appear, it's the result of one of Billy Graham's message outlines!

What I really learned from that, of course, was something I had studied and should have known all along: the Holy Spirit does the convicting. I was just a vehicle. God used me in spite of myself, and He did it in His own good time.

As Henrietta Mears said: "To be successful in God's work is to fall in line with His will and do it His way. All that is pleasing to Him is a success."

I ignored the busses that night and walked all the way home, praising the Lord that He had chosen to use me again. Yet even though I had great convictions about preaching the Word and wanted to serve Christ more than anything, I still had those terrible ups and downs.

106

13

Someday My Chance
Will Come

*The Lord is not slack concerning his promise, as some
men count slackness; but is longsuffering to us-ward, not
willing that any should perish, but that all should come
to repentance.*

2 Peter 3:9

During the nightly prayer meetings with others from
the assembly, I started writing down the thoughts I felt
I was getting from the Lord. I had pages full of notes,
many of them dealing with my own impatience. Here
we had about 130 Brethren preaching on the streets,
witnessing, passing out tracts, and visiting, but were we
really touching this massive city of 800,000?

There were a few evangelical churches, but we weren't
making a significant impact. We weren't even touching
the middle and upper classes. As the months went by,
we kept praying for big things, but our actions weren't
matching our prayers. I thought we should either quit
praying or start acting. We prayed, "Lord bless the
work," and we had thirty children in the outreach Good
News Clubs.

I thought we ought to do something for widows and

orphans, the way the Bible instructed us to. We needed to defend the people and win them to Christ. I decided that if I could choose any area in which I could do the most to affect the masses for good, it would be in evangelism. I began seeing myself as an evangelist then, while others still saw me as a young Bible teacher.

Brethren missionaries who gave me books also passed along dated copies of American Christian magazines. A copy of *Moody Monthly* in the 1950s caught my eye. It showed Billy Graham in the 1954 London crusade and told the whole story. What an impact that had on me!

Here I had heard that the end was near and that there would be no more revival, no more great masses of people coming to Christ. The assemblies would get smaller, and believers would just have to band together and defend the faith in the last days. But it just wasn't true! To say that the masses weren't turning to Christ, one would have had to ignore what Billy Graham was doing.

I tore out the color picture of Billy Graham and pinned it on the wall near my bed. My mother said, "That's idolatry." I knew it wasn't. I wasn't worshiping Billy Graham. I admired him, yes, but to me that picture represented what God could do through a man. And it gave a boost of hope to my growing dream to evangelize millions of Latin Americans.

I prayed that God would somehow use me to share Christ with many people, and even nations. Billy Graham's ministry proved that something was happening. God was moving. There surely was such a thing as mass evangelism, and it excited me.

One day when I was sick, the elders came to call on me and pray for me. They were shocked to see the picture of a man on the wall, and they told me so. Still, I talked about Billy Graham almost as if I knew him. I followed what was happening with him, because it made sense to me.

If there were more people on earth than ever, and God was not willing that any should perish (as 1 Timothy 2:4-5 and 2 Peter 3:9 clearly state), then many of them should be coming to Christ. I was enriched by these American magazines, and I was spurred to read books about Luther, Calvin, Wesley, Whitefield, Finney, Spurgeon, Moody, and Sunday.

Why couldn't we have widespread revival and see hundreds of thousands come to Christ? South America was so in need of it! It was happening in the United States through Youth for Christ and many other organizations, so it could happen here, as well. I believed my dream was not far off.

The Brethren had difficulty accepting mass evangelism, for reasons other than that they thought the Christian population would diminish in the last days. They were big on the local church and didn't believe in giving altar calls, basically because they felt that a person's decision for Christ under such circumstances might not be genuine.

A mass evangelistic crusade, on the surface at least, seems removed from the local church, though many evangelists, including myself, have since proved that it is a perfect extension and natural place of worship for the local body.

I wanted a part in proving that God was still powerful. The world is impressed by big crowds. No, I don't believe in numbers for numbers' sake, and, no, I don't believe in big crowds to show off how the hotshot evangelist can draw a crowd. A huge crowd is a credit to God.

I have been told that Moody's and Finney's converts were weak. Others told me that mass evangelism was not for our time. Still, I felt burdened by the Lord about it. Friends gave me the book *Revival in Our Time*, which discussed Billy Graham's 1949 Los Angeles crusade, the event that contributed to what Dr. J. Edwin Orr calls the mid-century revival.

"Why can't we see this in our country?" I wanted to know. A whole nation could be turned around with only a small percentage of conversions. Mass evangelism could lift a nation's moral and ethical standards. History bore that out.

My dream from all the reading and praying I had been doing was that Latin America could be reached on a large scale for Christ. We were doing such small works —not that there is a thing wrong with any of them. But if there is room for growth—and that means more converts—then let's get to it. Let's win the thousands. Let's start new local churches.

I believe in one-on-one evangelism. I practice it. I teach it. But it can only be a complement to the greater movement. History has shown that a nation of millions cannot be converted by one-on-one evangelism, because eventually the chain breaks down and the multiplication peters out. You can prepare the groundwork, but eventually it's necessary to move the masses, sway public opinion, influence the thought patterns of the nation and the media.

A nation will not be changed with timid methods. The nation must be confronted, challenged, answered, hit with the truth. We have nothing to lose and everything to win.

People wonder if my motivation in those days was at all ego-inspired. No, I don't believe I was thinking about making a name for myself. But people have choices. They can be successful; they can be failures; or they can be mediocre. Being second-rate is certainly dishonoring to God. He spews the lukewarm out of His mouth, as Revelation 3:15-16 tells us.

I accept the biblical sanction of God. I know I am ego-centered. But I'm not going to spend the rest of my life beating my breast and searching my soul. Nevertheless, I do ask the Lord, "If I get out of hand, or if I am in the way of Your greater glory, please put me down." And I have perfect confidence that He will do so.

I allow Scripture to search my soul. I would love to say that my motivation was just sheer love for widows and orphans, which was there, of course. But I am sure that there are mixed motives in my desire to reach nations. I will give that desire to God and pray that He will remind me who I am and who I am not.

My integrity will not allow me to say that I live only for the glory of God. I wish that were the case, and I want it to be that way, but I'm still human. I pray, "Lord, make everything I do pleasing to You," but that prayer is only good before the fact. If I have done something dishonoring to Him, He cannot be pleased with it.

I believe in the inherited corruption of the heart. The Lord knows all my motivations, even the basest. Slowly but surely He will chip away at any vestiges that dishonor Him, so I am at peace.

It's impossible to successfully wrestle your own ego down, because, when you're on the bottom, who's on top? Still you. Ray Stedman, pastor of the Peninsula Bible Church, in Palo Alto, California, says you need a third force that invades you, wrestles you down, and controls you. That force is Jesus Christ. Anyone who claims to have beaten his own ego is deceiving himself.

The more I prayed and read about mass evangelism, the more convinced I became that it was where the Lord wanted me. I shifted into high gear in my personal study, and since formal theological training and degrees were not encouraged by our elders, I knew I would have to be self-taught.

I loved keeping up on trends in evangelism, and I was addicted to the truth of the Word. I wanted to know theology. I wanted to know technique. I wanted to know it all.

A Navigators representative to Argentina, Norman Lewis, influenced my life, and memorization became a big part of my study. I organized my days just like a school day, breaking the morning into four one-hour periods, studying one subject for fifty minutes, taking a ten-minute break, then studying another subject. At one time I was studying three different Bible books and some general theology.

Someone gave me an old Moody correspondence course by R. A. Torrey, entitled *How to Work for Christ*. I ate it up. I didn't send the exams to Chicago, but I answered all the questions and memorized every verse in the entire eight-volume course. I spent an hour a day on that course and learned much about personal evangelism. Torrey covered everything from how to lead someone to Christ to how to deal with an agnostic. It was fantastic. There were even sections on passing out tracts, having prayer meetings, and making sermon outlines.

I still use the truths learned from that course in training counselors for crusades and television campaigns.

For the next two years, I studied several hours a day,

When we arrived in Bogota, Colombia, in 1964, we
worked with Overseas Crusades as missionaries,
training others in evangelism and church planting.

The typically beautiful Colombian countryside, as it
appeared in 1965.

"Luis Palau Responde," one of two daily radio programs begun in 1965, grew to reach an audience of an estimated 14 million in over twenty countries.

Preaching in Cali, Colombia, in 1966.

My wife, Pat, and I in our early days as missionaries, sharing in a street meeting in Colombia.

Despite open hostility toward evangelicals, a group of young Christians asked us to help them organize a citywide evangelistic campaign in Bogota, Colombia, in December 1966.

Ten thousand people paraded through the streets of Bogota, witnessing to their faith. For me, it was the fulfillment of a ten-year dream and prayer. The efforts of these young people were instrumental in opening up Colombia to the gospel.

My family in 1966: Pat and I with Andrew, Kevin, and Keith (L to R).

Our Mexico '70 Crusade in the Mexico City Arena was, in many ways, the catalyst that began to focus the attention of

many on what God was doing in Latin America. During the ten-day campaign, 106,000 people came to hear the gospel messages.

The 1972 Crusade Traveling Team consisted of:
(L to R) Marcelino Ortiz, Edgardo Silvoso, John
McWilliam, Bruce Woodman, me, Guillermo
Villanueva, Don Fults, and Jim Williams.

Preaching in the tropical rain during the first crusade
in the Dominican Republic in 1973.

Speaking at "Youth Quake" in Birmingham Cathedral, England, in June 1976. These meetings marked the early stages of our ministry in Great Britain.

I interpreted for Dr. Billy Graham when we traveled to Guatemala to provide help for victims of the 1976 Guatemala earthquake. (*Photo by Russ Busby, Billy Graham Evangelistic Association.*)

It is always very gratifying to challenge college students interested in missions, as here during the 1976 Inter-Varsity Student Missions Conference, held in Urbana, Illinois.

I had the great privilege of sharing the platform with Dr. Billy Graham and Rev. John R. W. Stott at the Urbana conference in 1976.

My mother, Mrs. Matilde de Palau, was a strong influence on my Christian life. She has been able to assist in the Family Counseling Centers at several of our crusades.

I am grateful for the superb Bible teachers that the Lord brought into my life, who taught and discipled me, helping me to prepare for an effective Bible teaching, as well as evangelistic, ministry.

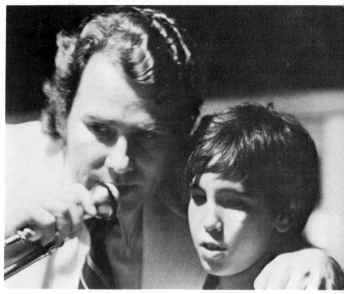

Though we specialize in mass evangelistic crusades,
our concern is for individuals to come to know Jesus
Christ personally.

Visiting with young people during the Team's 1977 Dominican Republic Crusade. Over 105,000 attended the two-week crusade, as reported in TIME magazine.

The Anglican Bishop of Llandaff joined us on the platform of the "Jubilee '77" Crusade in Cardiff, Wales.

During most of our crusades, the Team's "Responde"
television program is aired live on local and national
television networks. Viewers telephone in, seeking
biblical solutions to a variety of problems.

An evangelist
must be ready to
face times away
from his family
—times of long,
hard hours of
work on the
road.

Our team has produced two full-color English films.
In 1977 we shot footage for *God Has No
Grandchildren,* in South Wales.

In 1978, I appeared on "100 Huntley Street," the popular
Toronto, Canada, talk show.

Participating in news programs and talk shows often
provides me with opportunities to correct misleading images
of evangelical Christianity. Pictured here is Venezuela's
"Meet the Press" news program.

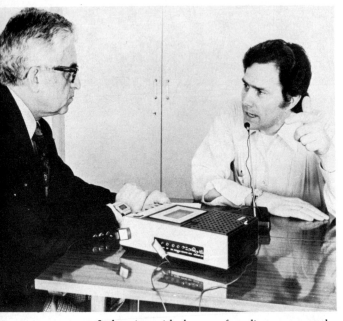

In keeping with the use of media to support the
Team's campaigns, Forrest Boyd, of International
Media Service (Washington, D.C.), interviewed me at
our 1978 crusade in Uruguay.

We had many Team members who worked on the
Uruguay 1978 crusade. My mother (standing in
front of me) came from Argentina to be with us for
the crusade.

In October 1978, we formed our own organization,
the Luis Palau Evangelistic Team, with headquarters
in Portland,
Oregon. Pictured
are the original
board members:
(L to R) Duane
Logsdon, Milton
Klausmann, me,
Don Ward, Dr.
Dick Hillis, and
Paul Garza.

The Palau Team has distributed more than 16 million pieces of literature during its 17-year history—including Luis Palau's five Spanish and seven English books.

The Guatemala Crusade traveling team included: (top, L to R) Paul Garza, Rev. Marcelino Ortiz, Rev. Jim Williams, me, Benjamin Orozco, Stan Jeter; (bottom, L to R) David L. Jones, Douglas Gaynor, Dr. Ruben Proietti, William Conard, and John McWilliam. (*Photo by Richard Ball. © Luis Palau Evangelistic Team.*)

In the most explosive campaign the Team has ever held, 18,916 people made public decisions for Christ, October 15-29, 1978. The two-week, three-city Bolivian Crusade attracted international attention when Bolivia's President, Pereda Asbun, and top military and government personnel attended the Presidential Prayer Breakfast we organized.

In 1978, and again in 1983, I was honored to speak at the National Religious Broadcasters Convention, in Washington, D.C. (*Photo by Ake Lundberg.* © *Luis Palau Evangelistic Team.*)

In 1978, 400 church leaders gathered in the Glasgow Cathedral, in Scotland, and invited me to speak on church growth principles and the future of evangelism. Between 1979 and 1981, we held four exciting crusades in Scotland.

The 1979 National Congress on Evangelism and nightly crusade meetings in Caracas, Venezuela, were held in the El Poliedro sports arena, with 65,500 people attending the six-day campaign.

During the Team's 1980 Glasgow area crusades, I spoke to members of the Scottish Presbytery in Hamilton.

More than 6,500 young people attended Spring
Harvest '80, a youth congress on evangelism in South
Wales. (*Photo by Ake Lundberg.* © *Luis Palau
Evangelistic Team.*)

The Festival of the Family Crusade, held at the Los Angeles Sports Arena in 1980, was aimed at reaching the four million Spanish-speaking people of the area. The crusade had a cumulative attendance of 51,329, and 1,945 inquirers were counseled. (*Photo by Ake Lundberg. © Luis Palau Evangelistic Team.*)

Over 11,000 crowded into Kelvin Hall, Glasgow, Scotland, for the closing meeting of the Luis Palau Scottish Crusade in 1981. This five-week crusade, the longest and perhaps most important in the Palau Team's history, had a cumulative attendance of 200,000, with 5,300 inquirers.
(*Photo by Ake Lundberg. © Luis Palau Evangelistic Team.*)

Nearly 2,000 people made public commitments to
Christ during the Luis Palau Greater San Diego
Crusade, Aug. 23-30, 1981. The crusade, billed as my
first English-speaking crusade in the United States,
included outreach to the area's Hispanic and Pan-
Asian populations and to military personnel.
(*Photo by Ake Lundberg.*)

Organizers and the press described our Helsinki, Finland,
Crusade (May 3-9, 1982) as "historical," because it was the first
time in 400 years that the State Church and Free churches
had cooperated
in a united
evangelistic
outreach.
(*Photo by
Ake Lundberg.
© Luis Palau
Evangelistic
Team.*)

On the closing Sunday of the Asuncion, Paraguay, Crusade (Sept. 8-2
1982), 1,690 of the 25,000 in attendance made public Christi
commitments—the most decisions ever recorded in a single Palau Tea
meeting. (*Photo by David L. Jones.* © *Luis Palau Evangelistic Tear*

On the closing Sunday of my eight-day Guatemala City
Crusade (Nov. 21-28, 1982), I spoke to the largest crowd ever
to hear an evangelical preacher in South America. Government

officials
estimated that
the crowd
exceeded
700,000
people. (*Photo
by David L.
Jones.* © *Luis
Palau
Evangelistic
Team.*)

How thankful I am for my wife, Patricia, who has been such a blessing and so supportive these past years. (*Photo by Ake Lundberg.*)

In April 1983, I had the privilege of having lunch with former terrorists in Belfast, Northern Ireland. These young men are now born-again Christians. (*Photo by Allan J. McCullough. © Allan J. McCullough.*)

The World-wide Ministries of the Luis Palau Evangelistic Team

1 Canada ■
2 United States ● ■ ● ■ ■
3 Mexico ● ■
4 Guatemala ● ■
5 Honduras ●
6 El Salvador ●
7 Nicaragua ●
8 Costa Rica ●
9 Panama ●
10 Haiti ●
11 Dominican Republic ●
12 Puerto Rico ●
13 Argentina ● ■
14 Bolivia ●
15 Venezuela ●
16 Netherlands Antilles ● ●
17 Colombia ●
18 Ecuador ● ●
19 Peru ●
20 Chile ●
21 Uruguay ●
22 Paraguay ●

23 England ■
24 Scotland
25 Wales
26 Ireland
       Northern Irela
27 Norway
28 Sweden
29 Denmark
30 West German
31 Belgium
32 France
33 Switzerland
34 Portugal
35 Spain
36 Italy ●
37 Finland
38 Greece
39 Australia

World-wide Ministries . . . Through the Mass Media

RADIO broadcasts by the Team reach millions of people daily with the gospel message. Cassettes of messages further expand the Team's teaching and follow-up work.

PUBLISHED WORKS by Luis Palau include a dozen books and scores of booklets available in several major languages.

ARTICLES by (and about) Luis Palau regularly appear in newspapers and magazines throughout the world.

TELEVISION call-in programs, holiday specials, follow-up programs and evangelistic films expand the world-wide ministry of the Team.

"Continente '75" blanketed the entire Latin American continent with the gospel of Jesus Christ by radio and television, reaching over 80 million people.

World-wide Ministries . . .
Together with Local Churches

SCHOOLS OF EVANGELISM and COMMUNICATIONS train national believers to reach their area for Christ using the most effective means.

COUNSELING training equips national believers in evangelism and family counseling.

FOLLOW-UP work conducted through local churches and the media focuses on discipleship training and church growth.

CONFERENCES encourage believers to grow in their walk with Christ and assist pastors in leading their churches.

Pat joins me at crusades more frequently, now that our boys are older. In March 1982, she spoke at the Newcastle, Australia, crusade.

Our family in 1982: Kevin and Keith in the back; Stephen, me, Pat, and Andrew in the front.

five days a week. Many days I nearly wept in despair when I had to pull myself away from the books and go to work. Along with that, I had all the service opportunities through the assembly, the radio program, the speaking engagements, and the weekly prayer meetings with my young friends. Sometimes I wonder how any of us persevered through those crises of wondering whether the gospel had as much power in our lives as it did in converting the lost, but God kept His hand on us.

I found myself often searching my heart. I would tell myself I could handle the pride if it were just mass evangelism on a local scale. One church, one town, one region—something like that. But I wasn't interested in mass evangelism in which I was the only evangelist. I was sort of forced into that kind of thinking, because it seemed so few others caught the vision. I felt that maybe I would be the only one out there doing it, anyway.

When I read about this new invention, television, in *Time* magazine, I knew it would eventually play a major role in world evangelization. I was fascinated by the technological and social possibilities of the new medium. Even in the United States it was fairly new and, in Latin America, nearly nonexistent. The magazine told how the cameras worked and how the TV personalities used TV to their advantage.

I began to pretend that my mirror was a television camera. I would preach into it, looking straight into my own eyes, assuming that—as *Time* said—the speaker looking directly into the lens of the camera gives the viewer a feeling of intimacy, the impression that the speaker is looking each viewer in the eye.

I made sure that my gestures were confined to the dimensions of the TV camera while practicing, thinking, praying, and wondering. I was convinced I would one day preach on television; I just wanted to be ready.

It would be years before I preached on television, but I was rehearsing in Cordoba, Argentina, South America, when television itself was in its infancy. Just as in the bank, when I read all the manuals and tried to learn everyone's job, I knew that someday my chance would come, and I wanted to be ready for the Lord to use me for His glory.

14

Sleepless Nights

. . . be filled with the Spirit.

Ephesians 5:18

I hardly knew where to turn. There weren't enough hours in the day to do all I needed and wanted to do. Working at the bank was getting in my way, but I couldn't just quit. I had no other source of income.

I wanted to see Latin America come to Christ on a massive scale, and although I could get very few to agree with me that it was right or even that it could be done, I tried to realistically evaluate the situation. I had no contacts and no money; hardly anyone outside Cordoba even knew who I was. All I could do was prepare and believe that one day my chance would come; God would make it happen. I didn't know how a door would be opened, but I knew one would.

Because of all of the street preaching and church work I was doing, I spent a lot of time on my knees, studying and praying. It was during this time that I began to envision, during prayer, reaching out to great crowds of people, people by the thousands, stadiums full.

It was as real to me as a prophetic word. I could not shake the mental pictures, so I just knew that one day it would take place.

At first I didn't know what to make of it. Was it just my imagination telling me that I wanted to be a well-known preacher? I decided it wasn't. I believed the Lord was laying on my heart what He was going to do. It had to be the Lord, because I was totally bankrupt of the resources needed to accomplish something like that.

I didn't even have the full backing of my local church, let alone all the other elements that would have to fall into place before great crowds would come to hear me preach. I knew that if it was ever to happen, and if I was going to have anything to do with it, it would have to be of the Lord. I could study and work and pray and do my own little thing there in Cordoba, but, beyond that, I was helpless without a miracle.

Some of us still-zealous young people were encouraged by the elders to go ahead and buy a large tent so we could reach people who wouldn't come to the chapel. As long as everything was done in good taste and we didn't give altar calls, it was more than all right with them.

One of the young elders, a construction worker, helped us buy the tent and set it up in one of the neighborhoods. It held a little more than a hundred people, so we advertised children's meetings in the afternoons and evangelistic campaigns in the evenings.

Early on, many of the Christians in the area came to support us and make the unsaved people feel more comfortable in a crowd. It was probably a mistake to get a tent that took so much work just to keep clean and in good shape, but we had fun and learned a lot.

I studied Torrey books for instructions and suggestions. His counsel on giving invitations was sound, but the idea that giving an altar call actually appealed only to emotions had been so ingrained in me that I agreed not to do it. We had heard many horror stories about evangelists who preached the gospel for twenty minutes and then begged people to come forward for twenty-five minutes.

Then there were the aggressive preachers who would ask the people who wanted to go to heaven to stand, and those who wanted to go to hell to remain seated. Those preachers apparently wanted to make themselves look better by pumping up their number of conversions, or at least manipulating people into making decisions. The Brethren were dead set against it, and I was too—at least that style of preaching—although history shows that God moves mysteriously and even saves people through their own unwise methods.

It was thrilling to be preaching the gospel to unbelievers, and I knew it was training me for even bigger and better things. They tell me I preached loudly and gestured expansively, as if I had a crowd of 10,000. It got to the point where all I wanted to do was study, pray, and then preach, to lead more people to Christ.

I had no peace about a girl I was dating. She was a wonderful, cultured, educated person, from a fine family in our church, and we were seriously considering marriage. But I just wasn't ready. I had no savings, and though, at twenty-four, in many ways I felt emotionally mature, I still got upset when things went wrong. *How can I get married when I am like that*? I asked myself.

The biggest obstacle, though, was that, in the back of my mind, I simply had the feeling that she was not the girl God had intended for me. I still felt very young, and while her family and everyone who knew us thought it would be great if we got married, I began to want out of the relationship. But I didn't want to hurt her, so I let it continue longer than it should have.

I probably encouraged her, simply by not ending it for a

good year longer than was wise. It wouldn't be over until I went to the United States, and even then I tried to take the easy way out. It would become one of the toughest and richest lessons of my young Christian life.

There are those who say that a preacher should not use his own failures as examples in his teaching and preaching. I disagree. It would be easy to leave this story about a disappointed young woman—and her disappointed father —out of my autobiography, but I have always tried to teach the Bible on the basis of what it says, as illustrated by my own experience.

That means that I must not hide my weaknesses. I don't want people to get the idea that because the Lord has blessed me in many ways and has used me for His glory to bring thousands to the cross, I am in any way above the ordinary struggles and battles of life.

I fail. I make mistakes. I struggle with the same sins and shortcomings everyone else faces. There are days when I wish that weren't the case. But when I finally found the peace I had searched so long for, I learned that God doesn't take away the temptations. There are still failures. He simply assures me that He has covered it all, and He gives me the power for future victories.

Anyway, I prayed a lot about my future with this girl, and I was not able to have peace about it. To me that was an answer from God. If you pray over something earnestly and don't have peace—in spite of the fact that everything else about the situation looks perfect—then God is probably trying to tell you something. Colossians 3:15 says, "And let the peace of Christ rule in your hearts, to which indeed you were called in the one body. And be thankful" (RSV). Although I didn't handle it correctly later, I had the definite leading that this was not the girl for me.

Meanwhile, I was reading books about evangelists of the past and how they moved out of their own localities and into preaching to the masses. Without fail, they started as unknowns. They had no contacts and no money. They were simply used of God. God did the work through them.

George Mueller spent more time in prayer and Bible reading than anyone I had ever heard of. He had been a leading Brethren teacher in England. And he never asked anyone for a dime. Perhaps there was hope for me, I decided. Just to be involved in a big campaign would have been exciting. I had no idea how soon it would happen.

Having been named general co-secretary of a national youth congress, I was invited to meet Jim Savage, a former Youth For Christ man, president of a seminary, and a representative of the Billy Graham Association. I could hardly believe it. I was invited to a meeting of 1,100 church leaders, where we would see films of Billy preaching and then would discuss whether we could sponsor his coming to South America for a crusade. I hardly slept nights.

My role with the youth department of the assembly had given me a more national platform, especially for speaking to young people, but I had been disappointed, too. Here I found that even some of the well-known speakers and Bible teachers we brought in could be dynamite with a message and then turn right around and put down a fellow preacher as soon as they stepped off the platform.

There were those, of course, who didn't do things like that. But I was shocked to find out how many did. In fact, I was drawn into the same type of cynicism and backbiting. I found that many people loved to hear me put down the others, and they said so. That quickly led to another roller-coaster experience of guilt for me.

I knew I was on the wrong track with that approach, even though it was giving me entree to larger, wider audiences. One of the reasons I didn't want that kind of reputation was because, deep down, it really wasn't me. What I wanted to do was to glorify God and call people to Christ. I didn't want to put other people down. For one thing, I wasn't sure anymore that our own group was the only one with the answers.

I had gone for so long, reading nothing but our literature, that when I finally branched out and found there were evangelical leaders in many groups and denominations who had something to say, it was a real eye-opener for me.

Don't misunderstand this. I don't feel I ever turned against my elders and teachers under God. I learned more Bible truth from the assemblies than anywhere else, ever. But I was beginning to see that there were other valid evangelicals who loved and served the Lord as much as we did. Not the least of whom was Billy Graham.

The day finally came when I joined many other church leaders in hearing Jim Savage speak about the possibility of Graham's coming to Argentina. But what impressed me most—besides the size of the crowd (as big as I'd ever seen for anything evangelical, and it was just over a thousand)—was a brief film of Billy speaking to Christian leaders in India.

The film revealed an unbelievable crowd, but the dramatic effect the camera left was that Billy was talking directly to us. Early in his message, which was not evangelistic, but directed at Christian leaders, the camera panned the whole crowd to show the tens of thousands.

Yet, when Billy got to the heart of his message, the camera zoomed in close to his face. There on the big screen he stared right into my eyes. He was preaching from Ephesians 5:18: "And be not drunk with wine, wherein is excess; but be filled with the Spirit." It was as if the crowd in India didn't exist. He was looking right at me and shouting, "Are you filled with the Spirit? Are you filled with the Spirit? Are you filled with the Spirit?"

And somehow I knew that was my problem. That's what gave me the up-and-down Christianity. That's why I had zeal and commitment, but little fruit or victory. When would it end? When would I find the answer?

I didn't know it then, but it wouldn't be until I had been in the United States for six months.

15

It's Not a Question of Call;
It's a Question of Obedience

Pray at all times in the Spirit, with all prayer and supplication. To that end keep alert with all perseverance, making supplication for all the saints.

Ephesians 6:18, RSV

Speaking engagements were becoming more frequent, and I was being asked to speak not only at youth meetings and rallies, but also at evening services in various churches. That is the evangelistic service in most Latin American churches, and we consider it very important.

Finally, some people were recognizing my bent for evangelism. Then came the mounting pressures. My mom, as spiritually sensitive as ever, kept encouraging me to leave the bank and start planting churches. She even had towns in mind that needed churches.

"Mom, how are you going to live? We have a lot of mouths to feed!"

"Luis, you know if the Lord is in it, He will provide."

"But I don't feel the call," I said. "I don't have that final call that tells me it would be all right."

"The call? What call?" she said. "He gave the com-

122

mission two thousand years ago, and you've read it all your life. How many times do you want Him to give the commandment before you obey it? It isn't a question of call; it's a question of obedience. The call He has given; it's the answer He is waiting for."

I feared she was right, but I wasn't confident enough in the Lord to quit my job just yet, even though I was becoming less enamored with banking every day.

One day in late 1958 I received a flier announcing a speaking engagement by two Americans, Dick Hillis, a former missionary to China and prisoner of the Communists, and Ray Stedman, a pastor from Palo Alto, California. I was afraid it might just be an anticommunist rally, but I was curious to see a pastor from California.

I went alone to the meeting, and afterward I noticed Pastor Stedman standing by himself. I introduced myself in English and was amazed when he immediately asked me a lot of questions and seemed genuinely interested in me.

I told him all about myself, my job, my girl friend, my motorbike, and my family. "I'd like to get to know you better," he said. I thought, *This guy's all right! He really cares.* He invited me to a Bible study with a few missionaries the next morning. I was flattered.

Years later Ray told me that when he first saw me, the Lord had impressed upon his heart to see that I got to the United States. He didn't know why and, of course, didn't even know who I was. When he discovered I was actively involved in evangelism, he knew his leading was of God.

The next day after the Bible study I gave him a ride into town on my motorbike so he could do some shopping, and we talked some more. "Wouldn't you like to go to seminary?" he asked.

"It would be nice, but I'm not sure I'll ever make it. I don't have a lot of money, and my church does not encourage formal theological education."

"Well," he said, "it could be arranged if the Lord wanted it." I couldn't argue with that. "How would you like to come to the United States?"

"I've thought about it," I admitted. "Maybe someday I'll be able to go, the Lord willing." I was just shooting the breeze. It never dawned on me that a minister from the United States would be able to arrange anything like that. I thought he was just speculating.

"You know, Luis," he responded, "the Lord may just will it."

The next night, after hearing Dick Hillis speak, I saw them both off at the airport. "I'll see you in the United States," Ray said.

"Well, the Lord willing, maybe someday," I said.

"No, Luis, the Lord *is* going to will. I'll write you from the plane."

To me, Ray Stedman seemed like a warm person, flattering, and a bit unrealistic. There was no way I was going to get to the United States within the next decade. It was out of the question. If the ministers there had as little money as the ones in South America, he wouldn't be able to help me. So why even think about it?

A few days later, his letter arrived with the news that he had got a few businessmen together who wanted to finance my trip to the United States so that I could study at Dallas Theological Seminary. It was a thrill—I had read about that school; its founder, Dr. Lewis Sperry Chafer; president, John Walvoord; and all its wonderful teachers—but I quickly got cold feet.

There was too much to do in Latin America. Besides,

I didn't want to spend four more years in school. And who would take care of my family? I wrote Stedman back and thanked him, but refused.

He wrote back quickly, assuring me that someone from the United States would be able to provide for my family, too. It was too incredible. I didn't know how to respond, and because other exciting events began to emerge in my life, I didn't answer his letter for several months.

Procrastination had always been a problem for me, but this was really rude. I simply ignored a couple more letters, and soon my life was busy with decisions and new open doors.

I confronted the bank branch manager with a few new policies I wasn't comfortable with and told him that due to my Christian testimony, I wasn't sure I could do everything required of me. Those practices weren't illegal, but they raised some ethical questions.

I knew I was taking my job in my hands, and the manager was not at all pleased. He reminded me of all the bank had done for me and all they had planned for me. Rather than agreeing that some of the practices might be considered less than ethical and ought to be changed, he insinuated that I was jeopardizing my career by rocking the boat. I knew if push ever came to shove and I was asked to do or say something I didn't feel right about, I would refuse, and that would be that.

My stock in the bank dropped overnight. I was living on borrowed time, and I knew it. No doubt the headquarters bank in Buenos Aires had received a report on me and would begin cultivating a new foreign-operations manager. It didn't take long, however, for me to discover that all of this had happened in God's timing.

About four days after my confrontation with the

manager, I noticed an American opening a new account. I greeted him in English and struck up a conversation. He was Keith Bentson, representing SEPAL, the Latin American division of Overseas Crusades. I told him I was a Christian, too, and we had a nice chat.

A few days later, when he came in to make his first deposit, he mentioned that he would like to know about any bilingual Christian man who might want to work for SEPAL, translating English material into Spanish for their magazine, *La Voz* (*The Voice*).

"You've got your man," I said.

"Who?" Keith asked.

"It's me." It had burst from me without a moment's hesitation. As soon as he mentioned the job, I knew it was for me.

"Oh, Luis, you'd better think about it and talk with your family. We're talking about a very, very small salary; no doubt much less than you're making here."

"I'll talk to my family," I promised, "but I'm your man. This is exciting. I'm sure it's of God."

Keith needed time to check me out, too, and that caused a few ruffles in the church. The elders didn't like the idea that I would be working with an organization that was interdenominational. A missionary lady I consulted also strongly advised me against it.

She reminded me that I had a good job and all the opportunities I wanted to serve the Lord. But I had already got my mom's blessing, and I would not be deterred. I was looking more for confirmation than advice, anyway, though I must admit I was surprised and disappointed by her reaction. It was years later that I really learned and accepted the biblical principle of more strictly following the leadership and authority of those over me in the Lord.

The only stipulation I made with Keith was that I be allowed to come in late on Monday mornings, because I had speaking engagements lined up for Sunday nights for weeks to come, and I wanted to be able to fulfill them. Some were as far away as seventy miles, and it was easier to come back the next morning on the bus.

Once we had that out of the way, and I got over the shock of the tiny salary offered, I was on cloud nine. I had finally found a way to get into full-time Christian work. There was a lot to look forward to, and I hadn't been so sure about God's leading in my life for a long time.

Four days after my confrontation with the bank manager, I gave him notice. He gave me my final check, asked me to give instructions to my fill-in replacement, and then I was free. Two of my sisters had found jobs by now, so having my salary cut by more than half would not hurt the family much.

I went from being close to the top at the bank to low man at SEPAL. But I loved it. I did a little of everything, including representing the mission and the magazine at conventions. I continued my tent preaching through the church on my own time, but one of the greatest lessons and blessings of those days came from praying with Keith Bentson.

After I had been at SEPAL a few weeks, he asked me to stay at the office after closing time one Wednesday night. He didn't want other staff members to think I was getting privileged treatment. He simply wanted to pray with me.

That first Wednesday night he prayed for me and my sisters and mother, then my church and all the elders by name. I was amazed at how informed he was, since he did not attend our church. It was exciting to hear him pour out his heart, imploring, "Oh, God, bless these men for Your service and Your glory!" It made me want to pray, too, so I did.

The next week he brought a map of the city of Cordoba and pinpointed the fifteen or sixteen local churches of the Brethren movement. Then he prayed for each church, literally one by one, by name and address and names of key leaders, if he knew them. It was as if we had taken a trip around the city on our knees.

He just poured out his soul, teaching me what intercessory prayer was all about. It was thrilling. We got into the habit of praying conversationally, back and forth, and often he paced the room as he talked to the Lord.

The next Wednesday his map of the city included all the evangelical churches of all denominations. He prayed for each one, incredibly knowing the pastor's name, in most cases. It really moved me when he prayed for other denominations. When Keith prayed for them, he confirmed something in me I had felt for years. I had always wondered why, when we were taught about oneness in Christ, that oneness shouldn't include devout evangelicals of other denominations. Now I was being taught the oneness of the Body through the fervent prayers of this devoted, committed missionary.

Well, as the weeks went by, Keith's map got bigger, first to encompass the state, and then the country, and then the nation. He knew how many towns there were and what percentage of them had churches. He prayed up a storm, and I was overwhelmed anew, each Wednesday night.

The meaning of Ephesians 6:18 began to sink in with enormous strength: "Pray at all times in the Spirit, with all prayer and supplication. To that end keep alert with all perseverance, making supplication for all the saints" (RSV).

All during this time, the tent ministry was growing because my friends and I pulled in people from other churches throughout the city. I had dreamed of having an evangelistic team, but I had no money, and I didn't know where I was going to draw the talent to help me. One night, it fell into my lap.

After the meeting, a handsome and winsome American named Bruce Woodman asked if I needed a soloist and song leader for the meetings. He was a missionary looking for a ministry and was eager to help out. I said sure. He told me he also knew a keyboard man named Bill Fasig, who had worked under New York evangelist Jack Wyrtzen; Bill could play the organ or piano for us.

Up until that time, our music had been an accordian, played by my sisters or a friend from our local church. Did Bruce and Bill ever make a difference! Bruce was a perfect emcee, song leader, and soloist. He could really get a crowd excited. He did it in the Spirit, too. And of course Bill Fasig has gone on to become a widely known artist and has played for Billy Graham through the years. In my mind, we had just graduated. Now we had a team.

I knew I wasn't that great as a speaker, and I kept working at it and studying. I breathed wrong, which made it hard on my voice. But many books by the old-time preachers such as C. H. Spurgeon and A. P. Gibbs (*A Primer on Preaching*) were full of advice on projection, sermon preparation, and anything else a budding speaker wanted to know. And when Bruce Woodman finally got through to me with counsel on how to breathe from my diaphragm rather than my throat, he probably added ten years to my speaking voice.

We were busy and happy and productive, and the really big break from the Lord was yet to come.

16

The Big Break

Let your conversation be without covetousness; and be content with such things as ye have: for he hath said, I will never leave thee, nor forsake thee. So that we may boldly say, The Lord is my helper, and I will not fear what man shall do unto me.

Hebrews 13:5-6

I had long been obsessed by the idea that we just needed a break, something dramatic, to open the way for mass evangelism on a large scale. Two things happened in 1960 that could be considered breakthroughs, at least for me.

The first was that Ed Murphy joined the staff of SEPAL. He was a missionary who worked with the national church.

The second was that Ray Stedman wrote me a stinging letter, telling me that not responding to his correspondence was irresponsible and rude. He made it clear that if I wanted to come to the United States, I could. I wasn't going to be forced to attend Dallas Theological Seminary or stay anywhere for four years.

I had told Ray that one of my big objections was the idea of spending four more years in classes and being almost thirty years old when I got out. "Too many people are going to hell, for me to be spending four more years reading books," I told him. "I can study at home. I am disciplined, and I enjoy studying. What I need is an opportunity to ask questions of some good Bible teachers and get answers to the really tough ones I haven't been able to resolve through my own reading."

I also wanted to learn more about the United States and what made Americans tick, after all I had read about that exciting country. It was a land of success, and I wanted to know why.

Ray's point, and he was right, of course, was that I should have kept the lines of communication open so he could assure me that all my questions would be answered and the obstacles overcome.

He told me there was a one-year graduate course in theology available at Multnomah School of the Bible, in Portland, Oregon, that might perfectly suit my needs, and that I could spend a few months before and after that school year as an intern at his church in California.

When he sent money for my mother, as a token of what they would do while I was there, and also enclosed a check to pay for my trip to Buenos Aires to get my passport, my excuses had run out. I had felt for a long time that God might want me to go to the United States to see more of the world and broaden my understanding, and now the door was wide open. I prayed about it and agreed to go.

Neither the assembly nor SEPAL were terribly excited about it, the latter basically because they feared I might never return to South America. They asked me to resign from my position with them before I left, because their policy forbade national missionaries from being sent out of the country while under their auspices. (They were concerned people might join the mission simply to leave their country to study and then wouldn't come back. Then SEPAL could be criticized for taking the national workers out of the country.)

Though reluctantly agreeing that I should go, SEPAL gave me a little sermonette on the subject that I should not let the United States enthrall me. "Your ministry is down here; this is God's will for you, in spite of how attractive the States are."

A few months before I was to leave, Ray Stedman set up a meeting for me with the president of Multnomah School of the Bible, Dr. Willard Aldrich, and his wife, who were visiting in Buenos Aires. Ray sent me some money and told me to show them the sights, interpret for them, and so on. It was his gift to them, but it benefited me even more. It showed me what wonderful people the Aldriches were, and it gave me a friend at Multnomah before I had even left for America—and an influential friend at that.

I had several months of service left with SEPAL before departing, and it was during the last month that Ed Murphy's strategy of church planting met with astounding success in a small town. I was right in the middle of it, and it was the perfect going-away present. If I had ever questioned the power of God, that experience erased all doubts.

There was just enough time left before I was to leave that nervousness had not yet set in about going so far away to a land of foreigners, who, I had heard, spoke English that was not exactly the same as what I had learned in British boarding school. I was excited, and it made me even happier and more eager in my work with SEPAL.

They were letting me do more out-of-the office evangelistic work, including preaching. That, combined with

132

the team work with Bruce Woodman and Bill Fasig, kept me going almost around the clock. I couldn't have been more pleased.

After much prayer, Ed Murphy and the rest of us decided upon the tiny town of Oncativo as the place we wanted to start a church. What Ed wanted to prove was that you could take a small band of Christians from a neighboring town and teach them how to plant a church in the next. If the new church was strictly planted by SEPAL, then it would be a SEPAL church, which was not the point of its efforts.

On the one hand, it would be too easy for SEPAL to take the responsibility and do all the work with full-time people. But that would not allow the area Christians to exercise their gifts and do what they were supposed to do. Besides, there weren't enough full-time missionaries around to keep the church going. We deeply believed in Ephesians 4:11-13 and intended to practice it implicitly.

So the plan was to visit a tiny church in Rio Segundo and see if we could get its members excited about planting a church in Oncativo, a few miles down the road. We asked the people at that small local church if they had ever taken the gospel to Oncativo. No one thought they had.

One of our men went on ahead to check it out, and sure enough, Oncativo appeared totally pagan. There wasn't an evangelical church anywhere. No one had ever seen an evangelical or held a tract in his hand, as far as we could tell. Five people from the small church in Rio Segundo agreed to undergo counselor training and to go with us as we tried to plant a church in their sister town.

One of the keys to our occupation of Oncativo was

133

the fact that we had three Americans with us: Ed Murphy, Keith Bentson, and Bruce Woodman, plus the editor of *La Voz,* Daniel Ericcson. They caused a lot of excitement in the town, because people wondered what they were doing there. However, they let us nationals carry the ball.

First we asked the mayor of the town if we could represent the evangelical population of Argentina in the annual May 25th Independence Day celebration and parade the next day and say a few words. He turned us down. We asked if our musicians could then join the parade and play some national songs. He turned us down again.

Strangely, we weren't discouraged in the least. To us nationals, even making such a bold request was something new and exhilarating. We were't going to fear rejection; we were going to plunge in. Finally we asked around for any foreigners or evangelicals, figuring that they would be more open to welcoming us to the city.

We were directed to a Swiss family that was indeed happy to see other foreigners. They ran a print shop in town, and Ed Murphy asked if they might have a spare room they could loan us for a meeting the next day. They offered a storeroom off the shop but insisted upon cleaning it up for us first.

In eating with them and sharing our mission, the Spirit began to work on the heart of one of the women, named Lydia. It was obvious that she was searching for God, and she was moved by what we had to say. She became the first convert in that town; she received Christ right at the dinner table. We thought of the Lydia mentioned in Acts 16:14, "whose heart the Lord opened."

The next day we knocked on doors all over town,

inviting people to a meeting at the print-shop store-room. Then in the afternoon our horn-playing Americans cut loose in a public park. They played march tunes and patriotic songs, drawing a crowd of curious Oncativans. Daniel Ericcson spoke for a few minutes and then turned it over to me.

I preached on Christ the Liberator, to fit with the Independence Day celebration, based on John 8:36. The theme was that if the Son shall set you free, you shall be free indeed. He will liberate you from your conscience, your chains, and the condemnation of sin.

Street meetings are usually pretty rough, but the people listened hungrily, and I felt a real freedom, almost as if I could have given an invitation right there. I had never done that, however, and anyway we wanted them to come to the meeting that night; I announced when and where it would be, and then we went to the Swiss family's home to hold our breaths and wait it out.

The room had space for about seventy-five, if we really packed them in, but we had no idea whether anyone at all would show up.

I nearly trembled with excitement, praying that God would send a few needy souls to us that evening. During my prayer I got the definite urge to give an invitation that night. It was so strong that I felt I would be sinning to disobey it. Then I just hoped for a crowd.

About seventy-five townspeople packed the place. I could hardly wait to preach, especially knowing that I would be giving the first bona fide public invitation of my life. Many of the people at the street meeting had appeared anxious to receive Christ, and I saw a few of them there that night.

I preached on John 10:28-29:

I give eternal life to them, and they shall never perish; and no one shall snatch them out of My hand. My Father, who has given them to Me, is greater than all; and no one is able to snatch them out of the Father's hand. (NASB)

It's a powerful passage of assurance that really speaks for itself. As I neared the end I felt free to invite people to receive Christ. I gave the invitation that night the same way I have now done it for years. I asked them to bow their heads and pray along with me silently if they wanted to receive Christ.

I prayed the simple prayer of confession, seeking forgiveness, and inviting Christ into the heart. Then I asked for those who had prayed with me to raise their hands to signify their decision. I counted thirty-five hands and nearly panicked.

So the critics were right! It is all emotion. These invitations were unfair. The people feel pressured, their emotions have been tampered with. I asked them to lower their hands.

"Let me explain again," I said, and I spent another half hour on the passage, clarifying every point, making sure they understood the significance of choosing a life with Christ. We prayed again, and I asked for hands: thirty-seven.

We held a meeting there every night and trained the new converts so that they could start their own church when we left. At the end of the week, seventy people had professed faith in Jesus Christ. We felt as if we had been on a journey with the apostle Paul to a virgin town that was hearing the gospel for the first time.

We didn't have to worry about leaving seventy brand-new Christians to flounder in their week-old faith.

Besides teaching them everything we could in a week—about baptism, witnessing, music, being elders, Communion, and preaching the Word—our friends from Rio Segundo had been revived themselves! They would be watchdogging the new church as if it were made up of their own sons and daughters. Which it was.

Both the churches in Rio Segundo and Oncativo multiplied themselves by planting churches in other nearby towns, proving Dick Hillis and Ed Murphy right: With a lot of work in the power of the Spirit and the blessing of God, indigenous churches would spring up.

I hardly had time to come down from that experience when it was time for me to leave for the United States. Many friends and my whole family saw me off at the airport in Buenos Aires for the first flight of my life. It was a tearful farewell, and my mother just couldn't get enough advice into the few minutes we had left.

As I was pulling away from her in my one-and-only brand-new black suit, she said, "Don't go into the cities, don't travel alone, watch out, don't get shot and stuffed in a trunk, and remember Hebrews thirteen, five and six!" She was worried about murder. I was worried about the plane ride.

17

California, Here I Come!

I have been crucified with Christ; it is no longer I who live, but Christ who lives in me; and the life I now live in the flesh I live by faith in the Son of God, who loved me and gave himself for me.

Galatians 2:20, RSV

The flight was horrible. The old DC-6 chugged up over the Andes Mountains, then settled in lower to take the strain off the engines. I was nervous every time we changed altitude. I learned what people meant when they talked about milk-run flights. It seems we stopped at every airstrip between Buenos Aires and Miami.

As we flew over the Caribbean at about twenty thousand feet I was thrilled at the sight of hundreds of beautiful sailboats. "Look at all those little white boats," I said in my best English.

My seatmate roused and leaned across to look. "Those are clouds, kid," he said.

I was exhausted, and my suit was a shambles by the time we landed in Miami, ten hours later than expected. Ray Stedman was wrong about being sure I could get a connection, so I was glad my brother-in-law had the foresight to give me the address of some Cubans he knew in Miami.

No one answered when I called them, so I took a cab to their place. I didn't know the money system, could hardly understand the cabbie, almost didn't get my change, and then didn't know I was supposed to tip him. I left him with about fifty cents.

I didn't even know how to call Ray collect, as he had instructed, but with help from the operator, we finally got things squared away, and I was on my way to San Francisco on a Delta jet. Now that was living! The airline gave away so many plastic spoons, salt packets, and postcards I couldn't believe it.

I arrived exhausted, scared, wondering why I had come, carrying one suitcase, and still wearing that new black suit, which didn't look so new now. I had no idea how out of place a tailored, black, South American suit would look in laid-back California. The plane landed with just about enough time for Ray's wife, Elaine, to pick me up and race me twenty-five miles down the Bayshore Freeway to the Sunday evening service at Peninsula Bible Church in Palo Alto.

And I do mean race! The speed limit was then seventy miles an hour, and I know she was pushing that at least a little. We rushed into the church after the service had already started, and I was marched right down the aisle and onto the platform, to the welcoming applause of the congregation. They thought I was so cute with my accent and my black suit; they were all wearing open-collared shirts.

I stayed with the Stedmans, and within a week I had a horrible toothache to go along with my homesickness. A dentist pulled three teeth and couldn't stop the bleeding for a week, until they diagnosed that I had a vitamin deficiency.

At least having my mouth stuffed with tea bags—and

whatever other home remedies they thought might help —kept me from debating with Elaine or anyone else who tried to talk to me. For some reason I was in an argumentative mood and would discuss theology and doctrine for hours.

I had come to the States to learn, but maybe I wasn't yet ready to admit that I didn't have all the answers. Ray and Elaine and their four daughters were so patient and understanding that their harmony pervaded the place, in spite of that fiery Latin who had invaded. Ray's humor kept everyone happy, and we all became fast friends.

Ray became like a father to me and even took to calling me his son when introducing me around. He treated me like a son, too, mixing a lot of advice and counsel, and even reprimanding, with his friendship. I learned as much from Ray as from anyone in the States. Mostly, his selfless consistency, his transparency, and devotion to the Word of God were an inspiration to me. I was amazed that someone could be so steady, so even, and so sharp. I've never had cause for disillusionment with Ray, and there aren't many men anyone can say that about. I know he was disappointed in me at times, but he was always quick to tell me straight out, and I admired him for that.

I've never forgotten the lessons I've learned from Ray Stedman, just from living with him and watching his life. First was his complete lack of a critical attitude. He does not talk negatively about anyone and shuts off the first hint of it from someone else. If anyone started to speak negatively about another person, he would simply say, "My, you have a critical attitude, don't you? You'd better get that settled."

Another lesson was his extreme patience under pressure, taking it in stride when someone was late for an appointment, even with his terribly jammed schedule.

Third, I was touched by his tremendous reliance on the power of Jesus Christ. He is not a high-pressure manipulator; he's just straightforward, open, quiet, and truthful, never resorting to double meanings.

Ray is not competitive or self-serving. I never saw him dress to impress or try to outdo someone. This was a good example of his Christlikeness, and I thought it was the way the Christian life ought to be lived.

Another characteristic was his interest in other people. He spoke like a man, not like a celebrity. He simply talked with power and seemed more like a man who was a preacher than a preacher who was a man.

I was also impressed by his expository preaching. He's one of the best I've ever heard, because he gives his sermons the study time necessary and delivers them in the most interesting, human, and often humorous ways.

Mostly I was impressed that he was the same at home as in the pulpit. Either he never let his hair down, or he always did. There was nothing hidden, no secret life. He was a great role model.

I've often heard him say, "If your reputation is OK with the Lord, it's bound to be all right with others. And if it isn't OK with the Lord, it doesn't matter, anyway."

That summer I also learned a valuable lesson from a visiting speaker from India. He was a high government official, and I wanted to find out from him the best technique for getting near to presidents and government leaders. "What's the method?" I asked. "What technique do you use?"

He put his arm around me and smiled. "Young man," he said, "there are no techniques. You must just love

141

them." At first I thought he was putting me on, withholding his secret. I have since learned that his was some of the wisest counsel I ever received.

I have met with leaders from all over the world since that time and sometimes am tempted to slip into persuasive methods or political and diplomatic protocol before I realize that what they need most and respond to fastest is love.

Sharing the love and claims of Christ with government leaders is one of the unique aspects of our ministry. Through the years, many presidents, mayors, and gospel leaders have listened as we opened God's Word and shared the gospel. "Pray for me," they often ask. "I need it."

Such men, because of the pressures of their positions and the types of lives they feel they must lead to feel successful, seldom feel genuinely loved. Many of them weep when I say I want to pray for them, no strings attached.

I believe that if God takes hold of the hearts and lives of a nation's leaders, that nation can be opened to the gospel and eventually be turned around to the glory of God. We've seen tremendous openings during our ministry.

Doesn't the Bible repeatedly remind us that nations that fear the Lord will be blessed by Him (see Deuteronomy 6; 1 Samuel 12; Psalm 25:14; 115; Proverbs 9:10)?

Two months with the Stedmans wasn't enough time to learn the American culture—how to chat and eat and behave the way the natives do—but it was all I had before going north to Multnomah School of the Bible, in Portland, Oregon. I rode there with Peninsula Bible Church associate pastor, Bob Smith, who was taking the one-year graduate course, too.

To this day I don't believe I've seen beauty anywhere in the world that compares to the big sky, lakes, streams, ocean, and trees along the route from California into Oregon. I was amazed at the orderliness of the traffic and the general cleanliness of the rest areas and parks. Every day I was becoming more impressed with the United States.

Multnomah is a very demanding school, and I found the first semester particularly rough. I had done a lot of reading, but not so much on biblical anthropology and the doctrine of the indwelling Christ. And that's what I needed.

I was still struggling to find more fruit in my personal spiritual life. I was frustrated in not being able to live out the life-style I saw in men like Ray Stedman and Bob Smith and several others at Peninsula Bible Church. Their lives exhibited a joy and release and freedom that I found attractive. The more I tried for it, the more elusive it became.

That made it frustrating when our Spiritual Life class professor, Dr. Kehoe, began every class—*every* class period—by quoting Galatians 2:20:

> I have been crucified with Christ; it is no longer I who live, but Christ who lives in me; and the life I now live in the flesh I live by faith in the Son of God, who loved me and gave himself for me. (RSV)

I had been hurt by an old friend in Argentina, who cynically made fun of the verses on victory. When I ran across a good book on the subject, my friend said,

"Well, I'd like to see how victorious that author would be if he was under a broken-down car, with oil dripping all over him."

I couldn't argue with that and fell into the same type of cynicism, mostly because I couldn't find victory myself. I figured he must be right; true victory wasn't possible. The Christian life must simply be a constant struggle. But the lives of Stedman and Smith and others didn't support that argument. I wanted what they had.

On my spiritual journey, it seemed every inch of the way was like clawing uphill and then sliding back down. Although I had experienced many times of blessing and victory, for the most part I felt the struggle was impossible, unbearable. I couldn't go on that way, especially when no one else knew about it. It was my secret, private death. I knew there was a limit to how long I could hold on, like someone hanging off the edge of a cliff, deciding that if someone didn't come soon, he would have to let go.

I was treated royally at Multnomah. The other students were nice and thought I was a friendly, winsome South American. They couldn't know the spiritual battles I was having. If I hadn't cared so much about serving Christ and preaching the gospel, I might have given it up at that point.

I was getting so annoyed at the teacher's quoting that same verse every day that I had to ask myself why. *It can't be a Bible verse that gets you so upset*, I told myself. *It must be you.* I decided that the verse was self-contradictory, hard to understand, and confusing, especially in English. I loved the school and the classes and the other students, but the pressure in my spirit was worse than ever. I wanted to be holy.

I still wanted to be a servant of the Lord, but the

battle was raging. Really raging. How does one find rest? Ray Stedman's favorite hymn was:

> Jesus, I am resting, resting,
> In the joy of what Thou art;
> I am finding out the greatness
> Of Thy loving heart.
>
> Thou hast bid me gaze upon Thee,
> And Thy beauty fills my soul,
> For by Thy transforming power
> Thou hast made me whole.
> (Jean Sophia Pigott)

I was teaching a Sunday school class and making a lot of friends, preaching in many churches around the area, even speaking in chapel. But in my soul I was desperate.

I was a sincere hypocrite. People always laugh when I say that, but I truly was, and it wasn't funny. Some hypocrites know they are hypocrites and want to be that way. They want to have two lives: one to show off at church and one to live in private. I simply wanted to be the person people thought I was.

If I were to describe myself in those days, I would have to say I was envious, jealous, too preoccupied and self-centered, and ambitious to a wrong degree. No amount of wrestling with myself would rid me of those sins. And yet I tried. I knew it was terrible, but I felt despicable; I hated the idea that I was a hypocrite.

I was smug about other speakers, silently rating their illustrations or delivery against my own. That left me feeling mean and ugly and petty. I had no victory. I was defeated. Even knowing what I was like on the inside, I still thought and behaved as if I were something special

145

on the outside. How I wanted release!

Then, on top of all that, I knew I had no guarantee of funds for the second semester. Though my grades were good, I was having trouble keeping up with all the reading in English. And though America and Americans were wonderful, I was about ready to forget it and go home.

18

What a "Brethren" Thing to Do

And be found in him, not having mine own righteous-
ness, which is of the law, but that which is through the
faith of Christ, the righteousness which is of God by
faith: That I may know him, and the power of his resur-
rection, and the fellowship of his sufferings, being made
conformable unto his death.

Philippians 3:9-10

Nearly three months into the first semester I told the Lord that if He didn't send the money for the second semester, I would take it as a sign to go home. I couldn't work with all the other pressures, and the lack of victory in my personal life made me wonder if I wanted to continue as a preacher, anyway.

I didn't expect anything from anybody. We had been taught that it was unspiritual to ask or hint for money, and besides, whom would I ask? I couldn't see why anyone should give me ten dollars, let alone a half year of schooling. A friend of Ray Stedman's had paid the first semester, but wished to remain anonymous. With the second semester only about a month away, I was pessimistic.

Over Thanksgiving I went to Tacoma to help with a ministry to military personnel. A Christian organization had a turkey dinner for them, and a few of us students were there to chat and play games and informally share the Lord. It was a good day, but I came away depressed.

I had hit a new low. The battle was a full-fledged crisis now, and on the way back from Portland, I decided I should plan on going back to Argentina. *As soon as the term is over, somehow I'm getting a plane ticket*, I told myself.

We reached Portland on Sunday afternoon, and I checked my mailbox for a letter from home. The only thing in the box was a plain envelope with my name on it. I assumed it was a graded paper.

There was no letterhead; it was unsigned; and it was typed. There was no way to tell who it was from. It read:

Dear Luis,

You have been a great blessing to many of us here in the States, and we appreciate what you have taught us. We feel that you deserve help to finish your term at Multnomah; therefore, all your tuition and books have been paid for.

Just check in at the business office, and they will finalize the papers. So you will be grateful to every American you have met or will ever meet, we remain anonymous.

I wish I could say I had been expecting it, but I can't. I had lost faith. Now I was beside myself with excitement, and there was no one for me to tell. I immediately wondered who had done it, and while I have my suspicions, to this day I don't know. All I could think of was, *What a "brethren" thing for someone to do.*

I was buoyed up once again by God's perfect timing. So He was still with me after all. Even with the defeat and the frustration I was feeling, He wanted me to know He was there and to hang in and stay at school. He had even more good things planned for me, all during the next few weeks.

The first was that I met Pat Scofield. Actually I had met her earlier in the semester in a group situation, but neither of us made any impression on the other. She was just one of the American girls. To her, I suppose, I was just one of the foreign students.

One night we had a class party at a home down the block from the school, and on the way I noticed several girls. "Are you going to the party?" I asked. They all said yes, and for some reason I said to Pat, "Can I walk you over?"

She said, "Sure." It was no big deal. We weren't even together at the party, but I became interested. She was fun and talkative and even a little loud—which I normally didn't like. People who know her today can't believe she used to be the life of the party and could really cut loose. (She denies it too, but it's true.)

I was quite taken with her. She seemed mature and smart, knew how to dress well, and in conversation I discovered that she was very spiritually sensitive. I don't know what she thought of me at first—she still won't tell me—but I began to look for her on campus. In fact, my window overlooked a walkway to the cafeteria, and I watched for her every morning and then just happened to pop out the door when she came by.

I never studied in the library, because people distracted me, but when I found out that she studied in the library, that's where I could be found, too—one eye on my book and one on the girl. I didn't know what had come over me. I had to take care of my mother, and I had big plans. Where did Pat fit in?

I continued to ignore letters from the girl in Argentina. In my foolish, naïve way, I thought she would get the hint and forget about me, but, of course, that was not the way to handle it. If I'd had any doubts about whether I was doing right by giving her up, however, they were gone, now that Pat was on the scene.

She finally caught on that I was interested, and we saw a lot of each other. There was nothing serious between us yet, but I certainly hoped there would be. I had been smitten, and when I learned she was going away over the Christmas break and had a few stops to make, I worried that one of those stops might be to see an old boyfriend. So I let her know how I felt. It wasn't anything dramatic or romantic, just my usual, straight-out Latin style. I wanted her to know that she was special to me, that I cared about her a great deal, and that I hoped we could spend a lot more time together after the holidays.

There were still a few days before Christmas break, and I was getting anxious for it to come, partly because I would be visiting the Stedmans again, but mostly because I was weary from my courses. My studies had been so intense, and I had taken almost solid Bible-book subjects for my electives. The nonelectives were Bible classes, too, so I was really getting my fill.

I have always loved reading and studying the Bible. But when you're getting that much of anything every day, sometimes more of it gets to your head than to your life. I was exhilarated about the potential with Pat, but when I thought about my own spiritual condition, I was depressed.

I had taken to sitting in the back of the auditorium during daily chapel, where we usually got another dose of exposition or missionary stories, daring the speaker to make me pay attention. If he was good, I'd honor him by listening. Otherwise I would daydream or peek at my class notes.

For one of the last chapel services before our break, our speaker was Major Ian Thomas, founder and general director of the Torchbearers, in England, the group that runs the Capernwray Hall Bible School. It was a challenge to make out all his words through a thick British accent and staccato delivery, but I had an edge on the rest of the students. And when he spoke and pointed a finger that had been partially cut off, I was intrigued.

Now here's an interesting man, I thought, probably just because he wasn't afraid to use that finger for gesturing. But as soon as he had me hooked, his short message spoke to me. I had been so hungry for answers to my dilemma that I had quit wondering where they would come from. I had all but given up, but, in twenty-two minutes, Ian Thomas got through to me.

His theme was "Any old bush will do, as long as God is in the bush." The essence was that it took Moses forty years in the wilderness to get the point that he was nothing. Thomas said that God was trying to tell Moses, "I don't need a pretty bush or an educated bush or an eloquent bush. Any old bush will do, as long as I am in the bush. If I am going to use you, I am going to use you. It will not be you doing something for Me, but Me doing something through you."

Thomas said that the burning bush in the desert was likely a dry bunch of ugly little sticks that had hardly developed, yet Moses had to take off his shoes. Why? Because this was holy ground. Why? Because God was in the bush!

I realized that I was that kind of bush: the worthless, useless bunch of dried-up old sticks. I could do nothing for God. All my reading and studying and asking questions and trying to model myself after others was worthless. Everything in my ministry was worthless, unless God was in the bush. Only He could make something happen. Only He could make it work.

Thomas told of many Christian workers who failed at first because they thought they had something to offer God. He himself had once imagined that because he was an aggressive, winsome, evangelistic sort, God could use him. But God didn't use him until he came to the end of himself. I thought, *That's exactly my situation. I am at the end of myself.*

When Thomas closed out with Galatians 2:20, it all came together for me.

I have been crucified with Christ; it is no longer I who live, but Christ who lives in me; and the life I now live in the flesh I live by faith in the Son of God, who loved me and gave Himself for me. (RSV)

You can't imagine the complete release I felt, as a result of that little chapel talk. My years of searching had come to an end. There would be many, many more problems that had to be worked out, on the basis of the principle in Galatians 2:20. But my biggest spiritual struggle was finally over. I would let God be God and let Luis Palau be dependent upon Him.

I ran back to my room in tears and fell to my knees

next to my bunk. I prayed in my native Spanish. "Lord, now I get it. I understand. I see the light at the end of the tunnel. The whole thing is 'not I, but Christ in me.' It's not what I'm going to do for You but rather what You're going to do through me."

I stayed on my knees until lunchtime, an hour and a half later, skipping my next class to stay in communion with the Lord. I realized that the reason I hated myself inside was because I wrongly loved myself outside. I asked God's forgiveness for my pride in thinking I was a step above my countrymen because I had been well-educated and could read English, and because I had spent so much time with Mr. Mereshian and prayed with Keith Bentson and worked in a bank and spoken on the radio and in a tent and in churches, and I got to come to the United States and mingle with pastors and Bible school presidents. Oh, I was really something, I had thought, but God was not active in the bush. I hadn't given Him the chance.

Well, He still had a lot of burning to do, but God was finally in control of this bush. He wanted me to be grateful for all the small hinges He had put in my life, but He didn't want me to place my confidence in those opportunities to make me a better minister or preacher. He wanted me to depend not on myself or my breaks, but on Christ alone, the indwelling, resurrected, almighty Lord Jesus.

I was thrilled to finally realize that we have everything we need when we have Jesus Christ literally living in us. Our inner resource is God Himself, because of our union with Jesus Christ (see Colossians 2:9-15). It's His power that controls our dispositions, enables us to serve, and corrects and directs us (see Philippians 2:13). Out of this understanding comes a godly sense of self-worth.

That day marked the intellectual turning point in my spiritual life. The practical working out of that discovery would be lengthy and painful, but at least the realization had come. It was exciting beyond words. I could relax and rest in Jesus. He was going to do the work through me. What peace there was in knowing I could quit struggling! Theologically, I knew better, but the experience made me feel as if I had just been converted, after trying to serve the Lord on my own for more than eight years.

Too many Christians live the way I lived all those years, because they believe that if they pray enough, read enough, and work enough, they'll be victorious. That's the essence of flesh, the essence of self. It cannot be done. We cannot work or earn our own victories through any self-effort, any more than we could work for our salvation.

I'll never forget the look on the face of an older missionary in Colombia, South America, some time later, when this truth dawned on him, too.

I'd been asked to speak to a group of missionaries at a conference, during our first year on the field. My theme was the indwelling Christ as our resource and power to serve.

Afterward, this old missionary gentleman invited me to go for a walk with him. Then, with tears streaming down his face, he told me, "Luis, I have been here on the field for over thirty years. I have worked for God as hard as I could, with every ounce of my being, but it's brought little but frustration. Now I see why.

"Until today, I don't think I have ever really known what it meant to allow the risen Christ to do the living in me. Thank you, brother."

My heart went out to this man, a genuine servant of the Lord, but one who had no victory in his life or ministry. His lack of victory had been evident. It was obvious that he had been carrying bitterness and ugliness in his soul, and there hadn't been much fruit in his ministry.

What makes the difference? Perhaps it sounds too easy: rely on the power of the resurrected Christ, rather than on self-control, where the struggle is almost unbearable. Rely on the indwelling power of the Holy Spirit, rather than on grim determination to hang on, which can be like killing yourself.

When temptation comes, turn to God and say, "Lord Jesus, you know I'm being tempted and that I cannot resist on my own. I'm relying on Your power, and I'm resting in You to turn my thoughts to something else.

"I have the mind of Christ, and therefore, with Your power, I will rely on You to give me the victory. I depend on Your strength and wisdom to serve."

That prayer changed me, and again God's timing was perfect. My most important life decisions were approaching.

19

Go Greyhound and Leave
the Driving to Me

My brethren, count it all joy when ye fall into divers
temptations; Knowing this, that the trying of your faith
worketh patience.

James 1:2-3

As one last gesture to prove my feelings for Pat, I
spent my last dollar on a set of tire chains for the car
she was traveling in over the holidays. It may not have
been very romantic, but I felt gallant.

I really missed her over Christmas and was anxious
to get back to school. But first there was the matter of a
good lecture from Ray Stedman. I told him all about
Pat, and he wanted to know if I had written to the girl
in South America to tell her it was all over.

I told him I hadn't even written to my own mother in
a long time, but that I would get to it. But that wasn't
good enough for Ray. Every time he mentioned it I
promised I would do it, but he would accept no promises. Finally one day he sat me down. "Look, Luis,
you've really got to write!"

Being the type of person who is tempted to put off
getting a haircut another month, even though I'm told I

156

need one, my immediate thought was, *Wait a minute. I'll write when I'm good and ready.* I didn't say that, of course, but as you can see, in spite of my spiritual awakening, I had a lot of growing up to do for a twenty-six-year-old.

"Don't worry, Ray, I'll write."

"It's going to hurt down there," he said. "The longer you prolong it, the more bad feelings you'll cause. You should write to her father, too, and just explain it to everyone. You could leave a trail of hurt people if you aren't careful. It's not good, and it's not right."

"Ray, when I get back down there I'll clear it up. I'll have a little chat with them, and it'll be all over." I had gone too far. Ray had heard too much. His eyes grew cold, and he put his arm around me.

"You know, my son, you really think you can solve any problem with that mouth." I started to object, but he shut me off. "Listen to me, Luis. One of these days you are going to dig a hole so deep with your mouth that not even God will be able to pull you out of it. Unless you shape up."

That hurt. No one had ever talked to me like that. I had talked to others that way, but to be on the receiving end was something else. It really shook me up.

"I didn't mean it that way," I protested weakly.

"Oh, but you *did* mean it that way, Luis. You said you would solve everything with a little chat, and that's exactly what you meant." He loved me too much to let me get away with it. It was the first of many stiff lectures I've received in my Christian life, and while they're painful, I have grown to thank God for the men who've dished them out.

The people I most respect are the men who have sat down and really had tough talks with me. I understand

157

that kind of honesty, and I feel it's of the Lord, at least after I've had some time to lick my wounds. Ray made me face up to the fact that my ego had to be brought to the cross, especially in that situation. It wasn't enough just to know the truth of Christ in me; I had to appropriate it and allow God to take me out of the way.

But Ray wasn't finished. He could tell by the look on my face that he had me, and there was more he wanted to communicate. "You are so self-confident that it oozes from your pores," he said. "Even the black suit that you showed up in was designed to impress people that you were a spiritual boy. Well, God can't stand self-confident people, and He'll not use you until you are selfless. You'll be nothing, you'll go nowhere."

The interesting thing was that he was wrong about the suit. To my knowledge I'd had no ulterior motive for buying a black suit. I could afford only one, and I had no idea how Californians dressed. It was custom-made, but I got rid of it, anyway, since it was out of place.

I was shocked and embarrassed that he had misinterpreted my black suit, but that didn't diminish the truth of his point. I knew he was right. I was so thankful that I had seen the light after Ian Thomas's chapel talk; otherwise, I wouldn't have been equipped to deal with this tongue-lashing. It took a few days for the shock to wear off, but I wrote my letters and recorded Ray's counsel. I couldn't have forgotten it if I had tried. That kind of chastisement from the Lord leaves a lasting impression.

I had waited too long to write the letters, and the girl's father contacted President Aldrich at Multnomah to complain about me. It was good that I had met Dr. Aldrich, and it was also good that he had a sensitive memory of his younger days. I admitted my mistake in waiting so long, and that was the end of it.

Another chat with Dr. Aldrich was in store, however, and it was the result of another girl friend problem.

The second semester was exciting, although a C in Hebrews brought my grade point average down a couple tenths of a point, to a 3.6. Pat could take some of the credit for that. I spent all the time with her that I could. By the Valentine's Day banquet, we were unofficially engaged. I didn't exactly ask her to marry me, though.

In my typical romantic fashion, as we walked under an umbrella in the Portland rain, I asked her if she would return to South America with me. She knew what that entailed. And I knew what her "yes" meant, too.

Then came the problem. The policy at Multnomah was that first-year students could not become engaged. I assumed it applied to the high-school grads who were just starting. Pat and I were in our mid-twenties, and I didn't think it should apply to grad students.

The dean of men thought otherwise. I argued that I had to make decisions about applying to Overseas Crusades so we could join as soon as the school year was out, but he was adamant. We sought the counsel of people we trusted, including Pat's parents, Willard and Elsie Scofield—whom I really loved from the first—and we were encouraged to appeal the rule.

I went back, but the dean refused. "If you get engaged, you will have to drop out."

"Fine," I said sharply, "then I'll drop out. But first I'd like to talk to the president, if you don't mind."

"Why do you want to do that?"

"Because I really don't want to drop out, and I don't think this merits it." We went round and round, and finally I said, "I'm sorry, but I must see the president."

I told President Aldrich that I loved Multnomah and wanted to stay, but that I would leave, if necessary, so we could become engaged. I had been offered the opportunity to apply as a missionary with Overseas Crusades to work in Colombia under my old boss, Ed Murphy, who was now field director there. First there would be missionary internship training in Detroit for seven months, and then two and a half months in Fresno to help in a Billy Graham crusade. Then there would be deputation. I was anxious to get going.

I wanted badly to be married, and I looked forward to the Graham crusade more than anything I had ever done. And I was excited by the prospect of working with Ed Murphy again, with the vision of taking a Latin American country for Christ. Well, Dr. Aldrich was convinced. If I waited, the whole thing would fall apart, and I would miss out on many of those opportunities.

"OK," he said, "we'll let you do it."

In Detroit, several months later, I went over someone's head in order to remedy a situation my way, and the Lord had to teach me another lesson.

Reverend Albert Wollen, pastor of the Cedar Mill Bible Church, in Portland, rushed us through his six mandatory premarital counseling sessions, and at the end of the school year I headed back to Palo Alto to intern for two months at Peninsula Bible Church with Ray Stedman. I bought his old '55 Buick and in August 1961 raced back up the coast, arriving just a few days before the wedding.

It had been a rough summer. We had utterly no money for phone calls, so all our contact was by mail.

We couldn't dream of inviting my mother—slightly worried about this woman in my life, who was neither a friend of the family nor a Latin—to come to the wedding, because of the costs. My sisters assured my mother that everything would be all right.

After we were married—with Ray Stedman sharing duties with Pastor Wollen (who is still the pastor at Cedar Mill Bible, our home church)—we took a two-week driving honeymoon down the coast, were interviewed by the Overseas Crusades board, and were accepted for missionary service. Then we hustled back to Portland to pack for Detroit.

My temper reared its ugly head in the first week of our marriage. Pat had been talking a lot about how her dad handled things—typical of a young woman reluctant to pull away—and I was starting a slow burn. Finally, on the way back she wanted me to drive straight through, rather than stop at a motel, because then she could see her mom and dad sooner.

"Well, I'll tell you what," I snapped. "If you want to see your father that badly, I'll put you on a Greyhound bus, and you can go see him." It was cruel, and I didn't deserve a wife so patient and loving. Whenever I make a fool of myself and we both know it, she doesn't rub it in, demand an apology, or go off and cry. She just leaves my comment hanging in the air to echo in my head until I'm as sick of it as she was to hear it the first time.

The trip across the country to Detroit was fun. Getting to know each other was exciting. My new wife probably wondered what she had got herself into, when my best-foot-forward courting approach gave way to the real Luis Palau, but she never admits that.

We visited the usual sites people see on their way

across the United States, all of them brand-new to me, of course. I was intrigued by Yellowstone National Park and by the Moody Bible Institute, which we saw after spending three nights in a Chicago YMCA with a lot of strange characters. We had no money for anything better.

In Detroit for seven months of missionary internship beginning in September, we were put up in the attic bedroom of an old woman's house. The plan was that we would work with a church and depend on them completely to support us. The program was designed to teach us to trust the Lord for our funds and to show us how to adapt to any situation. That turned out to be an understatement.

The director of the program, Mr. Fred Renich, was a wonderful man who taught us a lot at our weekly sessions in suburban Farmington. We went through several Navigators memory courses and also studied the epistles.

The problems, however, were that the church we served gave us very little, and the woman we lived with refused to put a lock on our bedroom door. She would burst in at inopportune times with a plate of cookies. It sounds funny, but you can imagine how we felt.

We were supposed to work under the pastor and do anything he asked, and then he would report to the mission about whether or not he thought we would be good missionary candidates. There was a lot of hard work involved (especially in an all-white church in an integrated neighborhood). Of course, the work was designed to weed out candidates who couldn't take a lot of thankless tasks.

It soon got to be too much for me, and I had thought I could do just about anything. In my mind, the project was going well beyond the bounds of credibility. A box had been placed at the back of the church, into which the congregation was supposed to put any contributions for us. One week we got a quarter and a few cans of food that someone didn't want. If a few friends hadn't sent us five dollars now and then, I don't know what we would have done.

We couldn't go anywhere or do anything. Our waking moments were spent trying to teach classes and organize programs, while literally wondering where our next meal was coming from. To me, that was what this internship program was all about. Pat and I had already developed our own ideas and independence. Now we were learning unconditional obedience, and it was rough.

Jumping to the conclusion that Mr. Renich knew exactly what was going on and approved of it, I thought Overseas Crusades ought to hear about it. I couldn't imagine any rational men sanctioning missionary life at this extreme. It was time to write a letter and get the situation taken care of. Luis Palau, the man of action, was about to move.

20

The First Epistle
of Saint Luis

But now ye also put off all these: anger, wrath,
malice . . . .

Colossians 3:8

I fired off a hot letter to Norman L. Cummings,
home director of Overseas Crusades, knowing that
would get quick action. I told him all about the situation at the church and our apartment and said, "If you
don't get us out of this within four weeks, we'll pack up
and go back to California. If you want us to resign
from the mission, we will; we must leave this place."

Cummings, of course, immediately wrote to Fred
Renich, demanding to know what in the world he was
doing to this young couple. He thought, as I did, that
enough was enough. Mr. Renich called us in.

I hardly let him talk, using the same resolve to leave
that I had in the letter. "Why didn't you come to me
and tell me before you wrote to your superiors?" he
asked.

I hadn't even thought of that. "I wanted action," I
said. "I figured that was the way to get it."

"Don't you see that this puts me in a bad light?" Mr.

Renich said. "It makes me look careless and insensitive. I look bad with Mr. Cummings and your whole mission. Don't you think if I had known all these things, I would have taken action?"

"Well, maybe I should have come to you first," I admitted.

"Of course you should have, and frankly, I don't like it."

"But I wanted action. I've had it up to here. We want to leave."

"You don't have to go home. We're going to rectify the situation and move you next week. But first I want to tell you something." He was about to become the second man God used to lovingly let me have it. "You are choleric," he said.

Before he could go on, I was on the defensive. I had never encountered that term, and I was racking my brain to figure out what he meant. I didn't even like the sound of the word. "What's that?" I asked.

"A choleric person always wants his way. You know how to go to just the right person to get action, and in the process you don't stop to think of how many people you step on, or how many you may even destroy. You don't care about that because all you care about is action.

"The problem," he continued, "is that you have a quiet wife. If you don't learn to put that choleric temperament under the control of Jesus Christ, you're going to walk all over Pat, and she just may not let you know. Then one day you'll have destroyed her, and you won't even realize it."

I was upset about not having known what *choleric* meant, but I had no argument. I was stunned, set back. I had taken it in the teeth again, and I had needed it.

"Think back on your life," Mr. Renich continued. "Go back to your room and think about all the people you've hurt, all the people you've stepped on, and perhaps all the spiritual corpses on the side of the road you traveled to get where you are today."

I felt battered and bleeding on the way back to our apartment. One of the books we were studying covered the four basic temperaments, so I studied cholerics. It described me to a tee. It took a long time for me to work the whole thing out, but for the remaining several months in Detroit, I was a different person.[1]

I evaluated everything I said or did on the basis of my temperament. I was amazed how it ruled me. And my memory was indeed full of people I had pushed aside without a second thought. I grew very close to Fred Renich and found him to be an excellent teacher. He wanted to help me learn to apply the principles of the indwelling Christ to my temperament and all my daily affairs: in marriage, in thinking, in emotions, in service, in preaching, in relationships. I had tremendous ground to make up.

The point was to control the choleric bent, not to eradicate it. I couldn't change what I was, but I could bring it under control—that is, God could, in the power of the indwelling Christ. Not long after that, Ray Stedman told me that *he* was a controlled choleric. I could hardly believe it. In my mind, his basic personality was as different from mine as night and day. If a choleric could be like Ray Stedman, there was hope for me.

1. If you want to learn more about your own temperament, I recommend Tim LaHaye's *Spirit-Controlled Temperament* (Wheaton, Ill.: Tyndale, 1966).

That internship training period turned out to be one of the most valuable seasons of my life. Because we didn't have children yet, Pat and I were able to really give ourselves to study and prayer.

An extracurricular project of mine was writing to many old friends and acquaintances to apologize for past actions. It was something I needed to do before I could feel too good about the truth I was learning about myself. It was one thing to go around happy as a lark because I was getting my spiritual life put back together, but it would be another if there were casualties still left behind.

I kept in touch with Ray Stedman during this time, so he would know that I was finally learning what he had been trying to teach me.

By the summer of 1962, we were ready to get on with our lives as missionaries. After a brief visit with Pat's family in Portland, we headed to Palo Alto for three weeks of orientation with Overseas Crusades. While we were there, we received the shocking news that Pat's mother had contracted polio. She was stricken severely enough that she is in a wheelchair to this day. Elsie Scofield has been an amazing source of inspiration to us, in that she seems to harbor no bitterness. She never complains and is so personable that it's easy to forget she's even in a wheelchair. She's a fantastic woman. Of course, Pat hurried back to be with her for a few weeks before we had to go to Fresno for the Billy Graham crusade.

Normally, new missionaries who have just completed orientation go immediately into their deputation work, raising the support necessary to send them to the field. But since I had to be heavily involved in evangelistic crusades and campaigns, Overseas Crusades (OC) decided it would be valuable for us to learn from the Graham team.

Actually I would have preferred to have gone to Colombia right after the Fresno crusade and deputation and begin campaigns as an evangelist, but OC saw that further down the road. My mission in Colombia, like everyone else's at OC, would be to plant churches. If evangelistic preaching for a crusade-style team grew naturally out of that, it would be considered as it came up.

I was so sure that evangelism was what I was called to that I was like a hawk at the Fresno crusade. I didn't miss a thing. I asked questions of everyone, kept a thick notebook on every detail, and learned the mechanics of mobilizing thousands of people. I tagged along with Bill Brown, the Fresno crusade director, and also visited Spanish churches in the area, inviting them to the July crusade in Ratcliffe Stadium.

Pat worked in special reservations, arranging for the large groups that came by bus and train. During the crusade itself she was to work at the counseling table, and I would interpret for the Spanish audience on one side.

At a precrusade breakfast we got to meet Billy Graham, and when he found that my ambition was to preach in evangelistic crusades in South America, he advised staying with the big cities. "Paul always went to the centers of population," he told us. "And Mr. Moody used to say that the cities were the mountains, and if you won the mountains, the valleys took care of themselves."

It was a thrill to talk to him, but I wish now we hadn't been too shy to have our pictures taken with him. I've always been a little embarrassed by the line about my being the "Billy Graham of Latin America," but if anyone wonders why our team's crusades resemble his in many ways, they should have seen us eagerly absorbing the basics in Fresno.

Then we went immediately into deputation work, all up and down the coast, speaking in churches where Ray Stedman knew the pastors, or taking any meeting OC set up.

It was a tough time, and yet a rich time because I got to know Dick Hillis. We chauffeured him to many of his speaking engagements, where he would often put Pat or me on the program first to give a testimony, then he'd preach the message himself. I believe that Dick is one of the most servantlike leaders I've ever met.

He's so much that way when you first meet him that you wonder if he can be for real. You think, *This can't be; it must be for show.* But I've known Dick for nearly twenty years, and he's the same today as he was then. He's the first one to help clean up the dishes or stack chairs or do anything else that needs to be done. He doesn't believe he's too big for any task or any person.

I was humbled by him. Pat and I used to sit and listen to his pithy one-liners, pieces of advice that were hard to forget. He was sold on discipling people, and I would guess that he's personally trained as many missionaries as anybody else.

He liked to emphasize "building a platform under the national." In other words, as a missionary, don't build a platform for yourself, build it for the national, so that he can speak to his own people.

He also said, "Are you worth imitating?" In other words, "Are you the kind of person who could say, 'Follow me?'" That hit hard.

Another of his lines that helped with the foreign missionary's culture shock was "It's not wrong; it's different."

If Ray Stedman is my spiritual father, Dick Hillis is my uncle. I couldn't have been more blessed by two more special, godly mentors than those two. And when I think of all the other people God has sent into our lives, I praise God for His sovereign design.

Pat became pregnant during that time, and by January of 1963—though she was only seven months along—suddenly she knew it was time to go to the hospital. I couldn't believe it. We were staying in the home of some friends while doing deputation work at Valley Church in Cupertino, California. I said, "You're kidding!"

She said, "Tell that to the baby," and off we went to Stanford University Hospital.

I had been waiting in the hallway for more than an hour when the doctor, a Christian friend from Palo Alto, came and told me that there were serious complications.

"What's wrong?"

"I'm not sure yet, Luis. We just have to pray."

I was scared to death. And I did pray. There hadn't been any problems during the pregnancy, though I admit I was concerned when she went into labor at seven months. The only other unusual aspect of the pregnancy was that Ray Stedman and the chairman of the OC board kept teasing Pat that she was going to have twins. I figured if the real doctor didn't say that, who were those two amateurs trying to kid?

I couldn't sit down. I kept trying to peek down the hallway to see where the doctor was. When it had been another hour, and he hadn't come out again, I feared the worst. Then he showed up again. He looked worried. "We're getting an incredibly strong heartbeat for only a seven-month fetus," he said, "and it is so irregular that I must tell you I'm not optimistic."

I was nearly in tears. "Is it that bad?"

"It's bad."

"Well, save her life," I pleaded. "Can you do that?"

"Oh, yes. She doesn't appear to be in any trouble. It's the baby I'm worried about. I don't know how the baby is surviving with the heartbeat we're hearing."

I could hardly speak. "I know my wife. I don't know the baby. If you have to make a choice, save her."

For two hours I prayed with friends. I got so tired of waiting that I finally assumed that we had lost the baby. Otherwise, the doctor would have come back. The thought of that hurt deeply. I paced and paced, praying and then watching for the doctor. When he finally arrived, he wore a huge grin.

"Congratulations!" he said. "You're the father of two boys!"

I don't remember anything after that, but our friends said all I did was jump up and down. The irregular heartbeat had really been two regular heartbeats.

Kevin and Keith were premature, less than four pounds each, and had to stay in the hospital for five weeks. It drove me crazy not to be able to hold them, and I'll never forget the day we finally brought them home. Their chances had been slim for a while and their breathing difficult, but they're healthy teenagers now.

Our next stop, later that same year, was Costa Rica and language school for Pat. Then we were off to Colombia.

21

Only Thirty and Feeling Old

Now thanks be unto God, which always causeth us to triumph in Christ, and maketh manifest the savour of his knowledge by us in every place.

2 Corinthians 2:14

Not long before going to Costa Rica, Ed Murphy and I attended a retreat in Colombia for that nation's evangelical ministers, sponsored by World Vision International. The timing was perfect, because we were able to speak a little and get to know all the key leaders. We received an official invitation from CEDEC, the acronym of an evangelical federation in Colombia.

We considered the experience something of a spying trip, on the order of the spies' venture into Canaan in the book of Numbers. We wanted to see if Colombia was a land of giants or flowing with milk and honey. I have to admit I was frustrated, already anxious to get going, to get our teeth into some work. But we were guests. Our day would come.

I felt dangerously near thirty, all of a sudden. It was as if life were slipping away. I wanted some action, to get moving, to see souls saved.

After a brief visit in the States, the family and I left for language school for Pat.

My mother had come all the way from Argentina up to Costa Rica to stay with Pat and the twins while I spent five weeks in Guatemala, preaching and teaching the Bible. It was an important and fruitful time for me, although afterward I determined that the family would not be separated for that long a period again, God willing. Only once since then have we been separated for longer than three weeks, and that was during the 1980 Great Britain rallies and crusades.

On the way to Costa Rica we had stopped in Guatemala for a few days and had met several key leaders who were of help during the five-week tour.

It was great for my mother to be able to meet Pat and see the grandchildren. The women hit it off well from the start, and Pat was happy to have someone she trusted to watch the boys while she spent the mornings at language school and the afternoons memorizing Spanish.

In Guatemala I preached primarily in Presbyterian churches but also in schools and special meetings. The friends I met and made there would one day allow me to return for tremendous crusades with thousands of people. In fact, I feel more welcome in Guatemala today than in any other country I have ever preached in. Guatemala is the country whose evangelical leaders felt it could be 51 percent born-again by 1982.

Looking back, I suppose I was still a very grim, determined young man. Trusting and resting in the indwelling Christ gave me great peace, yet I was very serious about wanting everyone else to have what I had. It was so new and fresh to me then that I can look back on my notes and remember what thrilling days those were.

When we finally arrived in Bogota, Colombia, in the

summer of 1964, I knew I was expected to be a regular missionary, training nationals in evangelism and church planting.

I didn't dare tell anyone that I considered this a stepping-stone and training for my crusades of the future. The goals of OC fit in perfectly with my dreams of mass evangelism, and the mission has always been biblical and flexible, so I saw little conflict. I needed the experience, so I was willing to start from scratch.

We started with what we called local church mobilization campaigns. The idea was that we should try to be catalysts to bring together the Body of Christ and stimulate evangelism. We wanted the man in the pew to learn how to share his faith, lead others to Christ, disciple them, and plant new churches.

This was basically the reason OC was formed. We felt that the more quickly we could mobilize the church, the more progress we could make in fulfilling the Great Commission. The basic theme, or motto, that Dick Hillis placed before us was "to stimulate and mobilize the body of Christ to continuous, effective evangelism."

The idea was to set up an office in the best possible location so that all Christians could feel confident and free to come and get acquainted with one another. We weren't in Bogota long before we began to feel that city was not the best place for our headquarters. Ed Murphy and I prayed for Colombia, finally realizing simultaneously that God had answered and would open the country.

I've had that experience only a few times in my ministry, but it is thrilling. You pray until you've "prayed through," and the Lord gives you assurance that He has answered and worked. You may not know how—and you may never know—but you know that He has.

(Daniel experienced this in chapters 9 and 10 of the book of Daniel.)

According to all reports, Cali appeared to have a more receptive climate for the gospel than Bogota did. One of the principles of effective church growth is that you go where the harvest is. That doesn't mean you despise sowing, but OC is basically a harvesting mission. We felt that the real harvest was in Cali, a town less than half the size of the capital, Bogota, which then had about 2 million citizens.

We moved around a little in Cali, finally finding an apartment and praying that we would get used to the culture soon. Pat never liked having a housekeeper, but one was almost mandatory to guard the house and to double as a babysitter when necessary.

When we settled down and began to work, our first effort was with a Christian and Missionary Alliance Church, where we held Colombia's first evangelistic street meetings. My old friend Bruce Woodman, who was now working at HCJB radio in Quito, Ecuador, came and played the trombone and led singing.

I shared the preaching duties with another Argentine-born evangelist, named Santiago Garabaya. It turned out that he and I had the same temperament. We were a couple of wild young horses who needed to be reined in continually and corralled by Ed Murphy. What a job for a field director: two Latin evangelists anxious to get rolling in big campaigns. How Ed survived us, only God knows.

Ed always stayed in the background as the silent prayer warrior, always insisting that the nationals do the work of reaching their own countrymen. We were glad to have him behind us, though, because, in the first street meetings especially, the local Christians did not want to get involved with us. They thought we were in for rough treatment from the public and the authorities. The situation in Colombia was touchy. Only a few years previously, evangelicals had undergone extreme persecution for their faith. Preaching in the streets, as we were doing, was very risky, if not foolhardy. But we were convinced that God was going to swing the doors wide open for evangelism in Colombia.

One day, while we were preaching to a small crowd, six formal religious leaders approached. One of our younger guys met them halfway across the square and defused them by telling them how wonderful it was that the evangelicals were having a meeting.

"What are they doing?" the six asked.

"They're speaking straight from the Bible."

"Oh, that is good," they agreed. And they went on their way. The current discussions over Protestants simply being separated brethren did us a lot of good in Cali.

Pat went to the meetings and baptismal services. We had wonderful times ministering together, something often lost as families get bigger and ministries require more travel. We talked for hours—I don't think we've ever got bored with each other. That was when she first started neutralizing my anger with her silence.

She was not vindictive or cold-shouldered. She simply would not try to argue and reason with a man who was angry. Early in our marriage I blew up at her when a walk to a park ended in our getting drenched by a rainstorm. After all, it had been her idea, and now we were soaked.

She didn't respond until weeks later, when I asked where she would like to go during some free time. "I think you'd better decide where we go this time," she said.

I praise the Lord that this was a couple of decades ago and that the Lord—along with giving me the perfect wife for my temperament—has allowed me to see victory in this area.

Pat has always been stoic. By the same token, she doesn't get carried away about the results of a good evangelistic campaign. That's just not her style. I might overhear her telling someone about it, but never bragging or acting overly impressed.

The next church we worked with was in a poor neighborhood called San Marcos. A group of fifteen believers grew to well over a hundred after we spent two weeks in revival services, evangelism, and training.

About that time Bruce Woodman got the idea that I should occasionally come to Quito to record a daily radio program. In a year or so we would begin the television counseling program "Responde." The radio programs are still heard every day, all over Latin America, by an estimated audience of 14 million. Even when he and I officially quit working together and he was not with HCJB anymore, those programs continued to be broadcast on a growing number of stations, which gave tremendous coverage to our campaigns and helped build the base for future crusades across the Spanish-speaking world.

Our ministry in Colombia continued to be successful, by God's grace. I learned to be used in a variety of ways, but all the while I kept appealing to the home office for more action in evangelistic campaigns. Whenever one of the board members, or the president, visited the field, I got him alone and pleaded with him to let me start my own evangelistic team and begin campaigning.

They admitted that they had started me small so I could learn many things, including humility, but they weren't ready to turn me loose for mass crusades just yet.

Garabaya was considered the better evangelist, and I the better Bible teacher. That may have been accurate, but I felt an evangelist should also be a good Bible teacher, so it certainly shouldn't have been considered my liability.

I was now into my thirties and felt as if opportunities in mass evangelism were passing me by. I had learned a lot and had big plans, but I couldn't do it on my own. It seemed logical to me that OC should allow such a crusade team within the mission, but they weren't sure I was ready for it yet. And they were probably right.

The first church campaign I was allowed to do on my own was at LaFloresta Presbyterian Church, in Cali, in September of 1965. I knew that if our strategy was going to work in big city-wide campaigns, it would have to work in the small local churches, too. LaFloresta qualified as just that. It had about sixty members.

We were invited by an American missionary, who doubled as their pastor. I took team member Joe Lathrop for leading the singing, and an inspiring young national named Libny Piñeda was my right-hand man. He had been helpful in street meetings in Cali, and I found him to be an enthusiastic, dedicated, prayerful teenager.

He and I prayed up a storm about that two-week campaign, finally breaking through and feeling certain that God had decided to bring revival to the church. The plan was that we would follow the Keswick Bible Conference outline and spend the first week working on the Christians. We felt that the first thing to do in inspiring the church for evangelism was to make sure the Christians were walking in the light and were up-to-date in their spiritual lives.

A Christian who is out of fellowship with God might do the work of inviting people to the meetings and cooperating with our efforts out of a sense of duty, or the realization that he will betray his spiritual bankruptcy if he doesn't. But, when he's out there on the street, rather than dying with Christ, he's more likely to be dying of embarrassment.

So I was going to preach on a different theme every night, spending the first five evenings on the possibilities of the Christian life. Libny and I read books on revival and evangelism, such as Oswald J. Smith's *The Revival We Need* and *The Man God Uses*, until we were so excited we could hardly wait. We were praying for big things.

The first night, I wanted the Christians to be tantalized by the possibilities available to them if they wished to get their spiritual houses in order, using 2 Corinthians 2:14 as a basis. Then, on the second night, I would cover why many Christians miss out on all those wonderful possibilities: because of sin, according to 1 John 1.

I believed in the Keswick approach: if you can provoke a crisis in a man's spiritual life, you can drive him back to God. I wanted the Christians to go home from the meeting so ashamed of themselves and repentant over carnality in their lives that they would be ready to be revived the next night.

The third night, I would speak on the cleansing work of the blood of Christ as the remedy for sin, even in the life of the carnal Christian. The point would be to get all of the guilty consciences cleansed and purified, and John 13 fit here magnificently. The fourth night was for dedication and consecration, and that would be the first time I asked for any public confession of the willingness to serve Christ anew, on the basis of Romans 12:1-2. The last night would focus on the ministry of the Holy Spirit.

The plan was precise and meaningful, and eventually we got it all in. But I nearly didn't get past the second night. God was not exactly working within our schedule. He had the fireworks planned for evening number two.

22
Breakthrough

. . . Woe to me if I do not preach the gospel!
1 Corinthians 9:16, RSV

I prepared those messages on my knees, beseeching God for revival. The first night I preached on the victory and holiness available to the Christian who is right with God. I wanted to raise the audience's expectations of what the Christian life could be.

The second night's message was entitled "The Spiritual Bankruptcy of the Carnal Church." I wanted people to recognize their sin and experience a spiritual crisis that would force a private encounter with their God; the next night I wanted them to come back overflowing from their experience.

First, I tried to shoot down all the reasons people used to explain their carnality: their mother-in-laws, their churches, their ministers, their finances, the world, and even political conditions. Then I pointed out all the sins and their root causes that keep us from God, from the tiniest to the grossest—from gossip to adultery.

That morning during prayer, both Libny and I felt that a breakthrough was coming, but we didn't quite expect what happened during that sermon. I was into the message and had explained the objective for the night. Then I used the passage in Matthew 5:23-24, about settling disputes with your brothers before you bring your offering to the altar.

Starting in on the little sins, I was ready to move into the big ones that destroy homes and families, but I never got that far. Suddenly a man stood up among the church's packed crowd of about two hundred. "Wait a minute!" he said. "This is enough!"

Libny, sitting on the platform behind me, immediately began to pray. He felt, as I did, that we were about to have either a scandal or a revival. "I'm an elder of this church," the man said. "But I've got to confess my sins right here. My family is a mess, and I'm a shame to this church.

"My wife and I don't get along, and my children disobey me. Look at me. I'm seated here, my wife's over there, and my children are back there somewhere. Wife, come here! Children, come here!"

They came to him, weeping and broken, and people all over the tiny, steaming, crowded sanctuary began popping to their feet to confess their sins. I was speechless and scared. I had asked for a revival, but this was a long shot from the tradition I had grown up in. I asked for the windows to be closed and for only church members and other Christians to remain. The confession continued.

In the middle of it all, a man rose and said loudly, "My turn! You know that young man on the platform?" he announced, pointing at Libny. "I caused his father's death. He died of a heart attack, but I am responsible, because when we were both elders we had a violent personal disagreement. There's nothing I can do about it now," he said, breaking down, "but I want to ask young Libny, right here in public, if he will forgive me on behalf of his father."

"Libny," I asked. "Are you going to forgive this man?" Libny went down to the man and embraced him.

What we had hoped and prayed for had happened. For nearly two hours, the congregation in that little Presbyterian church in the middle of nowhere publicly confessed its sins and got right with God. That threw my schedule off a little, but I have learned never to try to program God anyway.

Later in the week, when we asked for a public confession of their desire to present their bodies as living sacrifices to God, almost everyone in the church came forward. By the end of the second week, with the Christians revived and anxious to get on with the work of evangelism, our meetings were held outside in a patio area.

Libny, Joe Lathrop, and I could hardly sleep during those two weeks. We walked around the town at night, too excited to sleep, praying, and dreaming big dreams for the future. If God could do that, what else could He do? More than one hundred twenty-five people prayed to receive Christ, and about eighty joined that congregation. The church was in a state of revival for months on end, with spontaneous evangelism and joy.

During that time, one experience shaped a crusade policy firmly in our minds and hearts.

We were planning to hold a city-wide crusade in a Colombian city. The meetings were to be held in an outdoor stadium, but rain was almost a certainty. In those countries, when it rains, it doesn't just sprinkle; the heavens open, and everything is quickly drenched. Many poor people would be coming, and their clothing would not be adequate to withstand a rainstorm.

We prayed, we debated, we agonized. I couldn't stand to think of all those people sitting in the cold rain. Finally, we decided to cancel the first night's meeting. But it was too late. Even after spreading the word, busloads began pouring into the city from the countryside. "But, Brother Palau, we don't mind the rain," they told me.

That night, after the meeting, we walked the streets, talking about our decision. "Never again," we determined. "We will never cancel a crusade meeting like that. We will trust God and go on."

Later that same year, I flew to Quito to try an unusual idea of live counseling on television, rather than just preaching, as other Christian TV people did. We started with a short program, but the lines were hot, and people kept calling. By the end of the nightly three-week program, we were on the air for more than three and a half hours at a time.

It was exhausting, but invigorating. From the beginning, I never wanted to be accused of breezing into a town and doing a series of evangelistic meetings, then leaving everything up in the air. Right away we opened family counseling centers to follow up callers or to deal with those who saw the telecasts and either could not get through or were too timid to call. We tried the same program in El Salvador almost five years later, and for the brief run of the program, it had better ratings than anything else in that time slot.

We've found that this combination of the TV program, the crusade meetings at the stadium, and the downtown counseling centers makes a powerful impact on a city. The question-and-answer format somehow causes the television viewer to examine himself in the light of Scripture. We praise God for the many letters that we receive after the telecasts, saying, "Mr. Palau, when you prayed with that man, I knelt down in front of my television and prayed the prayer with you. *Gloria a Dios*, I feel clean again."

After the initial TV success in Quito, we began doing the program every few months, and then doing it in conjunction with crusades, so that people could begin to understand more of the gospel and its relevance to everyday life. The TV viewers might come to the crusade, and the crusade audience might tune in the program.

An exciting taped Christmas special, now aired on many stations, grew out of that program. For the Christmas season, the HCJB writers wrote thirty short spots, which I read as news stories concerning the events in Bethlehem and the surrounding area as if they were actually reports from Nazareth and Jerusalem and so on. It was very effective, and many stations in Latin America request the programs every December.

When our third son, Andrew, was born, in February of 1966 in Cali, I missed being in the delivery room because I fell asleep, and the nurse forgot to wake me up. Pat claims I didn't want to wake up for the birth, anyway, because I was squeamish. She's right; but, *really*, the nurse did forget to wake me!

The thing that bothers Pat is that if she could stay awake, why couldn't I? I tell her that I didn't have any labor pains to keep me awake. She doesn't buy that logic.

She and I were involved in ministry in exciting ways back then. We spent money we hardly had to help the churches and local groups set up cooperatives so they wouldn't starve. We even bought a sewing machine for a new convert so she could support her family with it.

One of the other missionaries and I wrote to his

home church in Michigan and borrowed $2,500 for some evangelistic work and promotion that we felt was crucial. Our mission came down hard on us for that, and rightly so, because we had a tough time paying it back. We were earnest, I'll say that. I was getting anxious to see us turn a corner and get into some true city-wide crusade evangelism.

Undoubtedly, my impatience and eagerness to get on with God's call was hard on Ed Murphy and the whole OC staff. It's a good thing they liked me and saw that I was truly committed to Christ and sharing His love. It was all they could do to keep up with their two restless Argentinian evangelists.

People were hurting. They needed Jesus Christ. I was impatient to get the gospel message out on a massive scale in Latin America. Why couldn't people understand how important it was to get moving? "Lord, let the wheels start moving!" I prayed.

During Easter week of that year, Garabaya and I were scheduled for evangelistic preaching campaigns—his in Cali before 8,000 people in a covered auditorium, and mine 200 miles away in the town of Girardot, with a crowd of about 1,300. I directed the training, promotion, and publicity and arrangements for Garabaya's crusade, while someone else handled the arrangements for mine.

At the last minute, I left the preparations for his and hurried off to preach at mine. It was exciting to be involved in both. Mine was by far the largest crowd I had ever addressed, and his was bordering on the kind of mass evangelism I had dreamed about for so long. We were both excited by the response of the Colombian masses.

I preached in a Presbyterian school for four or five

nights, and the experience was just enough to thrill me on the one hand and frustrate me on the other. It was a terrific week of evangelism and revival, but it made me want more than ever to give up everything else and go into full-time evangelistic preaching campaigns.

We were ready to aim for bigger things, but whenever I mentioned my goal, I got the same response: "You're a Bible teacher. Be a Bible teacher. Let somebody else be the evangelist."

My reply was, "No, life is going by too fast. I want to redeem the time. I'm more than thirty years old!"

The drive within me to preach the gospel, to proclaim Jesus Christ, was so strong that I felt, with Paul: "Woe to me if I do not preach the gospel!" (1 Corinthians 9:16, RSV). I still have the compulsion to keep on preaching to greater and greater audiences till all have a chance to hear.

So much still needs to be done! Every new generation needs to hear about Jesus Christ. Years later, while I was preaching in Great Britain, we were told that Europe is a post-Christian society.

In my opinion, either a society is Christian or it's pre-Christian. A land that once sent missionaries to other countries now needs missionaries itself, to bring its own people the gospel.

I enjoy Bible teaching. I did then, and I always will. But if we say that good Bible teachers don't make evangelists, then we're saying that evangelists aren't good Bible teachers. That's irrational. Personally, I prefer Bible teaching to evangelism. I have felt that evangelism was my duty, in obedience to the Lord, because there is such a vast need, and people are suffering. My wife and I would love for me to retire from the grueling campaigns so we could just travel together to Bible conferences, where I could teach the Word in a relaxed setting. I don't know why more men don't do that, because the churches so badly need to be ministered to on a constant basis.

Anyway, it would have been easy for me to develop a complex about my evangelistic preaching. Even when I was younger, remember, everyone wanted my young friend to be the evangelist and me to be the Bible teacher. I have a hunch they didn't think I was a good evangelist; and, you know, I probably wasn't.

I struggled over my messages. I spent hours and hours trying to figure out how I was going to make the people stay with me and think. I'm not the kind of evangelist who always just pulls out an old outline, adapts it to the present crowd, and gets up and talks. I'm not a natural. It doesn't come to me easily. I have to think through every aspect. Nor do I feel comfortable with just stories and gimmicks that enchant audiences but are not the gospel.

I wanted to be an evangelist because of the command of Christ. There has long been in me a compulsion to evangelize. Evangelism also gives me tremendous authority and a platform from which to influence the Body of Christ. When I preach in a town, many pastors come for consultation on issues, and I am able to exhort and encourage the Body at large that way. I believe an evangelist has an advantage over someone who is strictly a Bible teacher, in that respect.

Now that I look back on it, and this has been corroborated in private conversations, I think the men at OC were afraid that I could not handle the glory that can go along with being a successful evangelist. They weren't sure my Latin temperament was suited to the adulation that might result from it.

Every person God has put in my life has been a blessing, especially the ones I've chafed under. Those people were sent by God to disciple a sometimes over-eager young man. One, I learned later, returned from visiting the field and, hearing my "time's wasting" pitch, told the board, "We may have to clip Luis's wings."

I wanted to preach, felt called to preach, was committed to preach, and needed a team to see it happen. But the fear of God in me helped to keep my ego from getting out of hand. I knew I wasn't immune to the problems that any Christian leader might have, but I truly believed that if a person attempted to steal any glory from God, He'd remove His hand, and that would be the end of his ministry.

By that time, I was getting desperate to get moving, figuring it would take several years to expand from a local church to united campaigns and beyond. If I let the years slip by, I'd be an old man, still hoping and dreaming foolish dreams. I didn't want that to happen. I was ready to go out on my own, if necessary.

23

Berlin Summit

*. . . let patience have her perfect work, that ye may be
perfect and entire, wanting nothing.*

James 1:4

Ray Stedman was in Guatemala for a pastor's conference, so I flew to see him. "Be patient," was his
advice. That was like telling an amputee not to cry.

"How long must I sit around and sit around?" I
wanted to know. "If I have to leave OC and start on my
own from scratch, I may do it."

"Be patient," he repeated. "If God is in it, it will
happen when the time is right."

Just before attending the World Congress on Evangelism late in 1966, in Berlin, I began getting letters from
OC board member Vic Whetzel about considering Mexico as a fertile ground for mass evangelism. I had never
considered it before, but I gave it some thought. I
wasn't sure what he was driving at. Would I be asked to
switch fields?

One dark, cold afternoon in West Berlin, when the
congress meetings had let out early and the delegates
were milling around town, I received a call from OC
board members Dr. Ray Bensen and Dick Hillis. They
wanted to take a walk with me and to have a chat. We

walked for a long time before they got to their point.

"Luis," Dick said, "we feel you should go home on furlough in December as planned. Once your furlough is over, begin to develop your own evangelistic team with your sights set on Mexico. You'll be field director for Mexico, with your headquarters there."

For once I was speechless. A dream had come true. I am grateful to OC that they patiently worked with me. Who knows what would have happened to me or my ministry if they had let me go off on my own when I was making all that noise.

I had no connections or contacts in the States, outside my few friends on the West Coast. My major concern was whether I could have OC team member Joe Lathrop on my team. Dick and Ray agreed readily and asked what else they could do for me. I knew we would need a music man, too, and we arranged for Bruce Woodman to work with us, though he never officially joined the mission.

Dick Hillis told me that he hoped I would "become the greatest evangelist in the world." Coming from a man who was prayerfully concerned about any potential ego problems, that was a comment I knew exactly how to take. It reflected his attitude. He wanted nothing for my glory, but all for the glory of God. So did I.

Just before leaving Colombia for Argentina—where my new family would celebrate Christmas with my original family before returning to the United States and furlough—it was time to keep a promise I had made to a band of Christian young people who wanted to make an impact on Bogota.

Ed Murphy and I had met with little success in Bogota before setting up shop in Cali, so this was an exciting proposition for us. This national organization of evangelical young people had scheduled a parade and a four-day crusade in Bogota, December 8-12, 1966. "Even if we get killed, come what may, we'll do it," they told me, "if you'll help us." They knew the rally could shake up their country and open it once and for all to the gospel.

I advised them to set high sights for Colombia, to plan a presidential prayer breakfast someday, and to work to have an evangelical elected president one day. (Eleven years later, many of us were reunited in a Bogota hotel after the first presidential prayer breakfast for Colombia. They had waited a long time for that answer to prayer, and it was an emotional time.)

When I arrived in Bogota to help them back in 1966, I was amazed at what had already been done. Thousands of evangelicals were coming in from surrounding towns. There were several teams of three young people each (one to preach, one to sing and play, and one to pass out tracts, inviting people to the meetings), who toured the city, carrying their own boxes to stand on.

The plan was that they would slam the box down on a street corner; then the guitar player and singer would jump up and start the music, drawing a crowd. Meanwhile, the tract passer would distribute as many as he could while the speaker gave a three-minute testimony. They were through and running by the time the police came. They would run one block one way and then two blocks the other, set up the box, and do it again.

The parade was going to be a huge one. We allowed no more than four people in a row and spread them out so they stretched twelve city blocks. The kids had purchased radio time from one of the local stations, and Christian songs were played over the radio during the march. There were enough transistor radios among the marchers that the whole line could sing in unison, even though they couldn't all hear each other.

It was impressive but dangerous. The crowds began to swell. Twelve thousand people followed the parade (the next day's newspaper said 30,000) to the presidential plaza, where, we heard later, the archbishop peeked out his window to see what was happening. Police cars maneuvered to the front of the parade to clear the streets for us. For a second I was sure we were all in for it. I even motioned for Pat to get the children out of there. The president came out and asked Libny (always on the edge of our crowds) what was going on. Libny told him, and the president said, "If you can draw a crowd like this, you could get a president elected."

By the time I was ready to speak, 20,000 people had jammed the plaza. I was beside myself.

Three hundred people raised their hands, asking for salvation after my short message in the plaza, and several hundred more were saved during the meetings over the next four nights. The young people prayed that the rain would not interfere, even though Bogota had had rain every day for more than a month.

We were spared the rain, and in fact, once the black clouds parted and allowed sunshine in during most of the service. At the end of one of the meetings, I encouraged the song leader to hurry as the clouds rolled in. Just as we finished the final prayer and people stood to leave, the heavens opened!

What a way to end one mission term and start looking forward to the next!

I had been freed of wondering about and waiting for my chance to get into crusade evangelism on a larger scale. On furlough we spread the word everywhere that Bruce and Joe and I were a new team and ready to take Mexico for Christ.

During a missions conference in Idaho, I drafted a memo to the board of OC on the goals, objectives, and strategies of the Luis Palau Evangelistic Team; they haven't changed. That memo became a foundation paper for our work, stating that our objectives were: to preach Christ; to stimulate and mobilize the Body of Christ; to see hundreds, if not thousands, of young men go into the ministry; and to plant local churches.

The highlights of the next years, more than a decade, would fill the pages of two more books, and perhaps someday they will, but let me focus on events that most affected my personal and spiritual life.

For almost a year and a half we were on furlough and deputation work, finally arriving in Mexico in mid-1968. It was a rough first year, particularly on Pat and the three boys (and we had one on the way). Because of a colossal transportation snafu, we went without our furniture for a year and a half! At one point, I called my mother-in-law and encouraged her to invite Pat and the kids to Portland for four to six weeks. I said I would finance it, but that Pat must not know it was my idea. I think Pat suspected, and if she didn't know for sure before, she does now.

Basically with the help of a new OC man, John McWilliam, and Joe Lathrop we staged fourteen campaigns in Mexico in 1969 alone. The big one was in a bullring in Monterrey, where more than 30,000 heard the gospel in nine days, and 2,000 made decisions for Christ.

Although the crusade evangelism was finally launched, and God was blessing the work with conversions, those days were some of the roughest in our ministry. Money was low, and we had to wait and hope and pray that it would come in. You can learn a lot of spiritual lessons from that experience, but you can also find yourself living at an impractical level and wondering why.

The gigantic crusade we planned for and promoted at a baseball park in Mexico City was canceled at the last minute by the government. We were discouraged—all of us. I wondered if we would ever get on our feet. We vowed to have that big crusade in Mexico City, somehow, someway.

Our fourth son, Stephan, was born that November, adding a nice touch to a difficult year. Good thing Pat and I both love boys!

The next year, 1970, we heard that another religious group had drawn a big crowd to a convention, so we called our crusade a convention, too, and drew more than 106,000 people in ten days, doing very little advertising other than by word-of-mouth. In many ways, that crusade was the catalyst that began to focus the attention of many on what God was doing in Latin America.

Through all the attacks of the enemy and the early tough going, the team and Pat and I did not lose our zeal. I was thrilled with the opportunity to present Christ to Latin America. I couldn't remember when I hadn't had that dream. And now, slowly but surely, it was happening. Slow, because there was so much ground to cover, yet we kept to our excruciating schedule.

That same year Jim Williams—another new missionary and a graduate of Biola College and Trinity Seminary—joined the team. At first I was upset because I felt he was sent without my getting a chance to interview him or get to know him. First I fired off a letter to OC, asking why they sent me a man with whom I was unfamiliar. Then when he arrived he was so quiet, and had not really learned Spanish well yet, so I wrote a complaint to Ray Stedman.

Jim soon learned Spanish fluently and became an expert in counseling, specifically family counseling. He has been with me ever since and is vice-president of the team, handling the day-to-day Latin American operations and also heading up the massive counseling centers and community-service programs required in the big crusades.

From the crusade counseling-center ministry that Jim directs, training counselors emerged in every crusade city, and an extensive counseling manual was produced in Spanish and English. During every crusade, scores of people seek out the biblical advice that Jim and the counseling staff offer. Hundreds come to Christ, as they see Him as a solution to their problems.

Through the years we've added top key people, an individual at a time, until I have felt that we had a strong team of professionals.

We followed up on new converts; kept accurate records, helped plant churches, put everything on film and videotape, wrote brochures and booklets and books, taped radio and television programs, and set up programs for the needy. In addition, Jim Williams continued to engineer the massive counseling programs in each city where we held a campaign.

We ministered from El Salvador to Honduras, Paraguay, Peru, Venezuela, and Costa Rica. In 1975, we held a tough but exciting three-week crusade in Managua, Nicaragua, where the gospel was broadcast from one end of the Spanish-speaking world to the other through an amazing radio network. In the seventies, we began receiving invitations to preach the gospel in Great Britain and other parts of Europe. The doors just kept opening, and we excitedly kept going through them, eager to see what God would do next.

John McWilliam, a graduate from San Jose State College and Talbot Theological Seminary, took over the duties of crusade director and has continued to direct the Latin American crusades. Stan Jeter, a graduate of San Jose State College, joined us to work in the area of radio and television. Marcelino Ortiz, a pastor from Mexico and a graduate of the Presbyterian Theological Seminary and Polytechnic Institute of Mexico, became a Bible teacher at the team's pastors' conferences and an associate evangelist in many of the crusades.

Bill Conard, a missionary in Latin America for fifteen years and a graduate of the Moody Bible Institute and the Regent Study Course in Vancouver, British Columbia, became editor of *Continente Nuevo*, our Spanish magazine for pastors and Christian leaders. And God has continued to lead many other talented people to help us in the ministry of evangelism.

I was privileged to receive favorable press clippings throughout Latin America and was able to meet the leaders of many of the countries. All that did was intensify my love for Latin America and my desire to see every Spanish-speaking person hear the claims of Christ upon his life.

There would be meetings with Billy Graham—who has been very supportive of our ministry—and invitations to other continents, Europe and elsewhere, but as the outreach grew and became more international, I was still most moved by the contacts that reminded me of my childhood.

For a little less than two years, from 1976 to 1978, I served as president of Overseas Crusades, which I loved;

I was reluctant to give up that position when it was obvious that I could not devote enough time to both that and my preaching ministry. In October 1978, I left Overseas Crusades and set up the Luis Palau Evangelistic Team. Yet, even with all the opportunities that opened up for me and the fantastic times of fellowship and work with the board of OC, my fondest memories are the ones that hit closest to home. That includes two encounters during a visit to Argentina in 1977, a visit I shall never forget.

24

Not the Pride, but the Passion

Humble yourselves in the sight of the Lord, and he shall lift you up.

James 4:10

It's always a treat to see how my native country has changed, and also to see whether anyone remembers Luis Palau, the young dreamer who left there back in 1960. In 1977, some of the team members and I were there for Juventud '77, an explosive youth crusade.

At one of the meetings, a woman introduced herself to me, but she didn't have to. I recognized her immediately as one of the maids we had employed when I was a child in Ingenero-Maschwitz.

My sisters and I had made fun of this woman because she sang a slow, dirgelike song to the virgin Mary to counteract all the evangelical songs my mother sang around the house. We had not been nice to her, even though we really liked her. Years later, she told me now, she received Christ and began attending our local Christian Brethren assembly. She has been active there now for thirty years.

It was good to see her again, to hear her wonderful news, and to be able to apologize for the dumb things my sisters and I did when we were children. She and I had a good laugh over it.

On that same trip one of my aunts gave me a hymn-book Mr. Rogers had given to my father after their first evangelistic effort following my dad's conversion. I was to preach the message in the very chapel my dad had built and that I had attended during most of my child-hood, so the gift was especially meaningful to me. What memories flooded my mind as I sat waiting to speak.

I had a lump in my throat as I saw my little nephews—who looked so much like me more than thirty years before—sitting there on the pews. I leafed through that little hymnbook as I waited and noticed that Mr. Rogers had signed it, marking a page number for my father. I turned to the song.

I nearly broke into tears as my mind transported me back to Cordoba. I had been eighteen or nineteen when I suggested this very song for one of our youth meet-ings. I had suggested it flippantly, but as we had sung it, I remember being convicted and moved by it.

Translated from Spanish, the song went something like this: "How many sheep are wandering astray? Let us go and find them, in the name of the Lord. And there'll be great joy for whoever can bring them back to the Lord." It went on about sheep being caught in the thicket, and followed with a verse that goes: "What joy it would bring us to be able to say, 'Shepherd, we have been out looking for Your sheep, and finally we've found them after a thousand trials, and here we bring them into Your fold.'"

It is nearly impossible for me to quote that in Span-ish even today, because of the emotion it evokes. Somehow, I was overwhelmed by the lyrics and could hardly go on, knowing that God was calling me to find sheep that had gone astray.

Then, thirty years later, sitting in the church I had grown up in, to realize that this very song that had led to a deeper commitment was the same one Mr. Rogers noted for my father in his gift hymnbook—it was almost too much. I found it hard to preach. There was no taping or photographing that day, and it's just as well. That service stands out in my mind, as clear to me now as when I was there.

That day I realized anew the impact that the death of my father had had on my ministry. I want to see men and women who are in his former spiritual condition come to Christ and have their lives changed, so they can leave this earth singing, as he did.

I am moved by many motivations to be an evangelist. My dream is that people from other nations will look at a country that is being revived and ask, "What is happening over there?" And also that they will get the answer: "A nation has been turned around, and God did it."

I hope mass revival can take place on this earth again, as it once did. I believe we are heading toward the climax of history and that things are going from bad to worse, but that doesn't mean we should stop struggling and fighting for the good of the nations. What if the Lord doesn't return for three more generations? Or—hard as it is to fathom—thirty generations?

As I see it, we're in a last surge of evangelism, in which many hundreds of thousands of new Christians are being added to the fold every day. Just look how many millions have been converted in just the last fifty years! There are more Christians today than ever in history. I don't think the Bible teaches a defeatist philosophy. If it did, we should have given up decades ago. I am looking for a dramatic, cataclysmic return of Jesus

Christ, but until then, I will work and hope and pray for the salvation of thousands and the betterment of as many countries as possible.

I've always been intrigued by God's reaction to Abraham's petition for Sodom and Gomorrah (Genesis 18). Abraham prayed that if there were just a few righteous people left, God would spare the towns, and God agreed to withhold judgment for as few as ten. How far down the line will the Lord go in blessing a nation or city? How few righteous people must there be before He finally takes away His hand of judgment?

I believe we're soon going to see perhaps three nations in Latin America that will have a majority of evangelical Christians, professing biblical ethics and a love for Jesus Christ.

If that happens, I look to God to do what He promises: to send rain and harvest and healing. I don't see why it couldn't happen. It moves and excites me. It spurs me on. It's what evangelism is all about.

C. H. Spurgeon gave the challenge:

> We want again Luthers, Calvins, Bunyans, Whitefields, men fit to mark eras, whose names breathe terror in our foemen's ears. We have dire need of such. Whence will they come to us? They are the gifts of Jesus Christ to the Church, and will come in due time. He has power to give us back again a golden age of preachers, a time as fertile of great divines and mighty ministers as was the Puritan age, and when the good old truth is once more preached by men whose lips are touched as with a live coal from off the altar, this shall be the instrument in the hand of the Spirit for bringing about a great and thorough revival of religion in the land.

I do not look for any other means of converting men beyond the simple preaching of the gospel and the opening of men's ears to hear it. The moment the Church of God shall despise the pulpit, God will despise her. It has been through the ministry that the Lord has always been pleased to revive and bless His Churches.

Many people think evangelists are motivated by money or ego and not by the prospect of hundreds of thousands, and even whole nations, turned to God. Well, no one who knows me could ever say with a straight face that I am motivated by money. Surely there are many other professions that would allow me to live more comfortably. In fact, I was involved in one before I got into Christian work.

It's not hard to understand why people suspect preachers, and particularly evangelists, of having ego problems. We are in the limelight. Each of us is like the pitcher on a baseball team, alone on the mound, with the ebb and flow of the game in his hand. People could think we're the stars of the show.

We have publicity and admiration and support. And, yes, we have pride to battle. Somehow Billy Graham has —in my opinion—found peace and victory over this. For me, and for many of my colleagues, it is not so easy. Perhaps Billy has problems in areas where others of us have found victory. I don't know. But for me at least, pride can indeed be a problem.

One of the major ways I deal with my ego and pride is to remind myself just who I am and who I am not. I remember that without Christ I am nothing. When people compliment me on a message or sermon, I remember an admonition I once saw in a book. Although I appreciate their kindness and enjoy the fact that I have been appreciated, I remember that, first, people don't usually think through what they're saying—they're saying it because they think it is the polite thing to say; and second, even if they do mean it, they probably haven't heard the really great preachers of this world and thus cannot make a valid value judgment on whether or not a sermon was good.

So, although I appreciate the kindness and acceptance people might give, I don't take their praise too seriously. The thing that counts is my daily walk with God. I am so conscious of weaknesses—and, thank the Lord, my team members don't allow me to forget them—that I just praise God He has blessed our work in spite of me.

Many seminary students and other enthusiastic young men say, "Luis, I want to preach to crowds; I want to be an evangelist and win souls to Christ. How did you get your big break to hold mass crusades?"

There are no big breaks in mass evangelism. God leads in many small ways, and we learn obedience each time. Big doors open on small hinges. If you feel that God has called you to serve, be faithful to do everything He shows you to do. Luke 16:10 says: "He who is faithful in a very little is faithful also in much" (RSV).

Be humble. Ask God to overcome any pride and arrogance in your life. James 4:10 contains a promise: "Humble yourselves before the Lord and he will exalt you" (RSV). Seek after holiness. In Romans 12:1, we read the admonition to present our bodies to God as living and holy sacrifices. And, as Robert Murray M'Cheyne said, "According to your holiness, so shall be your success. A holy man is an awesome weapon in the hand of God."

I often tell young men about the difficulties: the days and weeks away from their families, the long hours of just plain hard work. I tell them that they need to study God's Word and read about the lives and work of other men and women of God. Daily time spent searching the Scripture and praying is a must. But, if they're serious about being used by God in full-time service, and if God is leading them, they'll find that out soon enough (1 Thessalonians 5:24; 1 Timothy 1:12-15).

Many evangelists burn out after just ten years, for one reason or another. It's not always pride or any sort of sin that does them in; more often they just get tired and give up. Frankly, that is often more of a temptation to me than to become proud.

Persistence is the key to keeping a youthful spirit and enthusiasm. I don't know how Billy Graham does it, but I would love to follow in his footsteps in this respect. Here he is, a grandfather in his sixties, yet he still works and acts and thinks and dreams with youthful exuberance.

I was with him in Germany a few years ago when he counseled a young man who had a team and wanted to be an evangelist. Billy cautioned him, "Watch out for pride, immorality, and money; and be sure to walk in the Spirit."

After Billy had finished encouraging him, the young German asked him in broken English, "Mr. Graham, would you bless me?"

Billy could have just put his hand on the young man's shoulder and said, "God bless you," or prayed a little prayer for him; but, no, he was serious and earnest in seeking God's best for this enthusiastic young servant.

Almost as if he hadn't heard the young man's request, Billy said simply, "Let's pray." He stretched out nearly prostrate on the floor on all fours. I was dumbfounded as he prayed with that young man he had known only a few minutes. He prayed his heart out, "Oh, God, bless him as he preaches Your Word and seeks to draw men to You—"

I was speechless after the young man left. Billy said, "Luis, you and I are in the public eye, and most people speak very highly of us. We must follow the biblical command to humble ourselves that, in due time, God may exalt us" (see James 4:10). That really touched me. Humility in private is true humility.

We have to live in the light of the cross, and that's why our team spends time in the Word every day (2 Timothy 2:15). The Bible says that some are "servants of Christ and stewards of the mysteries of God" (1 Corinthians 4:1, RSV). What a privilege. That is how I want to see myself as an evangelist.

The Bible also says that it is required of stewards that they be found trustworthy (1 Corinthians 4:2). This is one of the reasons I preach on personal purity and accountability anytime I speak to Christian groups. It is the Lord who judges us, many times using people who truly love us and see weaknesses in us. If God leads them, I believe their admonitions will be as gentle as the Holy Spirit is. The Holy Spirit is not in the business of loading down servants of God with guilt.

Satan accuses through false, sometimes undefined, guilt. God points to specific sin, convicting by His Spirit and promising change as we allow Him to work.

For all that I am and do, I believe God will take care of the judging of Luis Palau. I have peace in my heart that I honestly want to do the will of God. I want to win souls.

I will continue to call men and women to Christ, and

I hope to preach until my strength is gone.

> This is how one should regard us, as servants of
> Christ and stewards of the mysteries of God.
> Moreover it is required of stewards that they be
> found trustworthy. But with me it is a very small
> thing that I should be judged by you or any
> human court. I do not even judge myself. I am
> not aware of anything against myself, but I am
> not thereby acquitted. It is the Lord who judges
> me. (1 Corinthians 4:1-4, RSV)

Books That Have Influenced My Life and Ministry

The Bible

Lectures to My Students, by C. H. Spurgeon

The Burning Heart: John Wesley, Evangelist, by A. Skevington Wood

Ephesians, by August Van Ryn

Revival in Our Times, by William S. Deal

God in the Garden, by Curtis Mitchell

Continuous Revival, by Norman P. Grubb

Synopsis of the Books of the Bible, by J. N. Darby

A Commentary, Critical and Explanatory, on the Old and New Testaments, by Robert Jamieson, A. R. Fausset, and David Brown

Hebrews, by S. I. Ridout

Spurgeon—The Early Years—An Autobiography, by C. H. Spurgeon

Jeremiah, by F. B. Meyer

Philippians, by F. Lund

The Life of D. L. Moody, by William R. Moody

D. L. Moody, by John Pollock

The Autobiography of Charles G. Finney, by Charles G. Finney and Helen S. Wessel

The Pentateuch, by C. H. Mackintosh

Treasury of David, by C. H. Spurgeon

The Man God Uses, by Oswald J. Smith

The Revival We Need, by Oswald J. Smith

Fundamentalism and the Word of God, by J. I. Packer

The Memoirs of Robert Murray M'Cheyne, by Robert Murray M'Cheyne

Vision Statement

In dependence upon God . . .

We want to win as many people as possible to Jesus Christ throughout the world.

In dependence upon God . . .

We want to emphasize with the church the principles of victorious Christian living (Gal. 2:20), so as to stimulate, revive and mobilize the church to continuous, effective evangelism, follow-up and church growth.

In dependence upon God . . .

We want to influence Christianity world-wide, holding high the banner of biblical evangelism, so that the church's commitment to evangelism will never die.

Luis Palau
Evangelistic Team

P.O. Box 1173
Portland, Oregon 97207 U.S.A.
(503)643-0777

PRAISE FOR
A HOLLY, JOLLY MURDER
BY JOAN HESS . . .

"*A Holly, Jolly Murder* showcases Claire at her
lovable best, struggling with a mystery just as she
tries to widen her horizons by diving into the
middle of New Age elements."
—*Painted Rock*

"A pleasant, entertaining series addition."
—*Library Journal*

AND THE
CLAIRE MALLOY SERIES

"Ms. Hess goes about things in a lively style. Her
heroine, Claire Malloy, has a sharp eye and an
irreverent way of describing what she sees."
—*New York Times Book Review*

"Hess's voice . . . is one of the most distinctive of
the current generation of mystery writers—witty,
ironic and biting."
—*Bookpage*

"Hess's style—that of a more worldly Erma
Bombeck—rarely flags. Amiable entertainment
with an edge."
—*Kirkus Reviews*

MORE PRAISE FOR
THE CLAIRE MALLOY SERIES

"[A] tightly woven tale. . . . Hess knots deceit upon
deceit into this suspenseful story, whose tone is
lightened by Claire's quick wit and warm heart."
—*Publishers Weekly*

"Joan Hess has more than perfected her craft; she is
one of the most fun mystery writers around. Bravo
to the queen of bon mots."
—*Gothic Journal*

"Happy days are here again! Joan Hess is in top
form in her newest Claire Malloy. . . . Gloriously
funny and brilliantly plotted."
—Carolyn Hart, author of *Death in Paradise*

"I've long been a Maggody fan, but this is my
first meeting with Claire Malloy. I wish it had
come sooner. She is a delightfully funny, spunky,
down-to-earth lady with a fine sense of humor.
Let's have more of her."
—Patricia Moyes, author of *Twice in a Blue Moon*

"Hess's low-key humor and bull's-eye dialogue are
reason enough to read anything she writes."
—*Publishers Weekly*

A HOLLY, JOLLY MURDER

A CLAIRE MALLOY MYSTERY

Joan Hess

AN ONYX BOOK

ONYX
Published by the Penguin Group
Penguin Putnam Inc., 375 Hudson Street,
New York, New York 10014, U.S.A.
Penguin Books Ltd, 27 Wrights Lane,
London W8 5TZ, England
Penguin Books Australia Ltd, Ringwood,
Victoria, Australia
Penguin Books Canada Ltd, 10 Alcorn Avenue,
Toronto, Ontario, Canada M4V 3B2
Penguin Books (N.Z.) Ltd, 182–190 Wairau Road,
Auckland 10, New Zealand

Penguin Books Ltd, Registered Offices:
Harmondsworth, Middlesex, England

Published by Onyx, an imprint of Dutton NAL,
a member of Penguin Putnam Inc.
Previously published in a Dutton edition.

First Onyx Printing, November, 1998
10 9 8 7 6 5 4 3 2 1

CHAPTER 1

"My mother was a very strange woman," the customer said, "and so was my father."

In that we'd done no more than make bland observations regarding the weather, I was not prepared for her abrupt pronouncement. I edged behind the counter, wishing there was at least one other customer in my dusty bookstore. As usual, there was not. Farber College had ended its fall semester, and the earnest young students had fled home for the holidays. I was reduced to selling books to stray Christmas shoppers like the one standing in front of me on this gray afternoon. "Stray" was an appropriate word; she appeared to be in her sixties or early seventies, with wispy gray hair in a haphazard bun, an ankle-length print dress, sandals, heavy wool socks, and a scarlet cloak. All she lacked to fit the stereotypic portrayal of a gypsy was a gold tooth and a wart on her chin.

"Oh, really?" I said.

"It was due, I should think, to her unconventional childhood. Mumsy was never quite at ease among the cannibals." She wandered behind the paperback fiction rack. "She remained a vegetarian until she fell to her death some years ago."

I resisted the urge to pinch myself as I watched the

top of her head bobbling above the rack. "She fell to her death?" I said, futilely trying to come up with a scenario that entailed cannibals and trapezes.

"As did my father, as you must have guessed. Where do you keep the New Age books, dearie? All I'm finding are covers with buxom women in leather underwear and boots."

"You're in the fantasy section," I said, "but it's the closest I carry to New Age material. You might try one of the bookstores out at the mall."

This had to be the first time since I'd bought the bookstore in the old train station that I had discouraged a customer, and I could almost hear my liver-spotted accountant hissing in disapproval. There were months when business was adequate to pay the bills and make nominal contributions to the credit-card companies, but there were also months when I endangered my relationship with the various publishers, as well as with the local utility companies, the above-mentioned accountant, and my daughter, who has a black belt in consumerism.

The woman reappeared and gave me a reproving look. "I do not patronize the merchants at the mall. The place is permeated by a negative energy field that makes me queasy. I have often suspected that the music blaring from unseen speakers masks subliminal messages. My name is Malthea Hendlerson, by the way. What's yours?"

"Claire Malloy," I said. "Would you like me to find out if I can order books for you?"

"I have a list," she said as she began to dig through an immense satchel made of bright fabric patches. "This store, by contrast, has a very well balanced energy field. It must be situated on a ley line."

"Only if the railroad tracks qualify."

Malthea finally produced a scrap of paper covered with tiny writing. "See what you can do. I sense you have a very determined nature and will not allow yourself to be daunted by a challenge."

I put on my reading glasses and peered at the paper. *"Celtic Mysticism in the Second Century? Applied Magick? The Encyclopedia of Pagan Rituals and Initiations? Symbols of Irish Mythology? A General Introduction to the Fellowship of Isis? Pagan Spirituality in the New Age?"* Seriously daunted, I looked up at her. "I'm not sure I can locate these. They're not mainstream titles."

"Making the books difficult to acquire is an insidious form of censorship perpetrated by the religious right. After all, I am hardly a satanist."

I made sure the scissors and letter opener were not within her reach. Her expression was benign, almost twinkly, but during the course of my civic-minded attempts to aid the police in the apprehension of miscreants, I'd learned the wisdom of prudence. "Shall I call you if I have any success?" I asked.

"That would be very nice," she said. Her hand once again plunged into the satchel. I held my breath until it reemerged with a rectangle of stiff, if somewhat soiled, paper. "Ah, yes, I knew I had it here somewhere."

She put it on the counter, nodded, and sailed out of the store before I could respond. I picked up the dog-eared card and read: "Malthea Hendlerson, Arch Druid of the Sacred Grove of Keltria." Beneath this announcement were a mundane street address and a local telephone number—although, of course, the address might prove to be a vacant lot and the telephone attached to an oak tree.

I dutifully scanned the microfiche for the pertinent titles, found all but one, and called in the order to a distributor in Nashville. The woman at the other end may have sniggered, but she promised the books would go out that afternoon. I was wondering how the employees of the mall bookstores would have reacted to the Arch Druid of the Sacred Grove of Keltria when I was pleasantly diverted by a customer in search of a coffee-table book. He was more interested in size and weight than content. In that I had no reservations about selling books by the pound, I sent him away with the most expensive of the lot.

After that, diversions were few and far between, and by late afternoon I was reduced to watching the traffic crawl down Thurber Street. The merchants' association had done what it could to battle the magnetism of the mall, but we all knew it was a matter of time before the pasteurized chains put us out of business; wreaths on streetlights were no match for Muzak and parking. A few people were drifting into the bar across the street in anticipation of happy hour, which was much happier when the beer garden behind it was open and conversations could be conducted under a thick canopy of wisteria vines (and a thick haze of exhaust fumes).

I was somewhat pleased when my daughter, Caron, and her steadfast companion, Inez Thornton, came careening into the bookstore like a pair of dust devils. Caron has my red hair and fair, lightly freckled complexion, but at the moment her face was flushed with excitement. Inez was more muted; the two made a wonderful example of bipolar attraction. Inez is a placid lake, deep and sometimes unfathomable. Caron is, in all senses of the phrase, a babbling brook.

"We got the most fantastic job," she began, her hands swishing in the air. "You won't believe it! We not only get minimum wage—we get commissions, too! It works out to more than ten dollars an hour."

"That's a lot of money," I said mildly.

Inez nodded. "If we work ten hours a day until Christmas, we'll make as much as six hundred dollars— less taxes and withholding."

Caron began to pirouette. "What's more, we don't have to wear dweebish paper hats and ask people if they want fries. We tried all the boutiques and department stores, but they weren't hiring. Inez wanted to try the shoe stores, but I wasn't about to spend eight hours a day bent over smelly feet and end up with hoof-and-mouth disease. The lady at the gift-wrapping booth said we'd have to come back when the manager was there and wrap packages so we could be rated on speed and aesthetic effect—as if some snotty little kid's going to sit there Christmas morning and admire the bow instead of ripping into it. Give me a break!"

Although I wasn't at all sure I wanted to know, I forced myself to say, "What's this fantastic job?"

Caron twirled to a stop and gave me the vastly superior smile she'd perfected on her sixteenth birthday in hopes, perhaps, of being conscripted into the British monarchy. "We're working for a photographer at the mall. The girls who were working for her quit, and she was so desperate that she came up to us at the frozen yogurt stand and offered us the jobs. Starting tomorrow, we work from ten till eight. We each get a twenty-five-cent commission for every portrait."

"In a department store?" I asked.

"Oh, no," inserted Inez, who occasionally found the

nerve to undertake a minor role in Caron's melodramatic presentations. "We're assistants in Santa's Workshop. It's this gazebo kind of thing in the middle of the mall, with a bunch of fake snow, plastic elves, and Christmas lights. We collect money from the parents and steer the children up the steps to sit on Santa's lap."

"At which time," Caron said, regaining the limelight with negligent ease, "the photographer takes the shot, we stuff a candy cane in the kid's mouth and hustle him back to the rope, and then go for the next one. Santa gets regular potty breaks, but we can still run twenty to twenty-five kids through the chute every hour. Maybe more, if she'd let us use cattle prods. I don't think she will, though. She's anal."

"I should put in an application, too," I said. "Of course I'd have to go on unemployment on December twenty-sixth unless I was offered a permanent position at the North Pole."

"Doing what?" Inez asked, staring at me.

Caron grabbed her arm. "Come on, let's go to my house and look at fashion magazines. I am Sick And Tired of Rhonda Maguire feeling obliged to tell us the brand name of everything she wears from her sunglasses to her shoelaces. When school starts back up, she's going to look like a bag woman compared to us."

"Wait a minute," I said with a frown. "You are not going to spend every penny you earn on clothes. For one thing, you still owe me a hundred dollars for the traffic ticket and defensive driving course."

"I already explained it wasn't my fault," Caron retorted. "The whole thing was stupid."

"But also expensive," I said. "What's more, the other day I gave you ten dollars to put gas in the car. I did not intend for you to put in a gallon and pocket the change."

Her lower lip crept out as she considered her response. She eventually opted for pathos, one of her favorites. "Then you should have said so. I assumed you didn't want me to be the only student in the entirety of Farberville High School who had to stand in the hall and beg for lunch money—or root through garbage cans for crusts of bread and moldy carrot sticks."

"Or have pizza at the mall," I said, unimpressed by the performance. "The first one hundred and nine dollars of your wages have my name written all over them."

"That's a violation of the Child Labor Act."

"So report me." I made Caron hand over the car key, shooed them out the door, and went to find a guide to boarding schools in Iceland.

At six o'clock, I locked the Book Depot and drove home to the duplex across the street from Farber College. As always, I glanced at the venerable landmark that had housed the English department and provided my deceased husband with the privacy he required when tutoring distaff students in fields not related to twentieth-century American literature (with the possible exception of *The Tropic of Cancer*). On a winter night not unlike the present one, Carlton had had an unfortunate episode with a chicken truck on a mountain road, leaving me a widow without a viable source of income.

I still didn't have one, but life (mine, not Carlton's) had been . . . well, lively since then. Being suspected of murdering a local romance writer had led not only to the dawning of my talents as an amateur sleuth but also to an ongoing relationship with Lieutenant Peter Rosen of the Farberville CID. Ongoing and off-going, to be precise, since Peter has been known to object to my well-intentioned assistance in situations in which I've felt obligated to involve myself. I've never walked the mean streets in hopes of capturing a drug dealer or thwarting a mugger, nor have I advertised my services in the yellow pages. Things just kept happening.

As I let myself into the top-floor apartment, I could hear a heated fashion debate emanating from Caron's room. I plugged in the lights that decorated the runty Christmas tree in the living room and glumly regarded the few packages around its base. Caron had been much easier to gratify as a child; cheap plastic toys and new crayons had thrilled her, as had a tricycle gleaned from a garage sale.

These days, however, she had the eye of a real estate appraiser, and I was worried that my scant offerings—paperback classics, a sweater, a pair of earrings, and a CD that Inez had recommended—would fail to elicit delirious gratitude. A key to a red convertible, yes. Her very own copy of *Pride and Prejudice,* no.

There was nothing I could do about it short of holding up a convenience store, so I poured myself a drink, found the mystery novel I was currently reading, and retreated to the bathroom for a bubble bath.

I was immersed in hot water and genteel mayhem when Caron knocked on the door. "Peter called about five minutes before you got here," she said, making it clear that this constituted a grave intrusion on her right to privacy. "He was at the airport, and said to tell you he has to fly to Rhode Island to deal with his mother. He doesn't know when he'll get back to town."

"What's wrong with his mother?" I asked.

"He didn't say."

I listened to her stomp down the hallway and close her door with just enough forcefulness to convey her displeasure at being coerced into service as a social secretary. I wasted a few minutes speculating about Peter's family crisis, then took a sip of scotch and settled back to outwit Scotland Yard. It was not as difficult as one might surmise, at least for those of us endowed with perspicacity and a keen nose for red herrings.

Peter called the next afternoon. Since I was alone in the bookstore, we exchanged steamy sentiments involving potential physical entanglements before I asked him about his mother.

"She's getting married," he said morosely.

"What's wrong with that?"

"So now you're advocating marriage? That doesn't seem to be your attitude whenever I suggest that you and I give it a whirl. Something about compromising your independence and sacrificing closet space, I recall. Oh, and let's not forget shelves in the bathroom cabinet and razor stubble in the sink."

"That's different," I said.

"Why?"

Lacking Caron's talent for extemporization, I fumbled for an answer. "It just is, so let's not talk about it anymore. Doesn't your mother deserve companionship at her age? If she were blissfully married, she wouldn't be threatening to sell the mansion in Newport and move to a retirement community to be near her only child."

"It's more complicated than that. The guy's given

her so many flowers that the house looks like a funeral
parlor. She's gained ten pounds from all the fancy
chocolates and champagne. She gets all moony-eyed
when she talks about him, as if she were a ditzy adolescent with a crush on a rock star. In fact, Myron's the
only thing she's been talking about since she picked
me up at the airport last night. She didn't even ask
about my flight."

"Then they ought to be very happy together," I said,
feeling more forceful now that the topic was back on
the right track (or ley line)."

Peter sighed. "My mother and I had lunch with him
today. I could tell the moment I saw him that there's
something phony about him. He was more deferential
than the maître d', and oilier than the raspberry vinai-
grette on the salad. He was nervous, too. Only people
with guilty consciences are nervous around cops."

"That's not true. Whenever I pass a police car on the
street, I get a lump in my stomach because I'm sure
I'm inadvertently doing something illegal. Furthermore, you were probably glowering at him so furi-
ously that he was afraid you were going to stab him
with a butter knife."

"I wasn't glowering," he said huffily. "Don't I have
an obligation to scrutinize the man who wants to marry
my mother? His name's Myron, for pity's sake. What
kind of name is Myron? Have you ever met anyone
named Myron? He's probably a Mafia accountant."

"Why don't you ask him for a DNA sample so you
can determine if he's related to Jack the Ripper?"

After a moment of silence, Peter said, "I certainly
will run a background check before this nonsense gets
serious. My mother's too besotted to ask him anything

more illuminating than his preference for lemon or milk when she pours his tea."

"Give it your best shot, Sherlock. I'm sure you can dig up some dirt and destroy your mother's last chance for happiness. Think how grateful she'll be, knowing she was saved by her son, who chooses to live two thousand miles away and has to be reminded to send flowers on her birthday."

Instead of engaging in a civil discussion about the transparency of his motives, he hung up. I replaced the receiver and examined my own motives, which were by no means transparent. Peter is very attractive in a rugged, vulpine way. His bite is significantly worse than his bark; countless convicted felons would agree. When angered, he can be ruthless. When the anger's directed at me, he can be irrational as well, but at other times, his eyes turn to pools of golden brown molasses and his amorous expertise leaves me breathless. He's divorced, rich, physically fit, accustomed to picking up his dry cleaning, and devoted to old B-grade movies.

If he'd only stop battling the marital status quo, he'd be close to perfect.

I glanced up from my book when Caron exploded into the living room that evening. I opened my mouth to ask her about her first day in Santa's Workshop, but I didn't get a chance.

"That woman is a tyrant!" she said as she flung herself into a chair. "She is incapable of listening to reason, and she is a slave to her stupid manual. She probably keeps it under her pillow at night."

"What's the problem?"

"Costumes. I could Just Die right here and now. I

have never been more mortified in my entire life, including the time I was dragged to the animal shelter simply because of the gorilla suit. Adults have no flexibility. Not a shred."

Steeling myself to maintain a sympathetic look on my face, I said, "What kind of costume?"

"Reindeer, if you must know. Furry brown tunics, tights, boots, and a collar with a bunch of jingle bells— which means we sound as idiotic as we look."

"I'm sure you look adorable."

She crossed her arms and glared at me. "And these hoods with droopy felt antlers. Rhonda Maguire and Louis Wilderberry were at the mall with some of the other kids. Rhonda yelled something about Blunder and Stupid, and everybody started laughing so loudly that I'm surprised mall security didn't come racing down the hall. Even the tyrant thought it was funny."

"Oh, dear," I murmured, determined not to smile.

"Is that all you can say?"

I rubbed my chin to control my trembling lips. "I can understand why you were embarrassed, dear. It must have been ghastly. However, you're making a lot of money, and by the time school starts in January, everybody will have forgotten all about it."

Caron groaned. "I won't. I'll remain traumatized for life and spend years in psychoanalysis coming to grips with my scarred psyche. Christmas will become an annual ordeal that evokes an overwhelming sense of humiliation. Hearing 'Jingle Bells' will reduce me to tears. I might as well join a convent and save you the cost of college."

I could think of nothing to say as she dragged herself to her feet and stumbled down the hall to her room. Maternal platitudes would not have been appreciated when all she wanted was for me to offer to put out a contract on the evil Rhonda Maguire.

Both of us knew I was too broke.

Peter did not call back that evening. I wasn't exactly brooding, but I was feeling rather grumpy the following afternoon as I unpacked a shipment and found the books I'd ordered for Malthea Hendlerson. Out of curiosity, I flipped through several of them and learned that the original Druids weren't nearly as romantic as I'd assumed and had never pranced around Stonehenge for the benefit of camera-wielding tourists. They'd been members of the ancient Celtic priesthood, serving as scholars, judges, and philosophers. They'd utilized divination via animal and human sacrifices, but their traditions were oral and almost nothing was known about them. By the end of the fifth century A.D., they were history (so to speak).

The contemporary ones, properly known as neo-Druids, sounded like stepchildren of the 1960s' social insurrection. Like their predecessors, they had rites and rituals aimed at a pantheon of Celtic deities, but they'd replaced the grisly sacrifices with fir branches, cake, and drops of wine. One reference book declared contemporary Druidism to be an alternative religion; another declared it to be a path to spiritual enlightenment. I was unable to make much sense of the blithe references to metaphysical principles and festivals with peculiar names like Samhain, Imbolc, Beltaine, and Lughnasad. I was familiar with the less mysterious concepts of the summer and winter solstices and the spring and autumn equinoxes, although I had no idea what was de rigueur on such occasions. A photograph

of naked bodies cavorting around a bonfire gave me
a clue.

I found Malthea's card and called her. When she answered, I told her that her order had arrived.

"How splendid," she said. "Do you need instructions?"

"I don't think so," I said, staring at the photograph
in the encyclopedia. If I were struck with an urge to
dance around a bonfire in my birthday suit, I could
figure out how to go about it on my own.

"Most people do."

"I'm not into paganism," I said tactfully.

Malthea chuckled. "Instructions how to find my
house, Claire. My car is in the shop, awaiting a part,
and it's a bit too far for me to walk to the bookstore.
You may keep the books if you wish, and I'll come by
when I can. However, I was hoping to get some decorating hints for the holiday season. I do so love to deck
the halls with boughs of holly."

"You celebrate Christmas?" I asked, somewhat bewildered. "I wouldn't have thought Druids ... did
that."

"Why, of course we celebrate the birth of Jesus. We
also welcome Dionysus, Attis, Mithras, and Baal with
song and dance. We have an absolutely lovely ritual,
then share a splendid feast, with my special 'Tipsy
Tarts' for dessert. Why don't you join us this year?"

I took a deep breath. "Thank you for inviting me,
but I'll have to check my schedule. I have a daughter,
you see, and she and I always—"

"Rainbow and Cosmos will be delighted to make a
new friend. Morning Rose and Sullivan believe in home
schooling, and I often worry that the little ones miss out
on opportunities to socialize with their peers."

I had a feeling Caron would not appreciate being cast in that particular role. "Well, we'll see," I said. "If you'll tell me how to find your house, I'll drop off the books on my way home this evening."

She obliged, and an hour later I pulled up in front of a one-story beige brick duplex in a neighborhood that had once been staunchly middle class. Now the majority of the residences were rental properties that housed college students and marginal derelicts. Station wagons had been replaced with motorcycles, and porch swings with chairs salvaged from the local dump. Landscaping was mostly aluminum.

Malthea's duplex was tidier than the ones on either side, although the sidewalk was cracked and paint bubbled off the trim. She'd told me her apartment was on the right, but as I raised my hand to knock, the other door opened and she said, "Over here, Claire."

I obediently went into a living room crammed with chairs, a love seat, a bulging sofa, and a dozen teetery tables holding potted plants of every sort, from dangling vines to exotic cacti. The walls were covered with amateurish watercolor paintings and overly ambitious macramé hangings.

Malthea beamed at me as if I'd made it across a minefield. "This isn't where I live," she confided in a low voice, her eyebrows wiggling jauntily.

"It isn't?" I said.

"I have a cat."

"Do you really?" I murmured, wondering what on earth we were doing in someone else's home. I was not inexperienced in breaking and entering (I have an eclectic rap sheet), but I preferred to do so with adequate provocation.

"And a very fine cat she is," Malthea said. "Why don't you sit in this chair by the radiator and get comfortable? It's so drafty here that we might as well be outside."

It was indeed drafty where we stood, but I could feel a veneer of perspiration forming on my forehead. "Who lives here, Malthea?" I asked in a shaky voice.

"Her name is Merlinda. It's a play on Merlin of the Arthurian folklore."

"Merlinda who?" I persisted. "What are we doing in her home?" I did not add: and what have you done with her? I was glancing over her shoulder, however, and remaining close to the front door.

"I don't understand, Claire," Malthea said, her smile fading as she approached me. Creases appeared between her eyebrows and cut semicircles from the corners of her mouth. "I think you'd better sit down and have a cup of something. I'd hate to think of you driving in this condition. If you're coming down with a cold, I can fix you a very nice fresh gingerroot infusion with a touch of honey. Nothing's nicer than clearing one's sinuses."

I kept the bag in front of me as I edged backward. "I promised my daughter that I'd—have dinner ready when she gets home from work, so I'd better be on my way. I'll leave the books on this table and you can mail a check when you get the chance."

"At least a cup of tea," she said sternly.

"No, thank you," I said, groping behind my back for the doorknob. "It's so kind of you to offer, but I must be going. As I said, I'll just leave the books—"

The doorbell rang. Malthea froze, but I'm embarrassed to say I gasped as if a slobbering monster in a horror movie had just leapt out from behind a headstone. I glanced wildly at Malthea, then spun around and yanked open the door.

The situation did not improve.

CHAPTER 2

Standing on Malthea's or Merlinda's or whoever's porch was a teenage boy who exemplified every mother's nightmare. He was not exceptionally tall or heavy, but he had stringy black hair that hung to his shoulders like some species of slimy seaweed. His eyes were dark, close-set, and wary. His worn leather jacket was unzipped, exposing a black T-shirt with a depiction of distorted white faces and the words: SATAN RULES. To make matters worse (if such a thing were possible), he was holding a hammer.

"Who're you?" he asked in a deep voice that made it clear puberty was a thing of the past.

My mouth was so dry that the best I could do was croak, "Nobody, really. I came by to drop off some books."

"Why, Roy," Malthea chirped from behind me. "Do come in. Claire and I were about to have a cup of tea."

He didn't move. "Mr. Chunder sent me over to fix the back steps. I would've made it earlier, but I had to run some errands for Morning Rose. You know how she can be."

I wished I could slide into the bag between *Applied Magick* and *The Encyclopedia of Pagan Rituals and Initiations*. Malthea was right behind me, and the boy she'd called Roy appeared to have taken up permanent residence in the doorway. Neither of them had said anything remotely menacing, much less implied I was in danger of physical assault (one of my least favorite things). I did not, however, have a fuzzy feeling about the situation.

I turned around as I heard footsteps. Entering the room was a gaunt woman with a narrow nose and thin, colorless lips. Her gray hair was pinned up in a braided bun, but unlike Malthea's, not a wisp dared to stray. She inspected me through wire-rimmed bifocals for a long moment, then said, "What's going on in here?"

"Claire came by with some books I ordered," Malthea answered, "and Roy's here to repair the back porch steps. I was just suggesting we all have a cup of tea."

"With the front door wide open? This room is by no means easy to keep warm, and my heating bills are exorbitant. Can you imagine paying over seventy dollars a month to heat a one-bedroom apartment?"

I stepped aside to allow Roy to come into the living room. "I'll be on my way, if you don't mind," I said to Malthea. "There's a receipt in the bag."

"Do allow me to introduce you to two more members of our grove," she said. "This is Fern Lewis, my neighbor, and this is Roy Tate, who's currently living in Nicholas Chunder's carriage house. Claire owns a bookstore just down the hill from the campus. When I was there, I could feel it breathing."

"Nice to meet you," I mumbled mendaciously, inching toward the door in hopes of escaping before the unseen Merlinda burst out of a closet with a bloody ax.

Roy acknowledged the introduction with a nod, then

brushed past me, saying, "Is there a light on the back porch?"

"Come along," said Fern as she started out of the room. "It would have been much more convenient if you'd come here earlier, but I suppose I should be grateful that you came at all. I called Nicholas well over a week ago. It's a miracle the step hasn't given way and sent me crashing into the side of the greenhouse. I shudder to think of the cuts and abrasions . . ."

Her voice diminished as they went into the back of the house. Malthea shook her head. "Fern is still having difficulty coping with her husband's death. He was a very competent handyman who could fix anything. Now that her circumstances have changed, she's frustrated at the need to rely on others."

"I'm sorry to hear that," I said as I put down the sack and tried once again to retreat. "Please let me know if I can order books for you in the future."

"Of course, after hearing her story, I began to speculate about his death. It's not to say that men of a certain age don't have severe gastric attacks, but Fern grows some plants known to cause a variety of disagreeable symptoms. She's particularly proud of her lilies of the valley and euphorbia. She said she gave him nothing but meadowsweet broth. I can't help wondering, though."

"You believe Fern murdered her husband?"

"Suicide was more likely," she said darkly.

"I truly must leave now," I said with all the resolve I could muster.

Malthea sat down on the sofa and opened her satchel. "Let me pay you for the books. It was so thoughtful of you to drive all the way over here to bring them to me.

Are you sure you won't have one cup of tea before you go back out in the cold?"

The redolence of cash was too much to resist. "I can stay for a minute," I said, "but then I'm leaving. The total came to one hundred twenty-seven dollars and forty-three cents." I sat down on the other end of the sofa and smiled brightly at her.

"Let me put on the kettle first," she said, then left the room before I could protest—not that I thought it would do any good. I resigned myself to a cup of tea and a brief conversation about whatever wacky idea popped into Malthea's mind.

From the back of the house, I could hear hammering as Roy did the repair work under Fern's supervision, and from the kitchen, water running as Malthea filled the tea kettle. I'd come to the conclusion that I was in Fern's half of the duplex, so I wasn't surprised not to hear any whimpers or pathetic scratching from a closet that might be serving as Merlinda's temporary dungeon. All I had to do is gulp down the tea, get the money, and head home for a drink and a dose of the nightly news.

I was beginning to relax when the doorbell rang and I nearly slid off the sofa. As I caught myself, Malthea called, "Would you get that, please?"

Rather than pretend I'd been struck by an acute hearing affliction, I went to the door and opened it. The man on the porch stared at me for a moment, then said, "I don't believe we've met."

"Neither do I," I said.

"I'm Nicholas Chunder, the owner of this property. I came by to have a word with Fern Lewis."

I didn't have a response to that, so I waved him inside and closed the door. Nicholas Chunder was of the same generation as his tenants, but he was clearly in a much higher income bracket. He had a neatly groomed mustache of the sort favored by nineteenth-century politicians and military men. I hadn't noticed a limp, so I presumed the gold-knobbed walking stick he carried was an affectation, as were the ankle-length black overcoat and fur hat.

"Nicholas," said Malthea as she came into the room, "you're just in time for tea."

He gave her a small bow. "Not tonight, Malthea. I stopped by on the way to a genealogy meeting to make sure Roy repaired the steps. Has he been here?"

"He's here right now. Did you introduce yourself to my friend Claire?"

"Claire Malloy," I murmured, extending my hand.

He squeezed it briefly. "Delighted, I'm sure. If you will excuse me, the meeting begins at seven and I'm presenting a paper on utilizing the Internet to access documents around the world. It's quite amazing."

"Tell Claire all about it while I fetch the tray," Malthea said as she made another unanticipated exit.

In that my technological prowess went no further than calculators and microwave ovens, my smile may have been unconvincing. "Please do, Mr. Chunder."

"Are you interested in genealogy?"

I sank back down on the sofa. "I've been told it's a very popular hobby."

"You're Irish, I suppose?"

"Someone in my late husband's family must have been."

He winced at my offhanded reply. "I have traced my ancestry back to early-eighteenth-century Wales. One of my distant cousins was influential in the formation of *Uileach Druidh Braitreachas*." When I merely looked at him, he added, "It was the first meso-Druid group to be organized after so many centuries of disrespect and ignorance resulting from the libelous writings of the Romans."

"Claire's not a neophyte," said Malthea from the doorway. "She's a bookseller."

Chunder frowned at me as if I'd misrepresented myself. "Then you must forgive me for boring you," he said coolly. "I should not have assumed you desired to join the grove. Few people do because of the erroneous idea that Druidry is associated with black magic and animal sacrifices. That, too, goes back to the writings of Julius Caesar and others of the era."

Malthea shoved a cup in my hand. "You really should join us for the winter-solstice celebration so you can see for yourself that we harbor no evil within the Sacred Grove of Keltria."

"Or so you say," Chunder muttered as he ignored the proffered teacup and went to the front door. "Tell Roy that as soon as he's finished, he's to go home and wait for me. We have something to discuss. It may have a profound effect on the grove, Malthea. Do not be surprised if there's an upheaval in store for all of us."

"Whatever does that mean, Nicholas?" she asked as if she were a nanny humoring a recalcitrant child.

"The grove has been tainted by depravity." He thumped his walking stick on the floor, then bowed and left.

Malthea waited until the door closed before permitting herself a fluttery little sigh. "It sounds as if there is unpleasantness in the ether. Roy's a good boy at heart, but like so many of his peers, he has taken an unhealthy interest in certain aspects of the occult. I can tell Nicholas is upset with him, most likely with justification."

Curiosity got the better of me, as it's been known to do. "You mentioned that Roy lives in his carriage house?"

"Nicholas owns a large estate at the edge of Farberville. On the property is an old carriage house with an upstairs apartment. Roy's father and stepmother are cultural anthropologists at Farber College, and they took a six-month sabbatical to Borneo or one of those peculiar places. They didn't want Roy to miss school, so they arranged for him to stay with a family. When that didn't work out, Nicholas offered the carriage house as lodging." She peered into her cup as if deciphering the tea leaves. "If Roy's done something to upset Nicholas, perhaps I in my capacity as Arch Druid should intervene. We must maintain harmony and positive energy fields in order . . ."

The sound of the back door opening ended her musing. I hurried to my feet and said, "Just drop off the money at the bookstore after your car is fixed."

This time I succeeded, and I was at home pouring myself a drink when Caron came into the kitchen. "I thought you were supposed to work until eight," I said.

"I was." She opened the refrigerator and glumly studied its contents. "There's absolutely nothing to eat. Can we order a pizza?"

"Then why are you home so early?"

"I wasn't fired, if that's what you're thinking," she said as she took out a pitcher of orange juice. "This smells funny. How long has it been in here?"

"Not that long—and what happened at the mall?"

She replaced the pitcher and sat down at the table.

"Santa got sacked. Since nobody's going to pay fifteen bucks for a photo of a kid sitting on a chair, Mrs. Claus sent Inez and me home. If she can't find a replacement, I'm out of a job."

I took a gulp of scotch. "Let's start at the beginning. Santa got sacked? What did he do—bash Mrs. Claus with a candy cane?"

"I wish he had, but it was a lot worse than that. He's this old geezer they probably found living under a bridge. If I were a kid, I wouldn't get within fifty feet of him, but he was doing okay with the 'ho-ho-ho' bit and Mrs. Claus was keeping a real sharp eye on him. She couldn't follow him into the men's rest room, though. Inez and I both noticed he was weaving when he came back from a break, but we didn't dare say anything. I'd just wrestled these three-year-old twins into his lap when he started bawling about his misspent boyhood or something ridiculous like that. Before anybody could figure out what was going on, half the kids in line were bawling, too. Both twins wet their pants, and so did Santa. Mrs. Claus hustled him off to the employee lounge, and when she came back, she told us she'd fired him."

"Poor old Santa," I said.

"At least he can go back to his bridge. What am I supposed to do about all the clothes on layaway?" She realized what she'd said and hastily stood up. "I'll think of something. Maybe I can still get a job wrapping presents or pushing fries."

"Hold on," I said, aiming a finger at her. "Didn't I tell you that you weren't going to spend—"

"Mrs. Claus is going to the unemployment office first thing tomorrow morning to interview some guys. She's going to call us if she finds a replacement."

I let my finger drop. "Let me ask you about a boy I met this afternoon. Do you know someone named Roy Tate?"

"Where did you meet *him*?" she said in a horrified voice.

"I delivered some books to a customer's house. He came by to do some repair work."

Caron stared at me as if I'd described a casual social encounter with Hitler. "Roy Tate is a freak."

"A freak? He may not have been attractive, but he looked ordinary in the physical sense."

"Oh, Mother," she said, "you are so far out of it. A freak is someone who's all creepy and weird. Roy Tate has to be the freakiest guy who's ever gone to Farberville High. He drives an old hearse and hangs out in the basement by the boiler room. He never speaks to anyone, including the teachers. They kept giving him detention, but finally resigned themselves to his occasional grunts. Emily had to sit behind him in European history at the beginning of the semester, and she just about threw up every time she looked at his hair. She was terrified she'd get cooties."

"He didn't seem that bad," I said, "and he explained why he was late."

"Selling drugs at the playground, I'll bet," Caron said with a sniff. At some point preceding adolescence, she may have had a speck of compassion, but hormones had flushed it out of her system. "I cannot believe you're defending Mr. Mortician. Inez is going to absolutely howl when I tell her."

Her mood much improved, she went down the hall to call Inez. I accepted the futility of convincing her that nonconformity was not the worst of personal attributes; maturation rather than maternal enlighten-

ment would be required. I did feel a bit sorry for Roy
Tate, but there was nothing I could do short of inviting him for dinner. I wasn't anywhere near that sorry
for him.

I was heading for bed when Peter finally called.
Our greetings were chilly, but I decided to be magnanimous and forgive him for his previous childish
behavior.

"How's your mother?" I asked.

"Still jabbering away about Myron. She's eager to
elope, but I convinced her to think about it for a few
days. She may very well forget her promise to me,
though; she barely notices that I'm here. Maybe I
ought to change my name to Myron."

"Oh, Peter," I said with a flicker of irritation, "you're
behaving like a jealous toddler. Your mother is capable
of making up her own mind. If she wants to get married, she should hop on the next flight to Las Vegas
and haul Myron down the aisle of a wedding chapel.
Maybe they can find an Elvis impersonator to do the
honors."

"I don't trust him. He's probably after her money."

I did not point out that he'd ignored my astute
psychological diagnosis. "There's nothing wrong with
her wanting some excitement in her life. You yourself
were complaining that all she ever does is have her
hair done, shop, play bridge, and have dinner at the
country club. If Myron has swept her off her feet, more
power to the both of them."

"You're hardly in a position to encourage someone
to climb out of a rut," he said.

"Would you care to expound on that remark?"

"You get up in the morning and go to the bookstore.
If we don't go out, you spend your evenings at home

with a book. I'll admit you've stuck your elegant nose into some risky situations, but for the most part, you're in a rut somewhat deeper than, say, the Grand Canyon."

I was not pleased to be characterized as a total bore, even though there was an iota of truth in what he'd said. I could have pointed out the situations had been more than risky, but this might have led to another of his tedious lectures about meddling in police investigations.

I waited until I could trust myself not to bark at him, then said, "So I prefer as much order as possible in my life. What's wrong with that?"

"It's hypocritical of you to say my mother ought to elope when you won't even go to a movie until you've read a dozen reviews. The only times you've done anything remotely spontaneous were when you were hot on the trail of a murderer."

"That's not true," I said in such a cold tone that I hoped icicles were poking out of his receiver. "I happen to be a very spontaneous person when it suits me."

He snickered, fully aware it would infuriate me. "Do you have a block of time on your calendar marked off as 'be spontaneous from one till three'?"

"If you're quite finished, I suggest you spontaneously stick a fork in a light socket."

This time I was the one who terminated the conversation by banging down the receiver. I gave him a moment to call back and apologize, then stalked down the hall to my bedroom. When I glanced in the mirror above the dresser, I was surprised at how composed I appeared to be. Unlike Caron, I prefer to internalize my anger—an unhealthy habit most likely picked up from Carlton, who'd preferred sarcasm to histrionics.

I was still studying my reflection when Caron came into the room and collapsed across my bed.

"What were you shrieking about a few minutes ago?" she asked as she inspected her fingernail polish for infinitesimal flaws.

"Peter annoyed me," I admitted as I sat down beside her and massaged her back. "Was I really shrieking?"

"No, you were slightly strident, which is about all you ever are. When I tell my friends how you smacked somebody with a chair or barely escaped being blown up, they don't believe me. They think you're too stodgy for anything like that."

Great, I thought as I gave her neck a final (nonlethal) squeeze. According to popular consensus, I was in a rut, boring, stodgy, and incapable of raising my voice. Forty seemed too young for me to retreat to a rocking chair, but it sounded as though Peter, Caron, and her friends might beg to differ. They'd no doubt agree that knitting would be a suitable pastime—as long as the needles were too dull for me to hurt myself if I knitted when I should have purled.

I poked Caron's rump. "Call me in the morning if Mrs. Claus wants you back, dear. I'll close the store and take you and Inez to lunch in the food court at the mall."

"You won't close the store. Every time some emergency comes up and you have to go galloping off, you moan and groan about the sales you might be missing. I'll call you if Santa gets kidnapped or Mrs. Claus is found dead on the toilet, okay?"

I tried not to sigh. "Well, I do need every sale I can get. The post-Christmas season is bleak until the spring semester starts in the middle of January. Maybe I should close during that period. You and I can jump in the car and simply go wherever catches our fancy. The beach might be fun, don't you think? Or how about New Orleans? You've never been there."

"Oh, Mother," she said as she rolled over and gave me a piercing look, "you know perfectly well that we won't go anywhere. Spare me the long-winded excuses about Christmas bills and the checking-account balance. Inez and I are already resigned to cleaning out her closet. If I find that blue sweater I loaned her last year, I may pass out from the excitement."

I sent her away, then climbed into bed and tried to read. The words failed to capture me. I finally closed the book and spent several hours in critical self-examination before falling into restive sleep.

The following morning I felt somewhat proud of myself as I opened the Book Depot fifteen minutes later than usual, proving to one and all that I was not a slave to routine. Instead of automatically starting a pot of coffee, I sat down with the morning paper and turned to the entertainment page. There was a long column of movie offerings. I could go to any one of them I chose, I thought defiantly, even if I'd never heard of it. Or better yet, I could go to a country music bar, guzzle beer, and dance with bowlegged good ol' boys. I could respond to a personal ad and meet a stranger in a secluded spot. I could pull an Ambrose Bierce or a Judge Crater.

I was still entertaining myself with possibilities when the bell above the door tinkled. Entering the store was a petite woman with waist-length black hair and an exceedingly determined expression on what otherwise would have been a pretty face. Even in her wool coat and field boots she couldn't have weighed a hundred pounds; she would have made a perfect undercover agent in a junior high drug investigation. Trailing behind her were two small children of indeterminate gender, since they were swaddled in coats, mufflers, and knitted caps.

All three of them examined me from just inside the doorway. The woman finally said, "Are you Claire Malloy?"

"Yes," I said cautiously.

"Malthea Hendlerson told me you'd ordered some books for her. I'd like you to try to find one for me."

I felt a twinge of apprehension as the children disappeared behind the racks. Grubby little fingerprints do not enhance the value of books. "I'll do my best," I said. "Do you have the title and author?"

She glanced in the direction of her offspring, shook her head, and then came to the counter. "I'm looking for *Psycho-Sexual Transitions in Wiccan Initiation Rituals*. I'm not sure of the author, but I doubt the title's all that common."

An aroma of muskiness accompanied her. It brought back memories of my college days, when those of us who were adamantly antiwar staged demonstrations with temporary allies who wore flowers and beads in their hair and nothing at all on their feet. The woman across from me was much too young to have participated, and in fact was more likely to have found a bottle of patchouli oil in her mother's belongings.

"I'll try the microfiche," I said, glancing over her shoulder to check on her children, who were as silent as commandos on a covert mission. I slid the plastic sheet into place and scanned titles as quickly as I could. "No, I don't see it. Do you know the publisher?"

She shrugged. "A small press, I should think."

I took out *Books in Print* and started flipping pages,

mindful of minute rustling from the far side of the store. "Yes, here it is. I can order it from the publisher, but it may take several weeks to arrive."

"Mother!" howled a high-pitched voice. "Cosmos tried to bite me."

"No, I didn't, you pig-faced lump of dung!" said another. "But maybe I ought to."

The first speaker was not intimidated. "I'll yank off your penis, chop it into pieces, and throw them in the composter!"

The woman gave me a proud smile. "Children can be so forthright, can't they? They're blessed with a naive ignorance of societal conventionality."

I assumed this meant she approved of their nasty mouths and graphic threats. This further confirmed my hypothesis that she was the member of the grove who home-schooled her children. Since it was not a home I cared to visit, I said, "If you'll leave your telephone number, I'll call you when the book comes in and you can pick it up. As I said, it may be several weeks."

As the level of insults escalated from behind the rack, she unhurriedly wrote a name and telephone number on a piece of paper and handed it to me. "Do you have children?"

I winced as the rack shuddered. "A sixteen-year-old daughter." Who, in contrast to the present barbarians, was a veritable paragon of restraint and decorum.

"Such a perfect age," the woman murmured, looking into my eyes as though planting an idea in my mind.

It was not going to germinate, I thought as I watched her collect her children and leave. The musky smell lingered, but now it seemed to imply malevolence rather than flower power. *Psycho-Sexual Transitions in*

Wiccan Initiation Rituals was not likely to be a New Age version of the Girl Scout handbook. I picked up the piece of paper and read her name: Morning Rose Sawyer. One of the children had referred to his or her sibling as "Cosmos"; I couldn't remember the other's name.

Not that I cared, I concluded as I wrote up an order to Peanut Brittle Press and stuck it in an envelope. For that matter, I didn't care if the book ever came. My profit on a nine-dollar trade paperback would cover the cost of postage, but it would not impress my accountant.

I was straightening the cookbooks when Caron came into the store. "The tyrant called," she announced. "She found another Santa and wants us to report as soon as possible. Inez's mother has a meeting, so she can't take us to the mall. Can I have the car?"

"There's not much gas," I said as I gave her the key. "You may have to spend a couple of your own dollars if you want to make it home tonight."

She politely overlooked my ludicrous suggestion. "What's that awful smell?"

"It's from a customer who left a few minutes ago."

"Well, I didn't think you were wearing some peculiar perfume. All you ever smell like is talcum powder."

After she was gone, I tried to reimmerse myself in fantasies, but it was futile. What was wrong with smelling like talcum powder? It was preferable to smelling like ripened roadkill or rotten eggs. Peter had never objected, much less commented on it. He'd never given me a bottle of perfume, for that matter.

But he had, I remembered with a guilty start. I'd thanked him profusely, then tucked the bottle away in a dresser drawer. Maybe the time had come to shatter the aura of predictability that surrounded me like a scratchy wool blanket. In that I couldn't afford to enroll in a flight school or book a trek to Nepal, I took Malthea's card out of a drawer and dialed her number.

CHAPTER 3

What had seemed like a moderately eccentric thing to do the previous day seemed downright insane as I walked across the wet pasture. Frost crackled beneath my feet as though I was crushing glass. The diffused light from the eastern sky was adequate for me to avoid stepping in or on anything, although I was more concerned about snakes and mice than I was about livestock droppings. Minutes earlier I'd driven through a subdivision of treeless lots and prefabricated houses, but I was not at all convinced I wouldn't encounter a dinosaur, or at least a woolly mammoth, before the sun rose.

If the sun rose on places this desolate.

As per Malthea's instructions, I'd parked my car on a dirt lane in the company of a rusty van, an antiquated white subcompact, and a bicycle propped against a fence post. I would have dressed more warmly if I'd realized how far I had to walk. Okay, to be candid, I most likely would have stayed in my cozy bed until I heard Caron leave the bathroom after a ritual that was longer and more complex than anything Druids could ever dream up. I am not what is commonly called a morning person; the idea of hopping out of bed before dawn, jogging several miles, and arriving back home just as the newspaper is plopped into the front yard is inconceivable. I do not enjoy unnecessary physical exertion any more than I do bran muffins, and I prefer to stay in touch with my outer child, who does not care to sweat.

My shoes were making squishy noises by the time I reached the edge of the woods. My disposition had fared no better, and I sharply reminded myself that I was here by choice. Not a good choice, mind you, but without coercion of any kind. Malthea had been pleased, if not rhapsodic, when I'd called and accepted her invitation to attend the winter-solstice ritual. What I hadn't anticipated was that said ritual would begin at sunrise; the winter solstice, being a technical kind of thing when the sun reaches its most southerly point in the sky, can happen at any time during the day, including midafternoon. Malthea had informed me that they were using calculations from an eighth-century Celtic calendar. I hadn't thought they were relying on *TV Guide*.

An unfamiliar woman stepped out from behind a tree. Her anemic brown hair had been chopped off by what was clearly an untrained hand; uneven bangs obscured her eyebrows (presuming she had them). Her skin was sallow and scarred from acne, her cheeks concave, her countenance more sour than her thirty-odd years of life merited.

"Malthea asked me to meet you," she said. "I'm Gilda D'Orcher."

"Thank you. I wasn't quite sure how to find the grove."

"Those who genuinely come to seek enlightenment shall not stray. The Mother Goddess watches over us. Blessed be."

She turned and walked quickly into the woods. I followed as best I could, catching an occasional branch in the face and tripping over vines and rocks. There were no birds to be heard; birdbrained though they might be, they had enough sense to sleep in.

I was breathing heavily as we detoured around a fallen tree trunk and came into a small clearing defined primarily by oaks and scruffy firs. In the center was a stone altar made of two vertical pieces and a horizontal slab; it had been decorated with branches of holly and clumps of mistletoe. As far as I could see, there were no faded bloodstains or remnants of animal entrails on its surface.

Despite the imminence of dawn on what I gathered was a major holiday, the Druids were not in a festive mood. Malthea and Fern were on the far edge of the clearing, deep in a conversation that obviously disturbed both of them. Roy Tate sat on a log, his shoulders slumped and his hands twitching as his eyes flickered around the clearing. His hair was either wet or a good deal greasier than it had been when I first met him. Beyond him was the woman who'd ordered the book about Wiccan initiations; after a moment I remembered her name was Morning Rose Sawyer. The man beside her was small and wiry, his thin, receding hair a contrast to her profusive black mane. He stared at me as though I'd stepped in something in the pasture and brought an obtrusive fetor into the grove.

All of them, to my disappointment, were wearing conventional coats and gloves, including Malthea, who'd eschewed her scarlet cape for dowdy tweed. It was much too early to be confronted with naked flesh, but I'd been hoping for ornate robes and headdresses to spice up my subsequent accounts of my adventure (preferably interrupted by frequent gasps of admiration for my derring-do).

Gilda gestured at a stump. "Sit there."

"What's going to happen?" I asked her.

"How should I know? You'll have to ask the Arch Druid. She's made it clear *she's* in charge."

I went around the perimeter of the clearing and approached Malthea and Fern. In that I was not well versed in orthodox Druidic greetings, I opted for a commonplace, "Good morning."

Malthea gave me a forced smile. "I'm surprised to see you."

"Why should you be?" snapped Fern, her sharp chin quivering with annoyance. "You invited her, even though we have a covenant to ban skeptics. That was probably what pushed Nicholas over the brink. He's been fussing and fuming for the better part of a month, but he was not intractable. You must bear the responsibility for this, Malthea." Her eyes filled with tears, fogging up the lenses of her bifocals. "To think after all these years . . ."

"Now, now," Malthea said, patting Fern's shoulder. "We must not give up hope that Nicholas can be persuaded to change his mind. I may have erred, but Gilda and Morning Rose share the responsibility. Roy is not completely innocent, either. He refused to tell me why Nicholas was so angry earlier in the week. That well may have had something to do with the current calamity."

It seemed I had stumbled into something more multifarious than a sacred grove. "What's wrong?" I asked, as much to remind them of my presence as to meddle in the muddle.

Fern took a tissue out of her coat pocket and wiped

her eyes. "Forgive us, Claire. You're here in anticipation of our celebration to embrace the primacy of the Earth Mother and honor the Celtic deities. The 'calamity,' as Malthea calls it, has nothing to do with you."

I glanced at Malthea. "If it would be politic of me to leave, please say so. I won't be offended."

"There's no point in that now," she said with a shrug. Raising her voice, she said, "Roy, did you see Nicholas this morning? The sun will be up soon, and I don't want to begin without him."

Roy rose to his feet and came across the clearing to join us, walking with the same indolent slouch that was epidemic in the halls of Farberville High School. "I came directly here. There was a light on in the kitchen, so maybe he's having a last cup of coffee or something."

"Or he's not coming," added Morning Rose. "After what happened last night, he may have decided to boycott the ritual."

The Arch Druid hesitated, then threw back her shoulders and said with great regality, "Nicholas would never do that, no matter how upset he was. The cyclical celebrations are very meaningful to him. This is not to say he might not take petty pleasure in arriving at the last minute in order to alarm us."

Gilda glided up. "Perhaps someone ought to go ask him if he's coming. My shift at the hospital starts at eight, and it'll take me half an hour to get there on my bicycle." She looked at Morning Rose. "Did you put some kind of curse on him?"

"Of course not," Morning Rose said, ignoring Malthea's sudden intake of breath. "Sullivan has forbidden curses because of the children. Besides that, I don't know any specifically suited for this situation. Do you?"

Sometime between leaving my car and arriving at the Sacred Grove of Keltria, I'd lost my mind, I thought as I edged out of the circle of decidedly peculiar people. What's more, they were in the midst of a conflict among themselves that had unpleasant undertones. I'd hoped to come away with a diverting narrative, but at that moment all I wanted to do was leave without incurring any curses.

"Do you want me to go to the house?" asked the man who was apt to be Morning Rose's husband, or at least the father of her children.

Malthea nodded. "Yes, Sullivan, I think that's what needs to be done. If Nicholas does not intend to participate, then there's nothing to do but get on with it."

After he left, Malthea and Fern drifted away to continue their conversation. Roy resumed his seat and Gilda faded into the woods, leaving me with Morning Rose.

"Where are your children?" I asked her.

"At home. They got into a tussle last night and knocked over a bookcase. Sullivan was furious enough to ground them for two weeks. He doesn't believe that they should be allowed to express their aggressive impulses. I'm afraid they're becoming stifled. Cosmos, in particular, needs to act out his inherent urge to compete with his father for tribal dominance, which is all he's doing when he attacks Rainbow. She, on the other hand, must deal with her sexual attraction to her father and her resentment toward me." She touched a bruised semicircle below her eye. "She was so upset last night that she hit me. She cried afterward, but I assured her that she was only acknowledging her basic instincts."

I tried to hide my revulsion at her psychobabble. "It's a shame they'll miss the ritual."

"Perhaps not," she said. "Last year Cosmos ate so many tarts that he threw up in the van."

Malthea clapped her hands to get our attention. "The sun is going to rise with or without Nicholas's presence. I do not intend to allow him to put a cloud on this glorious day when we seek Herne, who at Samhain promised to protect us through the dark months of winter." She pulled off her coat. To my delight, she was wearing a silky white robe with embroidered symbols.

"What about us?" asked Gilda as she came back into the clearing, her smug expression leading me to wonder if she'd been casting the odd curse or two. "As I said, I'm going to celebrate in the manner I prefer."

Malthea frowned at her. "It was decided last night that Wiccan elements will be excluded from today's ritual. I believe we should continue to abide by that."

"Nicholas is the only one who objects," retorted Gilda, her hands on her hips, "and he's not here. I should be allowed to affirm my traditional beliefs. Go ahead and expel me from the grove. I don't care. I won't be here for Beltaine anyway."

"You'll catch your death of cold," said Fern, sounding more like a grouchy great-aunt than a joyful solstice celebrant.

"The first thing I did this morning was to cast a spell to protect myself from the cold," Gilda said, "and it's none of your business, anyway. I warned all of you when I joined the grove that I would continue to practice my religion."

I glanced at Morning Rose. "What's the issue?"

"Gilda wants to perform the ritual skyclad. So do I, but Sullivan would have a fit. He's incredibly surly when I insist on engaging in certain observances in the backyard. He thinks they're a bad influence on the children. He's being ridiculous, of course. Children come into the world without the artificial restrictions of clothing."

Sullivan staggered into the clearing. "There's been a terrible accident," he said in a raspy voice. "It's Nicholas. He's—" We all gaped at him as he leaned against the altar to steady himself. After a deep shudder that threatened to put him on the ground, he added, "He's badly hurt or even dead."

"Nonsense," said Malthea.

"When he didn't answer the doorbell, I went around to the back of the house to see if he might be in the kitchen listening to the radio. The door was locked, but I could see his body on the floor. There was blood."

Malthea gestured at Gilda. "It may well be a practical joke, but we must act. You hurry ahead on your bicycle and see if there's anything you can do. The rest of us will follow as quickly as we can."

No one commented on the sudden eruption of sunlight through the foliage as we ran toward the vehicles parked on the road. I could see Gilda pedaling across another pasture as I dove into my car and scrambled to find my key in the bottom of my purse. After a significant amount of maneuvering, we formed a procession and drove back to the highway, and then turned almost immediately on a driveway lined with poplars.

Nicholas Chunder's house wasn't a castle, but it was nevertheless impressive in its size and ivied stone facade. A separate building, also of stone and perpendicular to the house, was more likely to have sheltered cars than carriages, but it added a stately pseudo-Regency touch. I parked in front of a row of marble statues of bearded men and comely women, and beyond them, a nonfunctioning circular fountain. Sullivan, Roy, and Morning Rose were already running around the corner of the house as I caught up with Fern and Malthea.

"What are *you* doing here?" said Fern.

Rather than answer, I dodged around them and hurried toward the back of the house, where I saw Gilda peering through a window. Sullivan was seated on a wrought-iron chair, bent forward while Morning Rose held his head between his knees. Roy stood apart, with hands in his pockets.

Gilda straightened up. "He's lying on the floor, and like Sullivan said, there's blood on his face. What should we do?"

"Is the door locked?" I said.

"Yes," Sullivan whimpered. "I tried it earlier. The front door's locked, too."

Morning Rose released the back of his neck, picked up a flowerpot, and smashed the window in an unsettlingly proficient manner. "Roy, crawl through here and unlock the door." As he carefully climbed over the sill, she handed a small metal box to Gilda. "This is the first-aid kit we keep in the van. It's probably a little late for a Band-Aid and Mercurochrome. You'd better leave the smelling salts on the table for Sullivan."

Malthea and Fern arrived as Roy unlocked the back door, and with the exception of Sullivan, we all jostled our way into the kitchen. Gilda dropped to her knees and put her fingers on Nicholas Chunder's neck. I took a quick glance at his bloodied forehead, vacant eyes, and limp, outflung limbs. Suspecting it was a great deal more than a little late for a Band-Aid, I continued through the kitchen and into a hallway, where I found a telephone on an antique escritoire.

I dialed 911, explained as best I could what had happened and where the house was, and then returned to the kitchen in time to hear Gilda say, "I can't find a pulse."

"Don't touch him," I said. "I've called for an ambulance, and there's nothing we can do until the paramedics arrive. We need to wait outside."

"Oh, dear," groaned Malthea, the words bubbling from deep inside her. "This is dreadful. Nicholas was a stickler for propriety. It seems ... blasphemous to leave him in this undignified position. Let me find a blanket to cover him."

"No!" I said with such forcefulness that they all stopped staring at the body and looked at me. "The police will want the scene to remain exactly as we found it. They'll be upset as it is that the window's broken and everyone has trampled all over the floor. Now we need to move outside."

After I'd repeated this several times, Gilda rose and we retreated to the flagstone patio. Morning Rose hauled Sullivan to his feet and steered him across the lawn to a bench beneath a bower covered with dried vines. Fern sank down in one of the chairs and plucked at the buttons of her coat. Gilda announced she would await the ambulance in the driveway. The sun was above the treetops and shining brightly, but no one seemed in the mood to herald the dawn of the winter

solstice by embracing the primacy of the Earth Mother.
I most assuredly was not.

Malthea drew me aside. "Do you think it was necessary to summon the police? Nicholas had a heart condition that forced him to retire last year. Isn't it likely
that he had an attack and hit his head on the edge
of the counter as he fell?"

"All I know is that the police have to be notified in
this sort of situation," I said. "If he had a heart attack,
the autopsy will reveal it. Do you know who his next
of kin might be?"

"You'll have to ask Fern. She's been renting from him
ever since her husband passed away some ten years
ago. I myself moved into the duplex only two years
ago. I used to live in a little house of my own, but the
maintenance became too much of a burden. It was a difficult decision, but I finally sacrificed my view of the
cemetery and accepted Nicholas's offer." Her gaze
shifted to the kitchen door. "He was not the most
assiduous landlord, but I tried to be tolerant because of
his willingness to allow the grove on his property. I do
miss my midnight strolls among the headstones and
marble cherubim, however, and the ease in which I
could join funeral parties during interments."

I tried not to think how I would have reacted if a figure wrapped in a scarlet cape had appeared out of the
fog as Carlton's casket was being lowered. "Did Nicholas live alone?"

"I believe so," she said.

Roy, who'd disappeared during the transition to the
patio, came around the far corner of the house. "I
found a broken window in his study. There are foot-
prints in the flower bed, but they're so jumbled I can't
tell how many burglars there might have been."

"Burglars?" said Malthea.

"Looks like it," he said. "I told him he should have an alarm system put in or get a couple of dogs to patrol the grounds. I mean, a rich old guy living by himself in the middle of nowhere—that's asking for trouble."

No one refuted his final statement, or did much of anything until Gilda came back to the patio in the company of two paramedics with a gurney and an equal number of uniformed police officers.

One of the officers followed the paramedics into the kitchen, but the other, a shiny-faced boy who looked as if he were Caron's age, stopped and stared at me. His plastic name tag identified him as Corporal B. Billsby.

"I know you, don't I?" he said.

As much as I wanted to resort to nothing more than name, rank, and serial number, I managed a nod. "I believe we encountered each other last summer on Willow Street," I said coolly. "We were never formally introduced."

He took off his hat and scratched his head for a moment. "Oh, yeah, you're Lieutenant Rosen's girlfriend—the one who keeps butting into his investigations and trying to get herself killed. One of the dispatchers is keeping a scrapbook."

"Goodness," murmured Malthea, sounding awed and to some degree, appalled.

The other officer came to the doorway. "The homicide team's on the way. Keep an eye on things while I go meet the sergeant and let him know what's going on."

Corporal Billsby sized me up with such arrogance that I wanted to shove him into the nearest flower bed.

"Are you some kind of magnet for murder, lady? I've been on the force for six years, and I've only seen two cases. Funny that you were in the immediate vicinity both times, isn't it?"

"I wasn't in the vicinity this time," I said.

Malthea nudged me aside and opened her coat to expose her white robe with its colorful yoke. "Claire merely asked to participate in our winter-solstice ritual across the pasture in the Sacred Grove of Keltria." She raised her arms as if indicating a touchdown had been scored. " 'The geese fly high this solstice morn, the woods are bare, the snow is deep. We wait for Herne to sound his horn to wake his children up from sleep.' Isn't that lovely?"

"Yeah," he said as he pulled a notebook out of his pocket. "Is this one of those oddball cults where you all get naked and have orgies?"

Malthea swept across the patio in a bustle of white ripples and stuck her finger perilously close to his nose. "Your ignorance is shocking, young man. Druids worship nature, and we gather on holidays to invoke the inspirational presence of the Spirit. We chant, we dance, we meditate, and we offer benedictions to all the deities. We do *not* get naked, as you so crudely put it."

"And Wiccans rarely have orgies," said Gilda.

Corporal Billsby stared at her. "I thought she said you were Druids—whatever the hell that means."

"Well, I'm not, and if I could find a coven, I wouldn't be here. I prefer the structure and exclusivity of the Wiccan religion." She glanced at me. "We never allow gawkers to intrude on our ceremonies, and in particular, our initiation rites."

"Which are orgies?" said Billsby, visibly confused.

Gilda smiled. "That's an oversimplification of a religio-magical tradition that goes back more than five thousand years to the clay goddesses and cave paintings of the Neolithic era. Within the divine is a duality that is both male and female, and when the Great Mother Goddess and her consort, the Horned God, are reconciled ultimately in a divinity which is one, we achieve transcendency. It's as much spiritual as it is sexual. Want to give it a try some time, big boy? You can wear a mask and a cute little fur codpiece."

I wondered if Corporal Billsby might shoot me in the back if I attempted to dash around the house. It seemed likely, I concluded. His expression was that of someone awakening from a coma surrounded not by loved ones, but by large, green, tentacled creatures. Regrettably, I could tell he'd placed me in the latter group.

"Listen up," he said, backing toward the kitchen door. "No one moves till the sergeant gets here. Don't talk to each other, either." His eyes swiveled nervously toward Gilda. "And don't go taking off any clothes. The sergeant won't like it, and he'll already be pissed on account of getting a call at this hour."

I felt a wave of relief as I realized Peter would not be arriving momentarily to take charge of the crime scene. My presence at past crime scenes had never made his eyes light up and his lips curl into a smile of delight. One would think he'd appreciate the observations of an intelligent, perceptive witness, but that hadn't happened to date. On more than one occasion, he'd visibly bristled like a hedgehog. This time, I thought, I'd be spared the lecture and admonishments to mind my own business.

And there was no reason for me to involve myself in this investigation. I barely knew any of the Druids, and had met the victim only briefly. The winter solstice had arrived without dramatic fanfare, and all I wanted to do was to depart in the same fashion. However, Corporal Billsby had recognized me, so there was little hope my name would slip through a crack in the reports. The media would lapse into an unattractive feeding frenzy when details were made known to them; words such as "witches" and "pagan rituals" would dominate the headlines. The dispatcher could anticipate several new pages in the infamous scrapbook.

As soon as Billsby was safely inside the house, I sat down next to Malthea and gave her an encouraging smile. "Don't worry too much about this. The medical examiner is the only person qualified to attest to the cause of death. He'll probably determine that Nicholas had a heart attack and there was nothing unnatural about his death."

"But there was," she said.

My eyes instinctively widened. "Why do you say that? Does it have to do with whatever happened last night that resulted in what you referred to as a 'calamity'?"

"No one ever forgets where the hatchet is buried."

"I suppose not," I said carefully. "What exactly took place last night?"

"We gathered in Nicholas's living room to decorate for the climactic finale of our celebration to be held this morning. Fern and I brought bushel baskets of holly, ivy, and whatever greenery we could procure at this time of year. Morning Rose and Sullivan brought tinsel and string. Roy had cut down mistletoe from the oak trees surrounding the grove. We draped all the furniture with sheets, then hung garlands everywhere. It looked so peaceful, like a secluded glen on a snowy morning. I could sense the approval of the deities and the blessing of Mother Earth."

"But Nicholas was not happy?"

"I think he'd been exasperated by certain members of the grove for quite some time. He fancied himself to be a purist in matters of Druidry, although he based his interpretation on the nineteenth-century revival. That was absurd, of course, since they were heavily influenced by Freemasonry—and attracted some unsavory occult practitioners as well. 'Balderdash!' I said to him time and again. 'Rosicrucians and cabalists were no more Druids than the poets who frequented Mumsy's salon in Budapest.' "

I heard voices from the front of the house and made an effort to steer her back to the subject at hand. "What did Nicholas do that upset you and the others?"

"I was not upset, dearie," she said chidingly. "I was concerned. Fern, on the other hand, did seem agitated as we drove out here this morning. I clutched my crystal all the way so that its healing power might soothe her. It's so important to conduct rituals with the proper attitude, you know."

The voices were growing louder. I gave up trying to get a coherent response from her and moved across the patio to a neutral, and I hoped inconspicuous, spot. The first person to come around the corner was a rabbity little man with a medical bag. He went into the kitchen as Sergeant Jorgeson and several other men arrived on the patio.

Jorgeson was Peter's minion, which no doubt explained his dyspeptic nature. He gave me a discouraged look, then gestured at the rest of the crime-scene team to follow him into the house. I tagged along, and despite a scowl from Corporal Billsby, squeezed my way into the room.

"From the looks of it, I'd say he died maybe six to eight hours ago from a bullet wound to the chest," said the man I assumed was the medical examiner. "The shot was fired from less than three feet away. Any sign of a weapon?"

"No, sir," said the other uniformed officer.

Jorgeson squatted down to study the bloodied face. "He was beaten before he was shot." He looked up at the officer. "Anybody else live here?"

"No, sir. Only one bedroom appears to be occupied; the others are kinda dusty. But you ought to take a look at the front room. I don't know what this dude was into, but it sure wasn't interior decorating. It's spooky, if you ask me."

Jorgeson stood up. "Rather than asking you, why don't I take a look? Would you like to join me, Mrs. Malloy? You'll undoubtedly do it anyway unless I have you handcuffed to a tree."

"I did not come in here in order to interfere, Jorgeson. I simply want to ask that the people outside be allowed to wait someplace warm. Two of the women are elderly and beginning to turn a bit blue. Hypothermia is not conducive to cooperating in an investigation."

He gave me a dry smile, then said, "Billsby, you and Cliffern get their names and addresses, then send them to the station to give statements. I want all of them to be available the rest of the day if I have questions. Mrs. Malloy, why don't we have a look at the living room?"

As we went down the hall, I said, "Roy said there's

a broken window in Nicholas's study. Have there been other burglaries in the area?"

Jorgeson stopped so abruptly that I almost bumped my nose on his shoulder. Without turning, he said, "Mrs. Malloy, the only reason I've allowed you this much leeway is because you seem to have some idea of who these people are. Once you have shared that with me, you will be free to go home and have a nice hot cup of coffee. I'll need to get your statement when we have time. God knows I'd pay big bucks to be able to see the lieutenant's expression when he hears you were here. His nose will light up like that reindeer's."

"He's terribly worried that his mother is going to elope with a gigolo named Myron. There's really no reason to add to his troubles."

"I'm not going to lie to him," Jorgeson said as he resumed walking.

I caught up with him in the doorway to the living room. I'd planned on an insightful comment about the subtle difference between sins of commission and those of omission, but I found myself speechless. The room had been decorated as Malthea had said, and it did bear some resemblance to a forest glen—if said glen had been seized by hyperactive elves obsessed with pine-scented disinfectant.

"What's the deal?" Jorgeson asked me.

I told him about the aborted celebration in the clearing, stressing that my presence was motivated solely by my adventurous spirit and openness to novel experiences.

He raised his eyebrows. "Does the lieutenant know you're a closet Druid?"

"I am no such thing," I said. "Perhaps you don't need my cooperation after all. Start with the Arch

Druid. The only thing you're liable to get out of her is a long-winded account of her mother's childhood among the cannibals. The boy in the black jacket, known around the high school as Mr. Mortician, has a reputation for refusing to speak to authority figures. Fern's snappish, but Morning Rose will be happy to share her skewed take on developmental psychology, and—"

"Okay," he said, holding up his hand, "I get the point. Let's find a less leafy room where you can tell me who these people are and why"—he glanced into the living room—"they do whatever it is they do."

"So that you can tell the lieutenant how deeply involved I am?"

"You are obligated to cooperate fully with us, Mrs. Malloy. Anything less could be construed as impeding an investigation."

"Our definitions of 'fully' may differ, Sergeant Jorgeson. I will certainly give a factual accounting of any interaction I may have had with those people. It won't take long."

Peter would have had me hauled to an interrogation room and left me to ponder my transgressions over cold, oily coffee and a floor show featuring fleas.

Jorgeson grimaced. "All right, I won't say anything to Lieutenant Rosen, but I can't falsify the reports or drop your statement in the trash. When he gets back, he'll have to be briefed."

But only if the investigation had not been concluded to the prosecutor's satisfaction, I told myself in a slightly optimistic voice. Otherwise, Peter would have plenty of ongoing cases that he'd temporarily abandoned. Someone in the police department might take a wicked pleasure in telling him all the details of the case. I might even do so myself—when time has blunted the impact.

I nodded at Jorgeson. "Shall we take a look at the broken window in the study?"

CHAPTER 4

Jorgeson allowed me a quick look at Nicholas Chunder's study, but the room was unremarkable except for the broken shards of glass on the hardwood floor. It was all very masculine, as I'd expected. The desk was large, with a computer and printer protected by plastic covers, neat stacks of folders, and an expensive-looking gold pen and pencil on a block of marble. There were bookcases against three walls, an antique globe on a wooden stand, assorted leather chairs for visitors, and between the two windows behind the desk, a framed chart of a multilimbed family tree. Oak, no doubt, with lots of acorns.

"Six to eight hours ago," I said as we walked toward the kitchen. "That would put the time of death between midnight and two. I suppose after they'd decorated the living room, the others left and Nicholas turned off the lights and went to bed. When he heard the window break, he went downstairs to investigate. Bad decision."

"Could have happened that way," Jorgeson commented.

"Which means," I continued, "that the members of the grove had nothing to do with this."

"Didn't say they did."

I held in a growl of frustration. "They're not your basic Sunday-morning congregation, and their beliefs are out of sync with traditional theology, but that doesn't make them a gang of cold-blooded killers."

Jorgeson toured the front rooms and made sure all of his men were busily dusting for fingerprints, taking photographs of the scene, and measuring pretty much everything in sight. The paramedics had put Nicholas's body in a bag and transferred it to the gurney. The medical examiner mumbled a promise to do a preliminary autopsy as soon as possible, then followed the squeaking gurney out the door. We continued into a dining room with wainscoting, drab wallpaper, and a somewhat menacing chandelier above a table that could accommodate two dozen guests without any bumping of elbows.

We sat down next to each other rather than at opposite ends of the table, where megaphones might be required to communicate. Before Jorgeson could open his notebook, however, one of the officers came into the room. "I checked out the broken window," he said, shaking his head. "The dust on the sill hasn't been disturbed. Somebody broke the glass, but nobody came into the house that way."

"What about the locks on the doors and windows?" said Jorgeson.

"All the windows on the ground floor are locked, and the dead bolts on the doors are sturdy. We're still looking for signs of a forced entry. I'll be damned surprised if we find anything, though."

"The back door was locked when we arrived," I volunteered.

Jorgeson sat back and eyed the chandelier. "So the victim either admitted the perp, or the perp stayed around after everybody else on the decorating committee left."

For some odd reason, I was offended at his aspersion on the grove, since it was impossible not to share a sense of camaraderie with those with whom one rendezvoused before dawn. What's more, their potential as steady customers at the bookstore could not be easily dismissed.

"Isn't it more likely," I said, "that someone came to the door, posing as a stranded motorist, and asked to use the telephone? Besides that, he knew plenty of other people who might have been invited for a late-night drink. I'm sure he was a member of all sorts of organizations, like the genealogy society and the historical society and the"—it was getting tougher—"the Sons of the Celtic Revolution. He used the Internet, too. There have been numerous stories in the newspaper about people who strike up an acquaintance and then discover they're electronic pen pals with inmates in prisons and serial killers."

"Very eloquently put," said Jorgeson. "Tell you what, Mrs. Malloy—you go on home and write down anything you think might be helpful. Don't leave out any theories, including leprechauns, the CIA, and the Mafia. I'll send someone by later to pick up your notes."

"What about the others?"

"They'll be home within an hour. Until we get some feedback from forensics and the medical examiner, we can't do much more than try to get an idea of what happened last night. The weapon may turn up and be covered with lovely, legible prints. One of the neighbors out on the road may have seen a hitchhiker—or better yet, disgruntled Boston basketball players."

"Jorgeson," I said as I stood up and buttoned my coat, "you've been working too long with Lieutenant Rosen. Your feeble attempt at humor is indicative of the depth of your neuroses. Caron's announced she's entering a convent. Shall I inquire if it's coeducational?"

"Good-bye, Mrs. Malloy. Drive safely."

Vowing to order my own copy of *Applied Magick* so I could cast some ingenious curses, I went through the kitchen to the patio. The Druids were no longer present. I continued to my car and drove back to Farberville at an immodest speed, although I wasn't sure that ending up in a ditch would prove I'd climbed out of a rut.

I stopped by my apartment to change into dry shoes. Caron had left a note saying that—despite the indignity and source of further humiliation associated with the need to rely on public transportation—she'd taken the bus to the mall, and that she might linger after work to look at the Christmas decorations. Under no circumstances would she shop.

And I, of course, might get an apology from Jorgeson and a teary request to conduct the investigation into Nicholas Chunder's premature departure.

I drove to the store, started a pot of coffee, and sat down on a stool behind the counter to write down a few observations for Jorgeson. After nibbling the pencil and staring at a blank page, I concluded that I knew next to nothing about any of the Druids. I knew where Malthea, Fern, and Roy lived, but that information had already been recorded. All I really knew about Morning Rose and Sullivan was that they disagreed in matters of child rearing, curses, and skyclad performances in their backyard. Gilda rode a bicycle, worked at the hospital in some unspecified capacity, and trimmed her hair in the dark.

None of it seemed worth writing down, but I wrote a brief synopsis of what interactions I'd had on the slight chance that Jorgeson would keep his word, which meant Peter would not be immediately informed that I was involved in even the most minimal way. It would be best if the death turned out to be a suicide, but the team had not uncovered a weapon—and it was hard to envision Nicholas breaking the window, then beating his face on a kitchen counter before shooting himself with an invisible gun. He could have, I supposed, although my theory of a late-night visitor seemed more likely. Roy might have seen or heard something, including the shot; whether or not he'd share it with the police was debatable.

I paced up and down the aisles, pausing to rearrange paperbacks and tidy up the rows of thin yellow study guides that accounted for much of my income during final exams. When I realized I'd covered the territory more than once and was mindlessly tapping the edges of the same guides, I went into my cramped office and called Luanne Bradshaw, a divorcée of a comparable age who owns a secondhand clothing store and has been responsible for a couple of my forays into deduction.

"You'll never guess where I went this morning," I began coyly.

"Then there's no point in trying, is there?" she said, not nearly as enthralled as I'd hoped. "I'm having a few people on Christmas Eve for nog and nonsense. Caron's welcome to come, but she'll probably go into a coma at the suggestion. Can you and Peter make it?"

I told her where he was and why, then said, "He

sounded as though he'll stay there until either his mother stuffs a negligee in the pocket of her mink coat and vanishes, or Myron is exposed as a polygamist with weeping wives scattered across the country like fast-food franchises."

Luanne chuckled. "Maybe this'll cause him to re-think his position on matrimony and stop bugging you to tie the knot and don the gay apparel of leg-irons and joint tax returns."

"Maybe," I said, then changed the subject by telling her about Caron's job at Santa's Workshop. "Do you want to go to the mall with me this evening?" I added. "For fifteen bucks you can sit on Santa's knee and whisper your kinkiest fantasies in his ear."

"I might. What does he look like?"

"Well, Luanne, his nose is like a cherry and the beard on his chin is as white as the snow. When he laughs, his little round belly shakes like a bowlful of jelly. All in all, he's a right jolly old elf."

"Ho, ho," she said without inflection. "Pick me up at six and we'll check him out. Under all that fur and felt and excessive facial hair may well be a muscular bimboy who'll fill my stocking on Christmas Eve."

After I'd hung up, I realized I'd never told her about my early-morning activities. I was curious to find out what progress Jorgeson had made—if any—but I suspected he might not appreciate a telephone call any more than Peter would have. Malthea had not elabo-rated on her comment that Nicholas's death might not have resulted from natural causes, and had never really given me a clue as to the source of the friction the previous evening. Nicholas had objected to Gilda's desire to celebrate the winter solstice without "the ar-tificial restrictions of clothing," to use Morning Rose's phrase. The conflict, however, seemed more a matter of squabbling over policy than a calamity of measurable magnitude. What's more, the remarks in the grove seemed to imply Nicholas had emerged the victor.

I pushed aside the sparse notes and propped my face on my hands, wondering how I'd react if Peter came home and never again mentioned matrimony. Relieved—or rejected? Could our relationship continue indefinitely until the time came when we were more interested in sharing our beds with heating pads than with each other?

The telephone jangled me out of my thoughts. As soon as I'd picked up the receiver, Malthea said, "Would it be possible for you to come to my house? I just don't know what I should do, and Fern's no help whatsoever."

"I might be able to come by tonight," I said.

"That may be too late."

"Why, Malthea? I have a business to operate, and I can't leave a note on the counter asking customers to write themselves a receipt and make change from the drawer. I'd come back to empty shelves and an emptier cash register."

She snorted. "If that's your attitude, then I shall walk to the store. My arthritis will slow me down, but I should arrive there in an hour or so—unless, of course, it begins to rain. In that case, it may take much longer. At my age, I must be cautious about falling and breaking a hip. When that happened to a neighbor of mine, her husband put her in a nursing home and took up with a woman who allowed their Siamese cat to choke to death on a chicken bone."

I looked out the window at the cloudless sky, sighed, and said, "I can't stay more than half an hour."

"That should be adequate. I'll fix some sandwiches and we'll have lunch while we talk."

At noon I hung the "closed" sign on the door and drove to Malthea's duplex. I again raised my hand to knock on the door on the right; this time it opened before I could make contact. Malthea pointed at Fern's door, put her finger on her lips, and pulled me inside.

"I don't want Fern to know you're here," she whispered as she propelled me through the living room and into a cramped kitchen. "Sometimes I get very annoyed with her, as I'm sure her husband did before his excruciatingly painful demise."

"Why did you call me?" I asked bluntly.

"Sit right here," she said, gesturing at a dinette set with two place mats, forks, and paper napkins. "You do like tuna fish salad, don't you? Merlinda's very fond of it. I considered making deviled eggs, but it didn't seem right after what transpired this morning. The police officer assured me that he died instantaneously."

I assumed she meant Nicholas had died instantaneously, as opposed to Corporal Billsby. "What else did he say?"

"Not very much." She took a plate of sandwiches from the refrigerator and turned on the burner beneath an aluminum teapot. The telephone began to ring in the living room, but she seemed oblivious of the sound. "The young woman at the police department asked me a number of questions, but I couldn't really tell her anything useful. We finished putting up decorations shortly before nine o'clock, relaxed for a few minutes, and then said good-night and left. Fern's car was a bit balky, so we were still sitting there when

Sullivan and Morning Rose drove away and Roy went up the stairs to his apartment."

"Don't you need to answer the phone?" I asked.

"The caller will try again."

The rings stopped as if on cue.

Somewhat nonplussed, I returned to the topic. "Was Gilda there?"

"She'd planned to come on her bicycle, but Morning Rose insisted she ride with them. Yes, we were all there—our happy little grove. The eve of a major holiday is always so invigorating to the spirits, isn't it? We sang ancient pagan songs like 'The Holly and the Ivy' while we sat around the fire and had tankards of mead. Nicholas made his own every fall in preparation for Samhain, using honey from a very special apiary in Salisbury. I do hope I'll be able to find a recipe."

I waited until she'd poured boiling water into teacups and brought them to the table. "I'm sure you had a lovely evening," I said, grinding out the words as politely as I could, "but you and Fern alluded to some hostility that also took place. She was in tears this morning, and none of you looked the least bit like a 'happy little grove.' If you don't want to tell me what happened, that's fine. Did you tell the officer who took your statement?"

"No, I don't seem to think I did. That doesn't mean someone else might not have mentioned it. I hope not, though. Nonbelievers often have difficulty understanding the dynamics of a group such as ours. I'm sorry to have to say this, but Wiccans can be a teensy bit stubborn."

I pulled back my cuff to uncover my wristwatch. "I am leaving in eighteen minutes. If you desire, we can pass the time debating the recalcitrance of Wiccans or looking through cookbooks for mead recipes. You can expound on why Fern's husband might have sprinkled belladonna instead of blueberries on his cereal. It's entirely up to you—but in eighteen minutes I'm going to go out to my car and drive back to the Book Depot."

"It doesn't really have anything to do with last night," she said. "I'm concerned about Roy. He can't stay out there by himself, not at his age. When his parents left, they asked Sullivan and Morning Rose to look after him. Nicholas then took charge of him. Now I don't know what to do. It's impossible to get in touch with his parents, who're conducting field research in a remote area. There's no room for Roy here or in Fern's apartment, and neither of us has any idea how to deal with someone that age. My niece is well over thirty now, but when she was a girl, she was a quiet little creature who was more worried about braces and social clubs than—"

"When are Roy's parents returning home?" I asked as the tuna fish I'd eaten came to life and started struggling to swim upstream.

"Sometime in the spring. I know his outward appearance is not appealing, but underneath his belligerent posture beats a good heart. You were here when he came to repair the back porch steps, weren't you? He was very polite at the time."

"My daughter told me that he drives a hearse."

Malthea took a sip of tea. "Well, there is that. I should think it's nothing more than a petty affectation, shouldn't you? He's merely trying to make a statement."

The statement Roy Tate was most likely trying to make had to do with the role of Satan in secular society, I told myself as I finished my sandwich. "My suggestion is that you talk to Morning Rose and Sullivan about taking him back in until his parents return. That, or perhaps you and Fern can share one side of the duplex and let him live in the other. At this age, they don't need anyone to bathe them and tuck them in bed."

"No, I don't suppose they do," she said, "but we don't know about curfews and homework and pocket money and school lunches. What if he were to take drugs or drink alcohol?"

I picked up my purse. "You may feel you have some degree of moral responsibility for Roy, but you certainly have no legal one. The social services department can provide temporary shelter in a group home until someone can get in touch with his parents."

Malthea allowed me to make it to her front door before she put her hand on my shoulder. "I noticed an office at the back of your bookstore. Is there also a bathroom?"

"Yes, there is," I said, "and no, he can't." I forced myself to smile at her, noticing for the first time how pale and anxious she seemed. It was evident that Nicholas's death had caused her more grief than she was willing to acknowledge. I softened my tone. "I'll call Sergeant Jorgeson and ask him to contact social services."

"These homes cause more damage than good. What's more, Roy has told me that if he's placed in any kind of restrictive environment, he'll run away. He claims he has ample funds to leave the country."

"Why can't he stay with Morning Rose and Sullivan?" I asked. Desperation had added an edge of shrillness to my voice, but I was no longer concerned

that Malthea was on the verge of collapsing. Her
shoulders were rigid, her mouth tight, and her eyes
blazing as she tried to stare me into compliance. "I'll
go talk to them. After all, they were the ones desig-
nated by Roy's parents to look after him. If there was
some sort of problem, perhaps we can find a solution
so that he can return there."

Malthea closed the door in my face. I toyed with the
idea of banging on Fern's door and then clinging to
her ankles until she agreed to intervene. It wouldn't
have been dignified, I'll admit, but I was not about to
allow Roy Tate to sleep in the Book Depot for even one
night.

When I got back to the store, I took out the directory
and found the Sawyers' address. Walnut Street ran
through the Historic District, but it had its origin in a
seedier tract development, and their house number
seemed suspiciously low. Still, it was likely not to be
more than a ten-minute drive away, and if I took no
action, I had a pretty good idea who would show up
at the door of the store at closing time—with a backpack or overnight bag, as well as black candles, sticks
of incense, and whatever other paraphernalia necessary to open lines of communication between Farberville and Hades.

As I'd expected, the Sawyers lived in the south
end of town, but I was a bit surprised when I realized
the development adjoined Nicholas Chunder's estate.
Many of the boxy, semi-identical houses were abandoned, the yards surrounding them overgrown and
littered with beer bottles, papers, and the lumps of
sodden clothing one sees in such areas, as if pedestrians were unaware as shirts and socks dropped off
their bodies. The Sawyers' house was in no better

shape. A bicycle had been left in the middle of the yard, along with broken toys and a moldy stuffed animal of an indistinguishable species.

I locked my car and went up onto a splintery porch. A curtain twitched, then fell still. I waited for a moment, shifting uneasily and assessing the distance to my car, then reminded myself of Caron's likely reaction if I took in a foster child who drove a hearse. Coward that I am, I knocked on the door.

I would have preferred to deal with Morning Rose, but the day had been going downhill since well before dawn and I wasn't especially unnerved when Sullivan opened the door.

He stared for a moment, then pulled off discount-store reading glasses and cleaned them with a grayish dish towel, as if this simple ritual would reduce me to nothing more than a twinge of heartburn. He wore a T-shirt and baggy trousers; without a winter coat he was much thinner than I'd remembered. On the other hand, he wasn't any friendlier.

"I'd like to speak to you," I said hesitantly.

"What about?"

"Roy Tate."

Rather than invite me inside, he came out onto the porch and eased the door shut. "Then you've wasted your time and gasoline. I am not going to discuss Roy with you or the police or anyone else. My children and wife are forbidden to so much as say his name. Am I making myself clear?"

"Yes, but that doesn't mean I'm leaving. I drove all the way over here to try to find a place for Roy to stay until his parents can take charge. They left him in your care, didn't they? Do they know you broke whatever promise you made to them?"

"Probably not," he admitted, "but I didn't throw him out on his butt, even though I would have been justified. I found an acceptable place for him to live. Nicholas had him do odd jobs around the estate in exchange for rent, and his parents left money for food and necessities. I'll have to tell the Tates what happened when they get back in ten weeks, but I feel I did the best I could under the circumstances."

Guilt had weakened his certitude, and I deftly moved in. "Why did you make Roy move out of your house?"

Sullivan sat down on the top step and rubbed his temples. "I was opposed to him staying here to begin with, but his father's head of the department and I'm a lowly grad student with a family to feed. Rent's not cheap, even in this slum. One or the other of the kids is always at the doctor's or dentist's office, running up bills. I couldn't afford to jeopardize my assistantship by pissing off Dr. Tate." He paused as I sat down beside him, then continued pleading his case. "Roy's not a normal teenage boy. If I were his father—and thank god I'm not, by the way—I would have packed him off to some sort of adolescent treatment facility. His parents preferred to observe him as they would any aborigine from a diverse culture. They're big on nonjudgmental interpretation. That's what they said, but I used to wonder if they were intimidated by him—or even frightened."

"Mr. Sawyer," I said, "I don't want to waste any more of your time than necessary. I've seen enough of Roy to know he won't be elected president of his class. What did he do that upset you?"

"I told him up front that I wouldn't tolerate any hint of satanism in my home. Cosmos and Rainbow are too young to be exposed to practices that might lead them in an unhealthy direction. Roy agreed to this, but within a month I started finding evidence that he was doing as he damn well pleased. What's more, he was using drugs in his room. What if the children were to come across a bag of pretty green capsules? One evening I came home and found them playing poker on the porch. Do you know what they were using for chips?"

"Pringles?"

"Foil-wrapped condoms they'd found in Roy's drawer. Teenagers these days—they're more mature than I was, but maybe I was a hopeless nerd back then. Or maybe it's just Roy. He swaggers around and acts like a jerk, and for some reason it appeals to women. I guess it's kind of a disenfranchised antihero thing. You know, like James Dean in that tight black T-shirt with the sleeves rolled up and a cigarette dangling out of his mouth. It brings out the maternal instinct in women."

"Not this one," I said. "My only instinct was to buy him a bottle of shampoo."

Sullivan looked away. "But the most important thing was the children's well-being. Their mother believes they should have total freedom to explore their world, but I believe they'll thrive in a more structured environment with clearly defined limitations and an awareness of the potential consequences of their behavior. Which means, basically, that Roy was a bad influence."

"Was Morning Rose in agreement when you told Roy to move out?" I asked.

"Hardly. She seems to think she alone can save Roy from his perverted belief that he can empower himself through Satan. She *is* about the only person he says more than the absolute minimum to. All I ever got was a curt response to a question."

"Can she persuade him to obey your rules until his parents get back? He's smart enough to know that his only options are here or in a group home. Surely he can restrain himself for ten weeks."

"I have to think of the children," said Sullivan.

It occurred to me that Druids could be a teensy bit stubborn, too. "What sort of drugs was he doing? I could arrange for Sergeant Jorgeson to warn him about the consequences of getting caught with an illegal substance."

"The drug's not illegal. It's called 'Herbal Ecstasy' and can be bought at any health-food store or New Age record shop. It's supposed to be a stimulant and an aphrodisiac."

"An aphrodisiac?" I said. "Are you positive this is legal?"

"Look at the signs in the store windows along Thurber Street. It's legal for the moment, but the FDA's liable to ban it before too long." He flipped the dish towel back and forth, then added, "Do you understand why Roy can't move back here? My children spend all day being told they can do anything they want in the name of learning. Cosmos has already learned that grass burns quickly in the summer and goldfish can't survive with peroxide in the water. Rainbow obsesses on dead squirrels. I could search Roy's room every night, but I wouldn't be here when he got home after school."

I glumly watched a haggard dog slink across the yard and disappear under the house, wishing Roy Tate could do the same. "I understand your concerns, Mr. Sawyer. Malthea's worried about him being out there by himself with no supervision whatsoever—and if she knew about this drug, she'd probably be hysterical. Do you have any suggestions?"

Sullivan stood up. "No, and I don't care. He's a nasty piece of work, Mrs. Malloy. I was opposed to allowing him to join our grove, and nothing he's done has convinced me to change my mind. There are so few of us who consider ourselves to be pagans that we have to form some uncomfortable alliances. This one has proved to be an unholy one as well."

I could think of no rebuttal, so I settled for a nod and headed for my car. As I opened the door, I heard a child shriek, "Look, Daddy! I found a dead squirrel in the backyard! Did he eat poison?"

I opted to pass up the opportunity to conduct a spontaneous autopsy of the corpse and drove up the hill, trying to convince myself that someone else would deal with the Roy Tate problem. So what if he didn't want to be taken into temporary custody? No teenager would, especially when savoring the specter of living alone and doing whatever he wanted day and night. Caron might not enjoy the isolation, but I had a feeling it was precisely Roy's cup of Herbal Ecstasy tea.

I intended to go straight back to the store and immerse myself in paperwork until it was time to pick up Luanne. At the fateful moment, however, I failed to turn on Thurber Street and headed for the road that led to Nicholas Chunder's estate.

Clearly, the Druids were getting to me.

CHAPTER 5

This did not constitute meddling, I assured myself. I'd had more experience with teenagers than any of the others; I was the most likely contender to convince Roy that he could survive a few months in a group home without, as Malthea had predicted, becoming warped, bitter, and the victim of unspeakable abuse. I could also make it very clear that he would not be staying in the back of the bookstore or—I shuddered—at my apartment. Afterward, my conscience clear and my hands washed in true Herodian fashion, I could devote my energies to filing invoices, updating sales-tax figures, deciding which books to return to the publishers, and dusting the front window display of calendars and novels with Christmas-related artwork.

This all seemed so admirable that I was smiling as I turned down the driveway to Nicholas's manor house. Earlier in the day I'd failed to spot the brass plaque that identified the property as Primrose Hill. It had a pleasant ring to it, although it may have taken its name from some infamous Druid sacrificial site. Nicholas had hardly evinced a sense of humor, but I'd learned that Druids were a wily lot.

The front door of the house had been sealed by the police, and a cardboard sign threatened would-be trespassers with retribution. The murder was Jorgeson's arena, not mine, I told myself as I parked. The hearse was not in sight, but it might be inside the carriage house beside whatever more conventional vehicle Nicholas had driven.

At one end of the stone building was a flight of stairs. I was a bit breathless by the time I arrived on the landing and knocked on the door without allowing myself to question the shrewdness of my action. If Roy was gone, fine. If he was there and amiable, fine. If he was there but unwilling to talk, fine. The only option that did not fall into the 'fine' category would be if he was so angered by my visit that he shoved me over the railing. That would definitely be un-fine, as well as painful.

I was pondering this ultimate possibility when the door opened and I was met with a blast of noise from unseen speakers. I swallowed a gurgle and said, "I'd like to speak to you for a moment."

Roy was wearing his standard monochromatic apparel: black on black, and his T-shirt for the day was emblazoned with a fire-spitting skull. He scowled at me for a long moment, then said, "I'm kinda busy."

"Aren't we all?" I said as I squeezed past him and went into his living room. The furniture was cheap and utilitarian, the walls adorned with posters of bands with names like "Putrid Stench" and "Ebola." The music, to use the term loosely, was so loud that my skin crawled as if it were being pelted with sleet.

"Turn that off!" I said to my involuntary host.

He picked up a remote control and aimed it at an elaborate stereo system, cutting off a particularly graphic bellow of anguish. "Whatta you want?"

"Well," I said as I sat down and did my best to come

across like a sanctioned social worker, "we need to discuss your plans for the immediate future. Malthea doesn't think you should stay out here by yourself."

"So?"

"I spoke to Sullivan Sawyer. He's not comfortable with the idea of you returning to his house until your parents can make more permanent—"

"You've got a daughter, don't you?" he interrupted. "Red hair, loudmouthed, a real snob."

"My daughter's a sophomore at the high school. Her name is Caron and she's not a snob."

"Right," he drawled, then took a cigarette out of a pack and stuck it in the corner of his mouth. "What'd she say about me?"

"Nothing much," I said.

"She tell you what they call me?"

"I seem to recall something," I said, moistening my lips, "but we need to talk about where you're going to stay. I assume your parents have a house in Farberville. Can you stay there?"

"It's rented out." He scraped a wooden match across the tabletop, lit the cigarette, and sat back, clearly amused by my discomfort. "I don't think the Baptist minister and his wife would want me to move into my old bedroom."

"Do you have any friends you might stay with?"

"What do you think?" he said with a harsh laugh. "I've only been here four months. I used to live with my mom, but she got all freaked and sent me to live with my father and that bitch he married." He blew a stream of smoke at me. "Why's this any of your business?"

"Malthea thinks it's her business and asked for my help. You really shouldn't stay out here by yourself, especially after what happened to Nicholas Chunder. Whoever broke into his house may still be in the vicinity."

"I can take care of myself."

Dealing with teenagers can be like building a castle with dry sand. I pretended to consider his response, then said, "Nicholas was shot. Do you have a gun?"

"I can get one."

"It may be more difficult than—" I stopped as someone banged on the door. "Who's that?"

He gave me a contemptuous look as he went across the room and opened the door. Corporal Billsby stood on the landing, his expression leery and one hand resting on his sidearm.

"The sergeant wants you to come back to the station."

Roy flipped his cigarette over the railing. "What for?"

"The statement you gave wasn't adequate. Sergeant Jorgeson wants you to add some details, like what you might have seen and heard in the middle of the night."

"I didn't see a burglar lurking in the shadows outside the study—okay?"

"It's looking less and less like a burglary. Somebody broke the window to try to make it look like one, but the officers on the homicide team didn't just get off the turnip truck. The sergeant wants to know if maybe you heard the glass break and forgot to mention it."

I went to the doorway, nodded politely at Corporal Billsby, and then said to Roy, "You have to cooperate with the police."

Corporal Billsby did not seem to appreciate my well-intentioned support. "What are you doing here?" he demanded. "Is there a body in his kitchen, too?"

"I haven't looked." I put my hand on Roy's arm. "Do you want me to come with you?"

"I don't know," he said, making a weak effort to shrug off my hand. "I've never been in trouble before. Should I get a lawyer?"

Corporal Billsby crossed his arms and sighed as though the rigors of law enforcement were giving him an ulcer. "This is not some idiotic cop show. All the sergeant wants to do is go over your statement and ask a couple more questions like what time you went to sleep and if you saw anything out of the ordinary this morning on your way to that—that orgy or whatever it was. If you'd been more talkative in the first place, you wouldn't have to be doing this."

Instead of looking reassured, Roy turned pale and began to sway unsteadily. "I went to bed at midnight," he said numbly, "and I didn't see anything or anybody before dawn when I cut across the pasture."

"Are you okay?" I asked him.

He shook his head. "I think I'm gonna throw up."

Billsby retreated until he bumped into the railing. "Don't do it on me, punk. I just got my uniform back from the dry cleaner's yesterday."

I was no more inclined than he to be splattered with the dregs of Roy's breakfast, but I was in my maternal mode and unable to loosen my grip on his arm. "Can you make it to the bathroom?"

"Yeah, I think so." As soon as I released him, Roy turned around and stumbled across the room.

My maternal mode did not extend to holding anyone's head over a commode. I waited until a door slammed, then said, "Has Sergeant Jorgeson made any progress in the investigation?"

"No weapon's been found," Billsby said. "We searched the house and the grounds, but it could be anywhere by now."

"Was anything stolen?"

He squinted at me. "Why are you asking?"

I smiled sweetly. "Just passing the time while we wait, Corporal. Nicholas Chunder was obviously a wealthy man, and it seems likely that he had something worthy of being stolen. A coin collection, perhaps, or the family jewels. I guess he'd keep things like that at a bank, though. Was there any indication that any of the rooms had been searched?"

"He's the only one who could answer that. How long is it going to take for the punk to puke? I haven't got all day, fer crissake. I never got any breakfast, and it's getting on toward lunch."

"Feel free to check on him," I said as I stepped out of the doorway and gestured (rather gracefully, I might add) at the interior of the apartment. "I don't know where the bathroom is, but you can follow the sounds of retching. I'm sure a trained police officer can do that easily enough. We civilians lack your proficiency in such matters."

"Yeah, right." He came into the living room, paused to stare at the posters, and then went into a hallway. Seconds later I heard him roar, "Goddamn it! When I catch that kid, I'm gonna bounce him against a wall!"

This seemed to suggest Roy Tate was no longer available for a session at the police department. I picked up my purse and waited for Corporal Billsby to come storming back into the living room. His demeanor was not attractive when he did so; the blotches on his face did not flatter him, nor did the spittle on his chin.

Nor, for that matter, did the glower that he aimed at me. "You're in on this, aren't you?" he said in a voice almost as loud as the music had been when I arrived. "You asked all those questions to give him time to escape out the bathroom window!"

"I did no such thing," I said indignantly. "You were the one who was worried about your uniform and terrified you might have to shine your shoes tonight. I didn't hear you offer to escort him to the bathroom, either. That was really very negligent on your part, wasn't it? I do hope Sergeant Jorgeson's not too cross with you when he hears about this."

"Aw, hell," the corporal said as he collapsed on the sofa. "I've already got one reprimand in my file for roughing up a junkie."

"Then you should consider tracking this witness, shouldn't you?"

"There are at least forty acres surrounding this house. I walked most of them earlier today." Corporal Billsby stood up and slammed his hat back on his head. "Stay here, ma'am. I'm gonna call for backup."

"Roy Tate isn't a suspect," I said.

"Now he is."

Corporal Billsby had a point, I thought as I listened to him call the police department and squirm through an explanation of why he needed additional officers on the scene. He banged down the receiver, gave me a final glower, and hurried down the exterior stairs. I followed at a more decorous pace, wondering if I ought to call Malthea and report the dismal outcome of my mission. Presuming Roy was on foot and eluded the police, he was likely to be sleeping in the woods in the future.

I went onto the porch of the house and peered in the window at the shrouded living room. A strand of tinsel had come loose and hung like a thick silver snake. I tried to envision a blazing fire, tankards of mead, and a rousing rendition of a pagan hymn, but my thoughts kept returning to the bloodied corpse on the kitchen floor. Hardly convivial.

I went to the double doors of the carriage house and dragged them open. Although I'd anticipated the sight of the hearse, it still jolted me. It was long and sleek, with polished chrome accents and fringed curtains in the back windows. I stuck my head in the window in case Roy was hunkered on the floor of the front seat; all I saw were paper cups and crumpled cigarette packs. The key was in the ignition, but I was not tempted to drive around Farberville and drum up a little extra income.

Parked next to it was a burgundy Cadillac, indicative of Nicholas's more conservative taste. I made sure Roy was not hiding under either vehicle, then opened the door of a small room with a tool bench, a headless marble statue draped in cobwebs, and shelves piled with oddments such as flowerpots and wicker baskets.

Satisfied Roy had fled elsewhere, I emerged as a patrol car pulled up. Corporal Billsby came around the corner of the carriage house, unaccompanied by his errant witness.

"How'd the sergeant take it?" he asked the driver.

"About like you think he would, Billsby. Can you say 'school crossing guard'?"

Apparently Billsby couldn't. He waited until his colleagues climbed out of the car, then gave them a rambling account that characterized me as a cross between Ma Barker and Bonnie Parker.

"Look here," I cut in before I was cuffed and thrown into the backseat, "I have no control over Roy's past or present behavior. I came here out of concern for a minor whose parents are on the other side of the world. Sergeant Jorgeson should not have allowed him to continue to live here. Why weren't suitable arrangements made?"

"We aren't in the baby-sitting business," snapped Billsby. "Come on, guys—let's scatter and see if we can find this punk."

No one bothered to commend me for my virtuous motives as they walked between the two buildings. I waited for a moment to see if Corporal Billsby might return to order me to sit in my car or go back upstairs, then decided I'd been dismissed and drove back to the bookstore.

The telephone was ringing as I unlocked the door. In that there were many people with whom I did not wish to converse, including Peter, Jorgeson, and Malthea, I answered it with a guarded acknowledgment that this was indeed the Book Depot.

I'd overlooked Gilda D'Orcher.

"I need to talk to you," she said over the background clamor of voices and machinery. "My shift's over in an hour. Can we meet someplace?"

I was beginning to feel as if I was beset by a parasitic vine that was curling around my limbs. "I'm busy the rest of the day. The person you need to talk to is Sergeant Jorgeson. Would you like the number?"

"No, I need to talk to you, Mrs. Malloy. Can't you please give me a few minutes?"

"I'll be here until six o'clock," I said. "If you want to come by, you can."

She began to snuffle. "My bicycle's out at Primrose Hill. Fern gave me a lift to the police station and then to the hospital so I wouldn't be late. I meant to ask the Sawyers to bring it back to town in their van, but they left before I had a chance." The distasteful snuffling increased in volume, if not sincerity. "There's no way I can get to the bookstore before you leave. This is really important, Mrs. Malloy. I know you think I'm a crackpot, but please hear me out."

The metaphorical vine slithered up my back and twined around my neck. "I might be able to meet you at seven or eight tonight," I said.

"I guess that'll have to do," she said. "One of the orderlies lives in the trailer park, so I can get a ride home with him. It's on Appleby Road, and I live in the last unit on the left. I'll put a candle in the window."

I admitted I could find the trailer park and hung up, all the while cursing myself for being such an easy mark. Lacking the proper Wiccan vocabulary, I employed old-fashioned Anglo-Saxon expletives.

My only sale the rest of the afternoon was to my amiable science-fiction hippie, who was a relic of the sixties and a local institution. He ambled in and out of the store in his typical haze; I considered asking him if he knew anything about the local Druids, but his eyes were so unfocused that I was afraid my question might further bewilder him.

No police officer appeared to drag me to the nearest dungeon for impeding an investigation, and at six o'clock I locked up and drove to Luanne's store. She was waiting on the sidewalk, her hands buried in the pockets of a tatty fur coat.

"Do you think it'll impress him?" she said as she got into my car. "I realize that fur's not politically correct, but neither is a guy who denigrates children's self-esteem by categorizing them as naughty or nice."

"Get a grasp, Luanne," I said as I eased into the stream of cars heading up Thurber Street. "Caron described the previous Santa as an old geezer who didn't require makeup for his cherry-tinted nose. I doubt he'd have cared if your entire body was covered with fur."

"That attitude does not reflect the Christmas spirit of goodwill to men, especially the kind with admirable physical attributes and limitless financial resources. Speaking of which, anything more from Peter?"

"No, and I don't expect him to call anytime soon. Our last conversation did not go well. I suppose he deserves some credit for being concerned about his mother, but he's so blinded with infantile jealousy that he'd object to the pope."

"The pope's pretty old," Luanne said, ogling a pedestrian who met at least one of her criteria. "Pull over, Claire—he winked at me."

I kept going. By the time we arrived at the mall, I'd told her the entire Druid saga, which she found more amusing that daring. It took nearly half an hour to find a parking space, and only then did I succeed by stalking a woman laden with shopping bags.

The mall was jammed with shoppers. The organized ones clutched lists and darted between those with slack-jawed faces. Children were dragged along by grim parents bent on bargains. Strollers competed in an informal version of the Indy 500. The odor of sweat competed with perfume, popcorn, cedar, and recycled air. The worst of it, however, was the clash of carols from inside stores; the Little Drummer Boy was banging away over the warning that Santa was mak-

ing a list and Rudolph was being denied participation
in reindeer frivolities taking place away in a manger.
Cash registers jangled in kiosks in the middle of the
promenade.

"I don't know if I can do this," I said to Luanne as
we elbowed our way through the teeming masses, at
least one of whom was yearning to go home and
spend a quiet, uneventful evening with a novel.

"Don't be ridiculous."

She scooted around a line of swaggering adoles-
cents, forcing me to trot after her. The crowd coagu-
lated as we neared the food court, and our progress
slowed to a maddening crawl. New odors assaulted
us. I was amazed that anyone could eat in such a
raucous environment and not succumb to terminal
indigestion.

Luanne grabbed my wrist. "It's down this way."

After a few more minutes of weaving through a
maze of humanity, we found Santa's Workshop in a
pavilion in front of a department store. It was delin-
eated by a two-foot-high picket fence and festooned
with twinkling lights, faux icicles, and blankets of
cotton strewn with glitter. Plastic elves grinned maniacally from strategic points. On a stage partially surrounded by lattice sat the man himself; below him was
a camera on a tripod and the invincible Mrs. Claus.
There must have been forty or even fifty children in
line, each held in place by a parent. A few of the children were smiling, but most of them were pouting or
whining. Their parents reminded me of soldiers being
briefed on the eve of a critical campaign.

Luanne and I wormed our way closer to the gazebo,
and finally caught a glimpse of the two reindeer in

their tunics and antlers. Both appeared to be exhausted but determined to keep the line moving (and the bonus money flowing). While Inez consulted Mrs. Claus, Caron took a sobbing child by the hand, hauled him up the two steps, and deftly deposited him on Santa's lap. Thirty seconds later, she removed the child and Inez fetched the next victim.

"I can't make out his age," said Luanne, gazing thoughtfully at Santa. "Do you think he's padded or really that pudgy?"

"You'll have to fork over fifteen dollars for the answer to that," I said. "Furthermore, I don't suggest you try to cut in line. Those mothers are probably packing designer pistols in those imported leather handbags."

"I'll ask Caron about him. She and Inez look cute in a goofy way, don't they?"

"Don't tell her that," I said, watching as yet another child was positioned on Santa's lap. Mrs. Claus remained hunched over the camera, raising her head only to announce she was ready to take a photograph. All I could tell about her was that she had white hair (possibly a wig) and an ample rump (probably her own). As Luanne had said, it was impossible to make out Santa's features under the bushy beard, equally bushy white eyebrows, and fur-trimmed hat.

A girl of five or six, dressed in a red velvet party dress, ran up to the head of the line. "I'm next!" she screeched in a voice that imperiled the vases in a nearby jewelry store.

Caron rolled her eyes and said something to the girl, who in response shoved the boy next to her with enough force to send him sprawling onto the cotton. Mrs. Claus straightened up and gave Caron a stern look.

"I want to go now!" the girl repeated, stamping her foot with each word. It sounded as if this were a familiar assertion in her home, whether the issue was a glass of milk, a cartoon show, or a basic demand of nature.

"Wait your turn," said a mother in the middle of the line.

The girl's face was pink and her chin trembling. "I don't want to wait! I hate to wait!"

Luanne nudged me. "Guess who'll be getting coal and switches in her stocking."

Caron seemed nonplussed as angry mutters from those in line grew louder. Santa and the child on his lap stared at the crowd as if it were a mob in the making. The little boy who'd been pushed began to wail as his mother yanked him to his feet and brushed glitter off his knees. Shoppers formed a loose circle around the fence, no doubt intrigued by the diversion of violence.

The girl took advantage of Caron's momentary paralysis and darted through the gate. Inez started to reach for her, then timidly lowered her hand and stepped back.

"Where on earth is that child's mother?" I asked Luanne. "Surely she's not here on her own."

"Maybe the chauffeur's out in the limousine, waiting on her royal highness. As we know, her royal highness does not like to be denied the privileges of rank."

The girl was halfway up the steps when Caron spun around and went after her. She caught the girl around the waist, and to the crowd's enthusiastic approval, carried her to the fence and set her down outside it.

The girl froze for a moment, her eyes rounded, then took a deep breath and ran toward a woman in a fur coat that was in no way tatty. "Inappropriate touching, Mommy!" she screamed. "Inappropriate touching!"

CHAPTER 6

"I don't believe it," Caron said as we drove away from the mall. "There must have been two hundred people who saw what happened. All I did was pick her up, for pity's sake. From the way everybody reacted, you'd have thought I flung her across the mall like a red velvet bowling ball. Which, for the record, I considered doing."

I looked at her in the rearview mirror. "You didn't get fired, and that's the important thing."

"I'm not so sure I won't get fired in the morning. Mrs. Claus really bawled me out in the locker room. She'll stay up all night trying to find something in the manual."

Luanne turned around and leaned over the seat to pat Caron's knee. "She's not going to fire you this close to Christmas. She can't risk not being able to find a replacement."

"That's right," Inez said. "I mean, who else would agree to wear costumes like that and deal with an endless line of drooling babies and bratty kids? The pay's good, but I'll sure be relieved when we're done on Christmas Eve."

Caron flopped back in the seat and closed her eyes. "No kidding."

The ambiance was so oppressive that none of us spoke for the remainder of the trip. I dropped off Luanne and Inez at their respective residences, and a few minutes later parked in the garage beneath the duplex.

"Don't worry about it," I said to Caron, treading a fine line between sage and cheerleader. "The girl was just parroting something she'd been taught to say. She sounded like a robot from some science-fiction movie. There were plenty of witnesses who saw exactly what you did."

"Mrs. Claus said I should call the girl's parents to apologize. I told her I hadn't done anything wrong and I wasn't that much of a hypocrite. I expected to get fired, but she shrugged and left the locker room. I can almost hear her on the hot line to the home office asking for the approved procedure for dealing with rebellious reindeer. I'll probably be transferred to a strip mall in some podunk town where all the shoppers are first cousins."

I offered to fix her something to eat, but she said she wasn't hungry and limped down the hall to her room. Her lack of defiance unsettled me; she's always preferred a vigorous offense, no matter how illogical, and she's never held a smoking gun that couldn't be rationalized away in a nanosecond.

I was pouring a drink when the telephone rang. Its sound reminded me of the earlier call from Gilda D'Orcher and my promise to go to her trailer, and I was not enthusiastic when I picked up the receiver.

"How's it going?" asked Peter in a suspiciously jovial tone. "Have you been out Christmas shopping?"

"Luanne and I went to the mall."

"Anything else going on?"

All systems went on red alert, but I managed a care-less chuckle and said, "This and that. Any develop-ments with your mother and the diabolic suitor?"

"No, she keeps babbling about his virtues and he keeps taking her to expensive restaurants. He's been dropping hints about giving her an engagement ring for Christmas, but I made her swear not to do any-thing rash until . . ."

"Hell freezes over?" I suggested.

There was a profound pause during which I could hear only the rush of his breath on the mouthpiece. Finally he said, "Until Leslie gets here tomorrow and she and my mother can have a long talk about Myron."

"Leslie? Is she an old friend of your mother's? A col-lege roommate or sorority sister?"

"Leslie's my ex-wife."

"Excuse me?"

"You heard me. Leslie and my mother became close friends, and since the divorce they've continued to call and visit each other several times a year. When I told Leslie about Myron, she offered to come as soon as she could. I'm picking her up at the airport at noon."

My hand was trembling as I grabbed the glass and took an unladylike swallow of scotch. "Did your mother call her or did you?"

Peter took his time responding to my extraordi-narily reasonable question. "Yes, Claire, I called her. To answer your next question, I didn't know her tele-phone number off the top of my head. I found it in my mother's address book."

"Did you?" I managed to say with only the slightest trace of frost. "How convenient that she could drop everything and come dashing to your aid. She must be *very* fond of your mother."

He either missed the edge in my voice—or opted to ignore it. "It wasn't convenient. She had to make all kinds of arrangements and wheedle her boss into letting her take some days off. She called a few minutes ago to say her travel agent had scrambled around and found a seat on a flight tomorrow. I offered to pay for it, but she wouldn't hear of it. A ticket at the last moment costs a bundle."

I decided not to point out that Leslie may have believed that martyrdom was the first step to canonization. My knowledge of saints was limited to Saint John of God (booksellers) and Saint Patrick (green beer), but I figured no one had laid claim to the title of patron saint of ex-daughters-in-law. "It must have been difficult for her to find a baby-sitter on such short notice, too," I said, feigning sympathy for the woman who'd been married to Peter for twelve years and had remained intimate with his mother. I'd never even met his mother.

"Baby-sitter? Who said anything about a baby-sitter? The biggest problem was trying to find a kennel for Boris Godunov and Prince Igor, her Russian wolfhounds. Leslie's crazy about Russian opera and goes to St. Petersburg for the season every year."

"Isn't that fascinating?" I said. "I hope this impromptu visit doesn't interfere with her consumption of vodka and caviar."

"I'm sure it won't," he said blandly. "What else have you been up to besides the mall?"

Standing around a gloomy forest while water dripped down my neck lacked the glamour of the St. Petersburg opera season. "Selling books, that sort of thing," I said with matching blandness. "Do you have any idea how much longer you'll be in Newport?"

"It depends on Leslie's plans. Since she's making the effort to come and be supportive, I can't just toss her the car keys at the airport and take the next flight home. I'll be here for at least a few more days."

"No, I don't see how you can leave while Leslie's there," I said, hoping he hadn't caught the slight hiss in my voice when I said her name. Someone with Russian wolfhounds, no doubt pedigreed to the *n*th degree, would never be so vulgar as to hiss. "You must have a lot of catching up to do."

"The only reason she's coming is to talk to my mother," said Peter. "There's nothing more to it than that."

"Oops, someone's at the front door," I said. "I know you'll be busy over the next few days, so I won't expect a call. 'Bye."

I carefully replaced the receiver, freshened my drink, and made it to the sofa without any disasters. Leslie was likely to be a spontaneous woman, I thought as I pulled off my scuffed loafers and propped my feet on the coffee table. I tried to remember if Peter had ever mentioned where she lived or if she'd remarried. Anyone who jetted to St. Petersburg every year was not likely to have a menial, minimum-wage sort of job. She was apt to be a stockbroker or a network news anchor or an editor at a prestigious literary house that publishes the sort of books that everybody buys and nobody actually reads. That, or Anastasia incarnate.

When the telephone rang, I stayed where I was, my fingers crossed that I was not going to be regaled with an addendum to the litany of Leslie's selfless, magnanimous sacrifices, such as donating a kidney to an orphan or single-handedly funding a Kurdish refugee camp. I heard Caron answer it in her room, her initial enthusiasm almost immediately replaced with ill-disguised resentment. Seconds later she came down the hall and said, "It's for you. Would you please keep it short? Inez thinks she saw Marissa at the mall when— well, you know when. I may need her to testify when I'm tried for assault and battery. Is that a felony?"

"I don't know." I picked up the receiver. "Hello?"

"This is Malthea, Claire. You must come over here and explain what's happening. I'd put on the front porch light for you, but I think it's better that you arrive under the cloak of darkness. Park around the corner and watch out for rough spots on the sidewalk. We can't have any scraped knees, can we?"

"Absolutely not!"

"I'm glad you agree with me. I'll see you shortly."

Before I could get in a word, she hung up. I considered throwing the telephone through the nearest window, but the apartment was chilly enough without inviting in the December wind. I could have hurled my glass at the wall, but someone would be obliged to sweep up the broken glass—and odds were not good that it would be Caron. The obvious option was to turn off the light and go to bed; I'd been up since an absurdly early hour.

Wishing I'd never heard of *The Encyclopedia of Pagan Rituals and Initiations* or any of the other oddball titles, I put on my shoes, set the glass in the kitchen sink, and went to Caron's door. She was sitting cross-legged in the middle of the bed, gloomily keeping watch over the telephone in case it attempted to scuttle away.

"I'm going out for a few minutes," I said.

"That's fine. I'll just sit here in the dark while my future gurgles down the drain."

"I truly don't think you have any reason to worry, dear. Luanne was right when she said Mrs. Claus wouldn't dare fire you so close to Christmas. You'll be able to retrieve everything on layaway and humiliate Rhonda on the first day of school."

"The only person who'll ask me to the prom is Mr. Mortician. I can see myself in the front seat of the hearse, dressed in black with a calla lily corsage. I might as well ask him to drop me off at the cemetery, since my life is over anyway."

I could think of nothing else to say, so I left the apartment and drove to Malthea's. I parked in front of the duplex, sat for a moment while I reminded myself how annoyed I was at her, then marched up to the dark porch and rapped on the door.

"It's cold out here!" I called. "If you don't open the door in the next ten seconds, I'm—"

The door opened. Malthea eyed me for a moment, then stepped back and waited until I was inside before saying, "I thought we'd agreed you would arrive under a cloak of darkness, Claire."

"It's plenty dark out there," I said. "What's more, it's getting late and I still haven't had dinner. Here I am. What do you want this time?"

"Goodness," she murmured, "you sound as if you've had a difficult day. Let's do sit down and have some tea while we talk."

I stared at her. "A difficult day? I think that sums it up nicely, although I might have chosen a more forceful adjective—like nightmarish. What do you want, Malthea? If you've decided I should adopt Roy Tate, you can forget it. I went out there to help, and it back-fired. Now I quit."

"Some of us have forgotten our manners, haven't we?" She sat down on the sofa, crossed her arms, and waited until I'd reluctantly joined her. "I thought it might be better if I tell you what took place last night while we were decorating Nicholas's front room. Then, if you feel strongly that I ought to tell the police, I will do so—although I cannot see why it should have any bearing on the tragic accident that befell Nicholas."

"Okay," I said neutrally.

The telephone began to ring, but as she'd done previously, Malthea ignored it. "As of late there has been growing dissension in our grove. Each of us brings an individual philosophy, and eclecticism and tolerance are important tenets of contemporary Druidism. There are Orthodox Jewish Druids, Catholic Druids—"

"Malthea," I said. "It's eight o'clock. I'm tired and I'm hungry—and I'm not predisposed to listen to a lecture. My daughter is at home preplanning her funeral. The significant man in my life is picking up his ex-wife at an airport tomorrow." I bit down on my lip, took a calming breath, and added, "Just tell me what happened last night."

"All I was trying to do was present the situation so that you can grasp the—"

"What happened?" I growled.

"Nicholas owned many of the residences along this street, as well as apartment buildings and houses in other neighborhoods. He was so very kind about helping his fellow Druids find affordable, if not luxurious, housing. Fern has been paying the same rent for ten years, and the Sawyers pay almost nothing. That's why they were upset."

"Well, of course. I myself would be heartbroken if my landlord threatened to reduce the rent." I paused so that she could hear my stomach rumble. "Who wouldn't be?"

"Sarcasm does not become you," she said with a sniff. "To return to the point, Nicholas was vehemently opposed to any practices that fell outside his interpretation of unadulterated meso-Druidic tradition. He was forever grumbling about our two Wiccans and their somewhat quaint notions about matters of ritual. He observed Roy's drift into satanism with horror. He went so far as to object to the little herbal remedies that Fern concocts when someone is feeling unwell." She stood up. "This is all so difficult. I must have a cup of tea to give me the strength to continue."

She was out of the room before I could protest, which would have been a waste of perfectly good breath. I used up most of it with a drawn-out sigh, tucked a pillow behind my back, and resigned myself to incipient starvation. I was wondering how Leslie would have handled the situation when Malthea returned with a tray laden with the necessary accessories.

"Last night," she said as she sat down and poured the tea, "the room was thick with tension. Gilda and Morning Rose were sulking because of our decision to disallow them to perform the solstice ritual while skyclad. Sullivan was pacing about like a caged animal, shooting dark looks at the rest of us. Fern was complaining about the placement of the greenery and tinsel, the smoke from the fire in the fireplace, the effect of the dampness on her rheumatism, and Roy's lack of participation. I had to agree with her about Roy. He refused to so much as climb the ladder or tack a clump of mistletoe to the wall. It wasn't like him at all."

"That's not how you described it this afternoon," I said. "What happened to the pagan songs and tankards of mead?"

"I did everything I could to create a festive air, but it was almost impossible. I'd just proposed a toast to the rebirth of the Earth Goddess when Nicholas made his announcement. After that, I'm sorry to say, there was no hope that any of us could maintain even a facade of gaiety. Harsh words were exchanged. Fern was in tears as I helped her out to the car, and Sullivan drove away with so much fury that we were left in a cloud of dust. It was very inconsiderate of him."

"What did Nicholas say to upset your happy little grove?" I asked.

Malthea took a tissue out of her pocket and touched it to the corner of her eye. "Nicholas told us that he'd made arrangements to put all of his property, including Primrose Hill and his rental holdings, on the market. He'd decided to move to Wales and continue his genealogical efforts to trace his lineage back to the Celtic Druids at the dawning of the Christian era."

I thought for a minute. "You, Fern, and the Sullivans were renters. What about Gilda and Roy's family?"

"Gilda rents her trailer from the man who manages the park. I'm not sure about the Tates, but I suspect not. Their home is in a lovely neighborhood. Nicholas's properties are of a lesser quality and rented primarily to students, with the exception of a few retirees such as myself and Fern."

"I can understand why those of you paying minimal rent might be perturbed, but surely not to the extent of harsh words, tears, and abrupt departures," I said. "Farberville has a goodly number of low-income rental properties. Moving might be inconvenient and the rent might increase, but still . . ."

Malthea rose and crossed the room to look out the window at the dark street. "The Sacred Grove of Keltria is very dear to me, as are its members. I've always considered us to be a spiritual family, and assumed Nicholas felt the same way. He was so brusque last night, so uncaring. He refused to discuss it further and said we had thirty days to vacate the property. When Fern tried to convince him to reconsider, he ordered all of us to leave."

"Even Roy?"

"He said that suitable arrangements would be made," she said, not turning.

I could see her face reflected in the windowpane. Rather than sad or even distressed, she seemed to be battling to suppress an anger that might have rivaled Nicholas's purported display the previous evening. Her eyes were narrowed, her lips squeezed together, and her cheeks flushed. I could easily imagine her at the stone altar in the grove, intoning an ancient prayer as she raised a dagger above a sacrificial victim.

Neither of us had moved when Fern opened the front door and came into the room. She stared at me for a paralytic moment, then swallowed and said, "I didn't realize you had company, Malthea."

Malthea's shoulders relaxed, and her expression was cordial as she turned around. "Claire came by to discuss how best to deal with the problem."

"She did?" said Fern. She put her hand on her face

to conceal her mouth from my view and mutely communicated something.

"Frankly," Malthea said as she came to the sofa and took my cup and saucer out of my hand, "there's nothing any of us can do. The police are searching for Roy. He can't go too far without transportation, and I should think he'll turn himself in rather than sleep outside."

Fern began to twist her bony hands, squeezing the blood out of her fingers. "Don't let us detain you, Claire."

"Thank you for dropping by," added Malthea, conveniently forgetting who'd issued the directive.

Five minutes earlier I would have chewed off my leg to escape, but the scenario had taken a peculiar direction and I was tempted to resist being dismissed like a chastised child. However, I picked up my purse, nodded, and went out onto the porch. I hesitated, but when no one opened the door and begged me to come back inside, I continued out to my car. Curiosity may have been gnawing at me, but I told myself it was more likely to be the combined effects of inadequate sleep and an empty stomach.

As I pulled away from the curb, two figures emerged from Malthea's side of the duplex. By the time I'd turned the corner, they had scurried into Fern's side. I slowed down, then caved in and parked the car. Mindful of the irregularities in the sidewalk, I cautiously approached the duplex and went across the yard in hopes I could see Malthea and Fern in the living room.

The drapes were drawn, and there were no telltale shadows. From one of the nearby houses I could hear a television blaring, and in the distance, a baby crying. There was no indication of any kind of activity, nefarious or innocuous, in Fern's apartment. She'd been agitated, though, and dismayed by my presence. Why?

I eased into the side yard and found yet another set of closed drapes. A thorny branch raked my hand as I tried to move closer to the window, underscoring the folly of allowing my overly active imagination to stifle my common sense.

I resisted the impulse to dive into the rosebushes as a car drove by, and instead dropped to my knees and turned my face away from the glare of the headlights. Once the car had passed, I arose and continued toward the back of the duplex, hoping to see them through a kitchen window.

Away from the glow of the streetlight, the only illumination came from a curtained window in the house next door. I felt my way toward a particularly impenetrable shadow that proved to be a high wooden fence. I was groping for a gate when I heard a door open and Malthea say, "How did he get here?"

"I have no idea," answered Fern, "and I must say I was not pleased to find him under the potting table. I like to keep everything arranged in a logical order so that I can easily put my hands on whatever I need. He's moved several stacks of flowerpots and pushed the bag of sphagnum moss against the wall. I do not look forward to having to crawl under the table to retrieve it."

I had a fairly good idea who was under the potting table, but I wasn't sure what to do. If I returned to my car and drove to a telephone to call the police, Roy might be long gone before they arrived. And turning him in wasn't necessarily the right thing to do. He'd been frightened when Corporal Billsby appeared at his door, and he'd certainly behaved suspiciously by climbing out the bathroom window, but as far as I knew he hadn't been charged with anything. If in fact he had, Fern and Malthea could be charged with harboring a fugitive. I had no desire to find myself in a courtroom, testifying against elderly ladies. Peter would not be amused when he saw the headline: BOOKSELLER IMPLICATED IN DRUID CRIME SPREE.

Perhaps I could persuade Roy to turn himself in, I thought as I gave up trying to find a gate and headed toward the front of the house to determine if I could go through Fern's apartment. I'd reached the edge of the porch when I saw two dark figures advancing toward me.

"Hold it right there!" one of them said in a decidedly unfriendly voice.

"Keep your hands where we can see them," said the other. His voice, although no doubt meant to sound equally menacing, ended with a squeak.

I noted the light glinting off both their weapons and their badges, so rather than swoon or bolt for the bushes, I said, "Do we have a problem, officers?"

"I don't know what you have, lady, but we had a call about a burglary in progress."

"In this neighborhood?" I said skeptically. "Is someone stealing beer cans out of garbage bags?"

The officers considered this for a moment, then lowered their weapons and gestured for me to move into the light. Neither was familiar, which I found heartening; I'd experienced entirely too much of Corporal Billsby's charm at various moments during the day—and it was feasible he would seize upon the most feeble of excuses to shoot me.

"Let's see some ID," Squeaky demanded.

"My purse is in my car," I said. "I'd like to add that I came here at a friend's behest. She lives in there."

"So why are you prowling around in the yard?" he countered.

"I am not prowling," I said.

"Look," said his partner, "the lady who lives in the next house saw you go by her window. According to her, you were prowling. Maybe you'd better explain why you went to visit your friend who lives there"— he jabbed his finger at Malthea's door—"and ended up out here in the dark. Maybe you were checking to see if the windows were locked in case you wanted to come back later."

I plucked a dried leaf off my jacket while I tried to decide how much of the truth I was willing to relate. "As I was driving away, I realized I had something else to tell my friend. She was not in her half of the duplex, so I assumed she and her next-door neighbor were in the greenhouse in the backyard."

Squeaky leaped on this tidbit as though it were a morsel of ripe cheese. "And you thought you'd break in and make off with her grocery money! I think we'd better take you down to the station and hear more of your fascinating story."

"Sergeant Jorgeson isn't going to like that," I said.

"Why not?"

It was time for a brief moment in the confessional before I was faced with a long moment in a cell. "He's eager to interview a possible witness in a murder that took place early this morning. The witness, Roy Tate, is in the greenhouse, too. Why don't I wait here while you fetch him, and then we'll all go to the station together? If you'd like to stop for doughnuts on the way, I'll pay for them. Better yet, let's order a pizza."

The officers looked at each other. "I guess it can't hurt to see who's out there," Squeaky said at last. "You aren't gonna wait here, though. Show us how to get to this greenhouse."

I led the way to Fern's front door. It was not locked, so we proceeded through the cluttered living room. As we went into the kitchen, I nearly tripped over the sill as I saw Malthea seated at a small table and Fern taking porcelain cups out of a cabinet.

"Goodness gracious!" said Malthea, although her performance was less than convincing. "I thought you'd gone home, Claire."

"Who are those men?" asked Fern. "Did you let them into my house? Why would you . . . ? Oh dear, Malthea, they're policemen."

Malthea cocked her head and gave them a beady look. "You really must explain this, gentlemen. This is a private residence, and unless you have a search warrant, you have no right to barge in like this."

"She," Squeaky said, pointing at me, "claims there's a fugitive hiding in the greenhouse out back. You'd better show me where it is."

"A fugitive?" repeated Malthea. "What a quaint notion. Fern and I were out there only minutes ago, and we saw no one."

I shook my head. "Sorry, but I heard you and Fern talking about Roy Tate's unauthorized presence in the greenhouse. He needs to stop being foolish and cooperate with the police. If it turns out that he needs a lawyer, I'll make sure he gets one who's had some experience."

Malthea stood up and gestured dramatically at the back door. "Officers, go see for yourselves that there is no one in the greenhouse. Fern discovered a stray dog earlier in the evening, and asked me to accompany her to make sure the creature had not returned."

The two policemen dutifully went through the door. Malthea, Fern, and I waited in stony silence. I mentally reviewed the snippet of conversation I'd overheard and concluded that Roy—or someone else, albeit unlikely—had been in the greenhouse. It was clear from their demeanor that whoever it had been was gone by now.

"No sign of anybody," Squeaky said as he and his partner came back into the kitchen. "We're going. Lady, stay out of other people's yards—okay?"

Fern managed to step on my toes as she went past me to escort the policemen to the front door. I looked down at Malthea, who was celebrating her minor victory with a contented smile.

"Roy was here," I said coldly.

"Only if he's reverted to a past life and taken the form of a large yellow dog," she said. "I was an eagle once, and what a lovely life it was. Soaring in the sky, swooping down on unsuspecting rodents and sinking my talons into warm flesh—"

"Did you give Roy money?"

Malthea's smile widened. "To buy dog biscuits?"

"If you know where he is, you need to convince him to call Sergeant Jorgeson at the police station and arrange to be picked up. Otherwise, Jorgeson will have no difficulty obtaining an arrest warrant and putting out an APB."

"Roy is a child."

"No, he's not," I replied levelly. "He's old enough to be tried as an adult and sentenced accordingly—if he killed Nicholas. His behavior certainly suggests it."

Fern came back into the kitchen. "Claire, in the future I'd appreciate it if you do not bring men into my home without my permission. It endangers my reputation in the community."

I threw up my hands, literally as well as figuratively, and stomped out of the duplex and down the sidewalk to my car. I knew what I'd heard, and it wasn't a discussion about a yellow dog. Roy Tate had taken refuge in Fern's greenhouse. My exchange with Officers Unfriendly and Squeaky must have carried to the backyard and sent Roy over the fence.

Scowling, I yanked open the car door and settled myself behind the wheel. As I reached for my purse to retrieve the car key, a male voice (neither squeaky nor unfriendly) said, "I gotta talk to you."

CHAPTER 7

"Talk to me about what, Roy?" I said, annoyed with myself for not checking the backseat before I got in the car. It was something I always did, except, of course, when I'd been jerked around by a couple of gray-haired Druids.

"Start driving."

"Driving where?"

Roy breathed heavily for a moment. "I don't know. Just drive around and keep both hands on the steering wheel."

"And if I don't?" I said.

"I have a gun, Mrs. Malloy. I don't want to use it, but I'm in such deep shit already that it probably doesn't matter what I do." He thumped the back of my seat hard enough to rattle my teeth. "Let's go!"

I couldn't see him in the rearview mirror, so I had no idea if he was bluffing or not. It did not seem wise to press the issue. I pulled away from the curb and drove in the general direction of Thurber Street, where there might be a few cars and pedestrians. Roy had said he'd moved to Farberville only a few months earlier, so he might not have been aware that we were also headed in the direction of the police station.

"About last night," Roy began, cleared his throat,

and tried again. "You seem to have some inside edge with the cops. If I tell you what really happened, maybe you can explain it to them. I could tell from the way they were looking at me this morning that they think I'm some kind of psychopath who'd decapitate his grandmother for the price of a hamburger. I wouldn't be surprised if they dug up the flower beds at my father's house today in search of graves."

His supposition was likely to be accurate, but I saw no advantage in saying so. "Tell me what happened, Roy."

"Nicholas got pissed and yelled at everybody to get out of his house. Everybody did. I went up to my apartment, stuck a frozen dinner in the oven, and turned on some music. Around midnight, Nicholas knocked on my door and asked me to go back to the house with him. He was acting real odd, grinning at me and patting me on the back like I had colic. I could smell booze on his breath. I should have refused, but I was hoping maybe he'd changed his mind about selling all his properties. Living in the carriage house was a lot better than sharing a crappy little bedroom at the Sawyers' dump. Sullivan's a tight-ass, and Morning Rose fixes these weird vegetarian casseroles. Their kids give me the creeps."

"I'm sure it was an improvement," I said as I turned onto Thurber Street. Cars were scarce, pedestrians nonexistent. In the dark, the Book Depot looked more like an abandoned warehouse than a haven of intellectual enlightenment. I made a note to buy a few strands of Christmas lights—presuming the passenger in the backseat was not a psychopath who'd shoot a mild-mannered bookseller on a whim.

"So I was thinking I might not have to move out after all," Roy went on, "as long as I didn't do anything to set him off again. We went into the kitchen. He poured himself a glass of brandy and asked me if I wanted some. I said I didn't. He got all huffy and kept insisting until I finally said okay. Then he said for me to sit down at the kitchen table because there was something he needed to share with me. I was—well, I was getting really nervous at this point."

"Had he ever offered you alcohol before?"

"Never. He hardly spoke to me unless there was something he wanted me to do, like go down to the end of the driveway to get the mail or do minor repairs on his rental stuff." He tapped my shoulder. "Don't turn here, Mrs. Malloy. I'm not ready for the cops."

I abandoned my less-than-subtle subterfuge and drove toward the campus. "Okay, last night Nicholas was behaving strangely. You sat down as ordered— and then what?"

"Maybe I shouldn't tell you," he said in a voice that reminded me he was only sixteen years old. "You'll probably think it was all my fault. It wasn't like I was handcuffed to the table or anything. I could have gotten up and left. I wish I had."

"Why?" I asked softly.

"He started putting moves on me. You know what I mean? He put his hand on my knee, and then, before I could figure out what the hell was going on, he—you know—he was saying things and grabbing at my crotch. This never happened to me before. Girls, maybe, but not some guy older than my father! A guy, fer chrissake!"

All I could hope at that moment was Roy would not

be so overwhelmed with raw memories that he inadvertently squeezed the trigger. I heard the anguish in his voice, the adolescent uncertainty that he might have dropped a hint, might have done or said something to suggest that his true sexual identity was being suppressed. Whether or not it was did not concern me, and I certainly had not spent enough time with Nicholas Chunder to have formed an opinion about his.

I pulled into the football stadium parking lot, selected one of five hundred empty spaces, and turned off the engine. "What did you do?"

"I hit him. He sat there for a minute, then took a gun out of his pocket. I told him that all I wanted to do was go back to my apartment and go to bed. He started making this grotesque noise, like he was laughing but not really. I was so scared, Mrs. Malloy. You've got to believe me."

"Why didn't you run out the door at this point?" I asked.

Roy's fist bounced against the top of the front seat. "I should have, but I was petrified. He had a gun. It flashed across my mind that all he had to say was that I'd attacked him and he shot me in self-defense. I only hit him to make him leave me alone."

"Then what happened?"

"I went after the gun, and we sorta fell on the floor. The next thing I realized, the gun went off and he was breathing funny. I figured he could call himself an ambulance, so I went back to my apartment and tried to stay awake until somebody showed up. The brandy must have gotten to me, because I fell asleep on the couch. When my alarm went off at six, I walked across the pasture to the grove. I was praying like I'd never prayed before that Nicholas would come. You know the rest."

"I'll do what I can to help you," I said, easily imagining his version but not completely buying it. Nicholas Chunder had been an elderly single man, but I was not ready to stereotype him so neatly. Roy seemed distressed; however, he'd had time to rehearse. "If you're telling the truth, Sergeant Jorgeson can steer you through the maze of legal problems. He'll certainly sympathize with your reaction to Nicholas's advances."

"I should have pushed him down and run," he said glumly. "I know that."

"You're young. No one will fault you for what you *should* have done. Why don't we go to the police station now? I'll stay with you and do whatever I can until your parents get back from Borneo."

He began to whimper. "Would you do that for me, Mrs. Malloy? Like, nobody's ever done that before. My parents got divorced when I was ten, and my mother's an alcoholic and hooked on prescription drugs. My father married that bitch with all her dysfunctional relatives, so he's too busy to deal with me. Malthea's about the only person who cares about me."

"I'm sure other people care about you, too," I said, hoping he wouldn't demand a list of names.

"Look, why don't you talk to the police and see what they say? Let Malthea know, and I'll get in touch with her."

The car door opened and then slammed shut. Roy sprinted across the parking lot and vanished into the trees surrounding the admissions building at the top of the hill. As I sat, pondering his story, a campus cop pulled into the lot and stopped next to me.

"The lot's closed," he said. "Is something wrong?"

"I'm not sure," I replied truthfully.

I drove to my duplex, rerunning Roy's story in my mind. I reminded myself that I didn't know him well enough to judge his sincerity. I'd heard derogatory comments from Caron and Sullivan Sawyer, but for all I knew, Roy could have qualified for the title of patron saint of abused postpubescents—or at least those whose parents were on sabbatical in Borneo.

I was thinking all these muddled thoughts when I arrived at home and found a uniformed officer waiting for me on the doorstep. He was yet another member of the Farberville Police Department; I seemed to be going through the roster at an alarming rate.

"Yes?" I said.

"Where's Roy Tate?"

"I don't know. Maybe he's applying for admission to the college. That's where he was going when I last saw him."

"This isn't a joke," said the officer. "There's a warrant for his arrest."

I gave the officer a sketchy account of what had taken place at the duplex and in my car, omitting any mention of the gun Roy'd claimed he had. I would have to bear full responsibility if he used it on a rookie campus cop, but I didn't want that same cop to be so jittery that he shot Roy on sight. The phrase "armed and dangerous" can lead to such a result.

"I doubt he'll go back to Malthea's," I added, "but you might send someone to the Sawyers' house and Gilda D'Orcher's trailer. He doesn't seem to know any other people. Please let Sergeant Jorgeson know that I'll come by the station tomorrow morning."

The officer wrote down the names and left. I went

inside, kicked off my shoes, and punched buttons on the microwave to reheat that which had had nearly two hours to congeal into gelatinous glop. Caron's door was closed and her lights were off. I eased open the door to make sure that she was under the covers (as opposed to having gone undercover—an entirely different concept), then returned to the kitchen and retrieved the entrée.

At least, I thought as I mindlessly shoveled food into my mouth, my day had been anything but dull.

So there, Peter Rosen.

Jorgeson put down the stubby pencil and looked at me. "Do you believe his story?"

"Hard to say." I took a sip of coffee, shuddered, and set the Styrofoam cup on the corner of his desk. "That sort of thing does happen. Roy put on quite a show, but he's still just a kid and he certainly could have panicked when Nicholas molested him. Teenagers can be painfully self-conscious about their bodies. Every time Caron gets a pimple, she plunges into despair and spends hours staring at it in the mirror. That isn't to say she doesn't spend hours in front of the mirror when her skin is clear. If I'd let her, she'd put a mirror on the ceiling of her bedroom."

"Forensics didn't turn up anything useful," Jorgeson said, apparently inured to the toxic sludge that passed for coffee at the PD. "There were fingerprints all over the house, but that's usually the case. We'll match what we can to persons known to have been there that evening. The rest of them will be sent to the FBI, but I don't think they're going to come back with a serial killer. I can't see asking for prints from the membership of the genealogical society."

"I suppose not," I said, sighing. "I feel sorry for Roy. He's clearly unhappy and seems to go out of his way to be a misfit and a loner. Problems with both of his parents, a stepmother, a new school—those things can corrode any teenager's sense of worth. What'll happen to him, Jorgeson?"

"Nothing at the moment, since we don't have him in custody. It's a shame you didn't deliver him to us, Mrs. Malloy. He'd be talking to a lawyer instead of hiding in the basement of almost any building on campus."

"He *said* he had a gun; I wasn't inclined to find out if he did by daring him to put a bullet in my back. None of the other Druids have seen him?"

"They say not, but who knows? I can't figure out any of them. My wife and I go to church where there are pews and stained-glass windows, not bushes and squirrels." Jorgeson shuffled through a pile of reports, snuffling and wheezing like a bulldog. "Here's what we've got on the victim. Nicholas Chunder was sixty-eight, a retired doctor, an upstanding member of a couple of civic clubs. He was born and raised in Indianapolis, went to medical school in Chicago, and opened a private practice here after twenty-five years in a group practice back in Indianapolis. Not so much as a hint of scandal back there. His wife, an heiress with a considerable trust fund, died of cancer when she was in her early thirties. There were no children."

"Did he have family in this area?"

"We didn't come across anything in his files to suggest it. I spoke to his lawyer on the phone. He said the heir is a nephew in Terre Haute. Don't start wiggling your nose like that, Mrs. Malloy—the nephew was wounded in Vietnam and is a paraplegic. Besides, I thought we'd just agreed that Roy confessed to the homicide. Why would he do that if it wasn't the truth?"

"I have no idea," I admitted.

Jorgeson said he'd assure Malthea that Roy would be treated gently if he turned himself in. I drove to the Book Depot, made sure Roy wasn't hiding behind the boiler, and then started a pot of coffee and sat down at my desk while the Mr. Coffee machine groaned in what sounded like terminal agony. It was slightly after nine, which meant Peter would be drinking coffee, reading a newspaper, and no doubt keeping an eye on the time so he wouldn't be late picking up Leslie at the airport. I battled back an irrational urge to break into his house and search for a photograph of the blissful couple on their wedding day.

When the coffee was ready, I filled a mug and went up front to read the newspaper. A short article about Nicholas Chunder's murder had made the second page, but there was no mention of the Druid connection. It was only a matter of time before reporters heard rumors and started nosing around. Malthea might decide it would be diverting to be interviewed on the local news so she could proselytize to the non-tree-huggers. My name would surface. Despite my efforts to downplay my involvement in previous cases, I'd had a bit of publicity in the past. I could anticipate a good deal more than fifteen minutes in the limelight this time.

I spent the remainder of the morning wishing that Jorgeson would call to say they'd taken Roy into custody and arranged for a lawyer. At eleven o'clock (aka noon EST), I snatched up the feather duster and attacked the racks with heretofore unseen diligence. When my science-fiction hippie came into the store, I went for the dandruff on his shoulders. He retreated out the door and scurried up the sidewalk.

I was inking out pearly white teeth on the bridal page of the newspaper when the bell jingled and Malthea came into the store. "Claire," she said, "may I speak to you for a moment?"

I added a mole to a brunette's nose, then put the page and the pen in a drawer. "Have you heard from Roy?"

She shook her head. "No, and I'm terribly worried. That police officer who called this morning said only that Roy confessed to you. I'm at a loss to understand why he would do such a thing, and I was hoping you might tell me more about what he said."

"I'm afraid I can't go into detail," I said. "They were in the kitchen and got into an argument. The gun went off accidentally. Roy was too panicked to call an ambulance, so he . . ." I faltered as I realized what I'd just said. For starters, Roy hadn't been too panicked to break the window in Nicholas's study in order to make it look as though a burglary had taken place. Furthermore, the brandy bottle and glasses had been removed before our arrival. As had the gun. I doubted I would have been so coolheaded in a situation of that nature. Caron would have been on the roof in a matter of seconds, screaming for an ambulance.

"You're looking pale," Malthea murmured. "Why don't we sit down in the back?"

I followed her into the office and cleared off a chair for her. "Would you like a cup of coffee?"

"That would be nice. It's rather chilly back here. Could you turn up the thermostat?"

"Certainly," I said mendaciously, since I'd yet to find a way to influence the boiler. I made decisive motions with a gizmo on the wall, then poured two cups of coffee and sank back down behind my desk, still puzzling over the discrepancies in Roy's story.

Malthea gave me a concerned frown. "Is something vexing you, Claire?"

"A couple of the things Roy said don't support his version of what happened. I guess I'd better call Sergeant Jorgeson and make sure he's aware of them." I reached for the telephone, then noticed her birdlike expression and said, "After we've finished our conversation, of course."

"Well, there is one little thing I believe I should tell you. If you think it's important, you can pass it on to your friend on the police force. I failed to mention in my statement that I returned to Nicholas's house shortly after midnight."

I choked on a mouthful of coffee, nearly spewing it across the desk. "You did what?"

"After Fern and I arrived at the duplex, we said good-night and went into our respective sides. I made tea and was trying to distract myself with my tarot cards when I heard her back door open. I peeked out my kitchen window. Fern was inside her greenhouse, sobbing uncontrollably. I wanted to rush to her side to offer comfort, but I knew she would be appalled to be discovered in such an emotional display. Oh, if only Nicholas had been there to see her misery."

"Because she was going to lose her greenhouse," I said.

"Her plants and the Sacred Grove of Keltria are all she has," Malthea said, taking a tissue out of her satchel to wipe the corner of her eye. "She's tried other hobbies, but nothing fascinates her more than puttering around the greenhouse, misting and repotting and pinching off dead blossoms. She'd sleep out there if it were feasible."

"There's no way she could have it moved?"

"She has very limited financial resources, and will most likely have to settle for a subsidized apartment complex for senior citizens. She can take a few of her leafy friends with her, but not the special ones that require a carefully regulated climate." She took another swipe at her eyes. "Nicholas did a terrible thing when he told her she had to move within thirty days. What's more, he was overreacting to the disagreement between himself and the Wiccan faction. The ultimate decision as to what's allowed during our rituals is up to the Arch Druid, and I assured him that I would not vacillate from my stated position."

I jumped in before she could lapse into a discourse on the variations in pagan practices. "So you went back to Nicholas's house to talk to him, right?"

"I knocked, then repeatedly rang the bell. Nicholas enjoyed doing things on his computer. I never quite understood what he did, but he always said what satisfaction it gave him. I assumed he was too immersed to hear me, so I went around to the back of the house, planning to tap on his study window. To my surprise, the kitchen door was wide open. When I saw his body, I almost swooned, but I pulled myself together at the last second and took a more careful look at the scene. I felt exactly like Sherlock Holmes as I deduced what had taken place."

"And what did you deduce?"

Malthea stared grimly at me. "I knew no burglar had been responsible for Nicholas's death, since neither of them would have sat down and enjoyed a bit of brandy. Mumsy did that once and came close to being arrested." She waggled her finger at me to prevent me from interrupting. "Therefore, whoever had been there was someone Nicholas knew well enough to offer hospitality. A chair was overturned, indicating there'd been a scuffle. It was obvious that the police and paramedics had not been alerted or it would have been very crowded in the kitchen." Her eyes shifted away from me and her hand fell to her lap. "Roy came to mind."

I was beginning to suspect where this was going. "Malthea, did you decide to make it look like a burglary in order to protect him?"

"How clever of you, Claire. I washed the glasses and put them away, wiped fingerprints off the brandy bottle and returned it to its cabinet, and broke the window in the study. After a final inspection to make sure I'd missed nothing, I locked the door behind me and went home. It was rather late by then, and I wanted as much rest as possible before our celebration at dawn."

"And said nothing to the police, of course," I said wearily. "Don't you know it's wrong to remove evidence from a crime scene?"

"I have a duty to protect Roy, and I was convinced that whatever had taken place was not his fault. He's a good boy at heart. When he matures, he'll forget about this satanic nonsense and become a productive member of society. I did what was necessary for him to have that opportunity. It was the least I could do."

I had a flash of insight into Peter's reaction whenever I made assertions of a similar nature. I was always proved correct, of course, which made it all the worse. Perhaps after Leslie counseled his mother, she could counsel him, too.

"I think we're finished," Malthea said as she stood

up and headed for the door. "You might want to clean your coffeepot on a more regular basis. It will decrease the bitterness."

I trotted after her. "You absolutely must go straight to the police department and tell all this to Sergeant Jorgeson. He's not going to be happy, but he may handle it better if it comes from you instead of me."

"Do you think so?" she asked. "I was under the impression you and he are good friends."

"Not that good," I said coldly. "Will you promise to go there now?"

"I'd planned to go out to the grove and meditate. It's very peaceful out there, with the wind rustling the leaves and the shadows creating a lovely quilt."

"It won't be peaceful when the cops arrive to drag you to the police department."

"My, you are in a cantankerous mood, aren't you? Do take my advice about cleaning the coffeepot. It might improve your disposition."

She gave me a bright little smile and left. I considered chasing after her with the feather duster, then took a couple of breaths and refilled my cup with perfectly decent coffee. I decided to wait fifteen minutes before calling Jorgeson in order to give Malthea a chance to do the honorable thing. I would not have bet on it.

While I waited, I thought about her story. Like Roy's, it was plausible; she certainly could have taken it upon herself to lecture Nicholas. That she'd gone there at twelve-thirty at night would have seemed unremarkable to her. Neither, apparently, did tidying up the scene to suggest a burglary. I wondered if all Arch Druids were as protective of their underlings as she.

I finally called the police department and asked to

speak to Jorgeson. He came on the line with a martyred, "Yes, Mrs. Malloy?"

"Has Malthea Hendlerson arrived there yet?"

"The one who insisted on singing some song about holly and ivy when she gave a statement yesterday? The one who claimed her mother'd had an affair with Archduke Francis Ferdinand just prior to his assassination? Her?"

" 'Fraid so," I said, then related what she'd said.

He was silent for a long moment. "Jeez, what with all the cop shows on television these days, I'd like to think civilians have some idea of the word 'tampering.' Which planet has that woman been living on for the last fifty years? How could she calmly wash the damn glasses and wipe prints off the bottle? Gad, we're lucky she didn't haul the body upstairs and tuck it in bed!"

"Or bury it in the woods," I said, grimacing as I realized how effortlessly I could envision her doing it. "In any case, she's admitted what she did, and it explains a lot of inconsistencies with Roy's description of what went on in the kitchen ... with one exception. She never mentioned the gun."

"So the kid took it with him. As it happens, there's a major inconsistency you haven't heard yet. I checked with the medical examiner and there was virtually no alcohol in the victim's blood. He hadn't been drinking brandy when he was shot."

"What do you think that means?"

"I'd like to ask Roy Tate that very same question," Jorgeson said with a trace of acerbity. "Everybody on patrol is keeping an eye out for him. The campus security guys are checking the buildings, but it's gonna take them all week because so many of them are off

duty when the college is closed. We'll find him sooner
or later, and he'd better have an explanation."

I told him where Malthea might be, then hung up.
Malthea and Roy had both attested to the presence of
the brandy bottle and glasses in the kitchen, and Roy
had said he smelled alcohol on Nicholas's breath. But
unless the lab report was wrong, Nicholas hadn't been
drinking. He could have been pretending to be drunk,
I supposed, and hoping to bully Roy into joining him.

Or Roy and Malthea were lying about this one particular detail. Was everything else they'd said lies, too?
There were more than enough members of the grove
for a full-fledged conspiracy, presuming three Druids
(Malthea, Fern, and Sullivan), two Wiccans (Morning
Rose and Gilda), and one satanist (Roy) could collabo-
rate without coming to blows. Based on what I'd seen
and heard, it did not seem likely.

I felt sorry for Jorgeson. He clearly had no clue how
to deal with his less than conventional witnesses. Standard police procedure was no match for someone
who'd casually stepped over a corpse to put away a
brandy decanter—and hadn't thought it was worthy
of mention until the following day.

When the phone rang, I eyed it unhappily. Malthea
calling to say the gun was in the dishwasher? Jorgeson calling to report that Roy'd been killed in a shoot-
out with the campus cops? Gilda calling to berate me
for not going to her trailer? Peter calling to announce
that he and Leslie were getting remarried in the Winter Palace, with canine attendants?

Scolding myself for this ultimate petty thought, I
picked up the receiver and chirped, "Book Depot."

"Mother," said Caron, her voice low and hoarse,
"can you pick me up at the mall?"

"Sure. At eight o'clock—right? Which entrance?"

"Now, in front of Sears."

"What's wrong?" I said. "Did you get fired?"

"It's a lot worse than that. Please hurry."

She hung up. I did the same, locked the store, and drove to the mall, speculating about what she'd find worse than getting fired and having to sacrifice her layaway purchases.

I navigated through the crowded parking lot and pulled up in front of the appointed entrance. Caron was leaning against the wall, her arms wrapped around herself and her face lowered as if she could will herself into invisibility. She seemed to be having a degree of success; none of the shoppers streaming in and out the doors so much as glanced at her.

I rolled down the window and called, "Caron?"

She jerked her head up as though a bullet had hit the pseudo-stuccoed wall, then focused in on me and darted to the car. As soon as she'd slammed the door, she said, "Drive!"

I glanced at her, but she'd bent over and her face was hidden. "Okay," I said with a great deal more composure than I felt. I worked my way back to the stoplight and eventually escaped from the parking lot.

"You can sit up now," I said.

"What's the point in doing that?" she said, her voice muffled.

"Well, we're not being pursued by a car packed with heavily armed gangsters. Should I be watching for a police car?"

"No." She sat up, ran her fingers through her hair, and let out a grandiose sigh. "You're not going to like this."

"Did you get fired?"

"I think you can safely assume I will be within a matter of hours. Before I go on, you have to promise not to start yelling at me—okay?"

I turned into the bowling alley lot and stopped. "I promise not to yell at you. It's only a part-time job, dear, and you hated it. Some of the stores will hire temps after Christmas to help handle returns. You can find something."

"What I need to find, Mother, is a lawyer."

CHAPTER 8

I sat on the sofa, reading the document that Caron had taken out of her purse. "What's MultiPackaging, Incorporated, in Dallas?"

Caron was draped across a chair opposite me, her fingertips brushing the floor and her eyes closed for maximum effect. "That's the all-powerful home office, and it's more likely to be in Oz than Texas. They run Santa's Workshops in malls all over the South and Midwest. They also do this kind of crap with the Easter Bunny, as well as studio portraits and videotaping of everything from birthday parties and weddings to class reunions. You can hire them to come into the delivery room. That's the grossest thing I've ever heard."

"North Hills Mall is down as a defendant, too. Who's Winifred Portmeyer?"

"Mrs. Claus. I'm surprised they didn't go after Santa himself, although the only thing he did was watch."

"That's all I did," I pointed out, "and I made the defendants' list as your guardian." I began to read aloud. " 'Comes now Morgan G. Connolly, by and through her guardians, Suzanne and Eric L. Connolly, and for their complaint, state and allege the following, to-wit: that the parties are—' "

"Residents of the county, blah, blah, blah," Caron said, sagging further into the chair until she resembled an afghan. "What matters is they're saying that I committed assault and battery, that Morgan was bruised so badly and in such a state of hysteria that she had to be treated by a doctor. Can you believe this?"

I continued reading. " 'The plaintiff suffered various bruises and lacerations and other injuries to her person for which she is entitled to a judgment against the defendants herein in the amount of ...' " My throat squeezed up so tightly that I couldn't say the figure.

"One million dollars," Caron said for me. "Go on to the next page, Mother."

I forced myself to turn the page. " 'That, also, the plaintiff suffered great emotional distress and has been unable to sleep or attend school, which was intentionally inflicted upon her by the defendants, for which she is entitled to unspecified punitive damages in an amount to be determined by a jury.' This happened less than twenty-four hours ago! So she had a bad night and wasn't in the mood this morning for whatever fancy private school she attends. How can they claim she's been permanently traumatized? I'll bet right now she's contentedly eating ice cream and watching Disney videos."

"Or ripping limbs off her dolls."

I tossed the complaint on the coffee table. "What about Inez?"

"She is such a wimp. She wanted to leave with me, but Mrs. Claus went ballistic and made her promise to work through Christmas Eve."

"What did Mrs. Claus say to you?"

Caron's lip inched out. "Well, after the guy shoved the papers at us and left, she grabbed my arm, dragged me into the employee lounge, and started in on me about how it was all my fault. I reminded her that she'd just stood there like a tick on a reindeer's rump when the brat slipped by me. The conversation went downhill after that. I tore off my antlers and said I was leaving, and she said not to come back until she's talked to her supervisor."

"I'd better call a lawyer," I said, gloomily wondering about prevailing legal fees. Although Caron had come perilously close to the brink of criminal charges, she'd never before taken a plunge into the abyss. The summons and complaint stated that we had thirty days to respond, and I doubted an articulate, artfully composed letter from me would suffice.

"Is there anything to eat?" asked Caron, sounding like the last orphan in line at the workhouse.

I took some money out of my billfold. "Why don't you go pick up Chinese? The car key's on the kitchen counter."

"Yeah, okay." She curled her lip at the document, then went through the kitchen and out the back door.

I fixed myself a cup of tea, and then looked up the telephone number of the only lawyer I knew in Farberville. It was hardly my lucky day, but Franklin Adamson was in his office and unencumbered with a client.

"Merry Christmas, Claire," he said. "How's everything? Business brisk?"

"I suppose," I said, then told him about the summons and complaint. "The whole thing is absurd," I added. "The child may have a bruise or two, but she definitely didn't suffer lacerations. Okay, so she skinned her knee when she fell down while running to her mother. They're making it sound as if Caron chased her around the mall with a carving knife."

"Welcome to the wacky world of litigation. Who's their attorney?"

I flipped to the second page. "The child's father, Eric L. Connolly. I suppose that's why this was filed at the approximate speed of light."

"The holiday season's usually slow for us. I'm trying to think if I've met Connolly. The name's familiar. I'll see what I can find out about him. I'm going to switch you back to my receptionist so you can make an appointment. Bring Caron and the papers."

"Franklin, damn it," I said, "are you saying there's a grain of validity in this? I can't believe it. The child threw a tantrum because she didn't get her way—and we're being sued? If anyone deserves to be sued, it's Suzanne and Eric L. for raising an ill-mannered, egotistical monster!"

"Vent if you must, but make an appointment," he said, "and whatever you do, don't initiate any contact with the child or her parents."

I made an appointment for the next morning at ten o'clock, then decided tea was inadequate for the occasion. I poured a stiff drink, returned to the sofa, and retrieved the complaint. I could have gone to the store and reopened for an hour, but my mood was vile enough to frighten potential customers, who would then sue me for "great emotional distress" and future bouts of insomnia brought on by the lack of mystery novels on the bedside table. Heaven help me if one stubbed a toe while fetching a magazine.

Caron returned with an array of cardboard cartons and very little change. "I'm not hungry right now," she said as she unloaded the bags. "Inez said she'll call me as soon as she gets home. I don't know how she's supposed to deal with the kids by herself, but you know what? I don't care. I don't even care if a pointy-headed elf topples off the roof of the gazebo and embeds itself in Mrs. Claus's skull. It would be an improvement."

I was heartened to hear a more characteristic edge in her voice, but she'd not spoken in capital letters in two days. I smiled and said, "I'll put the food away and you can warm it up later."

"The prisoner had a last meal of moo goo gai pan and sesame beef," she intoned, then retreated to her room. The door closed with a tiny click.

I reread the complaint until I could recite every word of it, from the header to the date the notary public's commission expired. I wanted to call Franklin back and say, "You were kidding—right? No judge is going to even tolerate this nonsense in his courtroom—right? Oh, you had me going there for a minute, but we both know you were teasing me—right?"

Wrong.

An hour later, the telephone rang. I waited, assuming Caron would answer it, but it continued to ring. I picked up the receiver and said, "Hello."

"Mrs. Malloy, it's Jorgeson. We've got a problem."

"You have a problem, and I have a problem. However, we do not have the *same* problem unless you're being sued for a million dollars."

"Huh?"

"What do you want?" I asked.

"First, we found Malthea Hendlerson where you said and brought her in. She told me the same thing she told you. When I asked her about the brandy bottle, she insisted it had been on the table with one glass and the other glass was on the floor. She couldn't explain why the lab didn't find alcohol in the victim's blood and stuck to her story. There wasn't anything to do but let her leave."

"Is that your problem, Jorgeson? I could have told you that's what would happen."

"No, I was just telling you. The problem is another of those dadburned Druids. I put a man out at Nicholas Chunder's place to watch for Roy Tate in case he went to his apartment or tried to get the hearse. The officer caught Gilda D'Orcher trying to break into the main house. We've got her in custody, but she won't say anything except that she wants to talk to you. She's kept it up for a couple of hours. Doesn't want a lawyer, doesn't want to make a call, doesn't want coffee or anything to eat."

"Perhaps she'll change her mind after spending the night in a cell," I said without sympathy. "Your amenities are not on par with a luxury hotel. Give her a couple of prostitutes and drug addicts for cellmates."

He was silent for a minute. "I thought you'd want to talk to her, find out why she was breaking into the house. Listen, I've kept my end of the bargain. Lieutenant Rosen called this afternoon and I didn't mention your name when I gave him a synopsis of the case. I can't say what I would have done if he demanded particulars, but he seemed kinda distracted and didn't press me. This business with his mother must be getting him down."

"That would explain it," I said through clenched teeth. "I have an appointment in the morning. If Gilda hasn't capitulated by noon or so, call me at the bookstore and I'll think about it. Right now I have a headache and entirely too many other things to worry about—and not one of them is Lieutenant Rosen's mother."

I nibbled at the Chinese food and tried to finish a novel, but I found myself searching the complaint for fine print that would expose it as an idle threat or an unamusing practical joke. Lawyers were not notorious for that sort of thing, I told myself.

By eight o'clock I'd made little headway with the food or the fine print. My headache had eased, but I suspected it would rekindle itself in Franklin's office in the morning. I was considering a long, steamy bath when the doorbell rang.

I opened the front door and found myself looking at an unfamiliar woman. She was in her thirties, with short dark hair, a slender body clothed in a gray silk suit, and the resolute demeanor of someone intent on selling beauty products. "Yes?" I said.

"Mrs. Malloy, I'm Winifred Portmeyer. We need to talk. May I come in?"

She was already inside before she'd finished the question, rendering it moot. She sat down, crossed her legs, and opened a briefcase. "Is Caron home? She needs to be included in this discussion since it affects her, too."

"I'll get her." As I went down the hallway, I recalled my brief impression of Mrs. Claus bent over the camera and then straightening up to glare at Caron. I'd been right about the white wig—and wrong about the ample rump. I tapped on Caron's door, then opened it and in a low voice, said, "Mrs. Claus is in the living room."

"That's not funny," Caron said without looking up from the magazine spread across her lap.

"Sorry, dear, but she really is and she wants to talk to you."

"Tell her you came in here and found me hanging from the light fixture, my eyes bulging and my tongue blue. Threaten to sue her if she doesn't leave."

"Please come into the living room so we can get this over," I said. "I assure you I'm not any more delighted at the opportunity than you are, but she seems like the sort who will sit there all night."

"Let her."

After a few more exchanges of this nature, Caron threw down the magazine and trailed me back to the living room.

"Hello, Caron," the woman said smoothly. "Why don't you and your mother sit there on the sofa? Shall we get started?"

I sat down, but Caron remained standing behind the sofa, her arms crossed and her lower lip trembling. "Has Caron been fired?" I asked, attempting to regain some control of the situation, since we were in my apartment and not the corporate boardroom in Dallas.

Ms. Portmeyer nodded. "Yes, she has. I'll calculate her pay and she can pick up the check tomorrow. The cost of the hood will be deducted, as well as having the tunic dry-cleaned for the next reindeer."

"Good luck finding one," muttered Caron. "Talk about a stupid, demeaning—"

"And the lawsuit?" I cut in quickly. "That *is* why you're here, isn't it?"

"Yes, indeed," she said. She rummaged through papers in her briefcase, but as far as I could tell, she was doing so only to impress us with her professionalism. "I spoke with Mr. Longsterger in the Dallas office about this. He'll have to consult the legal department, but in previous cases of a like nature, MultiPack has settled with the plaintiff in order to avoid negative publicity. We wouldn't want the media to pounce on a story about someone suing Santa, would we? It could have a devastating effect on children too young to make the distinction."

Despite her slick presentation, I got the message. "MultiPack, as you call it, is going to pay off the Connolly family to keep them quiet?"

"I should think that will be the ultimate decision. Our insurance carries a liability clause. North Hills Mall has a similar policy and will most likely choose to settle, too. They prefer a reputation as a place where children are safe from physical injury and emotional distress."

"What about you?" asked Caron.

She flashed small white teeth. "As a MultiPack employee, the liability covers me from any lawsuit resulting from my assignment. I've been with them for fifteen years. I started out just as you did, then did a degree in business law, and went on to become an assistant regional season events director. We've used the same Mrs. Claus in Farberville for several years, but she was taken ill at the last moment and I stepped in as a replacement. Sacrifices must be made for the good of the corporation."

I gave her a cold look. "Caron was an employee at the time. Is she covered?"

"I'm afraid she isn't, since she was a part-time employee and therefore not entitled to any benefits. It's made quite clear in the contract she signed. I believe it's paragraph eleven, subsection four, item eight." Ms. Portmeyer closed her briefcase and stood up. "I'm glad to have met you, Mrs. Malloy. Caron, I enjoyed

working with you while it lasted. I hope you'll remember us fondly."

"Wait a minute!" I said as I stood up. "Let me make
sure I have this straight. You, MultiPack, and the mall
are bailing out of the lawsuit, leaving Caron and me to
face the possibility of a million-dollar judgment. Is
that correct?"

She held out a business card. "This has the telephone
and fax numbers of our legal department should your
attorneys wish to be in communication with them. If
Caron has misplaced her copy of her contract, I have
the original which can be placed in evidence. I can also
provide the manual given to her; it contains very precise guidelines on the policy of handling difficult customers. Physical roughness is explicitly forbidden."

Caron moved in front of the door, blocking Ms.
Portmeyer's withdrawal. "What was I supposed to
do, then? Let her go up on the stage and knock other
kids off Santa's lap?"

Ms. Portmeyer blinked. "Oh, no, that would have
resulted in a lawsuit, too. It's unfortunate that you
didn't take time to study the manual, Caron. You
would have made a fine senior reindeer in years to
come. Because of what happened, MultiPack cannot
continue any association that might taint our image as
a family-focused organization."

Caron looked as though she was ready to punch her
ex-boss in the nose, which no doubt would have resulted in yet another lawsuit. I hastily clutched her elbow and pulled her away from the door. "Good night,
Ms. Portmeyer," I said. "You'll be hearing from my
attorney within a matter of days."

"Good night," she said, then went through the doorway and down the stairs.

I released Caron's arm and told her about the appointment in the morning with Franklin Adamson. "Why don't you sleep in? I have a few things to do at the store, and then I'll come by and pick you up at a quarter till ten."

"I feel like I'm on drugs. I mean, this has to be a hallucination, doesn't it? One minute I'm a dorky reindeer, the next minute a defendant in a million-dollar lawsuit. Maybe we should just hop in the car like you said and take off—and never come back. Is there some kind of booksellers' underground railroad?"

"Good night, dear."

The session in the law office was more painful than an equivalent amount of time on a rack in a dungeon. Franklin emphasized the severity of the situation and the very real possibility of a judgment in favor of the plaintiffs. MultiPackaging and North Hills Mall were within their respective corporate rights to settle out of court for whatever amount was necessary to be detached from the complaint. What's more, we'd never find out how much they'd paid.

I'd brightened a bit when Franklin had said Caron was entitled—perhaps—to indemnification from Multi-Packaging. The crumb having been offered, he'd then snatched it away by adding that our lawsuit against them could drag on into the next century.

Caron was atypically subdued during the session, and was no more animated as we got into the car. "I'm sorry about this, Mother. Maybe I should have read the manual like she said."

"Don't be silly," I said, squeezing her shoulder. "I would have done the same thing, as would anyone. The manual is apt to contain nothing more than vague policies so that MultiPack can claim to have provided sufficient training for new employees. When you point-blank asked Ms. Portmeyer what you should have done, she didn't have an answer." I started the car. "Do you want me to take you to the mall so you can pick up your check?"

Caron sniffled rather endearingly. "No, Inez said she'd get it and come by tonight. Drop me off at Luanne's store. I think I'd better get used to wearing secondhand clothes."

I did as she asked, then continued to the Book Depot and took the "closed" sign off the door. This did not result in a mad rush of customers, alas, but eventually a professor I knew from the English department ambled in and we spent a pleasant hour deconstructing Dickens's *A Christmas Carol* over coffee. He bought a couple of sugary romance novels, claiming they were for his wife, but I knew her taste ran more to erotic time-travel fantasies.

No man is a hero to his valet—or to his bookseller.

Franklin had made it clear that there was nothing Caron and I could do except wait to see what developed. He would file our response (presumably, just legalese jargon for "did not!") and request copies of reports from the child's physician and whoever performed the psychological evaluation. Pacing and tearing out my hair were counterproductive.

"It could be worse," I said out loud, testing the level of conviction I could achieve without sounding completely deranged. Not much, I concluded, and I had a feeling I was going to be spouting that particular cliché many times over the next thirty days.

I needed a distraction. Although I'd lost all interest in the Druids, including Roy's current whereabouts and Malthea's motive for lying about the brandy decanter, I decided I might as well come to Jorgeson's aid and find out what Gilda wanted.

I dialed the station, and when put through to Jorgeson, said, "Do you still want me to talk to Gilda?"

"No, that's all right," he said. "She's not gonna be talking to anybody today."

"You said she specifically mentioned me."

"I went ahead and had her in a cell overnight. She got hold of a sharp object, maybe a piece of glass or something, and carved up her wrists. We took her to the hospital for a brief stop in the emergency room and at least twenty-four hours in the psych ward."

"Good grief," I said, stunned.

"There was another prisoner in there with her—just a woman who'd had too much to drink and broke a beer bottle over her boyfriend's head. The woman was still woozy, but she said Gilda was acting really weird and weaving around the cell, calling out long foreign-sounding names. It scared the woman so badly that she put the blanket over her head."

"Not an unreasonable response," I said. "Has anybody heard from Roy Tate?"

"Not yet, and I'm catching some hell from the captain. We've got around-the-clock surveillance at the victim's place, and patrolmen cruising past the Druids' houses every half hour or so. He's probably holed up at a friend's house."

"What about Gilda's trailer?"

"We've been there, and the manager promised to keep an eye on it. You know, Mrs. Malloy, I liked it better when you had other things on your mind. Why don't you go shopping or make a fruitcake?"

I didn't need to make a fruitcake; I was acquainted

with several of them, and in the middle of the afternoon, one entered the store, accompanied by her two well-bundled offspring.

"What's going on with Roy?" Morning Rose demanded as she came to the counter. "The police came to our house last night looking for him, and they've been driving by all day. Do they have evidence he had something to do with Nicholas's death?"

"They seem to think they do," I said. "Have you heard from him since yesterday morning?"

She shoved her children toward a display of cookbooks. "Go look at all the yummy food," she said, then turned back to me. "I called him yesterday afternoon to make sure he was all right. He's much more sensitive than anyone suspects, and prone to depression. It's a result of his studies in the realm of evil forces that are capable of toying with our individual destinies. He's seen things most of us have never imagined could exist, and is periodically overwhelmed with an agonizing sense of impotence and—"

"What did he say when you called?"

She took off her gloves and aligned them on the counter. "Not much, really. He wasn't especially fond of Nicholas, and in fact, a month ago he told me that there was something about Nicholas that made him uneasy. Nicholas affected others of us the same way. He was very private about his business and personal affairs. We saw him only on major holidays."

"He was your landlord, wasn't he?" I asked, straining to hear noises from behind the rack. "Didn't he come by to collect the rent every month?"

"Sullivan mailed him the check. No, Nicholas had a side of him that was every bit as sinister as Roy's demons. Who knows what might have gone on inside his house? He chose it for its isolation, he once told me. I intuitively realized that he didn't want anyone to see who visited him at night."

"Don't you think you ought to see what your children are doing?"

"They always like to explore a new environment on their own terms. Do you have any idea where Roy is?"

"No more than I do of what"—I braced myself to say the names—"Cosmos and Rainbow have found so fascinating. Please make sure they aren't damaging any books."

"They would never do anything like that. When I talked to Roy, he was terribly worried that he wouldn't be allowed to stay in the carriage house. He knew Sullivan wouldn't let him move back in with us. Because of his mother's substance problems, he was placed in foster homes several times, and he hated them."

"Where's his mother now?" I asked, increasingly concerned about the future salability of the cookbooks.

Morning Rose shrugged. "Roy doesn't know. When he first moved in with his father, he talked to her on the phone every week. Then, without warning, the phone was disconnected. Roy called a neighbor, who said his mother had packed her belongings and left town with a man she met at a nightclub."

"A tragic story," I said. "Will you please check on your children?"

"Oh, all right," she said sulkily, "although you seem to have an unhealthy obsession with their behavior." She disappeared around the rack, then returned with a smug smile. "They're sitting quietly, looking at photographs in cookbooks. A perfectly innocent activity, wouldn't you say?"

I was growing rather tired of being accused of sub-standard attributes. What's more, her children were quite capable of *licking* photographs instead of looking at them. I waited a moment to allow my irritation to subside, then said, "Has Roy ever mentioned any friends or fellow satanists in Farberville?"

"He doesn't make friends easily. His mother moved so often over the last six years that I doubt he has friends anywhere. I've never heard him mention any names."

"How did he become a member of the grove?"

Morning Rose made a vague gesture. "That was Malthea's doing, and I don't remember the details. She struck up a conversation with him and he attended our Samhain celebration at Halloween. No, that wasn't the first. He was with us for the autumnal equinox, which was about the time his father was informed that the grant was approved. They wanted him to accompany them to Borneo, but he refused." She picked up her gloves and twisted them. "I wish Sullivan hadn't made Roy move out of our house. None of this would have happened."

"Are you sure?" I asked. "Wouldn't Nicholas still have been upset by the intrusion of Wiccan and satanic practices?"

She gave me a cross look. "Oh, I suppose, but Roy would have been asleep in the upper bunk in Cosmos's room and therefore have had an alibi. Do the police suspect him just because he was conveniently nearby—or are they being prejudiced against him because of his religious beliefs?"

"You'll have to ask them. Look, Morning Rose, I think it would be better if you collected your children and left before one of them starts ripping out pages for souvenirs."

She leaned forward. "Do you swear you don't know where Roy is?"

As I stared at her, the rack of paperback fiction came crashing down on her back. I was amazed at the number of books that went flying through the air.

Simply amazed.

CHAPTER 9

It took the remainder of the afternoon to replace the paperbacks in a semblance of order. Morning Rose had hustled away her children without offering to help undo their damage. It was just as well, since I might have said something that would stifle the cognitive development of her ignoble little savages.

I was locking up when Luanne came into the store. "Caron told me what happened," she said in the breathy gush of a forties' actress. "Are you okay?"

"I'm not worried. All I have to do is make it out to the mall and ask Santa to bring me a million dollars for Christmas. Maybe I'd better ask for an extra couple of thousand to cover legal fees. Franklin dropped his rate to seventy-five dollars an hour, but he warned me it could add up, especially if we go to court. Start thinking about what you'll wear on the witness stand."

"Something modest, I suppose, with a high neckline and white cuffs. I've always fancied myself in a hat with a veil. Is that too British?"

I grinned at her, but it must not have been convincing because she gave me a hug and said, "Don't worry about it, Claire."

"Don't worry about it?" I laughed, perhaps a bit maniacally. I moved away from her and stared at the racks and shelves of books, all begging to be bought, savored, lovingly tucked on a shelf, and brought out again on occasion to be reread. "What if I lose the store?"

"You can marry Peter for his money and lead a life of self-indulgence. Breakfasts in bed, lunches at trendy cafés, candlelight dinners at romantic country inns. I got in a consignment last week that included a floor-length beaded dress. It's red, but you can still borrow it for the wedding. I know—we'll go for a theme! Peter can rent a Santa Claus suit and hire three-foot-tall groomsmen. I don't think we can persuade Caron to don a reindeer outfit, though. She's inordinately hostile toward the species."

I tried to hide the sudden pain that seemed to char my internal organs like a flamethrower. "No mistletoe in the bridal bouquet, okay?"

"Do you want to have a beer across the street?" asked Luanne. "Better yet, we can pick up tacos and a bottle of cheap wine, then go to my place to start working on a guest list. I've always regretted paying my daughter to elope and thus depriving myself of the opportunity to play bridal consultant. I adore bossing people around."

"Not tonight," I said, struggling to hold back tears. Like Fern, I have an aversion to being caught in a public display of emotion, and the last thing I needed was puffy eyelids in the morning. Puffy eyelids do not become me. "Where's Caron?"

"I offered her a ride, but she said she had some last-minute shopping to do."

"I hope she buys me the biggest bottle of aspirin in the drugstore," I said with a grimace.

After Luanne left, I took a last look at the paper-backs to make sure that lusty barbarian princesses had not crept among teapots and cats, then went home. Caron had come and gone; a note on the kitchen table announced that she was stopping by Rhonda Maguire's and then spending the night at Inez's house.

I had no appetite, but I forced down a few bites of moo goo gai pan while I watched the local news. A woman with stiff hair and capped teeth appeared on the screen, with the Primrose Hill house in the back-ground. I was relieved when she said only that a local doctor had been brutally slain in his home and the po-lice were investigating possible leads. The next seg-ment featured kindergarten children belting out an adenoidal version of "The Twelve Days of Christmas."

Fearing an encore, I switched off the television. The complaint lay on the coffee table in all its accusatory glory, but I ordered myself to ignore it. Perhaps I should have had dinner with Luanne, I thought as I roamed around the apartment, picking up books and then putting them down, taking a load of fuzz-encrusted dishes from Caron's room to the kitchen sink, rear-ranging tinsel on the Christmas tree, and basically do-ing everything I could in order not to imagine Peter and Leslie in an intimate setting. They were much more likely to be seated in his mother's formal living room, chaperoning the couple. Unless, of course, My-ron had whisked away his beloved to a restaurant, and Peter and Leslie were in a less formal room.

With no chaperons.

A major distraction was needed. In that I had no background in economics, balancing the federal bud-get was out of the question. It was too late to dash out for a dozen rolls of wallpaper and a bucket of paste.

I'd promised Franklin that I wouldn't so much as drive by the residence of Morgan, Suzanne, and Eric L., much less deposit a gaily wrapped box of manure on their porch. If I relented and went to Luanne's, eventually I'd tell her about Peter and Leslie, and then embarrass both of us with an unattractive bout of wailing and gnashing of teeth.

I found a notebook and sat down at the kitchen table to contemplate the cast of characters from the Sacred Grove of Keltria. I wrote down what I knew of Roy's background; none of it seemed very positive, from his splintered family to his alleged use of drugs. Fern's husband had died ten years ago, leaving her with a minimal income and a passion for all things botanical. I added what Jorgeson had told me about Nicholas Chunder. The fact that he'd been married did not have significant impact on Roy's credibility. The lack of alcohol in his blood, on the other hand, did.

I moved along. Sullivan Sawyer was a grad student in anthropology. Morning Rose home-schooled her children and prepared vegetarian casseroles. Gilda D'Orcher worked at the hospital, lived in a trailer, and traveled by bicycle (and broom, possibly). I drew a question mark beside her name as I tried to come up with an explanation for her peculiar behavior.

When nothing suggested itself, I wrote Malthea's name at the bottom of the page. I didn't need any more space, since I knew nothing about her except her address for the last two years. Had she lived in another state or in another part of town? Was she widowed, divorced, or steadfastly single? She'd spent more than a hundred dollars on books, so she had some discretionary income. From a pension or from selling nosegays of holly and mistletoe on the street?

I turned to a clean page and wrote down a timetable that began with the arrival of the group at Nicholas's house to decorate and concluded with Malthea's return after midnight. I wondered where the others had been during that period. Despite their indisputable idiosyncrasies, they were liable to have been performing commonplace rituals, such as watching television, reading, and sleeping. In Fern's case, misting plants; in Nicholas's, cruising the Internet. The Sawyers had children to be bathed, disarmed, and put to bed. Gilda might have been poring through dusty old volumes of curses for something suitably malevolent for Nicholas.

I kept coming back to Roy's confession. He'd taken a risk by hiding in my car so that he could tell me his story. His reluctance to do so at the police station was understandable. It just didn't quite play.

I was staring at my notes, my chin resting on a fist, when the telephone rang. It seemed as though every call lately had been disastrous, and it was tempting to let it go unanswered. However, Caron was not safely ensconced in her bedroom, so there was the possibility she might be calling about bail.

As soon as I'd said hello, Peter said, "Good, I caught you at home."

"Where did you think I'd be—down at the gym playing basketball with the college boys?"

"I thought you might be out shopping or having dinner with Luanne."

"I couldn't handle that much excitement. What do you want?"

He gave a rueful chuckle. "I was wrong when I said Myron was after my mother's money. He's rolling in it. He has a lodge in a ski resort in Vermont, and has invited all of us to go up there for Christmas."

"All of us?" I echoed.

"Yes, all of us. Leslie doesn't need to be back in her office until after New Year's Day, and the kennel's agreed to keep Boris and Igor. She's a serious skier. I, on the other hand, will undoubtedly break a leg and have to be brought down the mountain on one of those silly-looking sleds."

"I'm sure you're an excellent skier," I said.

"It's been a while. Anyway, I wanted to let you know not to expect me for nine or ten days. I'm sorry I won't be there for Christmas or New Year's Eve, but this will be a good opportunity to get to know Myron."

"I guess you already know Leslie—or has she changed since the divorce?"

I was hoping to hear how she'd gained a hundred pounds and lost her teeth, so I was disappointed when Peter said, "Not that I've noticed, but she only arrived this afternoon. Everybody's waiting in the limo for me, so I'd better say good-bye."

"Have a lovely time in Vermont, Peter." I hung up and sat back down at the kitchen table, ashamed of my acerbic remarks. He'd had the decency to pretend not to notice, but neither of us was fooling the other.

I was in the terminal stage of the Sour Grape Syndrome, and it was not pretty.

I debated calling Luanne and spilling out my pitiful plight, but decided against it. What I needed to do, I told myself resolutely, was to put all of this out of my mind and recover a modicum of self-respect by resolving Nicholas Chunder's murder to my own satisfaction. If Roy had committed it, then all I needed was an explanation for the enigmatic brandy decanter and glasses. This would require me to question him, which was a bit of a problem since no one knew where he was.

He'd taken refuge in Fern's greenhouse the previous evening and might have returned; it was not a night for camping out under a bush. Anyone dressed in black would have no problems avoiding being spotted by a cruising patrol car.

I put on my coat and went down the steps to the garage. I made sure Roy wasn't there, either, then drove to Fern's and Malthea's duplex and parked. Lights were on in both sides, but drapes were drawn. I approached with admirable stealth and found a slit that gave me a limited view of Malthea's living room.

She was talking on the telephone while toying with what I recognized as tarot cards on the table in front of her. Her expression was so absorbed that I was reluctant to interrupt her.

Fern did not respond to my repeated knocks. I went around the side yard to the gate. This time I found a latch, let myself into the backyard, and was pleased to see a glow inside the greenhouse.

The glass panels were milky with condensed humidity, but there was a hint of movement. I wasn't sure of the etiquette for barging into a greenhouse and startling its occupant into overmisting. I finally tapped and let myself inside.

Fern looked up at me. "Claire?"

My lungs were clogged with air so warm and wet that I could barely breathe. "Steamy, isn't it?" I croaked.

"Some of the tropical species require it," she said without inflection. "Is there a reason why you're here?"

Most of my resolve was leaking through my pores and forming beads of sweat on my surfaces. "I'm concerned about Roy. No one's heard from him all day. Did Malthea tell you what happened?"

"Some of it, yes."

"He needs to turn himself in," I said, fanning my face with one hand. The heat and humidity were more like an equatorial rain forest than a sunny island. Admittedly, the plants were thriving. Everywhere I looked I saw brilliant oranges, pinks, yellows, and reds. Leaves were dark green, tendrils thick and hardy enough to strangle a small dog.

Or a bookseller.

"I haven't seen Roy," Fern said.

"He didn't come back here?"

She gave me a pinched smile. "Wouldn't I have seen him if he did?"

Time for a new tactic, I told myself. "These are all so lovely, Fern. You must have a green thumb."

"They do thrive here, don't they? I used the last of the insurance money to have this built, and it's been a pleasure and sanctuary for me ever since." She put down a trowel and came around the edge of a table. "What will happen now? Will Nicholas's heirs sell the property?"

"I don't know, but probate takes a long time and you may not have to move anytime soon. Malthea said you were distressed about giving up your greenhouse." I waited a moment, then added, "I can see why. This is a different world, isn't it?"

"It's different," she said as if speaking to a particularly dim child. "Do you see these yellow berries? One of them can kill an adult in a matter of minutes. I find it odd that they're so attractive and yet so fatal. Mother Nature can be naughty." She pointed at a plant with spiky orange pods. "This is a castor-oil plant. The seeds are very poisonous."

I eyed it, then edged back toward the door in case it was exuding fumes. "Did Malthea tell you that she returned to Nicholas's house after the brouhaha?"

"I don't believe that," Fern said as she began to dig into the soil surrounding a feathery fern. "I would have seen her."

"You would have seen her drive away?"

"Is your hearing defective? I would have seen her at Nicholas's house, or at least passed her car on the road." She yanked the plant out of the pot and grimly thrust it into a larger one, seemingly oblivious of the soil spilling on her shoes. "I am more than capable of recognizing her car. It's dreadfully noisy and emits billows of black smoke. I don't know how many times I've told her to have the oil changed, but she's too stubborn. My husband stressed the importance of proper automobile maintenance. I have my oil changed every two thousand miles."

I frowned at her. "You went back to Nicholas's house the night he was murdered?"

"I just said so, didn't I?" She took the newly repotted plant to a sink and turned on the tap. "Setting the roots is a vital step in the process. It packs down the dirt and compresses air pockets. Air pockets can lead to bacteria."

I felt as though I had more than one such pocket in my brain. "Let's talk some more about this, Fern. When did you go back—and why?"

"I went back at eleven, and obviously in hopes that I might persuade Nicholas to change his mind. This business about the Wiccans was ridiculous, and he no more would have enjoyed living in Wales than he would in a dwelling made of mud and wattle. He was not friendly, but he invited me inside and allowed me to sit at the kitchen table. I suggested we talk over brandy. I could sense that he was uneasy, but I had little sympathy since he'd brought this crisis on himself with his childishness. He brought out the decanter and glasses and poured a bit for both of us."

"And drank it?"

Fern began rearranging a tray of seedlings in tiny pots. "I wasted no time in telling him what I thought of his petty display earlier in the evening. He spat out a mouthful of brandy and threatened to throw me out of his house. It was clear that he was beyond reason, so I returned to my car and sat until I felt calm enough to drive home. I am not accustomed to being treated that way. My deceased husband, rest his soul, was always solicitous of my feelings and never so much as raised his voice. Not, of course, that he ever had reason to do so."

I wasn't interested in the late Mr. Lewis, no matter how he died. "How long did you sit in your car?"

"Until I realized I was shivering not from shock but from cold. Ten minutes, I'd say."

"Did you see lights on in Roy's apartment?"

"I believe so, and I could hear the caterwauling that passes as music with today's youth. It's disgraceful. I don't know why their parents allow them to listen to such garbage. Music should have a melody and lyrics that contain no obscenities." She looked down at the rows and smiled to herself. "I'm finished for the evening, Claire. I suggest we walk through my apartment so you can leave through the front door like a proper guest."

Her rebuke was hard to miss, but I merely said, "It

is rather dark in the yard. There's something I don't understand. If you arrived at eleven, it sounds as though you left no later than eleven-thirty. Malthea claims she was there after midnight."

Fern shoved me out the door and flipped off the lights in the greenhouse. I thought she might ignore my question, but after a moment, she said, "Then my previous statement was in error. I was confused about the time. This has been so dreadfully upsetting that it's a wonder I can remember anything that's happened. The winter solstice is meant to be a glorious celebration, not a nightmare of rage and violence. You must excuse this lapse on my part."

She continued to apologize as she propelled me through the apartment, and I found myself on the front porch before I could get in another word. "Good night," she said, then closed the door. Seconds later, the lights in the living room went off.

Good night, Fern.

Malthea was still holding the receiver to her ear, but the tarot cards had been replaced with standard ones and she appeared to be playing solitaire. She spoke steadily for a few moments, paused to shift a card, and then resumed.

Gilda was not available and it was too late to drop by the Sawyers' house. I drove home, thinking about Fern's account of her visit. It explained the presence of the bottle and glasses, and also Roy's assertion that he'd smelled booze on Nicholas's breath. There was no alcohol in Nicholas's blood because he'd spat it out. It was all falling into place so neatly that I wouldn't have been surprised to find Morning Rose in my garage, ready to tell me how she'd gone back to Primrose Hill at precisely twelve-fifteen and taken away the murder weapon.

As I went inside, the telephone started to ring. It was not apt to be Peter, who was in a limo headed for a lodge in Vermont. Would he be sharing a bedroom with Myron, while his mother and Leslie shared the other one and stayed up all night, giggling and giving each other pedicures? If there were lots of bedrooms, how much tiptoeing might take place in dark hallways? Myron might be rolling in money, but what would Peter be rolling in?

I realized the telephone was still ringing. I picked up the receiver and waited silently.

"Mrs. Malloy?" said Jorgeson. "Are you there?"

I exhaled. "Yes, I'm here. It's eight o'clock, Jorgeson. Don't you ever go home?"

"I went home at five, and as soon as I got there, my wife dragged me out to the mall. It's how I imagine the Black Hole of Calcutta would be if everyone had American Express and Visa. Haggard faces, dazed eyes, twitchy fingers, bad tempers. Not a healthy place."

"Are you calling me to pass along your sociological insights into a great American tradition, Jorgeson? Couldn't you have waited until tomorrow?"

"Thing is, I got beeped in the middle of Sears. The murder weapon's been found, and I thought you'd want to know. It's registered to Randall Tate."

"Roy's father?"

"Randall ain't his dog, Mrs. Malloy. He's owned the gun for ten years."

"And you're sure it's the murder weapon?"

"The only thing I'm *sure* of is that my wife's still at the mall, buying everything that's left to teach me a lesson. You need any sheets? She's real fond of sheets."

I sat down and rubbed my eyes. "Where was the gun found?"

"In the hearse, which is appropriate in a screwball way. There's a compartment under the carpet in the back part. I dunno why, unless the funeral director needed a place for his wallet during the cemetery service—or he plucked watches and jewelry off his customers during the ride. Anyway, you see the problem, don't you?"

If I'd rubbed any harder, I would have peeled off a layer of cells. "Yes, Jorgeson, I see it. Nicholas didn't pull a gun on Roy. Roy took the gun with him when he went into the house. This seems a tad premeditated, doesn't it? He either sensed what might happen and armed himself, or he had an entirely different agenda."

"The real reason I called was to warn you, Mrs. Malloy. Randall Tate owns another handgun. All of his furniture and personal belongings are in storage, and it'll be a couple of days before we can determine if it's there. You need to be careful. Roy lied to you."

"That doesn't mean he's going to stalk me," I said, glancing uneasily at the kitchen window. "All I know is what these Druids insist on telling me. By the way, I listened to yet another casual confession this evening." I repeated the gist of Fern's story. "Tidy, isn't it?"

"That's what my wife puts in the toilet bowl," Jorgeson said without amusement. "I wish the lieutenant was here to figure these people out. I don't think even one of them is telling the truth."

"As in the whole truth, and nothing but the truth? I

don't think we've heard a pitiful fraction of the truth," I said. "What are you going to do about Roy?"

Jorgeson grumbled under his breath. "Same thing we've been doing, which is hoping to catch him on campus or walking down the street. We know where he's not—and that's about it. If he approaches you, Mrs. Malloy, don't offer him eggnog and cookies. Get hold of me or whoever's on duty. The boy could be dangerous."

I replaced the receiver and went into the living room. Roy's version of what had happened in Nicholas's kitchen might inspire an R-rated Disney film, but not a documentary. It had been holding up rather well until now; Malthea and Fern had covered a few glitches, and Morning Rose had volunteered several comments about Nicholas's questionable motive for living in isolation.

Only two more shopping days till Christmas, I thought as I gazed at the packages under the tree. I'd planned to give Peter a hefty book about the history of some football organization; for reasons unfathomable to me, he seemed enamored of bearish men knocking each other to the ground.

The book was among the other packages, meticulously wrapped and adorned with a big silver bow. Clearly he would not open it Christmas morning— or any other morning until January was under way. Leaving it there would only serve as a reminder of where he was.

I considered putting the book on a closet shelf, but even its unseen presence in the apartment would wear away at me like an endlessly dripping faucet.

I decided to take the book back to the store, and

then see if I could persuade Luanne to watch a movie rather than plan a wedding. If she persisted in harping on the subject (and she could be very persistent after a few glasses of wine), I would feign the onset of flu symptoms and allow myself to be ejected.

The wind was colder than it had been earlier, and gusting imperiously. Brittle leaves scratched across the floor of the garage. I quickly got in the car, started it, and gave it a moment to warm up. As I waited, I tried to recall the last time I'd had the oil changed. It was definitely more than two thousand miles ago.

The streets were almost empty as I drove alongside the campus and turned on Thurber Street. Anybody playing with a full deck (tarot or conventional) was at home, wearing warm bedroom slippers and munching popcorn.

I parked behind the Book Depot, grabbed the package, and hurried to the back door. My teeth were chattering by the time I managed to get the key in the lock and push open the protesting door. I stomped my feet to announce my presence to the nighttime denizens, some with six legs and some with brown fur, long tails, and an irksome habit of leaving traces of their presence along the baseboards.

It was tempting to unwrap the book and return it to its rightful rack, but that would be an admission of abject defeat by lovely, capricious, athletic, wealthy Leslie.

"Stop this!" I said loudly. "You are being more immature than Nicholas and Peter combined."

I dropped the book on my desk and went outside. I stood for a moment to let the wind batter me, hoping its frigidity would bring me to my senses.

When all it did was sting my face, I got in the car and reached for the ignition switch.

"Good evening," said a voice from the backseat.

This was getting old.

CHAPTER 10

"Where do you want to go tonight, Roy?" I said without bothering to return his greeting. "The lot by the stadium is closed, so we can't go back there. How about the police station?"

"What did the guy say when you told him?"

"He said that you ought to turn yourself in."

Roy grabbed my shoulder. "So he believes me? I mean, he understands that it wasn't my fault because Nicholas said he was going to kill me. All I was doing was protecting myself. You told him that, didn't you, Mrs. Malloy?"

"I repeated exactly what you told me. Why didn't you mention all the traffic in front of the house that night? It must have rivaled the parking lot at the mall."

I could hear him sucking on his lip as he thought about it. "I guess I had the music pretty loud. Once I thought I saw headlights, but I didn't bother to look out the window."

"Why would you?" I said comfortingly, if inanely. "Let's go to the station. Sergeant Jorgeson's off duty at the moment, but I can call him at home and ask him to join us. He'll want to question you tonight, and tomorrow he'll arrange for a lawyer from legal services.

Everything will be okay, Roy, and you'll have a place to sleep and hot meals."

"I don't need a lawyer. I already told you why it was self-defense. Any guy my age would have done the same thing. The kids at the high school may think I'm weird, but they sure as hell don't think I'm gay. I had a girlfriend while I was living with my mother. We had sex every weekend—and nothing kinky, either. You want her name and phone number? As long as her parents aren't in the room she'll tell you the same thing."

He was more agitated than I would have preferred. The whereabouts of the handgun used on Nicholas was known, but Jorgeson had made a point of mentioning the possibility of a second one. Roy's jacket had deep pockets.

"What's the matter, Mrs. Malloy?" he continued, thumping the seat. "I'll bet you don't believe me! Is that it? What's wrong with what I told you last night? You got problems with it?"

"Nothing major," I said, wishing I sounded more sincere. I am not adept at lying; normally, it's a praiseworthy attribute, but under the current circumstances, it was a distinct disadvantage. "I'm sure you can easily explain a couple of things that are a teensy bit confusing. You just now said why you didn't hear the cars drive up, and I believe you. The autopsy report said that there was no alcohol in Nicholas's blood, but one of your fellow Druids admitted that she was there before midnight and saw him take a mouthful of brandy." I realized I was babbling, but I couldn't seem to stop—even though I knew the most credible fabrications are unadorned. "We know who broke the window in Nicholas's study, and who put away the decanter and glasses. Most of the inconsistencies have been dealt with, Roy. You shouldn't worry about talking to the police. It'll be nothing more than a formality. You'll be released on your own recognizance tomorrow or the next day."

And the archbishop of Canterbury would elope with Princess Margaret.

This time his fingers dug into my shoulder and I could feel hot breath on my neck. "Who broke the window and put away the decanter?" he growled.

"Malthea. Fern was there earlier, when Nicholas got out the brandy and glasses. That was when he took a drink of brandy and then spat it out."

"They told you that?"

"Yes, they did. Do you mind if I start the car so we can get some heat?"

He released my shoulder and fell back against the seat. "Don't so much as move a finger, Mrs. Malloy. I've got to think here for a minute. I don't like this."

Neither did I, but I refrained from saying so and waited passively as the wind found ways to sneak in through the floorboard. I could see him in the rearview mirror, but it was too dark to discern his expression. His hisses and muttered curses indicated he was not in the best of moods.

I was on the verge of repeating my suggestion about heat when he said, "After I went out the bathroom window, they searched my place, didn't they?"

"They might have looked for some tips about where they could find you. If they did, it was because they were concerned about your welfare."

"Did they find the gun?"

"I couldn't say," I said, struggling to sound casual. Alas, even I heard a faint tremor in my voice.

He slammed his fist on the seat. "That's it, isn't it? That's the detail that's 'a teensy bit confusing,' as you put it. Damn! I knew I should have buried it in the woods! How could I have been so friggin' stupid!" He hit the seat again. I did not interpret it as a request for consensus with the assessment of his mental faculties.

"All of us make mistakes," I said. "I can think of several I've made lately."

"Shut up."

I shut up as he resumed hissing and cursing. Having never spent a significant amount of time in my car behind the Book Depot at night, I had no idea if patrol cars ever ventured into the parking lot. If I'd believed for one second that my forty-year-old reflexes were at all quicker than his sixteen-year-old ones, I would have attempted to scramble out of the car and run down the railroad tracks. However, I had no desire to be shot in the back or even tackled in the gravel.

"Okay," he said abruptly, startling me to the point I nearly yelped. "I'm gonna tell you the truth about what happened. I stole my father's gun back in the fall because some guys at school were giving me grief, and I used it to shoot Nicholas Chunder. First I hit him a couple of times, then I stepped back, aimed, and pulled the trigger. I would have shot him more than once if I hadn't freaked when I saw the blood. I rolled him over, thinking I'd take his wallet so the cops would jump on the burglary story, but I guess he'd left it in his bedroom."

"Why did you do it, Roy? He overlooked his personal dislike of your . . . ah, religious practices and allowed you to live on his estate. If you were short on cash, I'd think he or someone else would have loaned you enough to get by until your parents returned."

"I didn't kill him for spending money, fer chrissake! I killed him because of her. She made me do it, and there wasn't any way I could refuse. She's had this power over me since the moment we met. She took me out to the grove, just the two of us, and she drew a pentagram on my forehead with her finger. It burned so fiercely that I thought I was gonna pass out. You can't see it, but I can every damn time I look in the mirror. When I do something that she doesn't like, it turns bright red and begins to smolder. The pain's unbearable, like someone's pressing an ember against my skin."

I felt as though he'd knocked me on the head with a rock. "Who are you talking about," I asked.

"Malthea, of course. I know nobody will believe me, but I swear it's the truth. I'll swear on a bible if you want me to, or a whole stack of them. Malthea ordered me to kill Nicholas, so I did."

He began to whimper, and when I looked back at him, I saw him wiping away what I presumed were tears. I waited until he'd calmed down, then said, "Why would Malthea have done that, Roy? I haven't heard her say anything that implied she hated Nicholas so vehemently that she wanted him dead."

"You haven't been around her that much. Sure, she can come off like somebody's grandmother when it suits her, and she puts on a really good pretense of being scatterbrained and helpless. She's not, though. She may be the Arch Druid, but she's also a member of a secret cult called the Sisters of Illumination that goes all the way back to ancient Egypt and Babylon. Once a year they have a Black Sabbath and perform a human sacrifice."

"Malthea Hendlerson?" I said. "That's . . . hard to believe."

"I know it is," he said dispiritedly. "What happened was, when I first moved to Farberville, I spent a lot of time in that used bookstore up the street, just poking around for funky old stuff. I saw her there a couple of times, then one afternoon she came up to me and said we had to talk. She looked pretty harmless and I didn't have anything better to do, so I said okay. We drove out to the grove in her car. That's where she told me she worshiped Satan and could sense that I would make a perfect servant after she finished training me."

"Were you wearing a black T-shirt in the bookstore?" I asked.

He nodded. "I buy them at rock concerts because they're cool."

"What about the hearse? How long have you owned it?"

"The guy who lived down the street ran a funeral home. When he died last summer, I talked his wife into selling it to me real cheap. I get a buzz when people on the street stare at me. It wasn't like I was into satanism."

"Why don't you tell me more about what happened at the grove?" I suggested politely, as if we were discussing the merits of a movie.

"She pulled out a little pair of scissors and cut off a lock of my hair. She said she could use it to send this demon called Ambesek whenever I needed to be disciplined. I didn't believe her, but one night at the carriage house I was awakened by the stench of sulfur. I sat up and saw this—this eight-foot-tall creature with a hideous face, fiery red eyes, and huge hands. Its skin was covered with black scales that glinted like armor.

It dragged me out of bed, ripped off my shirt, and raked my back with its claws. I passed out on the floor. The next morning I thought maybe it had just been a really bad nightmare. I changed my mind when I saw the bloody marks on my back."

"Come on, Roy," I said, "you fell out of bed and somehow scratched yourself on the bedside table."

"I wish that was true, but she sends the demon whenever she's angry at me. Once she ordered me to steal a dog and bring it to the grove so she could slaughter it and drink its blood. I refused. That night the demon came and practically disemboweled me. She told me later that its formal title was Ambesek the Eater of Intestines."

It didn't matter whether or not he believed what he was saying; I was getting nauseated—and nervous. "Did you go to the hospital?"

"She said the demon could find me no matter where I was and not to get medical help. I bandaged myself as best I could. I was scared the wound would get infected, but she gave me this salve and it worked so well you can barely see a scar."

"When did Malthea order you to kill Nicholas?" I asked.

"She's been saying nasty things about him ever since the Samhain celebration at Halloween. He wanted everything to be done his way, and he and Malthea had an argument. I wasn't there, but she said he was hateful. You should have seen the look on her face the night before the solstice when he said he was selling his properties and moving to Wales. While the others were pleading with him, she took me out to the patio and told me what to do. I didn't want to, Mrs. Malloy, but she gave me a gruesome description of what Ambesek would do if I disobeyed her. You want to hear what she said?"

"I don't think so," I said. "If Malthea has this demon at her beck and call, why didn't she sic him on Nicholas instead of getting you involved?"

"She said I had to kill someone so I could participate in the next Black Sabbath. I knew I wouldn't live that long if I didn't do it. I went to my apartment, popped some pills to give myself the guts to go through with it, then went to the house and knocked on the door till Nicholas let me inside. You know the rest."

I still couldn't see Malthea as an evil dominatrix, and Roy had already proved himself to be a much more adept liar than I. "If you're so terrified of another visit from the demon, why are you telling me now?"

"I deserve to suffer for what I did. I've been trying to find spells that can protect me. If they work, they work. If they don't, then I'll be tortured until I beg to die. Let's go to the police station and get it over with."

I wasted no time starting the car. Although his story of demonic retribution was preposterous, I was not about to sit there in the dark and wait for an eight-foot-tall creature with fiery eyes to come ambling down the railroad tracks, swooping down from the sky, or popping up from the sewer drain in front of the Book Depot.

I was exhausted the next morning, having not been able to fall asleep until almost dawn. Jorgeson had permitted me to be present at the interrogation, but it hadn't lasted long. Roy's descriptions became increasingly graphic and filled with repugnant details; he'd shouted and cried and stormed around the room until Jorgeson gave up and packed him off to the psych ward for sedation and a seventy-two-hour evaluation. Gilda was already there in a padded room. I rather longed for one, myself.

After Roy'd been taken away, Jorgeson had asked me what I thought, and I'd told him that for the first time I could remember, I was out of opinions. He'd almost smiled.

Now, at nine in the morning, the sun was shining, but this was not enough to lure in the occasional pedestrian. I was hunting through the racks in hopes of finding a book about satanism when the telephone rang. The sound was not as harsh as a fiendish screech, but it had a comparable effect on me. There were a few people I was willing to talk to, but the converse list was very long and multiplying steadily.

Then again, it could have been Franklin with good news. I numbly picked up the receiver.

"Claire, this is Inez's mother."

Goose bumps rose on my flesh, but I managed a calm, "Is anything wrong?"

"I think the girls are up to something. They were acting odd last night, and her father and I agreed you ought to know about it."

This was a very forceful decision on Mrs. Thornton's part. She's as mousy as Inez and usually only faintly bewildered by the girls' escapades, but I never knew quite how much of the truth she heard from Inez. At this moment, I could almost hear her twisting her hands, which was alarming. I waited for a moment, then said, "What did they do?"

"Nothing, and that's what worries me. Last night when I picked up Inez at the mall, she told me about this ridiculous lawsuit and said she was going to quit her job, no matter how desperate Mrs. Claus was. I told her that she'd made the right decision. Well, Caron came over and the two locked themselves in Inez's bedroom for a long while. I could hear them talking and arguing. Then Inez came out and said she'd changed her mind about quitting. I was flabbergasted that Caron would want her to continue at Santa's Workshop, but it's obvious that she does."

"Hmmm," I said eloquently, in that I was in complete agreement with Mrs. Thornton's assessment. If in some way Caron could make a profit from unplugging someone's respirator, she would at least consider it. Not necessarily do it, mind you, but weigh the possibilities. Making life easier for Mrs. Claus, aka Ms. Portmeyer, would not have merited even fleeting consideration. And Inez, for all her meekness, has a streak of stubbornness that runs as deep as a vein of coal.

"It was odd," Mrs. Thornton continued, "and when they begin to behave oddly, they tend to end up in trouble. Inez will be applying for scholarships next year. She won't have much luck with a felony conviction on her transcript."

I could only commiserate, which I did for a few minutes. Once Mrs. Thornton was somewhat pacified, I said, "So where are they?"

"Inez had me drop her off at the mall. Caron said she was going to walk home. It all seemed so innocent, Claire, and I truly wish I thought it was."

We speculated aimlessly for a few minutes, then I replaced the receiver and sat down at the counter. I stayed there for most of an hour, making unattractive faces and finding myself unable to come up with a plausible explanation for Caron's behavior. I had little hope that she'd tell me the truth—unless she found it convenient. This rarely happened. She'd gone to Rhonda Maguire's house the previous evening, which in and of itself was worthy of a headline in the local newspaper. But why?

I was lost in thought when Jorgeson came into the store. He gave me a sour smile and said, "We interviewed Malthea Hendlerson. You ever seen a marble statue, Mrs. Malloy? She's a little less talkative than one of them."

"I can't see her summoning a demon and commanding it to disembowel a boy," I said. "You've met her, Jorgeson. I grant she's not your ordinary person, but she hasn't ever indicated she's that ... well, wicked. Did you ask the doctors to check Roy's back and abdomen for scars?"

"He's got scars," said Jorgeson as he went into the office and poured himself a cup of coffee. "But," he added from the doorway, "that doesn't mean they were inflicted by some fiend from hell. Could be an indication of past abuse from one of his parents, or even self-mutilation. He's a sick one."

"I won't argue with that. Is Malthea in custody?"

"She's been told to remain available until the shrinks evaluate the kid. I was expecting her to laugh at us, but she got real grim and said, 'So he told you that, did he?' No denials, no nothing. If somebody accused me of that, I'd be cussing up a storm and swearing I was innocent. We couldn't get another sentence out of her."

I shook my head. "It's impossible to figure her out, but that doesn't mean she's diabolic. She may be as sane as anyone else. Who's entitled to define what our senses take in and how we ought to process it? Look at this, Jorgeson." I poked a publisher's catalog on the counter. "You see what you call red, and you assume I see the same shade. We'll never know if we see something entirely different because we have no way to compare our input. We both agree that what we see is red, but who can say if we're actually receiving the same response in our brains? My red may be your green. We simply use the same term for what may be entirely opposite."

"What does this have to do with anything?" Jorgeson asked gently.

"Demons," I said. "My bout of indigestion may be Roy's fiend from hell ripping at his bowels. It's a matter of interpretation, of translation between his mind and his own concept of reality. He's disturbed; neither of us can argue with that. Is he genuinely disturbed? Who knows?"

Jorgeson seemed to sense he was dealing with a madwoman. He patted my hand for a moment, his face puckered, and then said, "You talked to the lieutenant lately?"

I tried for a stiff upper lip and a glib response, then poured out everything. I did not allow a tear to escape, but my demeanor was at best quavery and I resorted, albeit briefly, to a tissue in order to blow my nose in a ladylike manner.

"Leslie, huh?" said Jorgeson. "The lieutenant's never said much about her."

"What *has* he said?"

"Jeez, it's hard to remember." He stared into space and scratched his stubbly gray scalp. "She's a stockbroker, I think, and she breeds some kind of fancy dogs that are worth a bundle and win ribbons at competitions. One night when we were drinking beer, he showed me a picture of her. Blond, all the equipment— but not nearly as nice looking as you, Mrs. Malloy. You shouldn't fret over the lieutenant. His only concern right now is his mother and this guy named Myron. As soon as he gets it resolved, he'll come home."

"Unless the skiing is good," I said, not at all comforted by Jorgeson's sad gaze.

After he left, I called home to speak to Caron, but she was either in the shower or elsewhere. I hesitated to call Rhonda and try to get information out of her; she had the ability to spread gossip as easily as the rest of us spread peanut butter on bread.

Or caviar on toast.

I ordered myself to put aside self-pity and do something useful. If Caron spent the morning holding up banks, I'd hear about it eventually. I couldn't bring myself to confront Malthea until the images Roy had implanted in my mind faded to black and white. If I went to Fern's duplex, Malthea would spot me. It might be enlightening to talk to Morning Rose, but I didn't want her children doing further exploration and I couldn't close the store two days before Christmas.

My circumspection was rewarded when a few shoppers came in and browsed. One woman wanted a paperback for her daughter. Since she knew neither the title nor the author, but only that it featured a woman archeologist in Victorian times, we studied covers and discussed possibilities until I found one that met her criteria. A man needed a handyman's guide to replacing circuit boxes, having put up one too many strings of Christmas lights. Another wanted "anything a middle-aged woman like yourself would like." Three giggly junior high girls found a romance novel and paid me in dimes and quarters. They reminded me of Caron and Inez when they'd been in their Azalea Twilight phase, and this, of course, reminded me that an unknown game was afoot.

During lulls, and there were many of them, I pondered Roy's bizarre story. Was there any way at all that ditzy, kind-hearted Malthea could have ordered Roy to kill someone? She seemed to be genuinely concerned about him, but she was the one who'd introduced him into the Sacred Grove. It seemed logical that she'd feel some responsibility in loco parentis, with an emphasis on the *loco*.

I was calling home when my science-fiction hippie came into the store. He eyed me cautiously, then satisfied himself that I was unarmed. Despite his scruffy, crumb-encrusted beard, discolored bandanna around his forehead, and glazed eyes, he had a certain charm. As had, I supposed, Rasputin.

"Last-minute Christmas shopping?" I said.

"Yeah, I met this chick in a chat room and I want to get her something. From what she said, she sounds like a dead ringer for the woman on the cover of *Galactica Galore: Transvestite Empress of Andromeda*."

"You met her, but you don't know what she looks like?" I said, perplexed. "Were you blindfolded at the time."

"I don't think I was, but I may have missed something." He went behind the rack, and a subsequent thud informed me that he'd opted to sit on the floor. As long as a prissy matron didn't come in for an updated edition of Emily Post, it didn't matter all that much.

"Did you find a copy?" I called.

"Yeah, I'm just trying to decide if I want to lay out five dollars. For all I know, she could be a twelve-year-old boy. They do that kind of thing for kicks."

"What kind of thing?"

"It's hard to describe," he said vaguely.

I went to the end of the rack and looked down at

him. He was, as I'd expected, sitting cross-legged on the floor with paperbacks fanned around him. "Do you have a name?"

"Yeah, do you?"

"Yeah, I guess I do. May I ask you about a drug?"

He looked up at me. "I never thought you'd want to score. You're always so . . . well, I dunno . . . centered, like an earth mother. Things swirl around you, but you don't like even flinch. You ever read *Sidhartha*?"

So now I was reduced to a reincarnation of Buddha; I really needed to work on my image. "What do you know about a drug called Herbal Ecstasy?"

"It's legal, which is good. Twenty years ago I got picked up with less than a quarter of an ounce of pot, and you'd have thought I had bullion from Fort Knox the way everybody got fired up. All I was doing was—"

"Herbal Ecstasy?" I said.

"The main ingredient is mahuang. It's this organic stimulant that's supposed to work like ephedrine, but all it did was make me itch. I thought I was going to scratch off my skin."

"Does it cause hallucinations or psychoses?"

"Not that I've ever heard. It mainly fires up your central nervous system. The problem with the stuff is that you don't know what's in it besides the mahuang or how much you can take. A kid died of an overdose at a rock concert in Florida or one of those places, but the FDA still hasn't banned it. Makes you wonder what the world's coming to, doesn't it?"

"It surely does," I said dryly. "The book's my Christmas present to you. May it cement this relationship with the dead ringer."

He thanked me amidst a profusion of flying crumbs, then left before I could change my mind. He may have had another paperback or two in his army surplus jacket pockets, but 'twas the season. I might not have been blessed with lords a-leaping and swans a-swimming, but at least I had a hippie in a fuzzy fog.

Ho, ho.

Caron showed up in the middle of the afternoon. I was glad to see her, in that it indicated she was not in custody. She studied me appraisingly, then said, "Can I have the car?"

"To do what?"

"Nothing, really. I told Inez I'd pick her up after she gets off work at eight."

"Which will be in approximately six hours."

"Well," she said, studying the floor for inspiration, "I haven't bought a present for Peter, so I thought I'd go out to the mall and look around for something. Do you think he'd like a tie?"

I told her that Peter wouldn't be back until after New Year's Day, but did not elaborate on his present whereabouts and companions. "I'll make a deal with you," I added. "If you take over here for an hour while I run an errand, then you can have the car for the rest of the day."

"Are you going to pay me?"

"Only with the use of the car. Feel free to walk home and call the Department of Labor if you prefer. There's bound to be a toll-free number to report violations of this heinous nature."

"Oh, all right," she said with a sigh, "as long as nobody bothers me. We have to read some utterly suffocating book next semester for English. I might as well get started on it instead of watching the cockroach races in the back room."

"Good idea." I carried a pile of paperwork to said

racetrack, got my purse and coat, and came back to the front room. Caron was standing in front of the classics rack, looking as though she were on a scaffold awaiting the arrival of a hooded man. "By the way," I said ever so casually, "I was a little surprised that you went to Rhonda's last night. I thought you'd still be seething over her reindeer remark."

"I got over it."

"Was she having a party?"

Caron glanced at me. "If you must know, I needed to borrow something from her."

"Oh, really?"

"I wish you'd go run your errand so I can get to the mall before the parking lot is full. It's bad enough during the day, but after five everybody in the county descends like turkey vultures. You can almost hear the flapping of wings."

Having made no progress in unraveling this latest scheme, I went out to the car and drove toward the south part of town.

CHAPTER 11

Morning Rose must have seen me coming up the sidewalk, because she flung open the door before I reached the top step of the porch. "Has something happened to Roy?"

"Several things," I said. "May I come inside?"

"I guess so, but only for a few minutes. Sullivan went to the co-op to pick up mung bean sprouts and cheese. Do you know that the cheese sold in regular grocery stores contains animal by-products? Most of the yogurt does, too. Isn't that disgusting?"

Unable to respond with any sincerity, I nodded and went into the living room. No Druid touches were evident in the decor, which could be described as later-American thrift shop. Graduate assistantships appeared to be no more remunerative than they'd been in my day, when scavenged lumber, concrete blocks, and beanbag chairs had been our rejoinder to Martha Stewart.

"Sit down." Morning Rose gestured at a sofa with lumpy cushions and stained plaid upholstery. "I need to send Cosmos and Rainbow outside before we talk. They saw an old spy movie on television, and they've been eavesdropping like CIA agents ever since."

She left the room. I removed a headless Barbie doll and several potentially lethal slivers of plastic from the sofa, then sat down and listened to the muted sounds of her voice, interspersed with whining. Eavesdropping was not required.

"They always act as if they're being exiled to Siberia," she said as she came back and sat down on a wooden chair. "I insist they have at least two hours a day of fresh air and sunshine."

If I was obliged to stay home with Dennis and Menace all day, I would have opted for eight, maybe ten. "Roy turned himself in to the police last night," I began. "While he was being questioned, he became so upset that he was taken to the hospital."

Morning Rose stared at me. "I don't understand, Mrs. Malloy. Was he beaten?"

"I was there, and I can assure you that he was treated with kindness and concern. No rubber hoses or thumbscrews, just bad coffee and stale doughnuts. All Sergeant Jorgeson did was try to get a coherent story that explained why Roy shot Nicholas Chunder."

"Are you saying that Roy has confessed?"

"He claims that Malthea forced him to do it. It's hard to believe, though."

She was still staring at me as if I'd materialized from one of the numerous dust balls under the furniture and introduced myself as Farberville's resident Eater of Intestines and Disagreeable Children. "Malthea denies it, of course?"

"She refused to admit or deny the allegation. Sergeant Jorgeson is waiting for the psychiatric evaluation before he decides how to proceed. The allegation has some grotesque elements, but if she has that degree of influence on his behavior, she's in serious trouble."

Her gaze shifted away from me. "I've been afraid

something like this would happen ever since Sullivan and I joined the grove two years ago."

"How did that come about?" I asked, desperately hoping that Sullivan was mesmerized by an array of fresh, frozen, and for all I knew, pickled bean sprouts.

"Sullivan had a teaching position at a college run by a conservative religious denomination. We had no friends because we knew that one slip about our personal beliefs would lead to his dismissal. Cosmos and Rainbow weren't allowed to play with other children for the same reason. Everybody in the town was a potential enemy. Sullivan finally decided to get a doctorate so he could try for a job at a larger college where we might find a more enlightened community. When Nicholas came by with our copy of the lease, he noticed the titles on the bookshelves and invited us to attend a ritual. We were not pleased with the bickering and rigidity within the grove, but we ended up joining."

"How many were there of you two years ago?"

"About the same number, I suppose. Fern, Malthea, Gilda, Nicholas, and a middle-aged couple from California who moved to a commune in Oregon last summer. A newspaper reporter tried to infiltrate the grove, but Nicholas did a background check and we refused to allow her to participate. He was very adept at using his computer for that sort of thing. I prefer divination."

"You mentioned yesterday that Roy had joined the grove in September of this year," I said.

"Initially, Sullivan and I had reservations about Roy. He seemed to be so very ill at ease. I spoke to Malthea about it, and she assured me that he was merely intimidated by his lack of knowledge. She planned to

instruct him herself so that he could be formally initi-
ated when the time was right. Our celebrations are
open to everyone, but admission into the higher ranks
takes study and dedication."

Higher ranks—or lower circles?

"I gather that Roy got along better with you than
with your husband," I said.

She went to a front window and pulled aside a curtain. "It usually takes him only half an hour to go by
the co-op. Maybe he went by his office to pick up
something." She let the curtain fall back. "Sullivan can
be as prudish as Nicholas was. He is well suited for
Druidism, the patriarchal bastion of rationalism. Wicca
is intuitive and more feminist. He wants the sterility of
sunlight; I prefer the caress of moonlight."

"But you and he reached a compromise?"

"In regards to the children, we have. I do many of
my rituals in the backyard while he baby-sits. It's
worked out thus far."

"Is that what you were doing on the eve of the solstice?" I glanced at my watch. How many varieties of
sprouts could there be?

Morning Rose sat back down and smiled at me. "I
gather you want alibis rather than a description of the
Wiccan ritual. We arrived home a little after nine. I put
the children to bed, then went into the backyard for a
private welcoming of the birth of Horned God. He
will mate with the Goddess in spring, be sacrificed
and die in the autumn, and be reborn in the form of
himself at the next winter solstice. The Mother Goddess receives her strength from this, her power over all
that exists in both the physical and mystical realities.
Union and reunion are divine."

"Of course," I said lamely. "Why did you say that

you'd been worried that something like this might happen? Did you have a reason to think Malthea might have . . ."

"Gained control of Roy? Manipulated him into doing something dreadful? I encouraged him to confide in me. He wasn't very forthcoming, but I could tell that he was in the grips of a tremendous internal struggle. Terror doesn't begin to describe what I sensed. I don't know whose demons he was facing—but he was haunted by images so horrific that he was being driven crazy. From what little he said, I suspected Malthea was behind it." She took a shuddery breath, then stood up and began to pace across from me, her chin quivering as she struggled to maintain her composure. "I'm frightened, too. Sullivan refuses to acknowledge the possibility of demons, but I saw Roy's wound. I *saw* it, Mrs. Malloy, mopped away the blood, and put bandages on it. The physical scars are gone, but the spiritual ones will never go away. He needs help. I'm just not sure that doctors and shrinks can battle forces from the bowels of hell."

Stephen King, please pick up the white courtesy phone.

I tightened my grip on my purse and asked myself— not for the first time—why I'd voluntarily embroiled myself in these people's problems, when what they needed were soft-spoken therapists and mind-dulling drugs. In industrial strength doses.

"But what about Malthea?" I persisted. "Do you honestly believe she has control over Roy?"

Morning Rose let her curled fingers relax, and to my relief, sat down, saving me from a pinched nerve in my neck. She pushed her hair out of her face and leaned forward to peer earnestly at me. "Roy *believes* it, and that's all that matters. I've never met a demon, but he has. My time may come, and so may yours. Is reality what you accept—or what you deny because of your own primal fear?"

Having never had this conversation before, I was at a loss for a reply, glib or otherwise. I was reduced to looking at the floor when the door opened and Sullivan came into the room.

"What's going on?" he demanded.

Morning Rose clamped down on her lower lip, making it clear that she wasn't going to respond. I said, "Roy has confessed to killing Nicholas. He's in custody."

Sullivan dropped a grocery sack, presumably made from recycled paper, and leaned against the wall. "Roy confessed? I thought it was a burglar."

"The authorities have the weapon," I said. "It was registered to Roy's father. Did he ever mention owning a handgun?"

Sullivan's complexion was beginning to take on the cast of the dull beige sack on the floor, and he was reacting as though Roy were his firstborn son and successor to the throne. "Dr. Tate said he bought a gun when he did a stint on a reservation in Arizona back in the eighties. He wasn't into artifacts, but treasure hunters kept digging up sacred sites to get things to sell to tourists. It's often a battlefield to preserve certain cultures from so-called progress. Then again, maybe the only reason we preserve them is so that academics like Dr. Tate can write papers about them. Publish or piss off, as the saying goes."

"Sullivan!" said Morning Rose. "Have you been drinking?"

"Me?"

She glared at him, then made a quasi-successful attempt to soften her expression as she turned to me. "Mrs. Malloy, if you don't mind, I think I need to have a word in private with my husband."

"Don't mind me," I said with my customary grace and charm. "I was once married to someone who was known to detour by a bar on occasion. Go right ahead."

"Dada is blotto," sang a high-pitched voice from around the corner. "Dada is blotto."

"Can I have a pet demon?" asked another, somewhat deeper voice.

Morning Rose grabbed my arm and pulled me to my feet. "Thank you for coming by. Please let me know if there's anything we can do to help. Now, if you don't mind . . . ?"

I was on the porch by this time, and the grip she had on me made it clear I wasn't going back inside the house unless I was versed in sumo wrestling. I pulled myself free and said, "If there's anything else you want to tell me, call or drop by the bookstore."

She pulled the door closed behind her. "I would like an update on Roy. He's been through so much, and I don't believe that he realized what he was doing when he shot Nicholas. He doesn't need to go to prison, where he'll be abused by hardened inmates and tormented by his guilt. He's only sixteen. He can be saved, turned around, aimed in the right direction. At the moment, he's into drugs and some unhealthy philosophies, but he and I used to talk about poetry and light and goodness. Is there anything you can do for him?"

"I'll certainly try." I heard Sullivan bellowing at the children. "I guess I'd better go."

Morning Rose looked at me for an uncomfortably long moment, and then went back inside and shut the door.

As I drove toward Thurber Street, it occurred to me that by now Roy had proffered three versions of what had taken place on the eve of the winter solstice. The burglary version had held up only until Corporal Billsby had said there'd been no forcible entry into Nicholas's house. That evening, Roy had come up with the purported sexual-advances version. Malthea and Fern had conveniently stuck wadding in the cracks, and Morning Rose had dropped dark hints about Nicholas's secretive personal life.

The current version was a real doozy. I didn't know whether it would play in Peoria, but I doubted it would in Farberville, USA.

Caron would still have time to beat the crowd to the mall if I made a small detour, I decided as I turned onto a side street and made my way to the police station for the third time in less than a week. At this rate, I'd merit my own parking space in the lot next to the innocuous brick building. Lieutenant Rosen had one; the stenciled lettering on the sign was faded, but still legible. I considered yanking it up and tossing it in a Dumpster, then hurried inside before I gave way to the impulse.

"Is Sergeant Jorgeson here?" I asked the shiny-faced rookie at the reception desk.

"No, he's out at a crime scene right now. You want to leave a message?"

"Is he at Nicholas Chunder's house?"

"I'm not allowed to say, ma'am," the rookie murmured, his ears turning as red as geraniums.

"Please let him know that I'll be there shortly." I

went back out to my car before I could be detained on some fictitious violation.

Fifteen minutes later I parked next to a patrol car and a rather dismal car that was likely to belong to Jorgeson. After a brief argument, the uniformed officer at the door went inside to consult his superior, returned with a chagrined expression, and gestured for me to go inside. I found Jorgeson in the hallway, gazing pensively at an oil painting of one of Nicholas's long-departed ancestors. If the artist had accurately captured his subject, this ancestor had died of bad hair.

"Jorgeson," I said in the resolute tone of a brolly-wielding spinster, "I've had a thought."

"I'm sure you have, Mrs. Malloy. Oddly enough, so have I."

I overlooked this less-than-warm reception. "If Gilda D'Orcher was willing to risk breaking in, she must have been looking for something. It could be a pentagram drawn in chalk on Nicholas's bedroom floor, or proof that she's his illegitimate daughter and therefore entitled to inherit Primrose Hill and all the rental properties."

"Could be," Jorgeson said. "But I think we'd have noticed a pentagram the first time we searched. At the moment, we're going through all the papers in the desk. I'm more inclined to expect to find a bunch of boring letters to county courthouses and genealogical libraries than a birth certificate, but what do I know? I'm just a cop."

I glanced at the door of the study. "What about computer files?"

"We're not having much luck. Apparently, there's a way to put secret passwords on files, and no easy way to determine what they are. Maybe Chunder was an agent for a foreign power and was sending classified documents about military breakthroughs, or maybe he was into pornography and weird sex, or maybe he just liked to play games. Hard to know until my guy gets into the files. It could take days, even weeks."

"Was he really going to sell everything?" I asked.

"Now that we do know. He'd listed his property with a real estate agency, and was corresponding with a company in Cardiff. One of our college-educated boys says that's in Wales. I wouldn't know, myself. The most exotic place my wife and I have ever been is New Orleans. She didn't like it because of all the topless bars and drunks urinating in alleys."

"I don't blame her," I said, disappointed that nothing startling had been uncovered. I went to the doorway of the living room and looked at the artificial winter wonderland. A few strands of tinsel had fallen, and the greenery was turning brittle and brown. Two pewter tankards had been left on a shelf near the fireplace. It looked like the aftermath of a party awaiting the attention of a hungover host.

Jorgeson joined me. "Depressing, isn't it?"

"This entire mess is depressing," I said. "Roy's the same age as Caron. He's either psychotic or the most polished liar I've ever encountered. He must have done it, though. He's confessed twice now, and the weapon's damning."

"There's no doubt it was the weapon, and his prints were on it. There were a couple of smudges, but they've been identified as belonging to his father, who's been gone for three months."

"What about the brandy decanter?"

"We thought of that, too, Mrs. Malloy. It was in a cabinet over there, and covered with dust. No one, in-

cluding your friends, moved it or wiped off prints or
did anything with it before the murder. These people
are giving me a helluvan ulcer. They're all lying, and
I don't know why. We've got a perp, we've got a
weapon, and we've got a confession, which is enough
proof to dump on the district attorney's desk. The doctors and the prosecutors can determine if the boy's
competent to stand trial."

"What about Malthea?"

"The jury may have sympathy for the boy, but I
don't think they'll feel anything but revulsion for her.
Most people who serve on juries are parents or grandparents. They're not going to let her go free to find another messed-up teenager."

"Particularly if she won't defend herself," I said.

Jorgeson stepped into the hallway. "She may have
something to say if and when she's charged with first-
degree homicide, as well as impeding an investigation, perjury, contributing to the delinquency, and
whatever else the DA can find. His hemorrhoids flare
up during the winter."

I asked Jorgeson for permission to go to the grove.
He thought it over, shrugged, and told me to watch
out for snakes. I assured him I would, then drove back
to the main road and found the narrow lane that I'd
taken the morning of the solstice. If only I'd missed it
in the dark, I thought as my car slid from rut to rut like
an inept ice-skater. Or better yet, if I'd flatout told
Malthea that I was unable to get her encyclopedia and
other books. Aspirin, scotch, and gasoline would eat
up the profits from that transaction."

The pasture was no more appealing in the daylight
than it had been previously, although it was easier to
transverse. I found the tree where Gilda had waited

for me, ducked under a branch, and headed into what appeared to be the primeval forest.

I took a few false turns, but eventually floundered through a line of firs and found myself at the edge of the grove. Much of the greenery had fallen off the stone altar or been dragged away by rabbits to decorate their burrows.

I sat down on a stump and tried to picture the scene Roy had described. Had Malthea really brought him here and convinced him that she possessed the power to summon a demon? That she belonged to a secret cult that performed human sacrifices? Twinkly Malthea?

If Roy stuck with his story, he was apt to be sent away to a mental hospital until the doctors found the right balance of therapy and drugs. Malthea would spend the rest of her life in a prison. Fern might, too, since she'd implicated herself when she lied to me about the brandy decanter. She, like Malthea, had been familiar with Roy's initial confession and done her part to substantiate it.

Could that have also been Gilda's motive when she foolishly tried to break into the house? Had she intended to dust off the decanter and contribute a smeared fingerprint or two?

A shadow fell across the altar, reminding me that it was getting late. I stood up and brushed off my derriere, took a last look at the somber circle of oak trees, and was about to leave when I heard a crackling noise from somewhere behind the firs. Not the rustling of a small animal, mind you, or the fluttering of dried leaves in the branches, or even the blazing of a satanic furnace as something slipped out for a field trip.

At this time of year, bears were in caves and cows

were in barns. I'd noticed in the local paper that deer-hunting season had passed. Not at all pleased, I took refuge behind a somewhat inadequate tree trunk (I am svelte, but not so that I can be toppled in a light breeze).

Malthea stepped into the grove. In a heavy overcoat, gloves, and a scarf, she looked like an ordinary house-wife on her way to the grocery store for frozen peas and a can of cat food. This, however, was not a grocery store, and she was far from ordinary.

"I must speak to you," she said to whatever of my anatomy was visible.

I emerged, my face warm with embarrassment. "Have you been following me, Malthea?"

"Earlier this afternoon I parked across from your store, but each time I started to get out of the car, someone would go inside. I was ready to give up when you drove away. You've been as busy as a squir-rel in autumn, haven't you? First to the Sawyers' house, then the police station, Nicholas's house, and now here. Was it the desire for solitude that brought you to the Sacred Grove?"

"Something like that," I said.

She sat down on the stump I'd vacated and settled her satchel in her lap. "I'd like to hear exactly what Roy told you last night."

"You've been told the gist of it, and I don't see any reason to go into detail." I began to sidle around the perimeter of the grove, keeping an eye on her satchel. "If you want to discuss Roy's allegation, I'm sure Sergeant Jorgeson will be happy to oblige you. My daughter's waiting for me to get back to the bookstore so that she can have the car."

"I cannot discuss this with the sergeant until you

tell me what Roy told you," she said. "I was under the assumption that you wanted to help. This is your opportunity, if I am correct."

"I do, which is why I'm advising you to go to Sergeant Jorgeson."

"I can't do that," she said mulishly.

"Why not? Roy's told his side of the story, and you should be eager to tell yours. He wouldn't be undergoing a psychiatric evaluation if he were stable. Trust me when I say he's not. He may have started taking mind-altering drugs when he moved to Farberville, or he may have been experiencing schizophrenic episodes for years. How did he seem to you when you and Fern found him in the greenhouse?"

"Cold and hungry. He'd hoped he could sleep there for at least one night, but you ruined that when you returned with the police officers, didn't you? He barely had time to stuff a roll in his coat pocket before fleeing into the night."

Or into the backseat of my car, anyway. "Did he call you from a pay phone the next morning?" I asked her, still concerned about the contents of her satchel. Ambesek could not have fit inside, but a handgun scarcely would have created a bulge.

"What makes you think he called me?"

"I know he called you, Malthea. He told you what he'd told me, and you spotted his mistakes immediately. You came to the bookstore to do damage control. Later, after Jorgeson mentioned the lack of alcohol in Nicholas's blood, you and Fern hatched up another fabrication to cover it. You and she ought to be writing screenplays in Hollywood. She could have a greenhouse with every species of plant known to science, and you could buy several thousand acres with a grove in the middle."

Malthea picked up her satchel and rose to her feet. "All that is irrelevant. You must tell me what Roy said to you and the sergeant last night."

"And if I refuse?" I said, easing backward until my back hit a tree trunk. Forests would be more hospitable with fewer trees. "Will you summon a demon to coerce me?"

"When I first met you, Claire, you seemed like a calm, agreeable person. Lately you've been doing and saying the strangest things. Does the holiday season always disturb you this way? Mumsy had the same problem, which is why she took to opium so fervently. She claimed it was medicinal. To her surprise, the gentlemen from Interpol felt differently."

"I'm leaving, Malthea. We can walk back to the lane together, or you can stay here and meditate until you're blue in the face, which will be well before dawn."

Without waiting for her reply, I plunged back through the firs.

CHAPTER 12

When I got back to the Book Depot, Caron thrust out her hand and waited until I dropped the car key in it before saying, "Did you forget to mention that this errand of yours involved a trip to Another State? That's probably where the only empty parking place at the mall is by now. Is it in Montana or West Virginia? Is there a shuttle?"

"Did you have any customers?" I asked as I went in the office to hang up my coat.

"Yeah, a few. Is there any gas in the car?"

"Not enough to cross state lines, but ample to get to the mall and back. That *is* where you're going, isn't it?"

"That's what I said," she said, suddenly finding the need to align the pens and pencils on the counter like neatly toppled (and nutritionally challenged) toy soldiers. "We'll shop until nine when the mall closes, and then maybe get a pizza."

"I would have thought you and Inez were sick of the mall by now, particularly after what happened the other day."

She shrugged ever so innocently. "I'm not going to invite Mrs. Claus to share a pizza with us, if that's what you're implying. I don't ever want to set eyes on her or her manual again. Inez is going to meet me a little after eight by the fountain at the opposite end of the mall."

"Be home by eleven," I said, then stood by the window and watched her get into the car, twist the rearview mirror to inspect her makeup, and drive away. I was convinced she was up to something more insidious than wandering around the mall, but I couldn't begin to think what it might be.

I had a partial answer when an unfamiliar teenage girl with frizzy blond hair and unfortunately tight jeans came into the store an hour later. After a brief bout of stammering, she asked to speak to Caron.

"She's at the mall," I said.

"Drat! Even if I knew what she looked like, there's no way I could find her in that madhouse and we're leaving at five-thirty."

"You and Caron?"

"No," the girl said, wringing her hands like a heroine steeling herself to go up the dark, creaky staircase to the attic where things did not bode well for her. "I told her she could come over after supper, but now my mother's decided she wants to leave for my grandma's house as soon as she gets off work instead of waiting until tomorrow. I can ask my grandma's permission to make a long-distance call, but she'll most likely say no. She's so cheap that she unplugs all the lamps and appliances at night so they can't leak electricity."

"Would you like to leave Caron a note?" I said, pushing a piece of paper and a pencil across the counter and hoping I didn't seem overly eager.

Or rabid.

"It's kinda complicated for that. Can I just tell you?" I nodded with commendable restraint. "Darla Jean and I didn't up and quit, although we sure wanted to after Miz Portmeyer started nagging us all the time and bawling us out over nothing. I mean, it wasn't easy to keep the line moving, collect the money, and jam the photographs in the cardboard frames—all with mothers squawking because they didn't like the stiff smiles on their kids' faces and Santa getting lost every time he went to the rest room. Darla Jean said she'd work on her uncle's hog farm afore she'd put up with that again."

"You were fired?" I asked before she could launch into a discourse on the merits of a career in porcine husbandry.

"Miz Portmeyer said we took money from the cash box when her back was turned. How could we have done that? It's not like the costumes have pockets, and our purses were in our lockers. She just frowned and said that we must have passed the money to someone outside the fence. I was so mad I wanted to tell her to put one of those elves in a place where the sun don't shine, but Darla Jean started crying and I had to take her to the lounge before she made fools out of both of us."

"Was there money missing?"

"If there was, Miz Portmeyer took it herself. I don't see why she would, though. She always wore real expensive clothes and jewelry, and once she sent me to get something out of the trunk of her fancy sports car. Thirty dollars is nothing but lunch money to her. Anyway, that's what Caron wanted to talk about. Tell her I'm sorry, but I won't be back home until three or four days after Christmas, depending on how long my mother can put up with my grandma. It's usually not very long."

"Wait a minute," I said as the girl headed for the door. "How did Caron find you?"

"I don't know, and even if she'd found out our names, Darla Jean and I live in a little town about twenty miles from here called Maggody."

"I've never heard of it," I said apologetically.

"Nobody has," she said with a lugubrious sigh. "We had to write down our addresses and telephone numbers when we applied for the job, but I can't see Miz Portmeyer letting Caron copy down the information."

"Will Darla Jean be home tonight?"

"No, her family left yesterday to spend Christmas in St. Louis. I'll bet her grandma doesn't have a five-pound ball of rubber bands."

The girl, whose name I'd never ascertained, left the bookstore under her personal cloud of melancholy. No customers appeared after that, and at six o'clock I hung the "closed" sign on the door, locked up, and walked home to an empty apartment, an increasingly mangy Christmas tree, and a newscast that underscored the hazards of public transportation in underdeveloped countries. Vermont was not mentioned.

The following evening would be Christmas Eve. I'd promised the downstairs tenant, a retired professor who'd found himself divorced only recently and for reasons he'd not yet assimilated, that I would drop by his party, but I doubted I would any more than I would drag myself to Luanne's for an evening of cocktail-party chatter and squares of cheese on toothpicks.

The only thing that had any appeal was hearing what Caron had to say when she came home at eleven. It would require a healthy amount of inventiveness on her part to explain—without admitting to any misdemeanors, that is—how she'd found the names and

telephone numbers of the previous two assistants at
Santa's Workshop.

I wasn't sure what to make of the girl's story of being wrongly accused of theft. She'd sounded sincere
(and didn't everybody these days?), but Ms. Portmeyer must have been aware of the risk when she
fired them a week before Christmas. Without jingling
reindeer to facilitate the operation, profits would plum-
met and the home office might reexamine her position
on the heretofore ascending corporate escalator.

I was trying to decide on the best approach to persuade Caron to tell me what she was up to when the
telephone rang. I picked up the receiver with the same
eagerness I would a dollop of raw meat and said,
"Hello."

"Claire, this is Fern Lewis. I'm so upset I don't know
what to do. A woman from the hospital called to tell
me that Malthea's in the emergency room. I don't trust
myself to drive. Can you please take me there?"

I told her I'd pick her up in ten minutes, then
grabbed my coat and was halfway down the steps
when I realized the garage was empty. My half, anyway. I went back through the apartment and down the
interior front stairs to knock on the door of my nearest,
and at the moment, dearest neighbor.

He answered the door in his bathrobe and slippers.
"What a surprise, Claire, but I'm afraid you're early.
My little get-together is tomorrow. However, if you'd
like to come inside, I can offer you a tasty concoction
of cranberry juice, vodka, and crème de menthe. I like
to call it a 'Jingle Bell Bazooka.' "

"I need to borrow your car," I said. "Caron has
mine, and I don't know how to get in touch with her.
A friend is at the emergency room." When he hesi-

tated, I added, "The poor thing's quite elderly and frail, and she's never mentioned having any relatives in the area."

I may have been piling it on when I described her as frail, but he must have already had a Jingle Bell Bazooka or two because he blinked tearily, left the doorway, and returned a moment later with a key ring. I thanked him and hurried around the yard to the garage.

When I pulled up in front of the duplex, Fern was waiting on the porch. She wrinkled her nose as she climbed into the passenger's side of the VW Beetle. "Is it cigarette smoke I smell? I do hope you haven't picked up that filthy habit. My late husband used to sneak outside for an occasional cigar, and I always told him afterward that he reeked like an incinerator."

"I had to borrow the car," I said. "What happened to Malthea?"

"I wish I knew. The woman called me because my name and address are on a next-of-kin card in Malthea's wallet. It was just a precaution, and I never expected to be careening through dark streets like this."

I glanced at the speedometer. "I'm going twenty-three miles an hour, Fern. That does not qualify as 'careening.'"

"Perhaps you should step on it. Malthea may die before we get there."

I clenched my teeth and concentrated on shifting rather than stripping gears. As I parked in front of the emergency room, I saw two police cars at the end of the curb. A car that resembled Jorgeson's was in the shadows beyond them.

A succinct expletive entered my mind, in that it did not seem likely that Malthea had fallen off a curb or been stricken with a heart attack. I let Fern out of the car, parked, and joined her at the door. "It's going to be fine," I said, squeezing her shoulder.

"I've been fretting all day. Malthea refused to answer the door or her telephone. The curtains were drawn. I called over and over again. I was beside myself."

"I'm sure you were." I led her into the blindingly antiseptic environment of the emergency room. A multigenerational Hispanic family was grouped on two sofas; even the youngest child watched me solemnly. Beyond them was a woman holding a baby wrapped in a thin blanket. The only other person in sight was a young nurse with a clipboard and a harried expression.

"Malthea Hendlerson?" I said to her.

"She's been taken upstairs," the nurse said, flinching as an elevator opened behind us. "Are you relatives? We need some information about her insurance coverage."

"What happened to her?"

"I can't say. She suffered injuries, and once they stabilized her, she was transferred to ICU. We have her Medicare card, but we must know if she has a private insurer."

"Or what?" I demanded in what even I realized was an unnecessarily high voice. "Are you going to turn off the life-support system if she doesn't have insurance?"

Jorgeson appeared at my side, discreetly hustled me over to a soda machine, and hunted through his pockets for change. "Calm down, Mrs. Malloy," he murmured. "None of us needs to deal with hospital security just now. Why don't you sit and we'll talk?"

I sat. Jorgeson handed me a can and sat down beside me. "Here's all we know so far. Malthea went to

Nicholas Chunder's house sometime after we left at five o'clock. We haven't had anybody on duty out there since we took the boy into custody last night, but I did arrange for a patrol car to cruise by on a regular basis. The officers saw a light, went inside, and found her unconscious on the floor. Blow to the head. She's still out."

Fern, who'd given up badgering the nurse and was hovering nearby, made a gurgly noise. "Is she in a coma?"

"At the moment, she's merely unconscious," said Jorgeson. "We haven't ruled out the possibility that one of our local degenerates heard about the murder and showed up, thinking the house would be unoccupied. The light should have warned him off, though. These weasels are more scared of their shadows than your average groundhog."

I lowered my voice. "Then you think that it has to do with Nicholas's murder?"

"Hold on." He beckoned to a uniformed officer and asked him to escort Fern to the ICU waiting room. Once she was gone, he said, "Nothing was taken, and there're expensive objects everywhere you look. Anyone who'd gone there with the explicit intent to commit theft would have at least stuffed a piece of silver or crystal in his pocket."

I gazed at a greenish expanse of linoleum that brought to mind a stagnant pond. "Look on the bright side, Jorgeson—at least two suspects have been eliminated. Gilda and Roy are somewhere upstairs."

"If only they were. It seems that on this very afternoon, a Brownie troop came to sing Christmas carols and pass out cookies. The nurses and aides on the sixth floor decided that all their patients should be included in the festivities. A very kind-hearted gesture on everyone's part, to be sure. The door was left unlocked, certain patients became overtly emotional, two dozen Brownies started screaming, and Roy and Gilda managed to disappear. Nobody noticed their absence until supper trays were being distributed."

"I'd have thought security on that particular ward would be tight."

"Not as tight as it should be, obviously. Patients walk off the psych ward more often than the public's aware of, since the hospital administrators don't want negative publicity. Gilda and Roy aren't the only ones who slipped away this afternoon. We have APBs out on a convicted rapist and a guy who wears an aluminum-foil skullcap. Gilda works here, so she may have had help. Or maybe the Brownies were in on it."

I told him about my conversation with Malthea in the grove. "She must have lingered in the vicinity until you left, then entered the house to look for something. Could Gilda have gone back, too?"

"Yeah, or Malthea conjured up that demon with the foreign name and bad attitude."

"Have you located the weapon?"

He nodded. "Chunder had a marble replica of Stonehenge in his study. One of the chunks was found near her body. It'd been wiped off, but there was a trace of blood in a crack. Ironic, huh?"

"Very," I said dryly. "So Malthea was in the study when she was attacked? Was she searching the desk?"

"There's a cabinet in the corner. We'd already been through it and found nothing of interest, but she wouldn't have known that. Evidence suggests that she was kneeling in front of it and working on the lock with a hairpin, which would explain why she didn't hear this other person come into the room. Picking a lock requires a lot of concentration."

"So I've heard," I murmured. "What were they looking for, Jorgeson? No one could expect to find clues scattered about after your team went over the scene."

"No one in his or her right mind, anyway. The guy with the shiny cap would fit right in with this group."

"Thanks for the soda," I said as I stood up. "I guess I'd better find Fern and make sure she's not driving the ICU staff crazy." I took the elevator to the appropriate floor and followed stenciled arrows to the glass doors of the unit. A sign sternly forbade unauthorized visitors.

That being precisely what I was, I went into the waiting room across the hall. Fern was perched on the edge of a chair, her face grim with either concern or disapproval of the two androgynous teenagers sprawled across a couch in a corner. The latter was more likely, since they had nose rings and creatively styled purple hair.

I touched Fern's arm. "Have you spoken to anyone?"

"Only long enough to be told I'm not allowed to see Malthea. I'm of a mind to report that woman to her supervisor. Impertinence should not be tolerated."

"Give 'em hell, granny," said one of the teenagers. The other brayed in appreciation.

I stepped in front of Fern before she could launch an attack, verbal or otherwise. "Is she still unconscious?"

"They said that I would be informed of any changes in her condition. I couldn't tell which cubicle she's in or what sort of attention she's receiving. I really should be permitted to sit by her bed. She'll be frightened if she wakes up in a strange room and finds herself clad only in a flimsy gown. There are moments I wish I could cast an effective spell—or a curse that would teach that nurse a thing or two."

I sensed the stirring interest of the pair of eggplant heads in the corner. "There's a coffee machine by the elevator," I said. "I think you'll find a hot drink comforting."

"I only drink decaf after ten o'clock in the morning."

"There will be decaf," I said, tugging at her arm. "Afterward, I'll try to get information from the nurse."

Fern allowed me to guide her to the vending machines. I punched a button, waited while a stream of brown liquid dribbled into the cup, and then thrust it at Fern's trembling hand.

She stared at it. "I can't drink this. It's liable to upset my stomach."

I put the cup on top of the machine. "I can see how worried you are. Have you and Malthea been friends for a long time?"

"We met while we were in college. We both planned to teach secondary English, but my fiancé returned from Germany and wanted to get married immediately. He stayed in the army for the next fifteen years, and was stationed everywhere from Omaha to Manila. It was hard to remain in touch, but Malthea and I did our best with greeting cards and letters."

"What did she do?"

"Taught, of course. How else could she have supported herself?"

"She never married?"

"At one time, she was engaged, but the wedding did not take place. That's all I shall say concerning the matter."

I noted the rigidity of her expression and abandoned the intriguing topic. "How long has she lived in Farberville?"

"Twelve, perhaps thirteen years. She bought a small house and did volunteer work to keep herself busy. We rarely saw each other while my husband was alive. He was a deacon in the Baptist church and disapproved of her eccentricities. When he passed away, Malthea urged me to consider Druidism as an alternative to the orthodox traditions I'd followed since childhood. I attended a ritual and met Nicholas, who offered me economical housing and loaned me money from time to time until I straightened out my financial affairs. He went so far as to help with the paperwork that was required for me to receive a widow's pension from the military. How could he have been so compassionate back then, and so cruel the evening before the solstice?"

I wasn't sure how much further I could go without reducing her to tears, but anxiety had made her garrulous and I was not above taking advantage of it. Amateur sleuths cannot be slaves to scrupulosity. "Can you tell me exactly what happened that evening? Were you and Malthea among the first or the last to arrive?"

"Let me think," she said. "I do my best to be prompt, but we were a bit late because Malthea was so dithery. First, she forgot her sweater and had to go back inside. Nicholas's house can be drafty this time of year. We were all set to start off, and then she remembered a sack of holly she'd left in her kitchen. I was so annoyed that I refused to speak to her until we got there."

"The others were already there, then?"

"Roy and Morning Rose were in the living room,

acting as though they were at a funeral. While we were hanging up our coats, Nicholas and Gilda came out of the study. When I later asked her what they'd been discussing that had so distressed her, she mumbled something about needing to find another place to live. In my day, we were taught to speak clearly."

I did a mental review of the roster. "What about Sullivan?"

"He was a full half hour late. Apparently there'd been a problem with the children, and Morning Rose insisted that he put them to bed by himself. I believe she walked to Primrose Hill. She must have regretted her decision, because she seemed very unhappy."

"It must have been a tense evening," I prompted her.

"Oh, it was that. My annoyance with Malthea soon spread to all the members of the grove. Everyone seemed sullen and disinclined to participate. I had to speak sharply to Roy when he failed to fetch a stepladder at my request. Morning Rose and Sullivan had a whispered argument in the kitchen, and when they came back into the room, her eyes were red. Nicholas spent most of the evening in a chair by the fireplace, watching us as though we had designs on his knickknacks. I was deeply offended by his implicit accusation."

I spotted the teenagers sauntering down the hall toward us and nudged her around the corner and into a storage room filled with odoriferous cleaning supplies. "Did something specific happen that caused him to make his unexpected announcement?"

Fern clutched her purse on the off chance I was about to mug her with an ammonia bottle. "We'd finished putting up the decorations, and were seated around the fire, drinking that dreadful beverage Nicholas insisted on serving. Malthea did her best to lead us in song, but even I was infected with their gloom. I was about to suggest we leave when Gilda stood up and said that she intended to perform the solstice ritual as she pleased. As she *damn* well pleased is what she actually said. Nicholas came close to spilling his tankard. He began sputtering, but she told him that it didn't matter if she was kicked out of the grove since this would be her final celebration. Morning Rose laughed bitterly and said she might as well join Gilda. Sullivan grabbed her arm, and then Roy grabbed *his* arm, and the two began to grapple. That was when Nicholas exploded with rage. It was quite terrible."

"Why did Gilda say it would be her final celebration?" I demanded, my fingers crossed that the teenagers would not find us and make remarks that would send Fern off on a tangential tirade.

"I don't know. Shouldn't you find out about Malthea?"

"I'll try," I said. We went back to the doors of the ICU and waited until we were noticed.

The nurse who opened the door did not seem pleased to see Fern behind me. "I've already told you that I cannot discuss the patient's condition. That is the attending physician's prerogative."

"Not even with the patient's sister?" I said, hoping Fern was paying attention.

"She didn't say that earlier."

I tried to sound moderately smug. "Did you ask her?"

"She should have said so."

Fern cleared her throat, and in a voice well suited to a displeased schoolteacher, said, "You should have asked me. I was too distraught to respond to your

coldhearted refusal to allow me to sit beside my only
sister. If she should die before I have an opportunity to
hold her hand and reminisce about how we used to
make daisy chains in the meadow on summer afternoons, I may contact our youngest brother. He's an
attorney."

The nurse paled, then invited Fern to accompany her
into a curtained cubicle. I considered tagging along,
then decided not to complicate the ruse and returned
to the waiting room. I was relieved to have it to myself.

At least I had a better picture of what had taken
place between seven and nine o'clock on the evening
of the murder, I thought as I tried to make myself comfortable on the plastic upholstery. Gilda's threat to
turn up wearing nothing but an amulet may have trig-
gered Nicholas's outburst, but he'd already listed his
property with a real estate agency and contacted a
similar agency in Wales. It seemed likely that he'd
planned to delay his announcement until after the
solstice celebration for the same reason one doesn't
tell children about an imminent divorce on Christmas Eve.

But according to Fern, the Druids were already upset when she and Malthea arrived. Roy and Morning
Rose had been brooding in the living room, and Gilda
had heard something not to her liking in the study.
Sullivan had argued with his wife. The host himself
had been less than genial.

And why hadn't Malthea denied Roy's ridiculous
accusation? She could have been so taken aback that
she was momentarily speechless, but I'd practically
begged her in the grove hours later. Morning Rose had
seemed convinced that Roy had blindly obeyed Malthea's command to kill Nicholas. I wasn't.

I was not likely to find a listing for Sisters of Illumination in the telephone directory so that I could inquire into their membership role and annual observances. Surely law-enforcement agencies would have heard rumors if sacrifices, human or otherwise, were being performed in the area. There had been one such case concerning cattle mutilations in the county, attributed to almond-eyed alien vivisectionists, but the ensuing investigation had determined that a pack of feral dogs had been responsible.

I was still juggling ideas when a woman in baggy blue scrubs and plastic slippers came into the waiting room. Her hair was hidden under the sort of cap favored by surgical teams, but her sallow complexion could not be so easily disguised.

"Gilda?" I said. "What are you doing here?"

"It's as good a place as any. I'm waiting for someone I know to get off duty so he can give me a ride out to the trailer park. I'd be conspicuous dressed like this if I was walking down the road, but here I'm invisible. I was hanging around the emergency room when Malthea was wheeled in. What happened to her?"

I tried not to stare at the discreet bandages on her wrists. "She was attacked in Nicholas's study. Patrolmen noticed a light and investigated. Otherwise, she might have lain there for several days."

"What was she doing there?"

"The same thing you were," I said, "although you and she may have been looking for different things. What were you hoping to find?"

"Money," she said quickly. "He was a real miser, so I figured he'd have a lockbox in a desk drawer. If I'd known they had the house staked out because of Roy, I wouldn't have tried it."

"And that's why you wanted to talk to me the other evening? You wanted to ask me if I could suggest the most likely places to find a hypothetical lockbox? Then, after you'd been arrested, you thought my nonexistent license to practice law would facilitate your release? When I failed to bail you out, you attempted suicide? At the worst you would have been charged with criminal trespass, since you never made it into the house. I don't buy this, Gilda."

She sat down on the couch vacated by the teenagers, pulled off the cloth cap, and placed it carefully on the armrest. "You seemed like such good buddies with the cops that I thought you could tell me what was going on. It's only been three hundred years since the Salem witch trials. Wicca is something entirely different, but we're still lumped in with medieval practitioners with their black cats and evil eyes."

"Three hundred years is not the same as last summer," I said. "The Puritans are no longer monopolizing the city council and the school board, and no one except a lifeguard cares if you float or sink. You're not stupid enough to break into Nicholas's house for money. What did he have?"

She went to the doorway and stuck her head out, then sat down next to me. "Will you promise not to tell anyone?"

"I can't do that, Gilda. It's against the law to withhold evidence, and in any case, I'm not going to do anything that will muddy the waters. Did Roy tell you that he confessed?"

"Twice, he said," she said with a momentary smile. "Yes, we talked in the dayroom this morning. He killed Nicholas, Mrs. Malloy. He's ashamed of it, but he did it and he's willing to accept his punishment."

"Not so eager that he didn't escape this afternoon," I pointed out.

"There are things he must do before he turns himself in again," she said somberly. "He must conduct a final ritual in an attempt to protect himself from Ambesek. If it doesn't work, his body will never be found."

"Would you people stop this!" I waited until I'd simmered down, but whiffs of steam may have still been drifting out of my ears. "This is nothing but self-indulgent nonsense. Oh, I'm sure everyone who works here has heard rumors of your Wiccan practices, and therefore thinks you're terribly romantic. Salem witch trials? Ambesek? Demon-repellant rituals? Buy him a can of Raid and give me a break!"

"You're a skeptic," she said, pronouncing judgment from her plastic-covered bench.

"You can bet the farm on it. Now either tell me why you insisted on speaking to me, or see how far you can get after I call hospital security. Odds are not good that you can make it to an exit, but you may know of a door in the basement. Cast a spell and make yourself invisible. I don't care. A week ago I was minding my own business, and now I'm embroiled with a gang of delusional pagans. The man I care about is snuggled up in front of a fire with his ex–significant other. I'm being sued for a million dollars. My daughter's off committing a felony. Malthea's in ICU, Nicholas is in the morgue, Roy's in battle with a demon, and the best you can do is label me a skeptic?"

"Gracious, Mrs. Malloy," Gilda said, again checking the doorway for lurkers, "I'd no idea you were this upset. Shall I cast a spell to envelope you in a protective glow of love and warmth from the Mother Goddess?"

"That's it." I stood up and grabbed my purse. "I'm alerting security that you're in the building. Good-bye and good luck."

She caught my arm. "Okay, I'll tell the truth."

Not only would the archbishop and the princess elope, the pope would conduct the ceremony.

CHAPTER 13

"Then tell me the truth," I said as I allowed myself to be led back to the couch. This is not to say that I wasn't keenly aware of the distance to a bright red telephone in the hallway. No more than a whoop and a holler, so to speak.

Gilda's face puckered like a bulldog's. "Can this stay between us, Mrs. Malloy?"

"I've already said that I won't keep secrets from the police. If what you tell me is relevant, then I will certainly tell them."

"It's *not* relevant," she said. "It's nothing more than a rumor and it's not true. All the same, if it got out, it would cause problems. You can't believe the amount of gossiping that goes on in hospitals. The only person who'll keep a confidence is in a drawer in the morgue. Nurses, doctors, orderlies, secretaries, aides, cafeteria workers—everybody gossips."

"What's the rumor?"

"Oh, all right. A few years back, I was working at a hospital in Kansas City. I'm a pediatric nurse, so I deal with a lot of neonatal patients. Most of them are healthy and pink, but some are in bad shape and . . . well, not destined to lead happy lives. They're born with AIDS, or they're addicted to crack, or they have

deformities to their spinal columns and brains." She
moved away from me, her hands clenched and her
sallow skin now almost colorless. When she finally
spoke, her voice was tight. "Some of these babies die,
Mrs. Malloy. We keep them on respirators, we feed them
intravenously, we drain fluids from their cranial cavi-
ties, we do everything we can to keep them alive." She
spun around and looked down at me with strobelike
intensity. "But sometimes they die—and sometimes
it's for the best. Can you understand that?"

I held up my palms. "Sit down, Gilda. No one's accused you of anything."

"Nicholas did," she said bitterly. "He persuaded
someone in personnel to let him read my application,
and then used his computer to start a dialogue with
his colleagues at the hospital in Kansas City. They
were happy to pass along rumors about why I resigned. That's all I did. I wasn't fired, and there were
no charges brought against me. All he heard were lies.
If there had been any proof that I'd done something
wrong, I would have been charged."

I tried to keep my voice even. "If you were never
charged, then how could these rumors affect you?"

"That night in his study Nicholas told me that he'd
decided to 'clean off his desk,' as he called it, before he
left for Wales. He was not only going to inform the
head of nursing that I'd made no mention of the reason for my resignation on my application, he was also
going to put the word out all over the Internet that I
was . . . well, you know. A premature baby, not even
three pounds at birth, died last month. I wasn't assigned to that patient, but Nicholas said he was going
to retrieve the records and make sure I hadn't been
alone in the nursery on that night."

"And had you?" I asked softly.

"I was working the ward, but so were other staff. It's not uncommon for babies born with those kinds of complications to stop breathing. It happens, Mrs. Malloy. I had nothing to do with it. Nicholas said he was going to prevent me from ever again finding work as a registered nurse in any accredited hospital in the country. It's what I'm trained to do. It's all that matters to me."

Saliva was bubbling on her lips and her eyes were overly bright. I glanced at the doorway, hoping Fern would come to the rescue. I would have even welcomed the aberrant teenagers. As it was, I cast about for a soothing comment, and finally said, albeit with monumental inanity, "I understand, Gilda."

"No, you don't, and neither did Nicholas. I did everything I could to dissuade him, but he said that he would contact every state licensing board in the country. Boards administer a slap on the wrist to nurses who steal drugs. They issue a three-month suspension to nurses who expedite terminal cancer patients. But nurses who are rumored to have . . ."

To my astonishment, she collapsed across my lap and began to sob like a heartbroken toddler, her gulps and snorts loud enough to be heard on every floor in the hospital. I was torn between patting her on the back and rolling her onto the floor. I was not unsympathetic, but I'd learned by this time that if one of the members of the Sacred Grove of Keltria announced that the sun would rise in the east, I'd do better to be looking west at dawn.

I was still vacillating when Fern came into the room and stared disapprovingly at me.

"What ever is going on?" she demanded. "Have

you entered into an intimate relationship with an orderly, Claire? It is most inappropriate."

Gilda sat up and wiped her drippy nose on her wrist. "It's me, Fern."

"Oh, dear," she said. "I simply saw your ... buttocks, and leapt to ... oh, dear."

I stood up, effectively sending Gilda into an ungraceful tangle on the linoleum. "How's Malthea?" I asked Fern, ignoring the mutters from the region of my feet.

"She awoke some minutes ago, and although she was unable to speak, she was heartened by my presence. She'll be moved to a standard room in the morning, presuming she continues to show improvement. Why is Gilda rolling about like that?"

"She's upset," I said.

"We are all upset," Fern said sternly. "That is no excuse."

Gilda extricated herself up and crawled onto the couch like an intoxicated crab. "Malthea's vitals are stable?"

"A good deal more stable than yours," Fern retorted, then turned to me. "I should like to go home, if you don't mind. It's really quite late. I won't be surprised to find Malthea's cat on my doorstep, mewing piteously for her supper. She can make do with milk until I have a chance to pick up some cat food at the grocery store. This is all so inconvenient. Behavior like this does not become you, Gilda. I do hope this is not the consequence of some Wiccan spell."

Gilda and I looked at each other. When it became clear that she wasn't going to leap in, I said, "We were worried about Malthea, and now we know she's going to be all right. Our problem is what Gilda's going to do in the immediate future. I strongly suggest that she contact Sergeant Jorgeson."

She glanced at Fern, then whispered to me, "Does he know?"

"Know what?" said Fern.

"Not yet," I answered, "but it's a matter of time before his computer boys determine Nicholas's passwords and gain access to the files. It'll be better for you if you've already admitted all this."

"Admitted what?" Fern squawked, beginning to sound like a high-strung parrot with exceptionally acute hearing.

Gilda tried unsuccessfully to push her bangs out of her eyes. "There's more, Mrs. Malloy. I went back out there to talk to Nicholas."

"You people should have carpooled," I said irritably. "So were you there before Fern's purported arrival, after Malthea's purported departure, or sometime in between while Roy purportedly was shooting Nicholas?"

She ignored Fern's gasp and said, "The only person I saw was Sullivan walking across the pasture toward the house. He must have seen me, because he dropped to the ground like a sniper had nailed him."

"Sullivan Sawyer?" I said. "Are you sure?"

"He must have been going there for the same reason I was. When I knocked on the door of the study on the eve of the solstice, Nicholas was on the telephone. As I went inside, he said, 'As you wish, Sullivan,' and then hung up. He looked so angry that I pretended I hadn't heard anything."

"Eavesdropping is vulgar," inserted Fern. "I know you live in a trailer park these days. Did you grow up in one as well?"

"What if I did?" countered Gilda.

I clamped my hand on Gilda's shoulder to keep her on the couch. "Not everyone spends her childhood making daisy chains in the meadow, Fern. Are you ready to leave?"

"Poison ivy garlands seem more likely," Fern said as she buttoned her coat. "Yes, I am more than ready to leave."

"Then please wait by the elevator. I'll be there in a minute."

She opened her mouth to protest, then thought better of it and stalked out of the room. I listened as her footsteps diminished, then tightened my grip on Gilda's shoulder and said, "Did you speak to Nicholas?"

"I lost my nerve when I saw Sullivan. I pedaled home and stayed up half the night trying to find a spell that would prevent him from mentioning it at the celebration the next morning. It would have made Nicholas all the more determined to destroy me."

"What time did you arrive at his house?"

"I don't know," she said. "I headed out there at eleven, but whenever I saw a car coming, I dragged my bicycle into the ditch and squatted next to it."

"Did you recognize any of the cars?" I asked.

"I thought I saw hers," she said, pointing her thumb in the direction of the elevators. "There wasn't much moonlight, though, and I told myself I was mistaken. Was it really Fern? Had Nicholas threatened her, too?"

I briefly thought of Fern's deceased husband, then shook my head and picked up my purse. "You'll have to get a Ouija board and ask him yourself. Do you know where Roy is hiding?"

"Get your own Ouija board," she said, clearly offended by my remark. "Better yet, call a psychic at one of those one-nine-hundred numbers. You might get a real surprise."

"Roy needs to be in the psychiatric ward, Gilda. You said you talked to him earlier today. Aren't you worried that he might harm himself?"

She stood up and collected her green cap. "Group therapy three times a week isn't going to exorcise his demon."

I considering blocking the doorway, but to be honest, it was late and I was sick of them. "Will you go back to the sixth floor?"

"Like a good little girl?" Smirking, she pulled on the cap and tucked her hair under it. The result was lumpy but seemed to satisfy her. "No, I think I'll go out to the grounds, peel off these clothes, and recite the words of the Goddess. 'I who am the beauty of the green Earth, and the white Moon amongst the stars—'" She broke off as the doors of the ICU opened and a cart squeaked down the hall. "See you around, Mrs. Malloy," she said as she whipped past me.

"Not if I can help it," I retorted to an empty room. After a small debate whether I should straighten magazines and switch off the light, I went to the elevator and stood mutely next to Fern. We rode to the ground floor. The Hispanic family was no longer in the emergency room, but the woman with the baby was in the same place, partially covered with a blanket and snoring loudly.

I stopped at the reception desk and told a nurse about my encounter with Gilda D'Orcher in the ICU wing, then asked her to call security and the Farberville Police Department.

"I'd heard she was a patient on the sixth floor," the woman said with a malicious smile. "I'm not the only one who thought she should have been sent there a long time ago. The stories about her are enough to chill your blood. One of the orderlies swore he caught a glimpse of her in the basement with a black cat. Once she and her supervisor had an argument, and the very next day the supervisor slipped on a wet spot on the floor and broke her ankle."

I was hoping she would elaborate, but she picked up the telephone and punched a button. I pushed open the door for Fern and glowered at her back as she scurried toward the VW. Once we were buckled in and driving toward her neighborhood, I said, "Why did you go back to Nicholas's that night?"

Her nose rose imperiously. "I believe I've already explained it."

"No, you haven't," I said as I braked in anticipation of a red light. "The brandy decanter wasn't touched. The story you told me was at Malthea's behest, wasn't it? You and she were trying to help Roy. Why does she care so much about him?"

"I refuse to discuss it," she said with a sniff. "I have my reasons—and they are none of your business. I am very sorry you intruded on our winter solstice celebration, Claire. This is the first year we've had problems like this."

"Like murder?" I said bluntly.

"All this unpleasantness. Nicholas should have known better than to think he could . . ."

"Could what? Blackmail everybody? Could that be what put the damper on the festivities?"

"He was a gentleman. He would never stoop to that sort of thing."

"Then what?" I demanded, huffing and puffing and close to blowing her out of the car. "You did go there, although not to have a glass of brandy and a civilized conversation. Had Nicholas threatened to expose you, too?"

"Don't be absurd. I've done nothing wrong. You, on the other hand, are driving erratically. It's making me nervous. I can see I shall need a cup of valeriana tea before I can possibly fall asleep."

I gave up and drove her home without further attempts to elicit information from her. She might not have actually spent any time as a teacher, but she'd studied the techniques of classroom intimidation and paid careful attention.

"Good night," I said as I pulled up to the curb. "Can you drive yourself to the hospital tomorrow?"

"One would think." She climbed out of the car, gave me an enigmatic look, and went up the sidewalk to her porch. I waited until she was inside, then drove to the corner and obediently stopped in front of an octagonal sign requesting as much from me.

At this point, I'll admit, I craned my neck and made sure Roy was not hiding in the backseat. Rather than continue home, however, I pulled to the curb, cut off the engine, and sat back to think about what I'd heard—and what it might have meant.

If (with a capital *I*) Gilda had been telling the truth, Fern had been at the house and Sullivan had been going in that direction. What a busy night Nicholas might have had if he'd entertained each and every would-be caller. He must have begun to regret his announcement as cars, cyclists, and pedestrians crunched across the gravel forecourt in an endless parade. Which of them had been admitted? And what had he or she found? A blustery, self-righteous Druid or a corpse on the kitchen floor?

Roy should have been the central figure, but Malthea seemed to be popping up in the center of the vortex with every revelation. Thanks to Fern's uncharacteristic cooperation, I had a scanty notion of Malthea's history: college, a broken engagement, a career in teaching, retirement, volunteer work. Jorgeson might have a few more tidbits, but he wouldn't have ordered a full-blown background check on any of them unless fingerprints had matched a set in the FBI file.

At least I wasn't brooding about Peter, I told myself as I wondered if there was any way to get a set of Leslie's fingerprints. It seemed obvious that she was employed by the KGB, and used the trite St. Petersburg opera ploy to pass along state secrets to unshaven men named Vladimir and Uri. Myron was likely to be in on it. The wolfhounds undoubtedly had cyanide capsules embedded in their rhinestone-studded collars.

Clearly, I needed to go home and find something to read, if only the back of a cereal box or an insert in the newspaper announcing a Christmas Eve sale at a local discount store. I needed a cold drink and a hot meal. I needed to be sitting on the sofa when Caron came home.

Or maybe I needed a lobotomy, I concluded as I got out of the car, made sure the doors were locked, and walked back toward the duplex, careful to stay in the shadows.

Lights were on inside Fern's apartment; Malthea's, as expected, was dark. I asked myself where an Arch Druid might hide a front door key. Despite an escalation in the crime rate and admonishments from the chief of police, residents of Farberville continue to cloak themselves in a small-town mentality of trusting thy neighbor as thyself. However, there was no key under the mat or on the sill above the door.

I was groping the soil in a clay flowerpot when the porch light came on and Fern opened her door.

"Have you lost something?" she said.

I straightened up and brushed grit off my fingers. "My mind, for instance? I think that's obvious by now. No, Fern, I simply decided that I have to know more about Malthea in order to help her avoid spending the rest of her life in prison. She's maddening, but I like her."

"The rest of her life in prison?" Pulling a shawl more tightly around her shoulders, Fern came out onto the porch. "All she did was tell the police a little white lie about the brandy decanter. Surely that's not a crime that merits prison. A fine, perhaps, and certainly a scolding from a judge—but prison?"

"You haven't spoken to her today, have you?"

"No, I told you that when we first arrived at the hospital. Has she been accused of something?"

I gave her a short, sanitized version of Roy's latest confession. "And she wasn't in seclusion in her apartment, either," I added. "She followed me all over town this afternoon, then confronted me in the grove and demanded to hear exactly what Roy'd said. She refused to confirm or deny it. Sergeant Jorgeson had his doubts, but if the media get wind of this, the county prosecutor, who's never averse to publicity, may demand that she be charged. You'll have more tabloid reporters in your yard than you have dandelions in the spring. Your photograph—and Malthea's mug shots—will be on covers in every supermarket in the country."

Fern turned around and put her hand on the doorknob. After a long moment, she cleared her throat and said, "I was planning to pack a bag to take to the hospital tomorrow. Just a few things to make Malthea more comfortable, like her robe and slippers, toiletries, a crossword puzzle book. I'll get her key and do it now. If you'd like, you can come along."

Once we were inside Malthea's apartment, Fern murmured something and went into another room. I sat down at a small desk and began opening drawers. The first contained utility receipts, an expired library card, pencils with worn erasers, and a small box filled with discolored keys.

I moved along, discovering such keepsakes as matchbooks, calendars from the previous decade, postcards with illegible scrawls, packets of salt and pepper from fast-food restaurants, and leaky pens.

In the bottom drawer on the right, covered by notebooks and much-used folders, was a leather box. Feeling oddly guilty, I took it out and set it on the surface in front of me.

The top item was a neatly clipped newspaper article with a photograph of a smiling couple and a header that announced that Dr. Randall H. Tate and his wife, Dr. Brenda Cockburn-Tate, anthropologists at Farber College, had been awarded a grant from the National Geographic Foundation to study the Dayak of Borneo, an aboriginal people who lived in the tropical rain forests of the highlands. Dr. Tate was particularly interested in their centuries-old tradition of headhunting.

I put the article aside and took out a much smaller clipping concerning Dr. Tate's appointment as head of the department of cultural anthropology. Beneath it was a blurry snapshot of a man in his yard who appeared to be Dr. Tate at an age when he possessed a great deal more hair and at least one pair of bell-bottom jeans.

There were more snapshots of unknown people,

some grim and some smiling. The backgrounds were uniformly indistinct. I hurried through them, then froze as I came upon one of Roy. He was walking along a sidewalk, oblivious of the camera. After a bit of scrutiny, I decided that he was outside the used-book store on Thurber Street where he'd claimed Malthea had approached him.

Had she been stalking him?

I replaced everything in the box and returned it to the bottom drawer. I'd been through all the desk drawers, but Fern was packing at a charmingly slow pace. I went into the kitchen and eased open drawers until I found one filled with the sort of junk I keep in such a kitchen drawer. There were manuals from extinct appliances, virginal warranty cards, rubber bands, string, an empty roll of masking tape . . . and a brochure from an outfit called Psychic Confidantes. For a mere pittance of $3.99 per minute, any caller could, from the privacy of his or her own home, have a totally confidential session with a certified psychic. Answers to questions concerning romance, careers, and money were guaranteed one hundred percent.

Malthea must have believed this twaddle, I thought as I took out a deck of tarot cards and stared at the depictions of characters dressed in colorful costumes. Even "Death" was gaudy. Although I doubted conversations with a "Psychic Confidante" were covered by the rules of client confidentiality, it might prove difficult to subpoena a voice at the other end of the line with the name Divinia.

There was a 1-900 number written in ink at the bottom of the brochure. I copied it down on an old grocery-store tape, then put everything back and looked around for another place in which Malthea might have stashed something of note.

I was heading for the refrigerator (don't ask) when I saw Fern in the doorway.

"Did you find anything?" she asked.

"Photographs of Roy and a couple of clippings concerning his father. Why was Malthea so interested in them?"

"She was very disturbed when she first caught a glimpse of Roy in some shop, and asked the clerk about him. She did not lead him into satanism; she was trying to save him."

"Has she ever mentioned the Sisters of Illumination?"

"No, and she's never staggered in at dawn drenched in blood. That's all balderdash, and I'm disappointed that you would even ask such a question. She and I have a tacit agreement not to impose on each other, so I can't give you a detailed account of her daily activities. But I've never been given any reason to believe that she has an evil bone in her body. Roy has been experiencing nightmares, very likely drug-induced. He needs to be under the care of professionals."

I leaned against the counter and tried not to sound too frustrated. "Then why didn't she just say so?"

Fern looked away. "She is fond of Roy. I suppose she thinks her silence will in some way help him out of this dreadful mess. Is there any doubt that he shot Nicholas?"

"The evidence is there. What needs to be determined is if he's competent to stand trial. Once he's back in custody, there'll be a brief hearing at which his lawyer and the prosecutor will agree to a thirty-day period of observation at the state hospital. What happens after that is up to the psychiatrists."

"If he sticks to his story?"

"It's anybody's guess," I said honestly. "If a jury believes that Malthea took advantage of his vulnerability, she may receive a harsh sentence. He was very convincing when he told me. I almost felt as though I could smell a trace of sulfur in the air."

Fern picked up a small suitcase. "Then you are in need of a strong tonic to purge your system. I'd like to go to bed now. I doubt I'll get much sleep; I have many things to think about."

I trailed her out to the porch and watched as she locked Malthea's door, pocketed the key, and went into her apartment. The porch light flickered off. Being a perspicacious person, I realized that it was a not-so-subtle suggestion that I do the same.

As I drove home, I mulled over the significance, if any, of the two clippings and the photographs of Randall and Roy (*père et fils*, as it were). There was no way to question either of them and almost no point in questioning Malthea. Was it conceivable that she'd seen him drifting along Thurber Street and pegged him as a potential victim? Had the article about the Borneo sabbatical been in the newspaper before or after she approached him? Could Sullivan Sawyer have said something about his professor's son that led her to lurk near the bookstore and surreptitiously take the photograph?

I must have relied on automatic pilot because I was startled when I realized I'd parked in the garage. My car was not there, but Caron had more than two hours before she was due. I stopped by the retiree's apartment, handed him the keys and assured him that "my friend" was in good shape, then trudged upstairs.

Not more than two minutes after I'd turned on the lights and decided which frozen entrée might appeal, the doorbell rang. I stuck a chicken à la Popsicle in the microwave and went to the front door.

The man on the landing was a stranger, and decidedly strange. He wore a shabby overcoat bereft of most of its buttons, a beret that covered his forehead like a moldy blue pancake, and heavy, mud-caked boots. A backpack hung on one shoulder, a rolled-up sleeping bag on the other. His grayish yellow hair hung below his ears, and his white beard was scraggly and dotted with flecks of tobacco. Eyes that might once have been blue were faded into a dull, translucent gray. His nose, in contrast, was markedly red. There was a redolence about him— not of body odor or soured sweat, but of earthiness. I suspected bathing was not on his daily agenda.

"Ms. Malloy?" he said hesitantly.

"I'm Claire Malloy. Can I help you?"

He began to back away. "I knew it was a long shot, and I'm sorry to disturb you. The note was from some- one named Caron Malloy. I looked her name up in the directory and found a listing for 'C. Malloy.' I've been sitting on the wall across the street for most of an hour waiting for someone to come home. I was kinda hop- ing that . . . well, never mind. I could have used the dough, but that's how it goes. Have a nice evening, ma'am. I'll be on my way now."

"Wait a minute," I said hastily. "You had a note from Caron Malloy? Who are you?"

"I guess you could say I'm Santa Claus."

CHAPTER 14

"Won't you come in?" I said weakly.

"I don't want to disturb you. Do you know this Caron Malloy?"

"Rather well, I'm afraid. She's not here right now, but I'd appreciate it if you would explain why she sent you a note and promised you money. Would you like some coffee? It won't take a minute."

"That'd be nice." He dropped the backpack and sleeping bag on the landing and shuffled by me. "Nice place you got here, Ms. Malloy. Real comfortable and casual. I guess you decorated it yourself, huh?"

I gestured at the sofa. "Please sit down and I'll start the coffee. Shall I call you Mr. Claus, or may I be more informal and call you Santa?"

"I answer to Ed," he said as he sat down and pulled off his boots. Most of his blackened toenails were visible through holes, and one heel was covered by only a few crisscrossed threads. "Don't want to track up your floor any more than necessary. It's been a while since I was invited into a home like this. Most of the time I'm asked to wait on the back porch. Not that I mind, of course. I'll stand on my head and crow like a rooster if that's what it takes to get something to eat."

I caught the hint, and after I'd started the coffee,

made him several thick cheese sandwiches. When I returned to the living room with a mug and a plate, I
found him reading the complaint. It clicked rather
neatly. "You're the Santa who got sacked, aren't you?"
I said. "How did Caron track you down?"

"When I filled out some fool form, I put the Salvation Army shelter down as my address. That's where I
found a note late this afternoon." He chomped vigorously, and after several moments of masticating, said,
"Thanks, Ms. Malloy. I know I'm making you uncomfortable, so just tell me to leave when it gets to be too
much. I don't smell so good. I slurp when I drink coffee because of some dental problems. I can understand
why you don't want me to hang around and embarrass you in front of your neighbors."

"No," I protested, uneasily wondering how hypocritical I, an avowed liberal, was at heart. He'd been a
perfect gentleman thus far. He was down on his luck,
but amenable, polite, and a great deal more sensitive
than a lieutenant I knew on the Farberville detective
squad. "Caron was a reindeer for a few days. I suppose she wanted to ask you about your stint in Santa's
Workshop before she and Inez were hired. Did you
have a problem with Ms. Portmeyer?"

Ed wiped his mouth with a napkin. "Not like those
first girls had with her. They'd show up on time, put
on those idiotic costumes, and smile like gargoyles.
They weren't Fulbright scholarship material, but they
tried as hard as they could. It didn't matter. Ms. Portmeyer gave 'em hell all day every day."

"What about you?" I asked.

"You heard how I got fired, right?" He waited until
I'd nodded, then continued. "I have a problem with
drinking, but I really needed this job and I was being

careful. There may have been a day or two when I took a couple of swallows of whiskey, but facing a stream of greedy little kids and tight-assed mothers isn't all that easy. One kid gave me a notarized list, if you can believe it. Another wanted a week at a health spa. 'Ho, ho, ho,' I'd say, wishing I could turn my head and puke. But then along would come some kid who wanted a doll for his sister and a daddy who wouldn't hit them."

"The day you were fired, Caron said that she noticed you were unsteady."

"That I was, Ms. Malloy, and then some. I was cold sober when I got to the employee lounge that morning, mostly because I was broke. Portmeyer was in a real foul mood and started making nasty remarks about how sorry she was that she'd hired me in the first place. I was pretty sure I wouldn't last the rest of the week, much less until Christmas Eve, but I kept my mouth shut. Finally she left and I opened my locker to get out the Santa suit. Right there in front was a pint of whiskey. It wasn't my preferred brand, but I'm not as picky as I used to be."

"So you drank it," I said.

Ed took another bite of sandwich and washed it down with coffee. "Not right then, I didn't. I didn't dare go out to the Workshop with whiskey on my breath, not with Portmeyer waiting for one little mistake so she could fire me. I did okay most of the day, even with her watching me like a buzzard on a low branch. Every time I took a break, she'd follow me into the lounge and tell me how pathetic I was."

"What a dreadful woman," I said.

"It's amazing what you can put up with when you're desperate. Finally, late in the afternoon, she

told me I could take a break and then added in a real
sugary voice that I'd better make the most of it because it might be my last one. I figured I'd be fired at
the end of the shift. Since I had nothing to lose, I
opened the whiskey bottle. My nerves were so shot
that I guzzled it. You know the rest."

"Where do you think the bottle came from?"

"I wasn't in the mood to worry about it," he said,
sounding vaguely ashamed. "I didn't bother to use the
padlock on my locker. Anyone who would steal my
clothes needs them a lot worse than I do." He held up
his foot and wiggled his toes. "It might be time to go
by the thrift shop and treat myself to a Christmas present. Maybe I can find argyles this time."

"I wish I had some of my late husband's clothes," I
said, "but I gave everything away a long time ago.
How much did Caron promise to pay you?"

He tugged on his beard, surreptitiously watching
me as he pretended to think. Then he sighed and said,
"She didn't say, and I'd have settled for a couple of
dollars. However, you've been so kind and generous
that I won't accept anything. Like I said, most people
won't even let me inside. I guess they're afraid I have
fleas or lice. I do the best I can, but sometimes the shelter has to turn people away. Lots of women and children on the streets this time of year."

"Hey, Ed," I said, "would you like to take a bath
here?"

"I don't want to impose, Ms. Malloy. You tell Caron
that she can get in touch with me through the shelter if
she has any questions. You two have a real good
Christmas." He picked up the boots and started toward the door. "I'll put these on when I get outside.
Thanks for the sandwiches and coffee. It's comforting

to know there are still some decent people on the planet."

"Wait," I said as I scrambled to my feet. "It's not an imposition. There's a perfectly adequate bathtub begging to be used. Please let me do this small favor."

"You sure?"

I caught his arm and gently tugged him back inside. "I'm sure, Ed. You'll find clean towels in the closet and six or seven different types of shampoo. Caron never knows from day to day if she'll wake up with dry hair, oily hair, dandruff, or split ends. Help yourself and take your time."

He smiled. "Yeah, I worry about split ends, too."

Once he was in the bathroom and the water was gushing into the bathtub, I made sandwiches out of the remaining bread and cheese and left them in a sack next to his backpack. I crept back to the bathroom door and listened to contented splashing, then went downstairs and knocked yet again on the retired professor's door.

"You're still early," he said, waggling his finger at me. "Tomorrow at seven."

"Do you have any argyle socks?"

He looked blankly at me. "Argyle socks?"

"Yes. I'll replace them as soon as I have a chance, but I need a pair right now and it's too late to go to the store."

"Argyle socks?" he repeated.

"Santa Claus needs them."

"He does?"

"His are so full of holes that nine of his toes poke through. Please hurry; he'll be finished with his bath before long."

He licked his lips. "Santa, who is in need of argyle

socks, is taking a bath in your apartment. Is that an accurate assessment of the situation?"

I suppose he thought I'd been into a pitcher of my own creation, but I was reluctant to explain. "That, sir, is an accurate assessment of the situation. Do you have argyle socks or not?"

"Shall I wrap them?"

"No, that's pushing it. Just get the socks."

"Anything else?"

I thought it over for a moment. "A sweater would be nice."

"Argyle socks and a sweater," he murmured. "Does Santa need underwear and pajamas as well?"

The retiree looked like the sort to wear pajamas decorated with snowmen. "No pajamas," I said, "but underwear would be greatly appreciated. And a pair of lined gloves, if you have a spare."

"Mrs. Malloy," he began portentously, as though preparing to scold me for a poor semester test result, then shrugged. "Argyle socks, underwear, a sweater, and gloves. Any preference for the color of the sweater?"

Caron had gone through a brief period as a color consultant, but I hadn't paid much attention. "Just something heavy," I said meekly.

When I was back upstairs with the booty, I knocked on the bathroom door and told Ed the clothing would be on the floor outside the door. I then went into the kitchen, gazed longingly at the bottle of scotch I'd concealed behind the toaster, poured myself a cup of coffee, and called the police station. Jorgeson was not there, but the dispatcher promised to leave him a message that I'd called.

I was heating the entrée when Caron came in through the back door. "I'd like to speak to you," I said. "It seems you've been very busy for someone who was supposedly shopping at the mall."

"It was really crowded out there. Inez was so tired that I took her straight home. I'm famished. Will you stick something in the microwave for me?"

She made it out of the kitchen before I could reply. I was dutifully looking in the freezer when I heard her shriek; seconds later she skittered into the kitchen, and in a scandalized voice, whispered, "There's a man in the bathroom. He's taking a bath."

"It's the most logical room in which to engage in that particular activity," I said. "Do you want lasagna or beef tips with gravy."

"Mother, there's a man in the bathroom."

"You told me that, dear. Which will it be—lasagna or beef tips?"

"Why is he there?"

"Didn't you just say that he's taking a bath?" I said blandly. "If he were doing it in your bedroom, your alarm would be justified."

"Mother!"

I closed the freezer door. "You didn't recognize him?"

"No, I didn't recognize him—and I didn't stand in the doorway and introduce myself. Who is he?"

"Santa Claus."

"Why won't you answer my . . ." Her eyes widened. "Oh, that Santa Claus. How did he get this address? All I said in the note was that I'd go by the shelter in the morning."

"He found it in the telephone directory. How did you find *his* address, or those of the two girls who preceded you as reindeer at Santa's Workshop?"

"The shelter was a lucky guess," she mumbled, ner-

vously watching the doorway that led to the hall. "I
guess Ms. Portmeyer must have said something about
the other girls, like where they lived and stuff."

"Did you have any trouble finding the little town?"

"Why do you think I went there?" she shot back, no
doubt imagining herself tied to a stake as flames began to crackle around her feet. "I was trying to find a
Christmas present for Peter. It was unbelievable at the
mall. Inez said they took more than two hundred and
fifty photographs today. It's no wonder she had a
headache."

She'd managed to evade every one of my questions
thus far. I took a deep breath and tried again. "What
are you up to?"

"I can't tell you. Just trust me, okay?"

"I wish I could, but—" I broke off as the bathroom
door opened and a disembodied hand scooped up the
pile of clothing. I bit back a somewhat hysterical gig-
gle and reopened the freezer door. "Do you still want
something to eat?"

"Later," she said, glancing over her shoulder. "What
did he tell you?"

I gave her a recap of Ed's story, and then threw in
the anonymous ex-reindeer's for good measure. "Did
Inez search Ms. Portmeyer's briefcase?" I asked. "Is
that how you learned their names and addresses?"

"Not exactly. I didn't see a sleigh out in the yard
when I got home, so maybe I should offer to drive
Santa back to the shelter. Is that okay?"

"Whatever," I said, conceding defeat as graciously
as I could. I retreated to the living room, and was gazing blindly at the Christmas tree when Ed, aka Santa
Claus, came into the room. His hair was combed back,

his beard trimmed and glistening. The sweater was tight but serviceable.

"Argyles," he said appreciatively. "Practically new, too."

"Caron's back, and will drive you to the shelter if that's where you're going."

He nodded. "It's too cold to sleep outside, so I guess I'd better see if they've found any spare cots." He gathered his things and went back through the apartment. I listened to a sibilant conversation in the kitchen, followed by the sound of the door closing. I bleakly wondered if I should have insisted that he sleep on the sofa. However, altruism has its limits—and allowing an unknown man to stay in the apartment overnight was beyond the pale.

I poured the drink to which I was entitled and settled down once again. Not a silent night, nor a holy one. Malthea was in the ICU unit, and Gilda and Roy were loosed on a populace unschooled in spells and demons. Caron would continue to be evasive until it suited her own purposes to be otherwise. Ed would end up under a bridge. My downstairs neighbor was apt to be on the telephone with the landlord, doing his best to terminate the lease so he could move out during the night. Furthermore, I began morosely, then caught myself and took a gulp of scotch.

No furthermores permitted.

I forced myself to think about what Gilda had said. Nicholas had called Sullivan and had a conversation that left at least one of them angry. Later Sullivan had gone to the house. As had Fern. As had Gilda. As had Roy. As had Malthea, or so she'd said. Only one participant thus far had not yet admitted to a late-night visit.

I looked up the Sawyers' telephone number and dialed it. When a child answered, I asked to speak to its mother.

"Who's this?"

"Someone who will sneak into your bedroom and shave your head if you don't put your mother on the line," I said matter-of-factly. I don't think I meant it.

The receiver clattered as it hit the floor. Moments later Morning Rose said, "Hello?"

I identified myself, then said, "I was trying to get everything straight in my mind about the night Nicholas was killed. You went back there, didn't you?"

"Wait a moment," she said, then yelled at her children to go to their rooms or face the specter of no rice cakes with peanut butter. When she came back on, she sounded fatigued. "I was there, but not at Nicholas's house. I was worried about Roy. He was positively gray when the party broke up. I didn't want him to take off, or start in on drugs and do something he might regret. I knocked on his door, but he wouldn't let me in. I guess I should have beaten down the door and stayed with him until he came to his senses."

"This was when Sullivan thought you were in the backyard?"

"I guess so. He was in his office working on an article about contemporary paganism for some anthropology journal. Why are you asking me this?"

"Symmetry," I murmured.

"Are you okay, Mrs. Malloy?"

I could tell she wanted to ask me if I shared Roy's fondness for Herbal Ecstasy or more potent hallucinogens. "I'm dandy, Morning Rose. Is your husband available?"

"No, he left about an hour ago to get some research

material from his office. He's probably still there playing games on his computer. I've forbidden him to play any kind of militaristic games in the house; it gives the children the wrong ideas about global harmony and universal cooperation. Are you familiar with the writings of Marx and Engels, Mrs. Malloy?"

"Long before you donned your first environmentally correct diaper, Morning Rose." I hung up and sat back, wondering if I should contact each and every member of the Mormon Tabernacle Choir to find out who else had returned to Primrose Hill on the night in question. The crew of the *SS Enterprise*. The cast of whatever constipated musical was currently reigning on Broadway.

Caron seemed to be having problems finding the Salvation Army shelter, or perhaps in disentangling herself from Santa Claus. I wasn't especially worried about her, except in a generic sense. No police officers had loomed at the door thus far. No ambulances had wailed in the distance. Ed may not have been a CEO or a part-time brain surgeon, but I was confident that he was basically benevolent. If I was wrong, he would be sorry if he made an attempt to intimidate Caron into forking over money. He'd have better luck trying to wheedle her into promising him her firstborn child.

I listened to classical music drifting through the vents along the floorboards as I wandered around the room. It was not yet ten o'clock, and I knew no visions of sugarplums would be dancing in my head anytime soon. The telephone sat in splendid silence, but I kept glancing at it as if it might leap across the carpet and attach itself to my neck like a vampire bat.

I finally decided to walk off my tension. I wrote a note for Caron, then put on my coat and headed across the campus lawn. For the record, I was not worried that any of the Druids would spring out of the shadows and wrestle me to the ground, salivating wildly and wielding a butcher knife. That only happens in fiction.

I walked along the sidewalk, my hands in my pockets and my face furrowed unattractively as I tried to make some sense of the muddle. The most obvious—and simplistic—solution was to accept Roy's confession and write him off as a deeply disturbed kid. But why hadn't Malthea protested? Why hadn't she responded with indignation instead of doing everything she could to bolster Roy's various stories?

Moving briskly, I veered around the dark student union and headed in the general direction of the law school. The cold wind stung my ears and chapped my cheeks, but the sheer sense of motion felt good, as if I were accomplishing some minor Herculean task. And, yes, I seemed to be closing in on the social sciences building, where I might find a certain person blipping evil invaders on his computer.

There were several lights on inside the building. I went inside, paused to rub my hands together until they tingled, and then found a placard listing office numbers. Sullivan had not warranted an office of his own, but I was familiar enough with the ways of academia to suspect he would have a cubicle in the vicinity of the department. I took the elevator to the third floor.

The floor was adequately lit but very quiet. After several moments of questioning my wisdom—and determining that it was, as always, impeccably correct—I tried a couple of corridors and finally found one emblazoned with multicolored flyers announcing glorious opportunities to sift sand in Turkey or study the richly diverse subcultures of Paris and Rome. Airfare not included.

The sound of clicking keys indicated that at least one creature was stirring. I went through the main office and into a large room with tables lining the walls, a hodgepodge of chairs, stacks of papers and folders, a grid of overflowing mailboxes, and a graduate student hunched in front of a computer. On the screen entities resembling Ping-Pong balls drifted downward. One exploded.

Sullivan chortled. "Gotcha, you bastard."

"I hope I'm not interrupting," I said.

He spun around and gaped at me. "I—I didn't hear you come in. What are you doing here?"

"Morning Rose thought you might be here. Do you mind if we talk?"

"I've already told you that I don't care what happens to Roy. He confessed, didn't he? Why isn't that enough? Are the authorities waiting until he kills someone else before they arrest him?"

"They'd very much like to arrest him at this point," I said, "but he's unavailable. Why did you go to Nicholas's house after the disastrous party?"

My abrupt change of topic proved effective; he stared at me for a long moment, seemingly doing his best to ascertain what I knew—and what I didn't. I waited with the appraising stare of a distaff Perry Mason.

"Who says I did?" he said carefully.

"That doesn't matter, does it? Nicholas called you around seven o'clock. The conversation ended abruptly. You went there later to confront him."

"No, I didn't."

Perry Mason's witnesses always broke down on the stand and confessed seconds before the commercial.

Sullivan must not have been a fan of the show. "Yes, you did," I said chidingly. "A little after eleven o'clock, wouldn't you say? You came across the pasture on foot."

"So that was Gilda," he said, putting his elbow on the table and massaging his forehead with his fingertips. "I didn't think she saw me."

"Well, she did. What happened after that?"

"I don't have to answer your questions, Mrs. Malloy, but I will say that I did not set foot in Nicholas's house." He leaned forward and punched a button to shut down the computer, then stood up. "I'm going home. If the police want to talk to me, that's where I'll be. If you want to talk to me, too damn bad."

"Did Nicholas find out some dirty little secret about you?" I persevered as I followed him back into the corridor. "Did you falsify your résumé or forget to mention a felony conviction?"

"You are more than welcome to verify every name, date, and letter of recommendation included in my résumé. In the meantime, will you please just leave us alone? The children are already upset as it is. Nicholas allowed Cosmos to play on his computer. He gave Rainbow a robe that was supposedly an exact replica of those worn by Druid priestesses two thousand years ago. Morning Rose is worried sick about Roy. I'm more worried about what Dr. Tate will say when he gets back from Borneo and hears that I threw his son out of my house." He locked the office door, put the key in his pocket, and walked rapidly toward the elevator. "I have nothing else to say."

Amateur sleuths cannot be bashful. "If you didn't go there to speak to Nicholas, why did you? Certainly not to make sure Roy was not unduly disturbed, since you've made it clear you're not concerned about him. Morning Rose was, though. Were you following her?"

"*Nothing else*, Mrs. Malloy. Which word is causing you problems?"

I glanced at the lighted numeral above the elevator doors, trying to assess how much time I had. There were other people on the move in the building, but with only five floors, time was of the essence. "Morning Rose said she went to Roy's apartment but he wouldn't let her in."

"My wife was in the backyard, capering around stark naked and chanting. I was in my office at home."

"You just admitted Gilda saw you."

"Isn't she currently confined in the psychiatric ward? Not much of a witness, is she? Your only other witness claims to have been ripped apart by an Egyptian demon and admitted that he killed a man in cold blood."

I was casting about for an adequately scathing response when the elevator doors opened. Sullivan stepped just inside, blocking my entrance, and stood there glaring at me until the doors closed.

The elevator descended to the first floor, then came back up to fetch me. By the time I arrived outside, Sullivan had disappeared either down one of numerous dark sidewalks or around the building to the parking lot. The sound of a car starting suggested the latter.

"Jorgeson has the weapon," I said out loud as I headed home. "It belongs to Roy's father and has Roy's fingerprints on it. Roy confessed. Just because there was need of a pagan traffic controller before the murder doesn't mean that Roy didn't do it. A shoplifter in a grocery store doesn't negate an armed robbery an hour later."

A flutter of motion in my peripheral vision indicated my grousing had roused a couple who thought the lonely campus provided a safe place to advance their relationship. I did not apologize or make sure they planned to engage in safe sex, but instead continued along the sidewalk.

I stopped on the porch to collect my mail, the usual collection of bills and flyers, and opened the door.

A hand caught the door before I could close it.

CHAPTER 15

"Mrs. Malloy," Morning Rose said with enough ill-contained urgency to awaken drunks dozing on barstools across the street from the Book Depot. "Thank God you're here! I didn't know what else to do. I'm so frightened."

I'd put the poor retired professor through quite a bit already, so I motioned her inside. "Let's go upstairs," I said in a low voice. "Then we'll talk."

"There's no time for that," she said.

"Ah, but there is. I have no desire to go dashing into the night on some foolish mission, so I have all the time in the world."

"It's Roy. He's going to kill himself if we don't find him." She pulled a folded paper out of her pocket and offered it to me. When I didn't accept it, she said, "I found this under our front door. The minute that Sullivan got home, I hurried here. You have to read it. He's serious—"

"Call the police."

"I don't dare," she said as she sank to her knees and covered her face with her hands like a seduced maiden in a Greek tragedy who'd just realized the baby might be born with feathers. "The minute he sees them, he'll put the gun to his head and pull the trigger. He's sick,

Mrs. Malloy. We have to find him and get him back to the psychiatric ward where he can be restrained. How did he get out of there? Don't they realize he's suicidal?"

I plucked the letter out of her hand and read it under the glow of the forty-watt bulb the miserly landlord favored. Most of it was written in an illegible scrawl that would have exasperated Fern, but I could decipher the phrases "can't face the torment" and "better off dead."

"Just what are you planning to do?" I asked Morning Rose. "Roy left the hospital hours ago. He could be anywhere."

She looked up at me. "I think I know where he stayed after he left the carriage house."

"So alert the police. They're trained to deal with emotionally disturbed people. They'll walk softly and carry big butterfly nets."

"I'm the only person who can talk him into going back to the hospital. If anyone else approaches him, he'll snap like a twig. You have to help me save his life!"

"No, I don't," I said, shaking my head. "He's a confessed murderer and quite possibly a dangerous schizophrenic. I'm not about to go track him down in a dark alley and suggest he turn himself in. I've done that several times, and I'm tired of it."

"He's not in an alley," she said as she stood up and caught my hands. "I think Roy broke into one of Nicholas's rental properties. He's done repair work in many of them, and he knows which are likely to be empty over the Christmas break. You can stay in the van, Mrs. Malloy. If there's a light, I'll get out and ring the doorbell. As soon as you see Roy at the door, you can drive to a telephone and call the police. That'll give me time to convince him to come quietly." She squeezed my hands so tightly that I winced. "He won't hurt me. I can get the gun away from him and calm him down so that he won't—do something foolish."

"Jorgeson can arrange for an unmarked police car to take you around the properties."

"No," she said with a frustrated groan. "What if Roy looks at the car and sees an unfamiliar driver? He'll panic and blow out his brains. If he sees you, he might not be so impulsive. He's trusted you in the past. You don't have to set one foot outside the van. You'll be at least twenty feet away with the engine running. I wouldn't ask you to do this if I thought you'd be in any danger. What's more, the odds that we'll find him are infinitesimal. Nicholas owned houses and apartment buildings all over Farberville. I only know the few that Roy mentioned."

"Have Sullivan go with you."

"Roy knows how much Sullivan despises him," she said, lapsing back into urgency and doing so much damage to my hands that I could never become a renowned concert pianist (it was on my midlife-crisis list). "An hour is all I ask. If I haven't found Roy by then, I'll go home and light candles for him. He'll need all the help he can get."

"Let's not get overly dramatic," I said as I jerked my hands free before she completely mangled them.

"He's the same age as your daughter, isn't he? You wouldn't hesitate to save her, but Roy's mother isn't as compassionate. She got drunk every day and slept with anyone who'd have her. Roy came home from school one afternoon and found her in bed with the preacher from—"

"You've made your point. All right, Morning Rose, we'll drive by the rental properties and look for lights. Not all the tenants are students, however, and not all the students leave town for the holidays, so you're likely to find yourself apologizing to people for disturbing them at this hour. I will remain in the driver's seat. We will do this for no more than an hour."

"Oh, thank you," she gushed, looking as if she might give me a warm Wiccan hug.

I stepped back so abruptly I almost fell off the edge of the porch. "Where's the van?"

"Just around the corner. Please, let's hurry."

I followed her through the yard, debating if I should congratulate myself on this spontaneous enterprise or drive to the hospital and inquire into vacancies on the sixth floor. The van reeked of patchouli oil and dried peanut butter. It had a stick shift, but I'd mastered that earlier. "Where do we start?"

"Nicholas owned all the houses in our development," Morning Rose said.

"And the duplexes and houses on Malthea's street," I countered. "Let's go there, and work our way toward your end of town."

"Okay," she muttered, apparently having lost her missionary zeal between the porch and the passenger's seat.

I drove slowly down the pertinent street, noting that Fern's lights were on and Malthea's off. Almost all the other houses were dark, and there were only two cars parked along the curb in the four-block stretch.

"Roy could be inside any of these houses," I said. "What he's really interested in is somewhere warm to sleep. Maybe he realized that it wouldn't be wise to turn on the lights and advertise his presence."

"He's not thinking clearly."

"I agree with that," I said as I turned toward the south part of town. "Any other properties between here and your area?"

"Nicholas bought Malthea's house next to the cemetery. Roy mentioned that when he went there to rake leaves, the two girls renting it tried to get him to drink wine with them. Undergraduates, likely to go home for Christmas."

"Where's the house?"

She directed me to a narrow street that ran along the back side of the cemetery. "That's it, I think," she said, pointing at a shabby little house set well away from the streetlights. "Stop here and I'll check it out. Keep your door locked, Mrs. Malloy, and if anything strange happens, don't come after me. Get away and call the police."

I watched her creep across the yard, peer into a darkened window, and then vanish behind an unruly barrier of bushes. Five minutes later she had not reappeared. Nothing whatsoever, strange or mundane, had happened.

I turned off the car's engine and rolled down the window. In a more congenial season I would have heard crickets, birds, tree frogs, raucous music from the beer garden, and the mating calls of students in the apartment complexes on the next block. The only thing I could hear now was the rumble of traffic several blocks away.

I rolled up the window and looked at the cemetery beyond a crumbling rock wall. Moonlight glinted off marble and granite monuments as if they were chiseled blocks of ice. Wind riffled branches of trees that had been there longer than the current tenants.

Morning Rose did not return.

I hummed my way through the theme songs of *Gilligan's Island* and *The Brady Bunch*. I attempted the graduation processional but gave up after a few bars. I had a paperback in my purse (dedicated mystery fans always do), but I didn't have a flashlight and it was too dark to see the print, much less read it.

She did not return.

I contemplated how I'd explain her absence to her children on Christmas Eve. "Your mommy," I'd say, blinking back tears, "was a compassionate woman who sacrificed herself to save a young boy. She was an angel of mercy."

Still no Morning Rose.

Something was wrong, but I wasn't willing to leave the van to investigate. I finally decided to wait five more minutes, then go to the bookstore and call the police. They'd most likely find Morning Rose on the ground with a sprained ankle or wandering like a wraith through backyards at the end of the block, plaintively bleating Roy's name. I'd feel silly, but not stupid.

I was rehearsing my remarks to the 911 dispatcher when two clinging figures came slowly across the yard. As they reached the street, I could see that Morning Rose had her arms around Roy and appeared to be supporting him. He was hunched over as though he were in the throes of a violent gastric attack, his face masked by his hair, his arms limp at his sides.

"I found him," she called, "and he's agreed to be taken to the hospital."

The back door of the van slid open. She helped Roy inside, closed the door, and climbed into the seat next to me. "Everything will be fine," she said, twisting around to look at him. "You'll be safe. If they let me, I'll sit in your room the rest of the night, just in case you have . . . a nightmare."

The wisest thing to do was to get him to the hospital as quickly as possible. Rather than questioning Morning Rose about such minor issues as the whereabouts of his purported gun, I started the engine. "We should be there in fifteen minutes."

"I won't be safe at the hospital," Roy said dully. "Malthea's there, so she can tell Ambesek where to find me. I'm going to die. Why didn't you let me go without the agony?"

I pushed down on the accelerator. "Ten minutes, maybe less if we don't hit any red lights."

Morning Rose tried to smile. "You'll be fine, Roy."

I was about to reiterate the sentiment when I felt the barrel of a gun pressed against my neck. My foot slipped off the pedal, inadvertently hit the brakes, and brought the van to a shuddery stop in the middle of Thurber Street.

"Start the car," Roy said in a crisp, cold voice. "If that happens again, you can stand under the mistletoe and kiss your ass good-bye."

"Roy!" yelped Morning Rose. "You said you were unarmed."

"Yeah, but everybody knows I'm crazy." He increased the pressure on my neck. "Drive to the grove. I've got things to do that aren't permitted in the psych ward."

I did as ordered. Morning Rose sat silently, her hands writhing in her lap and her eyes lowered. I was as angry at her as I was at Roy, but there was no point in scolding her for falling for his ploy. Wiccans could be as obtuse as the rest of us.

"What things?" I asked Roy as I drove through town.

"I'll tell you when we get there. Now shut up and don't do anything impulsive, like run into a parked car. I don't want to hurt you, Mrs. Malloy, but I will."

"Haven't we been through this before?"

"Someone must have rewound the tape," he said. "Just drive—okay?"

We arrived without further conversation. I couldn't tell what was going through Morning Rose's mind, but I doubted she would be useful in a confrontation. Spells weren't likely to deflect bullets.

"Here we are," I said brightly as I pulled over to the fence. "Shall I pick you up later?"

"Get out of the car," Roy said, unamused. "Morning Rose, take the key. We're all going for a stroll."

It was not an appealing idea. I climbed down from the seat, went around the front of the van, and waited as Morning Rose pretty much slithered out of her seat. Roy caught her before she fell to the ground.

"Get a grip," he snarled. "I'm not going to sling you over my shoulder and carry you."

She touched his face. "You swore you'd go to the hospital, Roy. It's not too late. Why don't we all get back in the van and—"

She gasped as he lightly slapped her.

He waved the gun at the trees in the distance. "Let's go."

We stumbled across the pasture and into the woods. Roy prodded me with the gun whenever I faltered, and we eventually found the clearing. The altar reminded me of the gravestones in the cemetery, white and cold, eternally lifeless.

"What are you going to do?" Morning Rose asked Roy in a timid squeak.

"I hate to put it this bluntly, but I'm going to shoot Mrs. Malloy."

"What?" I said, staring at him. "What's your beef with me? I've been trying to help you ever since all this started, for pity's sake. I've listened to your confessions, held your hand while you were interrogated, and pleaded your cause with Sergeant Jorgeson. This is not the best way to express your gratitude, Roy. I don't expect flowers and candy, but a card might be in order."

"You know too much."

"All I know is what people have told me, and most of that has been untrue. I may not believe in demons, and I may have my doubts that Malthea's a priestess in some screwy cult, but . . ." I broke off and sat down on the stump, which was getting as familiar as my living-room sofa (although not as comfortable). "How do you know Malthea's in the hospital?"

For the first time since I'd met him, he smiled. "Maybe a little messenger from hell told me. Now move over there next to the altar. It's time someone put it to good use."

"I can think of no reason why I should cooperate," I said, staying where I was and crossing my arms. "You can kill Morning Rose and me, but you know perfectly well that you won't get away with it. If you're found guilty by reason of insanity, they'll lock you up in a hospital until you've quit foaming—then lock you up in a prison for the rest of your life. There won't be any 'sick little boy' defense."

Morning Rose moved toward my side, her eyes enormous in the shadowy light. "But that's what he is, Mrs. Malloy. Once he's had proper treatment, he'll be able to make a plea for leniency and serve only a small sentence. He's not a hardened criminal."

"Is that what you want as an epitaph on your head-stone?" I asked her. I grabbed her shoulders and spun her around so that she was facing Roy. Without releasing her, I added, "See that gun in his hand? He's going to shoot you."

"Let her go," Roy said.

She began to squirm, but I dug my fingernails into her flesh. "Or maybe he won't shoot you," I said slowly. "The only members of your group who know that Malthea's in the hospital are Fern and Gilda. I'm going to assume Roy has not been in communication with either of them this evening. He must have learned this from you, Morning Rose. How did you find out? Did you see the ambulance go up the driveway at Primrose Hill?" She nodded. "But that wouldn't explain why you knew it was there for Malthea. Was it because you were responsible for the assault in the study?"

Roy leaned against the altar, rather casually, in my opinion, for someone who intended to cover it with bloodstains. Without letting the gun bobble even for an instant, he pulled a cigarette pack and a lighter out of his pocket. "Very good, Mrs. Malloy. Now let her go."

"Not just yet," I said as my fingers began to protest. "Gilda told me that Nicholas had evidence that would cause her to lose her job and possibly face criminal charges. That's why she tried to break into the house earlier—to find the evidence. It's also why Malthea did the same thing a few hours ago, and, apparently, did Morning Rose. What is it?"

"You haven't proved I was there," said Morning Rose sulkily.

I shook her as I would a mysterious package beneath a Christmas tree. "Malthea seems determined to protect Roy, and not in order to hide any association with a satanic cult."

"Don't be so sure," he said as he lit the cigarette.

"But you did kill Nicholas," I continued. "Why?"

"Because," he said in a whiny falsetto, "I'm a victim, too. My father rejected me and my mother neglected me. The preacher used to beat me with a strap. I know I shouldn't have taken drugs, ma'am, but I was all alone and so confused. I guess I was beggin' for help."

"Roy," Morning Rose said, "this has gone on long enough. You've got a gun, and you should be able to find a way to use it."

I abruptly shifted my arms to her waist and grasped my wrists, pulling her against me. "The bullet will penetrate both of us. Waste not, want not."

"Don't make this any harder than necessary," he said as he approached.

"I'm not going to make it any easier than necessary," I said, calculating the distance. "I shouldn't do that, should I, Morning Rose?"

"No," she said in a thin voice.

"I didn't hear you," I said, vigorously administering the Heimlich maneuver to help her cough up a lie.

"No!" she wailed.

Roy was no more than a yard away, the gun a shade closer. I took a breath, shoved Morning Rose into him, watched both of them flounder backward against the altar, then darted into the woods. A shot ricocheted off a branch above my head, but I kept stumbling through trees and bushes. The sounds of thrashing and cursing made it clear that Roy was on his feet and coming after me.

It occurred to me that he was tracking me by the same noises. I crawled under a low fir, pulled my legs against my chest, and buried my face in decayed leaves and what smelled like the remains of a dead animal. The most minimal movement had exposed the amorous couple on the campus; I did not so much as blink. Footsteps crunched nearby, then moved away.

One of the egregious errors common to movies is for the fugitive to hear noises diminish, scramble to his or her feet, and go thundering onward, alerting the hunter to redirect the search. I stayed put, making no effort to do anything but listen for the most minute sound. When I felt the tingling onset of a sneeze, I clamped my nose between my thumb and forefinger and breathed carefully through my mouth. Something tickled my ankle. I told myself it was a leaf.

After ten minutes or so, a muscle in my calf began to quiver, warning me that a cramp was imminent if I didn't move. I stood up and wiped primordial ooze off my eyelashes and forehead. The road was to my right. Roy could be anywhere, but there was no future in freezing under a thicket. I kept a goodly distance between myself and the grove as I skulked from tree to tree like a spy in a cartoon.

When I arrived at the edge of the pasture, I could see the van where I'd parked it. Regrettably, this implied they were still in the vicinity. Loping like a hound, I made it to the road and squatted behind the scanty cover of a fence post. The van appeared to be empty. No one emerged from the woods behind me. I caught my breath, counted to ten, and then ran across the expanse of muddy ruts and flung myself into the stubble. I raised my head and peered over my shoulder, but the pasture remained a placid sea of weeds.

The stubble, on the other hand, was jabbing me most rudely in places never intended to be jabbed. Rather than make my way down the road, I decided to head for Nicholas's house. I could break another window if necessary, make a terse telephone call, and then hide in the garden until a patrol car came racing up the driveway. This would be one 911 call that required no rehearsal.

I took one final look at the woods, then ran toward the house, staying as low as I could and taking an impressive number of belly dives as I stepped in holes and caught my foot on obdurate vines. I was beginning to feel a bit optimistic when the headlights of the van came on and illuminated the pasture. I flattened myself and uttered a choice word.

After a moment, I looked back and saw a figure silhouetted against the headlights. Roy was halfway across the pasture and coming toward me. I couldn't see the gun, but it did not seem prudent to linger. I scrambled to my feet and ran toward the poplars delineating the driveway, fully expecting to feel an explosive pain in the middle of my back.

I arrived in the forecourt and paused. Roy would hear the breaking of glass and be inside the house before I could find the telephone in the dark. He would be less than empathetic. A bullet hit the front of the house, reminding me that I was unnecessarily exposed. The doors of the carriage house were ajar. I slipped inside and peered through the crack.

This time I could see the gun in his right hand as he came into the middle of the forecourt. He peered at the house, his head tilted as he listened for the sound of my footsteps. I edged backward and promptly bumped into the hearse. I remembered the storage room on one side, but it was very much a cobweb-festooned dead end.

The windows of the hearse had been down when I'd last looked inside it for Roy, and they still were. I slithered into it and crouched on the seat, praying the police had not removed the key from the ignition switch. My heart quickened as I felt it.

I eased into position in front of the steering wheel and located the pedals on the floorboard. Hoping Roy was the sort to keep his vehicle tuned and with adequate fuel, I switched on the engine. It began to purr most endearingly. My only chance to get it into reverse was to turn on the lights, and after a moment of fumbling, I yanked the right knob. The door behind me squealed as it was dragged open. I could see Roy's face in the red glare of the taillights.

I shifted it into reverse and jammed down the accelerator. Roy tried to leap out of the way, but he was only partially successful and went flying into the air, his arms flailing and the gun sailing into the darkness. I leapt out of the hearse. Roy lay a good ten feet away from the point of impact. Blood dribbled out of the corners of his mouth, indicative of internal injuries. I knelt and listened to his laborious breathing.

"Sorry about that," I murmured, then opened the back doors of the hearse. "Let me give you a lift back to town, Roy. It's the least I can do."

CHAPTER 16

"Would you rather have coffee?" Jorgeson asked as he handed me a can of soda from the machine in the emergency room. "The cafeteria's closed, but we can find a pot somewhere."

"I don't want anything," I said, exploring scratches and abrasions on my heretofore flawless face. It was well past midnight, and Jorgeson and I were the only people in the room. He was in need of a shave; I suspected I looked as though I was the loser in a mud-wrestling competition. I'd called Caron and made sure she was home; she'd been grudgingly pleased to hear from me. "What about Morning Rose? Have you found her?"

"Let me check." He went to the pay phone and had a muted conversation. When he returned, he said, "She called in a few minutes ago and demanded that we send dogs and a helicopter with searchlights to the woods to rescue you. The dispatcher assured her that everything was under control."

"I wish it were," I muttered.

Jorgeson overlooked my petulance. "What exactly did the staff say when you pulled up at the entrance in a hearse?"

"I told them the body was in the back. They were

hesitant to open the doors until I'd explained that I wasn't looking for the morgue. A sense of humor does not appear to be a prerequisite for employment."

His lips twitched momentarily, but he was too tired to produce a smile. "Okay, Mrs. Malloy, I have a reasonably clear idea of what happened. An officer will stay with Roy until we figure out what to do with him."

"Both of them may need demonproof vests. Can you assign an officer to Malthea's room, just to be on the safe side?"

"I've already done it. There's no reason for you to stay here any longer. I'll have someone drive you home. You'd better see if Caron can handle the bookstore tomorrow, because it's going to take a long time to get your statement. The prosecutor may decide to sit in on it. That means the media won't be far behind."

"They might have a better story if Roy truly were certifiable, but he's not. It's an act, Jorgeson. He's convinced that he'll be tried as a juvenile, incarcerated until he's eighteen or, at worst, twenty-one, and then be released. Presuming his father can afford it, an expert will testify about diminished responsibility and the effects of long-term abuse. Roy'll get a slap on the wrist. What he deserves is an Oscar."

"Best actor in a bad movie?"

"And the Oscar for best director should go to Morning Rose Sawyer. She was using him to reenact some Wiccan mythology involving the sacred marriage between the Mother Goddess and the Horned God, whatever that is. The sexual undertones have been obvious all along. Considering her track record, one shudders to think what might have resulted from this union." I disengaged a leaf from my hair and dropped it in a trash receptacle. "Sullivan suspected something, which is why he followed her. Nicholas must have seen her entering and leaving the carriage house late at night and realized what was happening. He was going to expose them before he went to Wales."

"Roy's only sixteen," Jorgeson said, grimacing. "She's thirty-four. That's sexual misconduct, or maybe even violation of a minor, a felony, if the prosecutor can show she was acting as a temporary guardian when the affair started. I can't see her going to prison because of it, though. He's twice her size and could buy liquor without being carded. A fragile boy he's not."

"She could hardly have consulted a lawyer, and she must have read about some recent cases in which the older woman received a substantial prison term. She had to worry about her husband, too. If he believed whatever evidence Nicholas had, he'd divorce her and get custody of the children. If you were a judge confronted with a diligent graduate student and a self-admitted witch who frolics naked in the backyard and seduced a teenage boy, what would you do?"

"So she encouraged Roy to kill Nicholas Chunder?"

I put down the can of soda. "Nicholas said something to them before the party, then went so far as to call Sullivan and repeat it. Morning Rose must have thought her only way to avoid prosecution and divorce would be if Roy killed Nicholas and, if necessary, confessed. When the burglary theory didn't hold up, and then the homosexual advances theory fell apart, they moved right along to the next one. You have to give them credit for flexibility."

Jorgeson picked up the soda I'd rejected and took a swallow. "But it required Malthea's cooperation. How could they know she wouldn't deny it? There was no way they could prove these ludicrous accusations."

"You'll have to ask them," I said with a yawn. "I'm not accustomed to being chased by a demon, Jorgeson. I need to bathe, dab cream on my cuts, take two aspirin, and go to bed. I'll call you in the morning."

"What were you babbling about last night?" demanded Caron as I hobbled into the kitchen the next morning. "Considering how awful you look, it's no surprise you were at the hospital. Shouldn't they have kept you for observation pending cosmetic surgery?"

I gave her a hooded look and poured a glass of orange juice. "Mr. Mortician decided to live up to his nickname, and did his best to let me be his first customer."

"Roy Tate? What were you doing with him?"

I told her what had happened. When she stopped sputtering indignantly (and swiping at a tear or two, although she will never admit it), I added, "It's over now. They got swept up into something that made them feel omnipotent and exotic—or maybe they were looking for an excuse to behave badly. If you must join a cult, dear, please let it be nothing more nefarious than a sorority. I'll have you kidnapped and deprogrammed in no time."

"Very funny," she said. "Are you sure you're okay?"

"I did damage to some muscles I didn't know I had, but I'll be fine in a day or two. Tonight's Christmas Eve. I absolutely have to stop downstairs and have a cup of cheer, and then I suppose I'll go to Luanne's party. You don't have to come along, but we will be having dinner there tomorrow afternoon."

"What time are you going downstairs?"

"Seven," I said, eyeing her suspiciously. My social

agenda is rarely of any importance in her overall scheme of the universe; the only time she inquires is when she's scheming to get the car. "Why?"

"No reason."

Although I knew it was futile, I waited for a moment in case she chose to be more forthcoming. She did not. I told her she'd have to open the Book Depot and stay there until I'd finished at the police department, and then compounded the crime by telling her she might be stuck most of the day.

Caron goggled at me as if I'd revealed a secret hankering to take up skydiving. "But I have important things to do. I haven't finished shopping. I just know Inez is going to get me this pair of earrings I found out at the mall, and that means I have to give her this dorky scarf that makes her look like she's being throttled by a paisley boa constrictor. And I haven't found anything decent for Luanne. I think she may give me this nifty beaded purse. I can't just give her a coupon to rent a video."

"I'm charmed by this display of selfless generosity," I said as I put on my coat. "Shall we go? I'd like to get this over with."

"I suppose."

She rolled her eyes and sighed all the way to the car, but restrained herself from attempting to convince me that shopping had priority over making a statement at the police department. An atypical display of maturity on her part.

"So," I said, frowning as I noticed how little gas was in the tank, "what did you and Ed find to talk about last night?"

"Nothing. I took him to the shelter and dropped

him off, then went to Carrie's for a few minutes. She has this really cool computer."

And I could hire eight tiny reindeer to pull the car to the gas station when I ran out of gas. "You must have had a reason for wanting to talk to him. You left him a note, after all." I paused to consider an earlier remark. "How could you have done that without knowing his name?"

Caron turned her head to look out the window. "He must have mentioned it. I just wanted to ask him a couple of questions—okay? We did not bond. The only thing we have in common is that we were both fired by a woman with plutonium implants. How long is this statement going to take?"

I dropped her off and continued to the police station. Jorgeson managed a wan smile as I came into his office. "We've got to start keeping regular office hours, Mrs. Malloy. My wife is so mad that she's threatening to book a Caribbean cruise. What am I supposed to do for three days while she throws up in the sink? Play shuffleboard with pink-haired ladies from Miami?"

"Is Morning Rose in custody?" I asked.

"Yes, and we're making some headway with the computer files. Chunder recorded every last detail, from what he spent on postage stamps to when he last spoke to his accountant. I won't be surprised if he kept notes about when he saw Morning Rose sneaking into the carriage house for late-night sessions. Last month he made a long-distance call to a seedy motel in Missouri, and not because he wanted a reservation. Someone there should remember them. It'll take a few days to reconstruct the evidence, but we will."

"How's Sullivan taking it?"

"He is not a happy man. He's admitted he thought

there might be something going on between the two of them, and that's the real reason he made Roy move out of the house. He told Chunder that his wife was just being supportive, but he knew she wasn't always in the backyard like she said she was. Corporal Billsby is not a happy man, either. We left him at the house with the two children. He's already called twice to beg for relief, but I think it'll be good for him. A young man like that can stand to build some character."

"And Roy?" I said, waving off a uniformed officer who was headed toward me with a cup of coffee.

Jorgeson rocked back in his chair. "He has a couple of broken ribs, a ruptured spleen, and a lot of bruises. When he's ready to be transferred back up to the psych ward, he'll remain under full security. The shrinks will wear him down eventually, and he and Morning Rose will be slathering the blame on each other like whipped cream on pumpkin pie." He took a couple of antacid tablets from a roll and offered it to me, but I shook my head. "Gilda seems to have packed up and left town. The manager at the trailer park thought he saw candlelight in her trailer late last night, but he was entertaining a widow. They were doing the lambada and he didn't want to lose the beat."

I imagined Gilda on her bicycle, a suitcase strapped on the back, her coattails flapping in the wind as she pedaled down the road in search of yet another hospital in need of her services. "What will you do about her?"

"We'll find her," he said flatly. "Now, Mrs. Malloy, we need your statement so you can get out of here. I hope the lieutenant doesn't blame this whole thing on me. That first morning I should have sent you home instead of asking for your help. You came damn close to getting yourself killed."

"I did no such thing," I replied tartly.

"Whatever you say."

"And the lieutenant has no one else but himself to blame for this. If he hadn't goaded me into doing something uncharacteristic, none of this would have happened. I hope you will make that clear when you speak to him."

He gave me the same sad look he'd given me when I'd blurted out my woes. "If he calls, I'll do my best."

I spent the next three hours relating the events of the previous evening, struggling to repeat verbatim conversations with Fern, Gilda, Sullivan, Morning Rose, and most painfully, Roy. Yes, he'd said he was going to shoot me. No, he hadn't said he was going to kill me, but his intent was hard to miss. No, Morning Rose hadn't admitted any collusion, but the headlights on the van had come on when Roy was already in the pasture. She'd driven away while I was loading Roy into the hearse.

By the time I was finished, my face felt as if it were caked with clay. My eyes were gritty, my tongue fuzzy with exhaustion. I declined Jorgeson's final offer of coffee and put on my coat.

He walked me to the front door, raised his hand as if to pat my shoulder, then thought better of it. "Merry Christmas, Mrs. Malloy," he murmured.

"You, too." I went to my car and sat for a long while, overwhelmed by the sheer nastiness of the crime. The only one of the Druids who'd behaved honorably was Nicholas Chunder, and he was dead. He'd been partially responsible, of course; he'd hoarded his information instead of simply informing the appropriate authorities. I hoped he'd enjoyed his final opportunity to flaunt his power over the members of the Sacred Grove of Keltria. It certainly hadn't ended well for him.

Caron would be chewing her fingernails by now, but I wasn't ready to spend the rest of the afternoon brooding over unanswered questions. I drove to the hospital, went through the conventional entrance, and asked a volunteer behind a computer for the number of Malthea's room.

The woman, seventyish and as petite and perky as any of Santa's elves, punched buttons, then beamed at me. "She went home this morning. I hate the idea of anyone spending Christmas in a hospital, don't you? Carolers come by, and the auxiliary decorates the nursing stations and puts candy-cane reindeers on the meal trays, but it's just not the same as being surrounded with family members and close friends."

I read her name tag and reciprocated with a warm smile. "May I use your telephone, Bea?"

"Normally, it's not allowed, but since it's so close to Christmas . . ." She looked as though she sincerely believed there was a manger in the nursery and shepherds keeping watch over their flocks in the parking lot. "Go ahead."

I called Jorgeson. "Do you know that Malthea left the hospital?"

"The officer assigned to her door called in a few minutes ago. She persuaded him to go down to the cafeteria to get her a cup of hot chocolate. Someone from housekeeping had just shown up to clean her room, so he figured she'd be okay for ten minutes or so. When he returned, her clothes were still there. He alerted hospital security, and they wasted an hour doing a floor-by-floor search for an elderly woman in a robe and slippers. I've sent a patrol car to her apartment to pick her up."

"Ask the officers to wait at the corner," I said. "Leaving the hospital without authorization is not a crime. I'd like to talk to her."

Jorgeson agreed. I hung up, thanked Bea, and drove to the duplex. I knocked on Malthea's door, and when no one answered, pounded on it with my fist until my hand throbbed.

Fern opened her door. "She's gone, Claire."

"Gone where?"

"I couldn't say."

I hit the door one last time, then let my hand fall. "Did you pick her up at the hospital?"

"Is that against the law?"

"No," I said. "May I have a cup of tea?"

"Yes, of course," she said, gesturing for me to come inside. "Malthea did indeed ask me to fetch her from the hospital. It was rather exciting to wait by the door, the engine racing, my palms perspiring; I felt like I was at the wheel of the getaway car during a bank robbery. I expected her to come running out the door with security officers hot on her heels, but she strolled out to the car and suggested we go home."

"In street clothes?"

Fern busied herself with the teapot. "Yes, I suppose so. She wasn't wearing one of those gowns that exposes one's privates to all and sundry."

"Gilda's doing?" I persevered.

"Gilda may be a Wiccan—and what an unreliable lot they seem to be—but she has deep loyalties to the grove. I'm not saying that she provided Malthea with clothes, but it might have happened that way. In any case, I brought Malthea home. Twenty minutes later she loaded several suitcases and boxes into her car, came to the door and hugged me, and promised to keep in touch. She made me swear to see to Merlinda. Before I could question her as to her plans, she left. Just like that."

A teacup slipped out of Fern's hand and shattered to the floor. She mumbled an apology and went into the living room. I picked up the sizable pieces, then found a broom and a dustpan and swept up the slivers. I found another teacup, fixed a tray, and took it into the living room, where I found her huddled on the sofa, a shawl around her shoulders.

"Here," I said as I gave her a steaming cup. "Malthea's not in any trouble, and neither are you. Morning Rose and Roy are in custody. It's over."

"What about Cosmos and Rainbow?" she asked.

"Sullivan may have suspected what was going on, but he won't be charged. You and Malthea knew, didn't you?"

"We weren't sure. We were worried that . . . Roy might be engaged in something beyond his years, but we couldn't ask him. It would not have been seemly for two old ladies to broach the subject. A boy his age can't believe that our generation ever experienced sexual intimacy. It makes one wonder where they think they came from, doesn't it? All this modern openness about sex, and they're clinging to storks and cabbage patches. Have they no idea what Adam and Eve did after they ate the apple?"

I paused, wondering if Caron had ever envisioned me in bed with her father. She most likely preferred to see herself as the consequence of immaculate conception.

"Why," I asked, "were you and Malthea so worried about Roy?"

"There was no one else to worry about him except the two of us. His parents had abandoned him, and he had no one else to fall back on for support and guidance. It would have been so much better if he'd gone to Borneo. He would have been much safer among headhunters than . . ."

"Why did Malthea leave?" I asked bluntly.

Fern pulled the shawl more tightly around her and took a sip of tea. "I don't know."

"Did she do it so she won't have to testify against him?"

"Testify about what?"

"Testify that she had nothing to do with Nicholas Chunder's murder," I said. "I know she didn't, and so do you. Why did you and she lie about it, Fern? He's a punk. He may have had a tough life, but so have a lot of other kids. My daughter's made it thus far with only a scrape or two. Families aren't perfect these days; we adapt to reality and do what's necessary to get by. I could understand if Malthea was concerned about Roy, but . . ."

"Of course she was," Fern said. "We both were."

"She's his grandmother," I said, wondering why it had taken me so long to arrive at the realization.

Fern snatched the teacup from my hand and banged it down on the tray. "That's absurd. Malthea never married, so how could she have had a child? Even if she had, the child would have been put up for adoption and that would have been the end of it. There could have been no reconciliation. If you don't mind, I'd like to go out to my greenhouse and mist the asparagus ferns. They require daily attention to maintain their vitality." She threw aside the shawl and stood up. "I will not be able to continue to live here in the future, Claire, so this had best be good-bye."

"Where will you go?" I asked as she literally propelled me to the front door.

"It's under control. Malthea left this for you." She pushed a folded piece of paper into my hand. "Good night, Claire."

The door closed in my face, and seconds later, the porch light went out. I stood there for a moment, trying to determine if I'd actually learned anything I hadn't already subconsciously suspected. Adoption papers were sealed; not even Jorgeson could ever prove that Malthea was the mother of one of Roy's parents, most likely Randall. Scrutinizing the photographs in the leather box would serve no purpose, even if it was still in the desk drawer. I knew it wasn't.

I wished Malthea had stayed around long enough to say good-bye, but I could understand her reasons for leaving. At some point, she would see an article in a newspaper that revealed the ugly plot and realize that she was no longer implicated. But perhaps by then she would have found a happier grove, where mistletoe and mead were abundant.

Something furry curled around my ankle, and I'm sorry to admit that I let out an unnecessarily loud shriek. Fern's door flew open and she came onto the porch.

"Merlinda?" she said, scooping up a bundle of black fur that resembled a cat. "Did she hurt you? Well, let's just have a nice saucer of milk."

This time the door slammed closed.

I walked slowly to the car, then paused under the streetlight to unfold the slip of paper. The writing was unsteady but legible: "As Mumsy always said, generalizations aren't worth a damn." Grinning despite myself, I glanced up at the moon and wished her well.

I went to the Book Depot and relieved Caron. She claimed some life-threatening need for the car. Rather than argue, I gave her the keys and went into the office, sat down, and tried to find a reason to call Jorgeson and tell him that Malthea had left town. She wasn't really a witness, I told myself—or at least not a vital one. The charges would not culminate in a trial. Plea bargains, minimal sentences, community service—and Morning Rose and Roy would be freed to resume their unhealthy alliance until she found another candidate for Horned God. Sullivan and the children would survive. I hoped Nicholas Chunder had left arrangements to have his ashes sprinkled in Wales.

"What's wrong with you?" asked my science-fiction hippie as he came into the store.

"Holiday blues," I said. "Need another book for your new friend?"

"No," he said, turning red in those patches of skin that were visible above his beard and below his beetlish brow. "I have something for you. I know that you think I steal books, and maybe I do, but not very often. Anyway, you don't ever embarrass me like some of the shopkeepers do. You don't snicker when I come in or trail me around like I was some sort of thief."

"Should I?"

"Yeah, maybe. Anyway, I wanted to give this to you." He dropped a tissue-wrapped package on the counter, then winked and went out the door.

I unwrapped the paper and found a crystal figurine of a magician, no more than an inch high (and there-

fore easy to slip into a pocket). I'd seen similar figu-
rines at the gallery just across the tracks, and made a
note to return it after Christmas. I would not explain.

Jorgeson came into the store late in the afternoon,
the tinkle of the bell above the door a good deal live-
lier than his expression. "Here," he said, handing me a
package wrapped in foil. "I want you to know how
much I appreciate what you went through. I was out
of my league, and you saved me from making a fool of
myself. We didn't always see things the same way,
Mrs. Malloy. You could have told me to take a flying
leap, but you didn't."

"Jorgeson," I said, "you didn't have to . . ."

"It's just a fruitcake. My wife said I should get you
perfume or something, but everybody likes fruitcake.
Right?"

"Absolutely," I said, nodding forcefully. "I love
fruitcake, and so does Caron."

He turned his back and picked up a paperback from
the rack. "The lieutenant called this afternoon. He's
going to take a three-month leave of absence. He said
he'd been under a lot of pressure and needed a break."

"Oh, really?" I said evenly.

"I don't think it means anything," Jorgeson said as
he turned around and looked at me. "Things have
been pretty hectic for the last couple of months. All of
us need a break, but we need our salaries, too. The
lieutenant's in a different situation."

"Independently wealthy, for instance?"

"I suppose he is. He said he's going to call you this
evening and explain things. I just thought I might
warn you so you won't . . ."

I realized he wanted me to say something, but I

picked up the package and looked at my distorted reflection. After he'd left, I took the package into my office, set it on the desk, making sure it was in the exact middle of the blotter, and went back out in hopes of selling one last book. I can offer no excuse for what I decided to do at that moment, except to say that I was somewhat lower than a pregnant sow's belly. I took out the scrap of paper on which I'd written the number of the Psychic Confidantes number and dialed it.

"Hullo?" said a squeaky voice.

"I'd like to speak to Divinia," I said.

"As soon as I heard the phone ring, I knew that," she said. "Can you hold on for a second?" She put her hand over the receiver and yelled, "Go vacuum in the bedroom, honey, on account of I got a call."

"Is this Divinia?" I asked.

"No, she ain't available. We've got this deal where all her calls are transferred to me when she can't answer. Are you one of her regulars?"

"Shouldn't you know that?" I asked.

"Oh, I do. Divinia's not doing so well at the present time, but she'll be on in a few days. What can I do for you? Got problems with your boyfriend? That's my specialty."

"What makes you think I have a boyfriend?"

"Everybody who calls Psychic Confidantes has a boyfriend. Tell me his name and I'll do a reading."

Although I knew the meter was ticking at approximately four dollars a minute, it was beginning to amuse me. "You're a psychic. You tell *me* his name."

"I don't got time to play games. Call Divinia when she gets back. In the meantime, don't trust what he says about other women, but don't be surprised if he shows up with a real nice Christmas present. He's real sorry about what he did."

"What did he do?"

"You don't want to know."

She hung up, leaving me holding the receiver against my ear and feeling foolish. I locked up and walked back to the apartment.

I had an hour before heading downstairs for a cocktail and mindless chatter, to be followed by white wine and more mindless chatter. I made a drink and took it into the bathroom, where I could find some solace in a bath and a book.

I was somewhat submerged in both when I heard the back door open and more than one pair of feet tromp into the kitchen.

"Mother?" called Caron.

"Yes, dear?" I replied without enthusiasm.

"We've got company. You'd better get dressed."

As much as I wanted to sink beneath the water and find out how long I could hold my breath, I climbed out of the bathtub and put on my clothes. They were not what I had intended to wear to the retiree's party, but I had no desire to be spotted sprinting down the hall to my room in the wherewithal. Skyclad, so to speak.

I was not prepared for the crowd in the living room. Caron and Inez were whispering by the door. Luanne was seated on the sofa as though it were a throne and she were awaiting an audience with an endless line of courtiers. One of them might have been Ed, who was hovering near the doorway to the kitchen.

"Hey," he said lamely.

Caron came over to my side. "Don't be mad at me, okay?"

"If I'd known we were having a party, I would have bought some eggnog."

"It's not a party."

Luanne looked back at me. "But it will be shortly, Claire. Come sit down next to me. Caron has something she wants to show you."

I glanced at Ed. "Shouldn't I make coffee or something?"

"Sit," Luanne said, slapping the cushion. "Caron has a Christmas present for you. You may be of the traditional school that believes presents can only be opened on Christmas morning, but we took it to a vote and decided that you deserve to receive it tonight."

"We?" I said as I sat down.

Ed cleared his throat; if he'd had a forelock, he would have tugged it. "I shouldn't be here, Ms. Malloy. I'll just be on my way."

Caron hurried across the room and poked him in the chest. "You'll do no such thing. I told you that I need a Santa Claus when I give this present to my mother. Is it asking too much for you to stay for ten or fifteen more minutes? I'll pay you for your time if that's what you want."

"You know that's not why I said that."

"Then let's not play Mr. Sensitive," she said acerbically. "Would it be too much trouble for you to sit down on the sofa?"

"Maybe I should stay over here," he said.

"Whatever." Caron turned around and looked at me. "I borrowed a video camera from Rhonda and made a tape. I think you'll enjoy it."

Inez slipped a cassette into the VCR, pushed buttons, and then stepped back. We all seemed to be holding our collective breath as static flickered and then materialized into a jerky scene of a child on a swing set.

"This," Caron said, "is Morgan Connolly, less than twenty-four hours after her supposed traumatic experience at the mall. Note, if you will, her smarmy smile and lack of reluctance to engage in strenuous physical activity."

"Caron," I began, "our lawyer said not to—"

"And here is Morgan, doing cartwheels. My goodness, was that a somersault? How could a child with these injuries perform so vigorously? Is it possible that she wasn't quite so injured as they claim?"

"One wonders," Luanne drawled. "She does appear remarkably fit, doesn't she?"

I knew something was expected of me, but I couldn't buy into their rosy glow. "This doesn't prove she didn't experience mental anguish. All it takes is one psychologist and—"

"And now what do we see?" Caron said as the flickering screen once again came into focus. "Why, it's Mrs. Claus knocking on a front door. The door opens, and it's Morgan's father, Eric Connolly. He's hugging her, and she's kissing him on the cheek. Now we have Suzanne Connolly, mother of the victim. She's hugging Mrs. Claus, too. Is this a warm reunion or what? You'd almost think these were old friends, wouldn't you?"

The tape dissolved into static.

"What's more," Caron continued as she positioned herself in the middle of the room, "it occurred to me that Morgan's performance was a bit too slick, as if she'd done it more than once. It hadn't worked the first time, so Ms. Portmeyer had to invent reasons to fire Santa and the reindeer. I didn't get a chance to ask the two girls if they recognized Morgan, but Ed did."

"That's right," he said. "Two days before I found the whiskey bottle in my locker, the same little girl pushed her way to the head of the line and then scrambled past the two reindeer and ran toward me. They just stared at her. She knocked over a couple of elves, kicked me in the shins, and yanked my beard so she ended up with a fistful of hairs. Portmeyer finally intervened and led her back to the fence."

"And found a set of new employees so she could try again," I said. "Let's gift-wrap the cassette before we take it to Franklin."

Luanne slapped my leg. "Party time! Come on, Ed, you can help me cut up cheese and crank up the gramophone. Caron, are you and Inez going to come?"

"No, thank you. We're going to another party."

"Whose?" I asked.

"Rhonda's having a few people over to string popcorn and dumb stuff like that. Trust me when I say I'll be home early."

I waited until Luanne and Ed had clattered down the stairs. "Why are you invited?"

Caron's lip slid out. "Why shouldn't we be? I mean, we may not be going steady with football players, but we don't drool when we drink cranberry punch."

Inez sighed. "Louis Wilderberry's sister told Emily that he's giving Rhonda a gold bracelet for Christmas. She'll probably be wearing it tonight so we can all go blind admiring it."

"There's more than one plum in the pudding," Caron said archly. "Or I guess there is, anyway. I've never had plum pudding."

I did not allow myself to be diverted into a culinary conversation. "Why did she invite you?"

"I decided that since it's the Christmas season I'd forgive her for all her bitchy comments. I went over to her house, and as a gesture of goodwill, offered to write her term paper for history."

"If she loaned you the video camera," Inez contributed, then edged around the back of the sofa. "I'm sure she would have anyway."

"What's the topic of this paper?" I asked Caron.

"Something about the influence of sixteenth-century exploration on the cultures in Latin America."

"You don't know anything about that. Are you planning to do research as a further gesture of goodwill."

"Don't make me laugh," said Caron. "Rhonda knows less than I do. She thinks they used to speak Latin, if you can believe that. I'll make up a bunch of stuff. As long as I stick in a lot of dates and peculiar names, she'll never know the difference."

"Her teacher will," I pointed out dryly.

"School will be out before Rhonda gets her report card. I'm thinking about getting a summer job in Zion National Park. I don't know where it is, but it sounds like the sort of place nobody can find, even with a map."

I gestured for her to sit down beside me. "Thanks for the videotape. That was smart work on your part."

"I thought so. Actually, Luanne had a couple of suggestions, like staking out Morgan's yard with the video camera, and Inez helped, too."

"By searching Ms. Portmeyer's briefcase?"

"Oh, no," said Inez. "The mall let her use a little office off the lounge. All I did was look at some folders on her desk while I was supposed to be getting a package of film. Looking's not the same as searching, Mrs. Malloy."

"No, dear," I said, "it's certainly not."

After they'd gone, I changed into a red fleece jumpsuit in honor of the holiday, did what I could to cover the scratches on my face, and applied bright red lipstick in hopes that it would make me look merry and bright.

I was unplugging the lights on the Christmas tree when the telephone started to ring. I straightened the packages, tucked the foil-wrapped fruitcake under my arm to give to Ed when I got to Luanne's, and turned off the living-room light. The telephone was still ringing as I went down the steps for a Jingle Bell Bazooka.

Don't miss the next

Claire Malloy mystery,

A Conventional Corpse,

coming from Dutton in 1999.

CHAPTER 1

It had thus far been a nice day, so the last thing I wanted to see was Sally Fromberger marching down the sidewalk, clutching her clipboard to her bosom. She was smiling and nodding at her fellow pedestrians; most of them managed to return the small courtesy with only a faint flicker of apprehension. There is nothing about Sally that suggests she might be a serial killer in disguise. She has a significant girth, bright yellow hair, rosy cheeks, and a perpetual glow of pleasure, as if beholding a hot fudge sundae. It must be the clipboard, I thought as I continued to arrange gardening books, flowerpots, and assorted tools in what I hoped would be an eye-catching display in the bookstore window.

Not that I wanted to catch eyes, mind you. I was much more interested in catching customers with platinum credit cards, and the law frowns on those who literally drag them in off the street. The Book Depot, situated in an old train station down the hill from the campus, certainly could use an influx. I suspect bookstores in college towns experience the same seasonal swings—a lull in January and February, followed by a flurry of activity before mid-term exams, and then a subsequent lull as the students pulled out their blankets and coolers to take advantage of the sunny spring weather. A young man's fancy may turn to love, or even lust, but not to literature. Not even Elizabeth Barrett Browning can compete with Budweiser when the tanning season arrives.

"Good afternoon," Sally chirped as she came into my bookstore and beamed at me. "It looks as though we'll have perfect weather for the conference, doesn't it? This very morning I had an enormous flock of robins in my backyard. There were also some darling little finches at the feeder."

I was tempted to put a flowerpot over my head, but instead descended from the foot stool and managed an amiable expression. "Would you like to buy a field guide to North American birds?"

Ignoring my admittedly silly question, Sally began to flip through the pages on her clipboard. "The steering committee met last night at my house to make sure nothing has been overlooked. Everyone attended except you and Dr. Shackley. Of course, he was presenting a paper at a seminar on the East Coast, so we could hardly expect him to be there." She glanced up at me with the expression of a robin assessing the worthiness of a worm. "Your role is vital, you know. The Thurber Farber Foundation for the Humanities has invested a great deal of money in our mystery convention. I'm hoping the board members will be impressed enough with the outcome to continue to fund us in the future."

"So am I," I said, wondering if I could persuade the foundation to fund me in the future, too. As much as I loved my dusty bookstore, I barely made enough money to keep my peevish accountant at bay and my sixteen-year-old daughter in designer jeans. The boiler at the back of the store hissed like a haughty dowager when pressed into duty; it was only a matter of time before it shuddered to a timely death—or exploded. One would think owning a bookstore was a suitable job for a widow, but there were moments when it seemed perilous at best.

Sally paused, in case I wanted to offer an explanation for my unexcused absence, then sighed and said, "Here are your copies of all the committee reports." She began thrusting pages at me. "Registration is approaching one hundred, and we anticipate a few more. Press releases have gone out to all regional media. The scheduling of panels is finalized. Your table will be in the back of the room in which the signings will be held, and you can start setting up Friday at four o'clock. Caron and Inez will be needed to fetch our authors from the airport beginning at noon. They are still willing to do this, aren't they?"

"For seven dollars an hour, they'd carry the authors on their backs." I set the papers down on the counter and attempted to look like someone with a very important chore awaiting her. "If that covers everything . . . ?"

"These are photocopies of the page proofs for the program book. They'll give you an overview of Farber College's first 'Murder Comes to the Campus.' I can't begin to tell you how excited I am, Claire. Just think of the luminaries who have agreed to be our speakers! I never expected such a response."

She didn't have to tell me how excited she was. Her face was flushed and her eyes were glittering; if the boiler didn't explode in the immediate future, she might, splattering the racks with bright red corpuscles. She clearly wanted to continue, but I clasped her shoulder and steered her toward the door.

"Why don't you go home?" I said in a concerned voice. "It's likely people are trying to get in touch with you. Your answering machine must be jammed with messages. All of us involved in the conference are so grateful for your attention to details, Sally. Don't let us down."

"It is a complicated project," she said modestly, then sailed out the door to badger some other innocent soul.

I went outside to admire my window display. It would not incite rabid gardeners to storm the store, but it might lure in a few green-thumbers. I most certainly was not one; the only things I grew with noticeable success were dustballs, mildew, and gray hair.

Satisfied with my efforts, I went into my cramped office in back, gathered up the checkbook and a stack of invoices, and sat down behind the counter to determine if there was any way to appease some, if not all, of my creditors. Will Rogers had never dealt with publishers. It was not an amusing way to spend a balmy afternoon, and I was gnawing on a pencil and mumbling to myself when the bell above the door jangled.

I put down the pencil as Caron and Inez came across the room. "How was school?" I asked in an appropriately maternal fashion.

Caron dropped her backpack on the floor and made a face reminiscent of a gargoyle. "School is such a bore. Everybody else on the entire planet is outside, soaking up sunshine, while we're incarcerated in that dreary prison. It's worse than the Bastille. I'm surprised the cafeteria isn't serving bread and water. What's more, the teachers seem to think their job is to torture us. All I was doing was looking out the window, for pity's sake. From the way old Crabapple jumped on me, you'd have thought I was skinning an armadillo."

Inez Thornton, a perfect counterfoil to my melodramatic daughter, stared at her. "Why would anyone skin an armadillo?"

"Boots," Caron said as she picked up the papers Sally had left. "I can't believe you're involved in this dorky crime on the campus thing, Mother. Why would anyone pay money to listen to a bunch of authors talk about where they get their ideas? Ms. McLair had this writer in to prattle to our class about poetry. I almost passed out from a serious bout of tedium."

I resisted an urge to snatch the papers out of her hand. "Authors can be interesting, dear."

"More interesting than dead armadillos? I doubt it." Caron went into the office and began to open drawers in search of my cache of chocolate.

Inez eyed me warily. "What time are we supposed to pick them up at the airport? I have an algebra test fifth period, and I sort of said I'd help decorate the cafeteria after school for the Latin Club banquet."

"Humanum est errare," I said. "You and Caron promised Sally Fromberger a month ago that you would work Friday afternoon, all day Saturday, and Sunday until noon."

"Yeah, a month ago," Caron said as she emerged empty-handed and picked the pages up once again. After flinging the irrelevant ones over her shoulder, she paused for a moment. "There's no reason why both of us have to make every run to the airport. We'll divvy them up so you can practice pinning up your toga. Who's this Laureen Parks, Mother? Is she an utter bore?"

"Laureen Parks," I said with admirable restraint, "has made a significant contribution to the mystery genre. She's written over sixty novels of romantic suspense."

Inez blinked solemnly. "Like when the heroine hears a noise in the attic and goes to investigate? I never could figure out why she doesn't call the police on her cell phone."

"She can't afford one," I muttered.

"Give me a break," said Caron. "This author's got to be really old to have written all those books. Inez, you get her. You can tell her how you used to obsess on Azalea Twilight's gushy books."

"That was a long time ago," Inez retorted stiffly. "At least two years, and you read her books, too."

Caron did not deign to respond. "Then, at one-fifteen, somebody named Sherry Lynne Blackstone. You'll have to get her, Inez. I absolutely cannot make polite conversation with somebody named Sherry Lynne. I'd feel obliged to drop her off at a trailer park or a bowling alley."

I glared at my darling daughter. "Sherry Lynne Blackstone is responsible for a goodly portion of your wardrobe. Her books have sold steadily for fifteen years. They're a bit too cozy for my taste, but she has a loyal following of cat fanciers."

Caron raised her eyebrows. "Do her cats type clues?"

"Sometimes," I admitted, "but I've been told there are a dozen web sites devoted to Wimple, Dimple, and Doolittle. Their pedigrees, what they prefer to eat, that sort of thing."

"Wimple, Dimple, and Dolittle? That sounds like a sleazy law firm. I may barf."

"Then go outside," I said, resuming my glare. "Sherry Lynne Blackstone is considered to be an outstanding practitioner of the cozy genre. She's rumored to be gracious, which is more than I can say for certain people."

Caron looked down at the schedule. "And we have Dilys Knoxwood at two o'clock. What kind of name is *Dilys*? It sounds so scatty. If I were named Dilys, I'd find myself twirling like a bow-legged ballerina at every opportunity. Inez, you—"

"No," Inez said with surprising firmness, considering whom she was up against. "I can't leave in the middle of fifth period. All you have is study hall."

"Dilys Knoxwood," I intervened, "writes a very popular series in the classic British tradition. Her books are considered to be the epitome of the genre introduced by Dame Agatha Christie in the nineteen-twenties."

"She's not on the list," Inez said, peering over Caron's shoulder. "I guess she'd be pretty old, like my grandmother. Maybe older."

"Okay," Caron said, "I can deal with this decrepit creature just so you can take your stupid algebra test. You have to get the next one, though. I'm not about to deal with some guy named Walter Dahl. Who are these people, Mother?"

"His books don't sell well for me," I said, "but he receives radiant reviews in the literary journals. In my opinion, his characters are riddled with neuroses and spend most of their time arguing about the Freudian implications of their motives. I prefer a butler with a well-deserved grudge or a pregnant parlor maid."

Caron gazed coolly at me, then looked at Inez. "If this guy doesn't mind hanging around the airport, I could grab him, Dilys, —and . . ."—her composure evaporated—". . . Allegra Cruzetti. Oh my gawd, Inez—Allegra Cruzetti! Can you believe it? Why would she come to Farberville? She's famous! Did you read her last book?"

Inez was blinking at me as though I'd added Moses to the list as an afterthought. "I thought *Courting Disaster* was the most thrilling book I've ever read. I had this history paper due the next day, but I started reading and just couldn't make myself stop. There's this beautiful young prosecuting attorney, and she's going after this guy that may or may not have murdered his mother, and he claims—"

"I've read it," I said to quell the impending hysteria. "Competent, but that's about all. Cruzetti hopped on the bandwagon at the precise moment to garner maximum attention and a Hollywood deal. A year from now, the hot topic will be angels with bad attitudes or cats with cleavers."

"Allegra Cruzetti," Caron sang, clutching Inez's arms in what must have been a painful vise. "Just think what Rhonda Maguire will say when she finds out I picked up Allegra Cruzetti at the airport. She thinks she's so hot because her father met Carl Sagan at some dumb conference. He never made the bestseller list, did he? Allegra Cruzetti's been on the *Oprah* show. She was on the covers of *People* and *Newsweek* magazines. She's a real author, not some dorky mystery writer. Rhonda will Absolutely Die. Do you think Ms. Cruzetti would mind if we stopped by the high school for a minute? Ms. McLair's teeth will fly across the room."

I held up my hands. "Under no circumstances will you use Allegra Cruzetti to undo whatever damage occurred today in your English class. Your mission on Friday is to collect the authors from the airport and deliver them to the Azalea Inn. On Saturday, you and Inez will be available to drive them back and forth from the campus as they desire. On Sunday, you will take people to the airport, and then help me pack up whatever books are unsold. This is going to be an uneventful conference to celebrate the current popularity of mystery fiction. The atmosphere will be calm and dignified, as befitting the occasion. Nothing will go wrong."